MACROECONOMIC THEORY

This book is a comprehensive survey of the recent journal and monograph literature on macroeconomic theory. It covers the consumption function, the demand for money, the production function and the investment function. For the four "functions" the survey covers the main contributions – both theoretical and empirical – since 1960, along with some notes on important earlier work. The material is developed in a model-oriented fashion with considerable documentation (and a large accompanying bibliography).

Chapter 1 includes a standard IS–LM model as well as surveys of the aggregation "problem" and disequilibrium economics as it applies to macro problems; these topics are presented here as basic to the entire study. Chapter 2 develops material on the consumption function, from Keynes to Rational Expectations; there is considerable reference to monetary influences on consumption and some new material on interest rates and consumption. Chapter 3 surveys the demand for money, concentrating on "general equilibrium", "asset", and "transactions" theories; again, there is new material on the term structure of interest rates and the demand for money. Chapter 4 covers the production function, concentrating on functional forms from the Cobb–Douglas to the Trans–Log; there is also a section on the role of money in the production process. Chapter 5 surveys the literature on the investment function; here the coverage is very broad indeed, including sections on fixed investment, inventory investment, and "investment in housing", as well as a section on financial influences on investment. Of course, the well-known flexible accelerator and Neoclassical models are featured. While full-scale discussion of growth models seemed unnecessary, in view of slow developments in the field, it was felt that the financial material could use a going-over, in view of recent developments.

Douglas Fisher is Professor of Economics and Business at North Carolina State University, Raleigh, North Carolina, USA. He formerly taught at Concordia University, Montreal, Claremont Graduate School, the University of Durham, Pomona College, the University of Essex, and Queens College, New York.

He is the author of *Money and Banking*, *Monetary Policy*, *Monetary Theory and the Demand for Money* and *Money, Banking, and Monetary Policy*, as well as numerous articles and reviews in professional journals.

By the same author

MONEY AND BANKING

MONETARY POLICY

MONETARY THEORY AND THE DEMAND FOR MONEY

MONEY, BANKING, AND MONETARY POLICY

MACROECONOMIC THEORY

A Survey

Douglas Fisher

Professor of Economics and Business
North Carolina State University

St. Martin's Press New York

St. Martin's Press, Inc., 175 Fifth Avenue, New York, NY 10010
Printed in Hong Kong
First published in the United States of America in 1983

ISBN 0-312-50329-6

Library of Congress Cataloging in Publication Data

Fisher, Douglas, 1934–
Macroeconomic theory, a survey.

Bibliography: p.
Includes index.
1. Macroeconomics. I. Title.
HB172.5.F53 1983 339 82-5767
ISBN 0-312-50329-6 AACR2

To my wife

Contents

Preface

This book is the first of two volumes surveying recent developments in macroeconomic theory and policy. The purpose of this survey is to try to piece together a consensus of the current state of macroeconomics as an aid to both graduate students and professionals in the field. The survey is "representative" on most topics, but since it was my intention to capture all of the main themes - and to identify the players as far as possible - it is certainly fair to charge against my account any important omissions. Similarly, it would be a miracle if no serious errors remained, considering the volume of material covered, and I certainly accept full responsibility for these. Even so, the reader should appreciate that certain material, mostly of a policy nature, is reserved for the second volume of this study.

There are several themes to this survey which should be briefly noted here. One is that I view economic "theory" as fully worked only when the empirical record is in; as a consequence, my survey of theory contains considerable reference to the empirical work, although on a selective basis. A second is that monetary aspects of macroeconomics receive greater emphasis than one customarily finds in "theory" surveys; this is not entirely a matter of taste in view of my belief that standard macroeconomic theory is made more general thereby. Finally, the reader will soon note that many of the traditional disputes in the literature are played down in this survey; again, it is my belief that a more productive *modus operandi* is to survey the major macroeconomic models, as they were developed and tested, and to eschew what I feel is distracting (and often illogical) controversy.

1 An Introduction to Macroeconomic Theory

1.1 OVERALL INTRODUCTION

The body of written material styled "macroeconomics" has expanded rapidly since 1960, inspired by technological breakthroughs, the ceaseless controversy between what essentially seem to be "conservative" and "liberal" points of view, and the obvious urgency of the problems of inflation, unemployment, and the rate of growth (in most countries). While the literature has grown - exploded really - there has been a tendency toward fragmentation and, regrettably, a tendency to forget all but the most recent and most striking results. There is, consequently, a continuing need to assess the state of the art in macroeconomics - both in its theory and in its policy - and in this spirit what is contained here is a synthesis across the major parts of the subject and a retroactive but selective survey going back some twenty or so years. What is hoped is that this will provide density to the mainstream of macro-material, insight into the current literature, and some hints as to where it all might be going.

This first of a two-volume survey of macroeconomics is intended mainly for graduate students and scholars in the field. In this volume - titled *Macroeconomic Theory: A Survey* - we will cover, for the most part, the traditional "functions" of standard macro-theory. These are, of course, consumption, the demand for money, production, and investment, and each chapter is a survey of many of the major pieces of work currently available; it is arranged topically and chronologically according to the style of the actual work being covered. The second volume, to be published in due course, is titled *Monetary and Fiscal Policy: A Survey* and, generally without much repetition, will be directed toward what might be described as an "optimal macroeconomic policy". In a sense then, this first volume contains much of the standard "macroeconomic theory" material, while the second volume could be titled "macroeconomic policy", but with the understanding that considerable omission is necessary in each case to avoid "double-counting".

Several broad initial points need to be made before we launch our survey of the theory. For one thing, since this study is model-oriented rather than controversy-oriented, it would be difficult to get a reading on the status of the monetarist-Keynesian debate (for example) here. The models, further, are laid out in terms of their structure and their conclusions and usually are not repeated, section-to-section or chapter-to-chapter, except in the event of a significant change of direction. Note, especially, that the derivations of the results are provided only rarely and then are generally done only once in the book, although the model itself may appear in several places. Furthermore, the reader should note that this is not a textbook, but a study of certain parts of macroeconomics; in this sense no attempt has been made to knit everything together or to be all-inclusive, although within the projected companion volume many of the policy aspects of the entire macroeconomic system are discussed (and presented in a more integrated fashion). It might seem, therefore, as if important omissions have occurred in this volume, of, for example, aggregate supply and macro labour theory, of money supply theory, and of price and quantity index number problems, but the decision has been made to include these topics in the policy volume for what one hopes are obvious enough reasons, and to stick to consumption, money demand, production, investment, and growth in this particular study.

The remainder of Chapter 1 is an introduction to the rest of the volume. It presents a short "prototype" macro-economic model - pretty much in the style of Patinkin (1965) - as well as two sections containing material basic to the entire survey. These are on "disequilibrium economics" and on "the aggregation problem".

Chapter 2 surveys the literature on the consumption function, from the familiar Keynesian-style models up to the recent rational expectations forms. More attention to derivations - both statistical and mathematical - is paid here, and there is considerable discussion of empirical results, especially in the notes. Chapter 3, on the demand for money, reorganizes the traditional macro-micro literature both around schools of thought and around models (essentially transactions and asset demand models). There is, in this chapter, some original work on the term structure approach to the demand for money and, again, some reference to empirical results. Chapter 4 surveys the literature on the production function, and the partly overlapping Chapter 5 surveys the investment function literature. These two chapters are more technical in nature, and both the theoretical and empirical work has a strong microeconomic flavour to it, as is the style in this literature. Indeed, it seems necessary to return to some of the questions of aggregation raised originally in Chapter 1 in view of the results of empirical work on (especially) production functions.

1.2 A BASIC MACROECONOMIC MODEL

Before we begin the task of surveying the literature on macroeconomics, that is to say, before we deal with the individual macroeconomic functions in Chapters 2-5, it is important that we should set down a simple and basic macroeconomic model sufficiently general in its design to enable us to capture some of the important variations of macroeconomic theory (and even policy) which one encounters in the literature. Approximately, we will begin with a general, but non-stochastic, model which has a structure which most economists could accept - not, of course, as the last word, but as a fair representation of expository models of this sort - and then go on from there. What we will do in this first chapter is to set up the structure of the model, where the main use of the model concerns the clarification of basic theoretical propositions in economics. The model presented is not very complicated - better ones abound in the literature - but it is necessary to make some basic points and to present some extensions involving the dynamics later in this chapter, and something needs to be set down at this point.

1.2.1 COMMODITY MARKETS

Let us begin by clarifying several notational devices which we will attempt to employ throughout the book (except where it becomes impossible). We will refer to items measured in current monetary units using an upper case designation (M = nominal money stock) and items measured in constant monetary units using a lower case designation (m = real money stock); this applies whether the concept referred to is a stock or a flow. We will refer to observed (market) nominal interest rates as i and (usually) unobserved real interest rates as r; the difference in this case is either the actual or the expected rate of inflation (depending on the context). When it is necessary to use matrix algebra, we will usually refer to a vector as, e.g. $\tilde{r}$ (a vector of real interest rates, perhaps differentiated by term-to-maturity), and matrices will be identified by capital letters. Finally, in this chapter and in several other places, we will refer to the partial derivative of (e.g.) the function $U(y, i, \text{etc.})$ with respect to the arguments y, i, etc. as U_1, U_2, etc. (or, on occasion, as U_y, U_i). We will, though, use the subscript in other ways; thus, time subscripts and definitions will also be subscripted (as in M_{pt}, which is "permanent" nominal money balances measured at time t). The context should permit such ambiguities to be deciphered readily. Full consistency over the entire study, given the range of our coverage, would require development of an unconventional notation which is highly undesirable in a survey which sticks as close to the literature as this one does. Thus, we will be faced with a few inconsistencies, chapter-to-chapter, but generally not within each chapter.

We begin with the consumption function. Let us argue that individuals plan their current consumption on the basis of where it fits into their lifetime income profile and do so in accordance with that part of their net income which they expect to receive regularly. That is, let consumption depend on disposable real income (y_D) - recognizing that a better formulation would have permanent income (as discussed in Chapter 2). It is also conventional to include an interest rate in the consumption function, especially in the event that the underlying rationale for the function is a dynamic consumption plan (as ours has been); but when one does that, certain problems arise. On the one hand, when the interest rate changes, individuals, who will have specific preferences for present versus future consumption, will re-evaluate their consumption plans, increasing current consumption, for example, when the interest rate falls because future consumption will seem less valuable at a lower interest rate (this is a "substitution effect" in the microeconomic terminology which is appropriate here). On the other hand, when the interest rate falls, one's current income is reduced to the extent that one has interest-earning assets; on this account both current and future consumption may well fall. Finally, any fixed interest assets which the consumer owns will rise in value when the interest rate falls, and this expansion of wealth could increase current consumption. This last effect on consumption is referred to in the literature as the "interest-induced wealth effect". On net, then, we cannot say in advance which will dominate, although we may well expect an interest rate to matter. But it is worth noting that it is common practice to take this effect as negative, sometimes on empirical grounds, and we will not hesitate to do this, as required.[1]

There is yet another aspect to the interest rate/consumption problem, and this involves the real rate of interest. The rate of interest which one observes in the market is a nominal rate of interest (i) and represents an underlying real rate (r) and a mark-up for the expected inflation rate $(\dot{P}/P)_e$ where $\dot{P} = dP/dt$. The real rate here is an *ex ante* concept (an expected real rate) and represents the trade-off between present and future opportunities (whether they be consumption or, below, investment) in "real" terms. Approximately it is a measure of the real productivity of capital (whether invested in producer or consumer goods). Now when one borrows money in order to finance present consumption (or investment), one does so by issuing a personal bond which is itself usually denominated in "nominal" terms; that is to say, most bonds or credit arrangements do not contain a purchasing power clause. That being the case, if there is actual inflation over the course of the loan, the borrower will pay back in depreciated dollars - will, in effect, return funds which are "shop-worn" to the extent of the rate of inflation. Since both borrowers and lenders will tend to perceive this influence, there will arise in the course of the market dealings between borrowers and lenders an average or market consensus, based on the expectations of both borrowers and lenders, of what sort of inflationary "premium" should be tacked onto the underlying "real" rate of interest to represent the collective view. In a nutshell, equation (1.1) also holds in our model,

$$i = r + \left(\frac{\dot{P}}{P}\right)_e \qquad (1.1)$$

where $(\dot{P}/P)_e$ is the expected inflation rate.

Now by and large - or, more accurately, in the aggregate - consumers who expect a particular rate of inflation will expect their nominal incomes to increase along with the increase in the average level of prices (and thus along with the inflation in their budgets). Quite simply, this occurs because all of the proceeds from inflation will tend to be distributed to the various economic agents - the workers and owners who create the products - who are themselves the consumers in the economy. Only in the event that there is some leakage - for example, into the government sector because tax rates are not correctly indexed - will this not be the case. Thus, the appropriate interest rate for all of the calculations described above is the real rate of interest expected to rule over the period in question. Indeed, the same comments will broadly apply to the investment function and will not be repeated. Note that the real rate of interest described here is an *ex ante* concept and presents some special problems of measurement in view of the fact that both right-hand terms in equation (1.1) are expectational variables and clearly are not readily observable (especially on macro data).[2]

The last variable to be included in the consumption function is initial real money balances. If the sum of consuming units receive a surprise, either in their estimates of the initial quantity of money in the system (M_0) or in their estimates of the price level, then they will (it is assumed here) react to this surprise change in the value of their money holdings by altering their consumption in the same direction (not, of course, dollar-for-dollar); this is a version of the real balance effect so common in neoclassical representations of the macroeconomic system. We will use M/P and not "surprises" in M/P in our consumption function, but our rationale is for only surprises to matter. This topic is discussed further in Chapter 2 under the heading of "rational expectations". The result, then, is a consumption function of the form of equation (1.2).

$$c = c(y_D, r, \frac{M_o}{P}) \tag{1.2}$$

The investment function presents somewhat of a problem to us since it is pretty clear from the literature that it may be best to try to express this function in an explicitly dynamic sense. Let gross investment be defined as the change in the capital stock $(\dot{K} = dK/dt)$ plus the replacement at rate δ of old capital; this is

$$I_g = \dot{K} + \delta K \tag{1.3}$$

where I_g is measured in real terms (we have already used the letter i). Subtracting δK from both sides, then, we have net investment defined as the change in capital stock $(I = \dot{K})$. Now strictly speaking the way to proceed is to define desired net investment as dependent on a time-weighted average of the past desired capital stocks as in the following difference equation.

$$I^* = \beta(W)(K_t^* - K_{t-1}^*) \tag{1.4}$$

This, is, for example, how Jorgenson (1965) has it in his (neoclassical) investment function, and this is how we proceed in Chapter 5. We may also present a function which is parallel to that used for consumption and justify it (see Chapter 5) in terms of a "vintage" neoclassical investment function; such a function appears as equation (1.5).

$$I = I(y, r, \frac{M_0}{P}) \tag{1.5}$$

Here again we have the real interest rate (r), the level of real income, and initial real money balances. We assume that corporations do not pay income taxes.

What remains in the spending sector is a characterization of the role of the government. We will argue that the decision to spend on government projects is a non-economic one (they will want to spend without limit) which is made into an economic problem by application of a constraint. That is, suppose the government can control its real expenditures at the level $g = \overline{g}$ but that it is constrained in this choice by the need to raise funds. It can raise funds by income taxes on nominal income, where $\overline{a}_1$ is a constant tax (it is negative in the case of an exemption), and $\overline{a}_2$ is some kind of average tax rate.

$$T = \overline{a}_1 + \overline{a}_2 Y \qquad \overline{a}_1 < 0; \overline{a}_2 > 0 \tag{1.6}$$

Note that we could add a term to equation (1.6) in order to express the imperfect indexation of personal income taxes - but we will forbear in the interest of simplicity.

The government, we will assume, can also raise funds by bond issue to the private sector (dB_g) and/or by the creation of high-powered money (dH). The latter is, in the United States at any rate, equal to currency provided by the Federal Reserve plus the level of reserves held by commercial banks at the Federal Reserve. It is termed "high-powered" because it tends to have, when expanded, a multiplied effect on the level of (e.g.) M1 - narrow money - and loans. Under present conditions in the United States, this M1 multiplier generally lies between 2.0 and 3.0.

Putting the elements of the financial constraint together, we have the following expression for government expenditures as expressed in real terms.

$$\overline{g} = \frac{\overline{a}_1}{P} + \overline{a}_2 y + \frac{dB_g}{P} + \frac{dH}{P} \tag{1.7}$$

Here we see that a rise in the price level affects government spending positively to the extent that the tax is not perfectly indexed (from $\overline{a}_1/P$ with $\overline{a}_1 < 0$) and negatively by reducing the spending power of either a given deficit (dB_g/P) or an addition to high-powered money (dH/P). These propositions seem valid, although this is far from a necessary way to model the government's role (although it is necessary to have a budget constraint here).

The last component of the spending part of the macroeconomic model we will consider is "net foreign spending". We may take real exports (E_x) as exogenously determined, clearly; real imports also obviously create domestic incomes and so should be included in total spending. On the other hand, real imports depend on domestic incomes and interest rates, etc., and so another function needs to be provided here. Imports will consist of both consumption and real capital investment flows, so two functions ought to be specified, but we will simplify things and adopt equation (1.8) as our import demand function (in real terms); we apologize for the use of I for investment and I_m for imports.

$$I_m = I_m(y, r, \frac{M_o}{P}) \tag{1.8}$$

Imports create incomes abroad and, consequently, are a withdrawal from the domestic income stream. The term $(E_x - I_m)$ describes the net contribution of the foreign sector. Finally, note that for simplicity we are using y instead of y_D in this equation.

The sum of real spending in our model, then, is given by

$$y = c + I + g + (E_x - I_m); \tag{1.9}$$

it is defined in real terms. Substituting into this equation from (1.2), (1.5), (1.7), and (1.8), and noting that y_D is equal to y minus income taxes, we have

$$y = c(y - \frac{\bar{a}_1}{P} - \bar{a}_2 y, i - (\frac{\dot{P}}{P})_e, \frac{M_o}{P}) + I(y, i - (\frac{\dot{P}}{P})_e, \frac{M_o}{P}$$
$$+ \frac{\bar{a}_1}{P} + \bar{a}_2 y + \frac{dB_g}{P} + \frac{dH}{P} + E_x$$
$$- I_m(y, i - (\frac{\dot{P}}{P})_e, \frac{M_o}{P}) \tag{1.10}$$

This is an IS curve in y, P, and i (the nominal interest rate) with $(\dot{P}/P)_e$ exogenous and dB_g, dH, $\bar{a}_1$, and $\bar{a}_2$ as potential policy control parameters. If, further, we assume no deficit financing for the government, treat exports as a constant, and hold the price level constant, we may calculate the total derivative of equation (1.10). This provides an expression in the slopes and original parameters of the model as in:

$$dy = c_y[dy(1 - \bar{a}_2)] + c_i di + I_y dy + I_i di + \bar{a}_2 dy - I_{my} dy - I_{mi} di \qquad (1.11)$$

In this event, then, the slope of the IS curve is

$$\left.\frac{di}{dy}\right|_{dP = 0} = \frac{c_y(1 - \bar{a}_2) - (1 - \bar{a}_2) + (I_y - I_{my})}{I_{mi} - c_i - I_i} \qquad (1.12)$$

which, ignoring the foreign sector, would be negatively sloped if $(c_y - 1) < 0$ and $c_i, I_i < 0$. Note, though, that for an open economy, a rise in $(E_x - I_m)$ - whether it is more exports or fewer imports - will tend to shift the IS curve to the right.

1.2.2 FINANCIAL MARKETS

A standard demand for money, in real terms, could be that appearing in equation (1.13).

$$m_d = m(y_D, i, \frac{M_o}{P}) \qquad (1.13)$$

We again assume that disposable permanent income is the appropriate income proxy, and we include the nominal interest rate directly as an argument. The latter is used because in addition to losing the opportunity of alternative investments (in r), the money holder's wealth is expected to deteriorate at $(\dot{P}/P)_e$. For the supply of money we will take the following approach. Define money to be narrow money (currency plus deposits) as in

$$M = C + D \qquad (1.14)$$

Furthermore, define high-powered money to be currency plus the reserves of the commercial banking system as in

$$H = C + R \qquad (1.15)$$

Then, dividing (1.15) by (1.14), we have an expression for the money stock in terms of three "determinants" of the money stock; these are C/D, R/D, and H, reflecting, respectively, the contributions of final money holders, the commercial banks (at least in the event that the actual reserve ratio is greater than the required reserve ratio), and the central government (or central bank).

$$M = \left[\frac{\frac{C}{D} + 1}{\frac{C}{D} + \frac{R}{D}}\right] H = kH \tag{1.16}$$

Assuming away the banking system, for convenience only, we might impose a 100 per cent reserve on deposits; this implies that $R/D = 1$, and thus $M = H$ - that is, there is a one-to-one correspondence between money and high-powered money. It also implies, since the private sector choice of C/D is now irrelevant to the determination of the money stock, that we do not need separate demand for currency and demand for deposit functions (C/D is not, in practice, a constant). Of course, if C/D and R/D were actually constant, so that the expression $[(C/D) + 1]/[(C/D) + (R/D)]$ is also constant (let k be this constant which is referred to as the "banking multiplier"), then the following analysis goes through in any event.

H, in our presentation, is subject to the control of the monetary authorities (recall that we had dH as part of the government's budget constraint). It certainly can be asserted that it is a policy-instrument (at least in the United States) which is at least occasionally moved in response to changes in employment (L), the price level or inflation rate, and the level of the nominal interest rate, as in equation (1.17); we assume "stabilizing" adjustments, even if these are potentially inconsistent.

$$H = H(P, L, i) \qquad -1 < H_1 < 0; \; H_3 > 0; \; H_2 < 0 \tag{1.17}$$

In particular, a rise in the price level produces a partial reduction of the money stock, and a rise in the *nominal* interest rate produces an increase in the money stock, on the interpretation that such a rise represents a "tightening" of financial markets. A rise in employment would, under stabilizing assumptions, produce a partial (at least) reduction of H.

Combining (1.17), after deflating by P, with (1.16) and (1.13), we have equilibrium in the money market described as follows.

$$m\left(y_D, i, \left(\frac{M_o}{P}\right)\right) = \frac{k}{P} H(P, L, i) \tag{1.18}$$

This equation replaces $[(C/D) + 1]/[(C/D) + (R/D)]$ with k, a parameter, and equates two stocks, money supply and money demand. Note that the price level effect on the supply side is composed of a scaling factor ($1/P$ multiplies the equation) and a stabilizing factor (in the list of arguments in

H). If price level stabilization were all that the authorities attempted, then one might expect perceived inflation to produce the correct stabilization reaction. But, in fact, both L and i receive the attention of the authorities (and so, too, may a balance of payments variable) - the latter possibly inappropriately - thus presenting us with the possibility that significant shocks to L and I will produce policy responses which "destabilize" the price level. In particular, a supply side shock may well create an undesirable alteration of employment (L) and a monetary response which accelerates inflation and raises the nominal rate of interest (i).

Equation (1.18) is a stock equation, and our previous results for spending were in the flow dimension. H, the stock of high-powered money, does appear in the earlier model, in the budget constraint of the government, but in the form dH. For one thing, this implies that monetary policy has direct fiscal policy implications. More importantly, we have a stock-flow problem which can be evaded in several conventional ways or, at the cost of some complexity, can be dealt with directly. Firstly, we should note that there are already bonds in our model, as reference to the government budget equation should make clear.

$$g = \frac{T}{P} + \frac{dB_g}{P} + \frac{dH}{P};$$

here dB_g is the supply of new government bonds. Indeed, we have used the interest rate in our model at various points, and this, too, implies the existence of a bond to provide the opportunity cost. The term dB_g refers only to the addition to the stock of bonds while, of course, there is a quantity of government bonds outstanding (call it B_{go}) to which, in any period, is added dB_g. The decision to hold money in equation (1.18) is taken in consequence of the rate of return on the alternative; this alternative is $B_g = B_{go} + dB_g$ in effect. Now the private sector also can issue new bonds, call them dB_p, for which there is also an existing stock B_{po}, whence we have $B_p = B_{po} + dB_p$ as the total of such, where B_{po} is taken arbitrarily at the beginning of the period. B_p and B_g, then, are "stock-flow" concepts, but they differ in that the B_p are "inside" bonds, such that when the consolidated private sector bond market is in equilibrium, $B_p = 0$, while B_g is "outside" bonds with a positive quantity in equilibrium. We will, though, take advantage of an evasion known as Walras's Law (see below and in Chapter 3) to eliminate the bond market. This assumes overall equilibrium, in effect as a constraint, which enables us to eliminate the market of our choice (the bond market in this case).

We have a stock-flow problem remaining, and that involves the supply and demand for money, both of which were given in stock terms. One way out of this is to apply an additional constraint, in the form of equation (1.19), which is the well-known equation of exchange.

$$MV = Py \qquad (1.19)$$

This expression, as written, could be interpreted as using V - the average number of times money is used in servicing the flow of money national income - to convert the stock (M) into a flow. Taking this as an identity, then, we can think of M or of m, in any of the following equations as adjusted in this fashion and as a flow. Velocity is not here taken as a constant (since Py/M can clearly vary in our model). An alternative, which is less precise - and possibly a little less satisfying - is simply to interpret the functions of m and H as referring to the services of money demanded and supplied, an assumption which also ducks the stock-flow problem.

There is, however, a further constraint needed on account of the fact that we have an open economy in which $(E_x - I_m)$ can have any sign. In particular, we can have private capital flows, and we can also have money flows between nations, such that equation (1.20) also must hold, to describe balance of payments "equilibrium".

$$(E_x - I_m) + (E_c - I_c) + (E_H - I_H) \equiv 0 \qquad (1.20)$$

This relation says that the sum of the balance of trade, the balance of capital flows, and the flow of money internationally $(E_H - I_H)$ must add up in a properly constructed balance of payments. Any two of these three balancing items must be analyzed in our model, and we must allow that an import of money from abroad, arising if the capital flow does not exactly offset the goods flow, will expand the domestic money supply as if it were high-powered money. We can drop the capital flow $(E_c - I_c)$, and we have already included $(E_x - I_m)$ in the IS curve, so the remaining problem is to put down behavioural functions for E_H and I_H. It is beyond the scope of this chapter to analyze the behavioural equations behind E_H and I_H, but we should note that I_H represents a flow of foreign currencies inward (approximately into the bank accounts of domestic money holders) and E_H represents the converse. We should note that these money flows will arise in the event that capital flows do not offset goods flows, and the former, clearly, will depend on domestic versus foreign incomes and interest rates. That being the case, so too will $(E_H - I_H)$.

We will evade those issues here, however tempting it is to broaden the model in this fashion; instead, we will add this component into the LM curve. The first thing to note is that $(E_H - I_H)$ is already in the flow dimension, and thus it does not require any sophistry to get it into conformity with the other financial variables. We will argue that it is, directly, a form of high-powered money, and so we will enter $(E_H - I_H)$ directly into equation (1.18), suitably premultiplied by k (since it is high-powered money) and deflated. The result is equation (1.21).

$$m(y_D, i, \frac{M_o}{P}) - \frac{k}{P}H(P, L, i) = \frac{k}{P}(I_H - E_H) \qquad (1.21)$$

Thus, if exports exceed imports and capital flows do not offset this so that funds $[(I_H - E_H) > 0]$ are absorbed into the monetary base, then in so far as these funds are not absorbed into the domestic money balances or there is no reduction of the domestic stock of high-powered money (we call this "sterilization"), then there will be monetary spillover (and inflation, *ceteris paribus*). A balance of payments surplus, that is to say, shifts the LM curve to the right.

We may, as before, use our definition of disposable income to produce an equation for the LM curve parallel to equation (1.10). This is

$$m(y - \frac{\bar{a}_1}{P} - \bar{a}_2 y, i, \frac{M_o}{P}) = \frac{k}{P}H(P, i, L) + \frac{k}{P}[I_H(i) - E_H] \qquad (1.22)$$

where we provisionally assume that money outflows are exogenous and $\partial I_H/\partial i = I_{Hi} > 0$. Totally differentiating equation (1.22), we obtain (1.23), with the further assumption that L and the price level are constant:

$$m_y[dy(1 - a_2)] + m_i di = \frac{k}{P}H_i di + \frac{k}{P}I_{Hi} di \qquad (1.23)$$

This produces the usual LM curve, with an adjustment for taxes and for foreign capital flows.

$$\left.\frac{di}{dY}\right|_{dP = 0} = \frac{(a_2 - 1)m_y}{m_i - (\frac{k}{P}H_i + \frac{k}{P}I_{Hi})} \qquad (1.24)$$

This has a positive slope (for $a_2 < 1$, $m_i < 0$, $H_i > 0$, and $I_{Hi} > 0$, all as assumed). Indeed, an "exogenous" increase in foreign funds, as a result of a shift of export demand, will shift the LM curve to the right. Since the IS curve also shifts to the right, the net influence of the "positive" goods outflow is expansionary on real income, *ceteris paribus*.

Finally, let us note that we can solve our system - and produce the slope of an aggregate demand curve - with the price level varying. To do this we can take the total derivatives of equations (1.10) and (1.22) and eliminate the change in the interest rate (di). The result would be an expression for dP/dy in terms of the slopes and parameters of equations (1.10) and (1.22). This is expressed in very general terms in equation (1.25), where $\tilde{Q}$ is a vector of parameters from the structural equations.

$$\frac{dy}{dP} = AD(\tilde{Q}) \tag{1.25}$$

We exhibit the aggregate demand curve in this form because we have no further use for it in this study, other than for cross-reference purposes.

1.2.3 AGGREGATE SUPPLY

In recent years there has been a strong interest in "supply side" economics, and this section represents an attempt to include a small amount of that material here. The starting point is the aggregate production function, which appears as equation (1.26).

$$y = \phi(K, L, \frac{M_0}{P}) \tag{1.26}$$

In this function we argue that y (we assume $y = x$, where x is real output) is produced by two factors of production - capital and labour - supplemented by real money balances. The latter appear as a factor of production as this function is written, but there are alternatives, as discussed in Chapter 4. For now, we can argue that M_0/P saves time in the production process.

We will, in what follows, take the capital stock as fixed $(K = \bar{K})$ since our working assumption is clearly that of a short-run analysis. y, then, in equation (1.26) represents a flow of both consumer and investment goods, produced by a stock of labour and a stock of capital (K) which is large compared to the flow $(I = dK/dt)$. From this formulation we can move directly to the labour demand function since, of course, that function can be derived directly from equation (1.26). In particular, if the firm successfully equates the value of the marginal product of labour to the wage rate, then the condition

$$\frac{W}{P} = \phi_L \tag{1.27}$$

must be met, where the (marginal product) function ϕ_L has as its arguments L and M_0/P. Thus, the demand for labour is given by

$$\left(\frac{W}{P}\right)_s = \phi_L\left(L, \frac{M_0}{P}\right) \tag{1.28}$$

where it is expressed as the real wage supplied (this notation is a little unorthodox, but since W/P disappears anyway, it is innocuous - and fits the wording of the paragraph more exactly).

The principal contribution of "supply side" economics, it seems, has been the appearance of a good deal of formal analysis involving the supply of labour in the standard macroeconomic model. The Phillips curve, in some ways, represents the first of these efforts, and its demise, following first the attack of the Friedman-Phelps "expectations-augmented" Phillips curve and then the "rational expectations" theory, has generally involved the expectations of workers. In particular, it now seems reasonable to argue that the labour supply function reacts to expectations about the price level - because fixed nominal wage contracts are frequent - and, since these expectations may well be inaccurate, the opportunity exists for an influence on labour supply (and hence on aggregate supply and employment) from the price level. This is not the place to go into great detail about the labour supply function and its rationale, but suffice it to say that the labour supply function, too, can be written in terms of a real wage demanded, as in equation (1.29).

$$\left(\frac{W}{P}\right)_d = Z(L, P) \qquad Z_P < 0,\ Z_L > 0 \tag{1.29}$$

Here $Z_P = \partial X/\partial P < 0$ implies that if there is an increase in the price level (matched by an increase in W, the nominal wage), then workers, not fully perceiving that the real wage has not changed, will increase their offer of real labour services to the labour market. This formulation captures the spirit of the "expectations-augmented" Phillips curve approach without, of course, putting any explicit price expectations into the picture.

Equilibrium in the labour market is then given by the following:

$$\phi_L(L, \frac{M_o}{P}) = Z(L, P) \qquad \phi_{LL} < 0 \tag{1.30}$$

We may totally differentiate (1.30), as before, ignoring the monetary element, in which case we have

$$\frac{\partial \phi_L}{\partial L}dL = \frac{\partial Z}{\partial L}dL + \frac{\partial Z}{\partial P}dP \tag{1.31}$$

This provides us with the following (after adopting a more convenient notation):

$$dL = \frac{Z_P}{\phi_{LL} - Z_L}dP \tag{1.32}$$

The total derivative of the production function, then, is

$$dy = \phi_L dL$$

in which case, after eliminating dL, we get the slope of a simple aggregate supply function of

$$dy = \frac{\phi_L Z_P}{\phi_{LL} - Z_L}dP \tag{1.33}$$

Here with the parameters having the signs assumed above, we see that the slope of the aggregate supply function is positive. Of course, in this very simple formulation there is no influence from the price level if $Z_P = 0$ (i.e. if workers adjust to inflation immediately), in which case the aggregate supply function is perfectly vertical. In any event, the combination of equations (1.33) and (1.25) - or rather that of the underlying models - provides an explanation of the determination of income and the price level in the static (and short run) aggregate demand-aggregate supply model.

1.3 SHORT-RUN DYNAMICS IN AN IS-LM MODEL

It is the purpose of this section to produce some results in an area - short run and disequilibrium dynamics - in which the most we can say is that research is offering "promising" conclusions. Part of the problem is that the analysis of the properties of even moderately-sized systems by the methods discussed in this section often requires solutions to higher order differential equations. Thus, while we may use the analytical methods for dynamic analysis at all levels of disaggregation, we cannot, except in very simple textbook cases, actually examine the stability properties of a proposed system (or, for that matter, readily employ the "correspondence principle" to help in the determination of the predictions of the model). But the general principles of the methods can be illustrated in two-by-two and three-by-three cases, and the advantages for both interpretation of data and for empirical work on the many derived economic relations in popular use in macroeconomics is easy to document. There are, though, severe econometric problems especially with regard to (a) lags in adjustment and (b) the proper way to interpret data which cannot be taken as equilibrium observations. We will have something to say about this here although it does stray from our major theoretical topics; we will also discuss the topic further in Chapter 5, under the heading of Housing "Investment".

We will begin with a summary of the Patinkin (1965) version of the problem and then turn to the standard Tucker (1971) and Barro and Grossman (1971) reformulation of the model; we will also briefly consider some extensions, further criticisms, and append some brief notes on recent empirical work, such as it is. Before turning to the macrotheory, though, we should briefly discuss the short-run disequilibrium context in a basic microeconomic framework, as a way of clarifying the concepts involved. In Figure 1.1, for example, we have a standard micro-paradigm, with the price set at $P = P_1$, which is arbitrarily a non-equilibrium position.

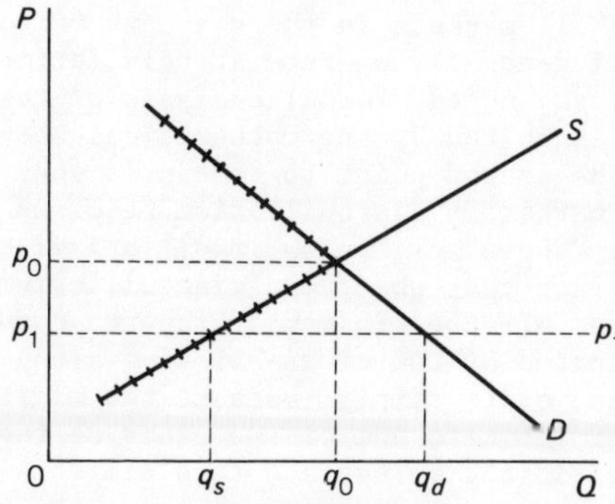

Figure 1.1 A simple disequilibrium situation

Here price is "below" equilibrium, such that the quantity demanded is unequal to the quantity supplied. A simple rule for adjustment, then (expressed arbitrarily as a time derivative), is

$$\frac{dP}{dt} = K_1(q_d - q_s) \qquad K_1 > 0 \tag{1.34}$$

where K_1 is an adjustment parameter. Quite simply, the assumption here is that if the quantity demanded is greater than the quantity supplied, then prices will tend to rise; this is a "Walrasian adjustment" as compared to a "Marshalian". In the latter, the dependent variable is the change in quantity, and the independent is the difference between a "demand price" and a "supply price". In the case described in equation (1.34) - as the curves are drawn in Figure 1.1 - equilibrium will be restored if we start at a position away from equilibrium (at P_1). Alternatively, then, we can retain the rule in equation (1.34) but suppose that the supply curve is also negatively sloped but is flatter than the demand curve. In this event, if we take up a position away from equilibrium, the dynamic equation (1.34) will move us yet further away from equilibrium (for $K_1 > 0$), and the "system" is unstable.[3]

There are two major points in the foregoing which we should retain as we venture into our macroeconomic version. One is that the stability properties of each sector will depend on both the nature of the adjustment proposed and on the structural parameters (the slopes) themselves. Indeed, this point generalizes to the proposition that even if all markets are assumed to be stable (in the combined sense just described), one cannot necessarily claim stability of the combination of all markets in the standard macroeconomic models. We will generally operate at this latter level although, as already noted, formal analysis of the stability properties is inhibited by the mathematical complexity of the problem. The second point to retain is that the formal analysis of a market in disequilibrium requires that we know whether we are "above" or "below" equilibrium; this is the result of the fact that observed (disequilibrium) data are necessarily read off the minimum of the two curves in Figure 1.1 as is indicated by the cross-hatching along those two curves; this is, quite simply, because the minimum represents the upper limit to one or the other of the economic agents involved in the market and this limit is binding. This means, since we are planning to carry the parameters of the underlying functions right into the dynamic equations (in combination with the adjustment parameters K_i), that we will observe sign-switches in the event that it is reasonable to suppose that the market switches from "above" to "below" equilibrium as it adjusts. This possibility provides interesting econometric problems, although we will avoid these in much of the theoretical discussion in this chapter.[4]

1.3.1 SOME BASIC RESULTS FOR DISEQUILIBRIUM MODELS

In order to clarify the nature and potential of the disequilibrium and short-run methods, we will begin here with a summary of Patinkin's (1965) integration of Keynesian and neoclassical economics. The model has four sectors: a commodities sector, a labour market, a bond market, and a money market, along with a technical relation - the production function - linking the factor market(s) to the product market. The product market has a consumption and an investment function (equations (1.35) and (1.36)), a money demand and a money supply function (equations (1.38) and (1.39)), a bond demand and a bond supply function (equations (1.41) and (1. 42)), a labour demand and a labour supply function (equations (1.44) and (1.45)), and a short-run (fixed capital stock) production function (equation (1.47)). Each of the four markets also has an equilibrium condition (equations (1.37), (1.40), (1.43), and (1.46).

$$c = c(y, i, \frac{M_o}{P}) \qquad c_1, c_3 > 0; c_2 < 0 \tag{1.35}$$

$$I = I(y, i, \frac{M_o}{P}) \qquad I_1, I_3 > 0; I_2 < 0 \tag{1.36}$$

$$c + I \equiv F(y, i, \frac{M_o}{P}) = y \tag{1.37}$$

$$m_d = L(y, i, \frac{M_o}{P}) \qquad L_1, L_3 > 0; L_2 < 0 \tag{1.38}$$

$$M_s = M_o \tag{1.39}$$

$$L(y, i, \frac{M_o}{P}) = \frac{M_o}{P} \tag{1.40}$$

$$B_d = iPH(y, \frac{1}{i}, \frac{M_o}{P}) \qquad H_1, H_3 > 0; H_2 < 0 \tag{1.41}$$

$$B_s = iPJ(y, \frac{1}{i}, \frac{M_o}{P}) \qquad J_1, J_2 > 0; J_3 < 0 \tag{1.42}$$

$$B(y, \frac{1}{i}, \frac{M_o}{P}) = 0 \qquad B_1 \lesseqgtr 0; B_2 < 0; B_3 > 0 \tag{1.43}$$

$$L_d = Q(\frac{W}{P}, \overline{K}) \qquad Q_1 < 0 \tag{1.44}$$

$$L_s = R(\frac{W}{P}) \qquad R_1 > 0 \tag{1.45}$$

$$Q(\frac{W}{P}, \overline{K}) = R(\frac{W}{P}) \tag{1.46}$$

$$y = \phi(L, \overline{K}) \qquad \phi_1 > 0 \tag{1.47}$$

Note that this model has a very standard set-up and that the *a priori* sign expectations are the usual ones, with one exception; this is that we assume that the real balance effect on bond demand is opposite in direction to that on bond supply, and that the supply adjusts further as the firm replenishes (for example) money balances lost due to price level changes. We will not use this restriction in what follows, but it is part of the Patinkin dynamics.[5] Note that the bond involved is assumed to be an "inside" bond (a bond based on private debt), and hence equilibrium (equation (1. 43)) occurs when bond excess demand is zero.

The labour market is written in such a way that the quantity of labour and the real wage are determined there under fairly general conditions. Identifying this quantity of labour as the "full" employment labour force, we may carry it forward to equation (1.47) as y_f; equation (1.47), that is to say, then determines full employment real income. The remaining three sectors are then sufficient to (over-) determine the two remaining endogenous variables, the interest rate (i) and the price level (P); with the assumption of Walras's Law, however, where Walras's Law is taken to be a further restriction on the solution which makes one of the three markets redundant, we have a unique solution to the system. Walras's Law is given as equation (1.48).

$$\frac{M_o}{P} - L(y_f, i, \frac{M_o}{P}) \equiv [F(y_f, i, \frac{M_o}{P}) - y_f] + B(y_f, \frac{1}{i}, \frac{M_o}{P}) \tag{1.48}$$

Note that we have an identity here, as our discussion implied.[6]

Points to the right of an IS curve represent excess demand in the commodities market (i.e. $F\ [\ ] > y_f$); this excess can be eliminated, holding the interest rate constant by reducing wealth (via a rise in the price level) so that consumption and investment demand decline. This justifies equation (1.49) as an adjustment equation in the spirit of equation (1.34).

$$\frac{dP}{dt} = K_4[F(y_f,\ i,\ \frac{M_0}{P}) - y_f] \qquad (1.49)$$

While this equation also says that a rise in the price level will result from an excess demand in the commodity market, we are using it in a more narrow sense: equilibrium (which we assume here) in the commodity market requires that a price rise accompany excess demand, to deflate that demand. Note that it will be impossible to follow the material in this section if the distinction just made is not carried through (it does not matter in this particular case). To pursue the point, in an equally unambiguous context, if we have disequilibrium in the bond market, as shown in Figure 1.2 at $(1/i)_1$, that disequilibrium can be eliminated if the bond price rises (or if the interest rate falls).

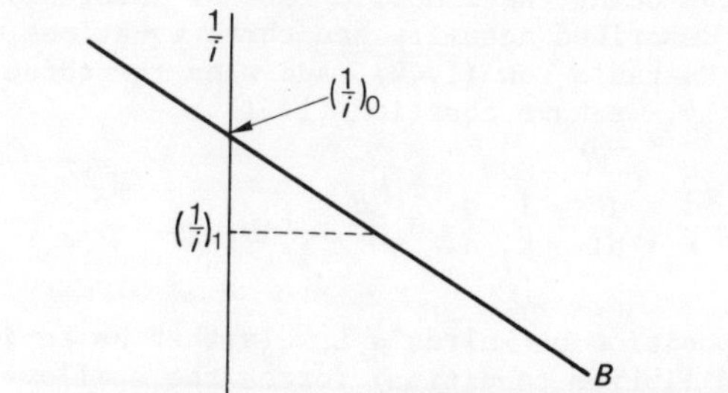

Figure 1.2 The (net) bond demand curve

Since we are assuming this happens, we will write this as equation (1.50); this is equivalent to the statement that a bond excess demand produces a fall in the interest rate.

$$\frac{di}{dt} = -K_1[B(y_f,\ \frac{1}{i},\ \frac{M_0}{P}) \qquad (1.50)$$

As noted, though, this coincidence will not be maintained for the indirect effects between markets under equilibrating assumptions.

The two adjustment equations, (1.49) and (1.50), represent a Patinkin-style parody of the Keynesian model (much as Keynes was represented by the macro-textbooks of the 1950s and 1960s). That is, prices were presumed to rise if an inflationary gap opens up $(F[\;] > y_f)$, with no direct influence from the bond market, and the interest rate changes in response to pressures in capital markets (note that we can have either the money or the bond market here without altering any of our conclusions). Of course, some Keynesians may well have preferred to hold prices constant in equation (1.49) - much as Friedman depicted them in his well-known 1970 - 1 articles - and substituted dy/dt for dP/dt there, but, as just stated, this is a Patinkin parody (and it does not matter which we have for most of the points we are about to make). Indeed, the presence of a real balance term in each equation is distinctly non-Keynesian, even though it is possible to find such a concept in Keynes's work.[7]

Equation (1.50) would appear to put the liquidity trap in its strongest light, for if the system is in the trap, then (further) disequilibrium in the bond market (induced by open market operations in the inside bond) would not affect the interest rate and would not, because of the construction of equation (1.49), spill directly over into commodity markets (the only link being the immobile rate of interest). But the system just described actually has three equations, (1.49), (1.50), and Walras's Law (1.48), and when the three are solved jointly, we have equation (1.51).

$$\frac{1}{K_4}\frac{dP}{dt} - \frac{1}{K_1}\frac{di}{dt} \equiv \frac{M_o}{P} - L(y_f, i, \frac{M_o}{P}) \qquad (1.51)$$

That is, imposition of Walras's Law (either as an identity or as an equilibrium condition) forces the spillover from an excess supply of money onto both the commodity and bond markets; in a nutshell, even in the liquidity trap when $di/dt = 0$, there will be price level effects so long as prices are not rigid (an absurd idea!), and there is a real balance effect. Thus, a distinction between Keynes-versus-the-neoclassics, on this interpretation, boils down to the role of the real balance effect (versus, if you will, the liquidity trap) and Walras's Law in undermining the strict Keynesian position. Note, though, that Keynes himself can be read as stressing the inappropriateness of Walras's Law for macro-applications, a point which if granted goes a long way toward rationalizing his approach.[8]

1.3.2 A MORE GENERAL DISEQUILIBRIUM MODEL

Parochial disputes aside, however, the possibility exists of employing a useful methodology and a general model which permits more interaction in order to achieve some results in macro-dynamics. Let us rewrite our adjustment system as equations (1.52) and (1.53), in this case allowing cross-effects to occur between the two markets (we still employ the assumptions of our previous section).

$$\frac{di}{dt} = -K_1B(y_f, \frac{1}{i}, \frac{M_o}{P}) - K_2[F(y_f, i, \frac{M_o}{P}) - y_f] \qquad (1.52)$$

$$\frac{dP}{dt} = K_3B(y_f, \frac{1}{i}, \frac{M_o}{P}) + K_4[F(y_f, i, \frac{M_o}{P}) - y_f] \qquad (1.53)$$

All K_i are positive. We have already achieved signs for K_1 and K_4, and so it remains to work out signs for the "off-diagonal" K_2 and K_3 under stabilizing conditions in each market.

For K_2 we can proceed as follows. Assuming $B(\;) = 0$, then if we have a condition of excess demand in the commodity market such that we are at point $\tilde{a}$ in Figure 1.3, then supposing the price level does not adjust at all, we must follow the arrow back to the IS curve, as shown.

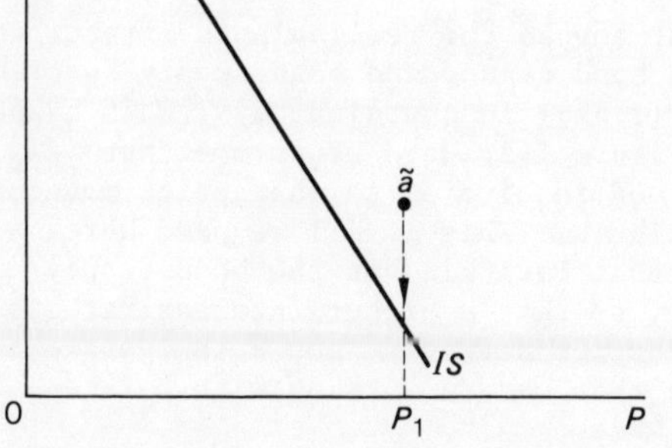

Figure 1.3 <u>The IS curve and the interest rate adjustment</u>

Here we see the conflict in the interpretation between our stabilizing assumption (we must follow the arrow and validate, in effect, the excess demand by lowering the interest rate) and what we normally might expect to happen in commodity markets. That is, we might normally anticipate that an excess demand would push interest rates up, not down. Of course, we are not really contradicting that statement which is derived presumably from a different (and dynamic) model; we are, instead, introducing a kind of limited dynamics into a basically static model, and we are bound by our limitations in this respect.

To obtain the sign for K_3, we note that we are at a position of excess demand in the bond market but that (for simplicity) an interest rate adjustment is not permitted to clear it. This is shown as point $\tilde{a}$ in Figure 1.4.

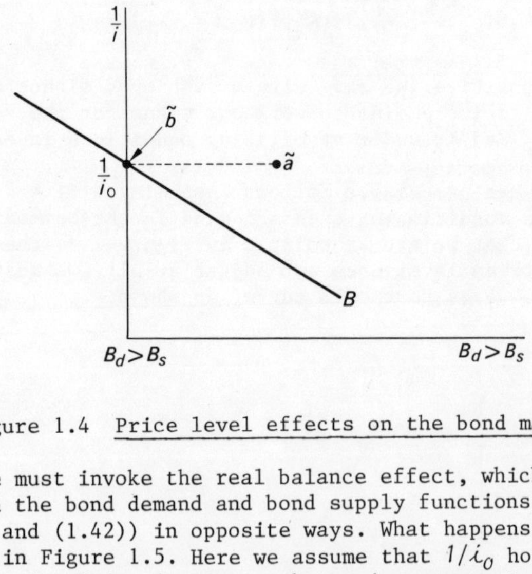

Figure 1.4 Price level effects on the bond market

Here we must invoke the real balance effect, which operates on both the bond demand and bond supply functions (equations (1.41) and (1.42)) in opposite ways. What happens is illustrated in Figure 1.5. Here we assume that $1/i_0$ holds, as in Figure 1.4 and inquire as to what price movement will restore equilibrium. This is all we need here, although we note again that Patinkin has the bond supply curve shifting yet further, so that a higher interest rate is required (this interaction between i and P is ignored in what follows). Note that we are working with B_d/P and B_s/P along the horizontal axis.

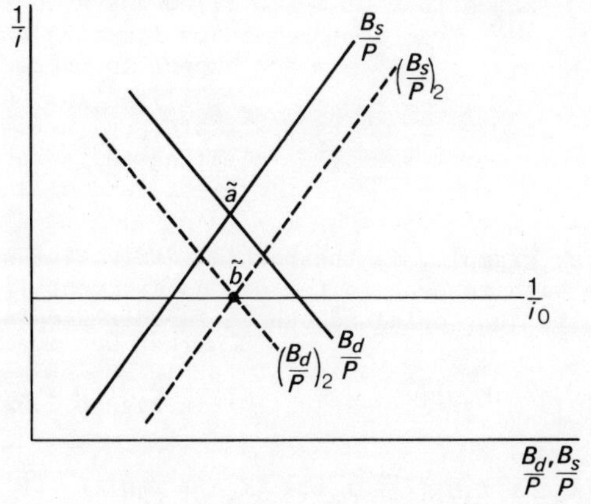

Figure 1.5 The operation of the real balance effect in the bond market

Following Patinkin (and Samuelson, 1947), we can now form linear approximations for our adjustment equations, with the approximations being taken away from the equilibrium [$(i - i_0)$ and $(P - P_0)$]. That is, we can write equations which are analogous to the total derivatives of the system, as given by equation (1.54); here we have inserted the equation numbers to save space.

$$\frac{di}{dt} = \frac{\partial(1.52)}{\partial i}(i - i_0) + \frac{\partial(1.52)}{\partial P}(P - P_0)$$
$$\frac{dP}{dt} = \frac{\partial(1.53)}{\partial i}(i - i_0) + \frac{\partial(1.53)}{\partial P}(P - P_0) \quad (1.54)$$

We can think of this system as representing the implicit dynamics of the system (1.52) and (1.53) in the neighbourhood of equilibrium. Full interaction is permitted in the calculation of the partial derivates. Carrying out the calculations in equation (1.54), we obtain directly equations (1.55)

$$\frac{di}{dt} = [\frac{K_1B_2}{i_0^2} - K_2F_2](i - i_0) + [\frac{K_1B_3M}{P_0^2} + \frac{K_2F_3M}{P_0^2}](P - P_0) \quad (1.55)$$

and (1.56).

$$\frac{dP}{dt} = [-\frac{K_3B_2}{i_0^2} + K_4F_2](i - i_0)$$

$$+ [-\frac{K_3B_3M}{P_0^2} - \frac{K_4F_3M}{P_0^2}](P - P_0) \qquad (1.56)$$

Here B_2, for example, is the partial derivative of the net bond curve with respect to the second argument $(1/i)$.

The results just obtained can be further simplified into

$$\frac{di}{dt} = (-K_1a - K_2b)(i - i_0) - (K_1e + K_2d)(P - P_0) \qquad (1.57)$$

$$\frac{dP}{dt} = (K_3a + K_4b)(i - i_0) - (K_3e + K_4d)(P - P_0) \qquad (1.58)$$

where $a = -B_2/i_0^2 > 0$, $b = F_2 < 0$, $e = -B_3M/P_0^2 < 0$, and $d = F_3M/P_0^2 < 0$ according to our *a priori* restrictions on the signs. Forming a characteristic equation as in $A\tilde{x} = \lambda\tilde{x}$, we have that

$$\begin{vmatrix} -K_1a - K_2b - \lambda & -K_1e - K_2d \\ K_3a - K_4b & K_3e + K_4d - \lambda \end{vmatrix} = 0$$

such that

$$\lambda^2 + g\lambda + h = 0 \qquad (1.59)$$

for

$$g = K_1a + K_2b - K_3e - K_4d$$

$$h = -K_1K_4ad - K_2K_3be + K_1K_4be + K_2K_3ad$$

Equation (1.59), then, has roots

$$\lambda_{1,\,2} = \frac{-g \pm (g^2 - 4h)^{\frac{1}{2}}}{2}$$

and in spite of our *a priori* restrictions on slopes and on the adjustment parameters (all individual markets were assumed to be stable), the possibility exists that the overall system is unstable. That is, the possibility exists that the roots will have non-negative real parts (note that we obtain oscillation, as well, if $-4h > g^2$).

We may, then, consider several direct results in this framework. For one, if the interest elasticity of the spending functions is nil, then $b = 0$, and we have stability as long as K_2 and K_3 are small. Of course, in the "Keynesian" case discussed above, K_3 and K_2 are equal to zero (so that $g > 0$ and $h > 0$), and we have, in effect, *a priori* stability (another non-Keynesian result which we can attribute, in effect, to the application of Walras's Law). A third case of some interest occurs when real balance effects are ruled out so that B_3 and F_3 are zero. In this case equations (1.57) and (1.58) collapse into two simpler equations in $(i - i_0)$. Both equations (1.57) and (1.58) would then depend on the interest rate disequilibrium, and this arrangement would provide the strongest potential for the liquidity trap, since a stalemate would then exist if the interest rate were unable to move. Finally, we note that if we are willing to assume overall stability, then, by Samuelson's correspondence principle, we can work backward from the characteristic equation to establish an additional restriction on the coefficients of the system.[9] This would permit additional leverage of a theoretical nature in the event that we were short by one sign in our *a priori* work.

There is another aspect to the foregoing that we should mention at this point, and that involves the speed of adjustment out of equilibrium. Keynes, as it turns out, is associated with the idea of sticky prices and yet at the same time with Walrasian adjustment as it is described in equation (1.34). Thus, even if one cannot turn off the adjustment - as described in this section - equilibrium may be slow to arrive and may involve long-term quantity constraints (i.e. may involve protracted unemployment). The distinction raised here is important; not only does Keynes accept a Walrasian style of adjustment, but also he feels that the adjustment is slow to unfold. Both positions represent a departure from the (essentially) neoclassical position widely taken at the time Keynes wrote. Keynesians (e.g. Tobin, (1975)) have frequently underscored this price rigidity - too often on empirical grounds - but much of the literature has neglected the Walrasian character of Keynes's work.[10]

1.3.3 THE BARRO-GROSSMAN DISEQUILIBRIUM MODEL

Patinkin points out in his book (1965) that disequilibrium can be represented as excess supply in the product market, and in this case, the case in which firms cannot sell all of their products, they will accordingly demand a smaller amount of labour services. In this case all economic agents are "constrained" in their decisions, and so the result is a constrained choice of "effective" rather than "notional" demands and supplies. The underlying rationale, here, is supplied by rigid prices, and so, it is clear, much of the Barro-Grossman-Clower work has to be interpreted as Keynesian in spirit, although recent work (by Drazen, 1980b) is moving away from rigid prices as a rationale for quantity-constrained demand. Note that one still must explain why (if they are) prices are rigid if economic agents can gain by adjusting them.

A general quantity-constrained four-sector disequilibrium model - in the style of Barro and Grossman (1971) - is the following: it is due to Tucker (1971),

$$c_c^* = c_c\left(r, \frac{W}{P}, \frac{M_0}{P}, \pi, c_d^* - c, \frac{B_d^* - B}{rP}, L_s^* - L\right) \quad (1.60)$$

$$c_p^* = c_p\left(r, \frac{W}{P}, \frac{M_0}{P}, y, c_s^* - c, \frac{B_s^* - B}{rP}, L_d^* - L\right) \quad (1.61)$$

with similar equations for B_d^*/rP, B_s^*/rP, L_s^*, and L_d^*. The appearance of constraint terms is rationalized with reference to sticky prices, and producers are assumed, here, to be concerned with expected sales (represented, simplistically, by the level of real income, y), while individuals are concerned with real profits (π) as well as real wages and the real interest rate. Most importantly, each equation has an appropriate disequilibrium term expressing that the optimizing decision is taken under constraint; the actual quantities determined, then, are

$$c = \min\left(c_d^*, c_s^*\right)$$

$$B = \min\left(B_d^*, B_s^*\right)$$

$$L = \min\left(L_d^*, L_s^*\right)$$

with the stock of money determined as a residual (via Walras's Law): this particular specification is often referred to as the "short side" model of disequilibrium. Here we should note - in contrast to the Patinkin model that we discussed in detail - that the Tucker model will switch terms and signs - either c_d^* or c_s^* - as one moves above and below equilibrium. This creates some interesting econometric problems (some of which we will return to below and again in

Chapter 5.[11]

The Tucker model, as noted, is actually a lineal descendant of the more commonly cited Barro-Grossman model, although Tucker has earlier work as well. A typical applied paper in the Barro-Grossman sequence is one written by Grossman (1971) dealing with the differences between the loanable funds and liquidity-preference theories of interest and the quantity and expenditure theories of price determination. Basically, the argument is that many distinctions in the literature, such as that between "loanable funds" and "liquidity preference", are the result of incomplete dynamic specifications. Thus, consider a market economy with a medium of exchange (money). Each commodity traded in this economy has its own market (in which it is traded for money), but money does not have its own market, since its "market" is merely derived from all of the other markets for commodities. More particularly, if the bond market were in equilibrium and the derived money market were not, the standard neoclassical position is that the price level would take up all of the adjustment (relative commodity prices being unaffected by assumption) with the interest rate unaffected. Out of equilibrium, however, both the price level and the interest rate would adjust.

In contrast, Grossman argues that all of the "effective excess demands" in the standard model should depend on disequilibrium in each of the markets, assuming, of course, that prices are rigid in the short run; then, whether one is to talk of loanable funds, liquidity preference, etc. depends on specializing the disequilibrium process and not simply on the underlying structure of the economy. In fact, to generate one of these particular theories, what one can do is eliminate one or more of the disequilibrium "spillovers" from market to market. In Grossman's words,

> A *priori*, the dynamic loanable-funds, liquidity-preference, quantity, and expenditure theories all turn out to be consistent with the structures of exchange in a monetary economy. Which better approximates reality depends upon choice-theoretic behavioral parameters which determine the pattern of spillover (1971, p. 946).

The following represent the standard (textbook) positions, expressed in terms of adjustment coefficients (K_i).

Dynamic Classical Model (loanable funds)

$$\frac{dr}{dt} = -K_2(B_d - B_s)$$

$$\frac{dP}{dt} = K_3(M_d - M_s)$$

Dynamic Keynesian Model (liquidity preference)

$$\frac{dr}{dt} = K_1(M_d - M_s)$$

$$\frac{dP}{dt} = K_4(y_d - y_s)$$

Dynamic Neoclassical Synthesis

$$\frac{dr}{dt} = -K_2(B_d - B_s)$$

$$\frac{dP}{dt} = K_4(y_d - y_s)$$

The foregoing assume that individuals are actually able to buy and sell any quantity they wish at prevailing prices; but in disequilibrium (as in Keynes, 1936, or Clower, 1965) they cannot - they must, for example, "false trade" - and spillovers occur between markets as dissatisfied customers seek to spend all their funds. The approach is the "dual-decision" framework; it involves recognizing that (e.g.) an individual who ends up with unspent money balances from commodity transactions, if he perceives the situation, will purchase more bonds (and money) and, indeed, will actually exceed his desired holdings of bonds. The two decisions concern the original demands and when to "jump the queue" and make a disequilibrium purchase. Under these hypotheses the dynamic processes become

$$\frac{dr}{dt} = - K_2(B^*_d - B_s) + \sum_{i=1}^{n} \alpha_i(x^*_{id} - x_{is})$$

$$\frac{dP}{dt} = K_4(y^*_d - y_s) + \sum_{j=1}^{n} \beta_j(z^*_{jd} - z_{js})$$

where the indices (i, j) are over the spillovers from all other markets (x_i, z_j), and the α_i, β_j are the other adjustment parameters. Thus, if there are no spillovers, we have the neoclassical synthesis etc., and one can readily show that the three "models" are special cases in their dynamic forms. Grossman argues that this puts to rest the liquidity preference, loanable-funds debates (on this interpretation) as merely special assumptions about disequilibrium dynamics; another more recent paper along the same lines is by Ferguson and Hart (1980).[12]

We have noted that the Keynesian model (of sticky prices) has a Walrasian dynamic interpretation; we should also point out (although the bulk of the discussion occurs in Chapter 2) that sticky prices can form a rationale (a) for inserting current income into the consumption function, (b) for unemployment cycles, and (c) even for underemployment equilibrium. This is, generally, because sticky prices could rationalize disequilibrium adjustment, i.e. could rationalize the appearance of "effective" quantity constraints in final spending equations. How this works out is explained by Clower (1965), Leijonhufvud (1968), and Barro and Grossman (1971), but one is still hard-pressed to find strong theoretical support for the idea,[13] and the "stickiness" of price can also be debated in terms of an optimal amount of price rigidity. There has also not been a lot of successful empirical work on the general "quantity-constraints" approach, and in a recent symposium (AER, May 1979) some of the creators of this literature discuss why this is so. The principal specific constraints mentioned in the disequilibrium models usually concern fixed nominal contracts; this would seem to justify Keynesian-style "sticky" prices and wages (and quantity adjustments), but efficient labour markets theory - even with contractually sticky prices and wages - does not provide a convincing explanation of persistent unemployment if only because such wage agreements are often altered, are often vague, and, in any event, are entered into "rationally", perhaps as Grossman (1979) suggests, being a device to shift risk from workers to employers. Thus, says Barro (1979), one must look at "deeper elements" such as imperfect information, imperfect factor mobility, or transactions costs, and these seem less likely to have major cyclical impacts. Along these lines Howitt (1979) suggests that one has to examine particular markets as to how they are organized (for example, individual traders, specialists, broad economy-wide agreements, etc.); he opts for the existence of specialists who (for a charge) actually break the link between buyers and sellers so that actual markets tend to operate as if they are always cleared, even in the face of supply and demand fluctuations. Such specialists would appear to the extent that other arrangements (e.g. unemployment) tend to use more resources (in the absence of certain types of externality). In this sense the "rigid price" constraint model of Barro-Grossman merges with the pure Walrasian model; see Drazen (1980a) for a summary of this literature (and some suggestions for further research). Grossman (1979), finally, stresses the idea of market participants failing to acquire relevant information and feels that work on "implicit contracts" provides the best avenue for future work.

What this amounts to is that successful empirical work on the relevance of "non-market clearing" has to await some further micro-underpinnings, themselves fairly unlikely to have convincing macroeconomic applications. There are cases (of course) in which price rigidities are clearly binding on market participants, and here empirical work has had some success. In one such paper, Howard (1976) applies the Barro-Grossman model to Russian data. Howard notes that the Barro-Grossman paper (1971) implies that the repression of inflation by means of price controls has the undesirable side-effects of increasing saving and of decreasing labour supply (with attendant multiplier effects on output). This seems a promising approach to take to the Russian data, where the "quantity constraint" is the quantity of consumer goods available; the three functions of the model are the labour supply, the demand for free market goods, and the demand for real saving. Howard feels the model fits very well and succeeds in exposing several ways in which the Soviet price control approach creates spillovers, especially onto saving (which it decreases!). This result has not gone unchallenged, and both Katz (1979) and Nissanke (1979) have reworked the study (Howard's model was on the simplistic side), Katz on the Russian data and Nissanke on the Polish; the former actually obtains a reversal of the sign of the savings effect.[14]

With regard to other markets and to cases when rigid prices are not necessarily the motivation for disequilibrium, our material is not very considerable. One exception is a study by Bowden (1978) on the demand for money under "persistent disequilibrium". First of all, one must note that while price rigidities present a rationale for determining functions with quantity constraints included in them, another interpretation of disequilibrium is that actual adjustment is to purely "notional" (unconstrained) variables. The former, which is Barro-Grossman, relies on inaccurate expectations or information; see the discussion in Drazen (1980a), as well as that in Bowden (1978). Indeed, Bowden (p. 130) argues that

> there is no unique theoretical demand for money function and no unique path to equilibrium. Instead, it is an empirical matter as to which combination, of many possibilities, of demand and supply functions and disequilibrium

dynamics best fits the available data.

Bowden opts for a Keynesian demand for money with the only binding constraint being the supply of labour. The estimation required is complex (he has an income identity and a money supply function), involving a combination of two stage and indirect least squares, and the results were not very satisfying, although the "diseconomies of scale", low (negative) interest elasticity, and long adjustment he found are certainly common enough in this particular literature.

We will continue the subject of disequilibrium - and consider some of the econometric problems in passing - in various parts of the remainder of this book. Disequilibrium will appear in our sectoral chapters, notably in the discussion of housing investment in Chapter 5, and various comments on the literature on the demand for money, consumption, production, and investment will reflect concern with the interpretation of standard results when disequilibrium may be present. There will be rare, but revealing, empirical results scattered about as well, the rarity reflecting the lack of literature (or, if you wish, the difficulty of the task confronting the econometrician).

1.4 THE AGGREGATION PROBLEM: SOME GENERAL ISSUES

In recent years there has developed an extensive - and growing - literature on the micro-foundations of macroeconomics which has attempted to sort out the conditions under which microeconomic insights may be relevant to macroeconomics (on both the theoretical and policy levels).[15] But there is also a traditional literature, which has a remarkably complete set of proved propositions, that we should look at; this is the literature on the "aggregation problem in economics". In this section we will take up some points of general interest, leaving the discussion of specific empirical results (and a few more theoretical propositions) to Chapter 4, on the production function, and, in passing, to Chapter 3, in the discussion of the definition of money. The reason for this somewhat awkward division is essentially that the main part of the empirical record has been generated in production studies or on the demand for money.

One reason we should enter into such a discussion at this point is the very practical one that the theorems we will be looking at here (and in Chapter 4) are not very encouraging to those who would operate macroeconomics as a kind of applied microeconomics. In spite of this, one still notes a widespread practice in macroeconomics of employing concepts that only seem to be precisely defined in the micro-literature, in order to motivate the discussion. Thus, to pick on Keynes for no particular reason, the propensity to consume is based on a "fundamental psychological law": money is held to satisfy a "liquidity preference", and investment spending is partly motivated by the "anticipation of future profits". In addition, one notes that it is the fashion (usually referred to as a "micro-foundation approach") to restate, sometimes self-consciously, the traditional macro-structural relations - e.g. the consumption function - as optimizing problems for representative economic agents. In either case, aggregation problems are often simply ignored, as if the idea of a "representative economic agent" were totally unambiguous from either a theoretical or an empirical point of view. Perhaps the best example of an area of current interest in which these problems are largely ignored is that of the literature on the causes of inflation, particularly as those causes emanate from the labour market (either as "cost-push" or "job-search" propositions).[16]

Actually, we have been approaching the problem as if the aggregation problem only concerned an aggregation "over" economic agents (consumers, producers, money holders) when in fact there are three main areas of concern; these are

(a) aggregations over commodities,
(b) aggregations over agents, and peripherally (for this chapter),
(c) aggregations over financial goods;

and in the following we will be pursuing a line laid down by Leijonhufvud (1968). We will consider (a) and (b) at some length in this book and occasionally extend our discussion into empirical questions, but before doing that, we should consider some general principles. For one thing, whatever the aggregation being considered ((a) to (c)), the aggregation produces a gain in terms of simplicity and a cost in terms of the suppression of potentially relevant information. Ideally, the suppressed information should be either (a) irrelevant under any condition or (b) irrelevant in practice (i.e. under some reasonable conditions), although these ideals really only set the limit. In practice one has to pay a cost - either kind of "irrelevance" is a matter of degree - and it will generally not be easy to assess just what this cost might be (although often one can disaggregate to some extent, in order to run an empirical verification).[17]

With regard to consumers, for example, we find that we can write aggregate demand functions "over" prices and the sum of incomes if there are no distribution effects. Thus, if all individual demand functions are linear and if all are homogeneous in income, then distribution effects become irrelevant (it does not matter who has the income), and condition (a) applies. On the other hand, if all other parameters (e.g. the variance) except the mean of the income distribution are fixed and if all Engel curves ($c = f(y)$) are linear, then in practice all distribution effects are irrelevant, as in condition (b). We can distinguish condition (a) from condition (b), in this example at least, because condition (b) can be approached empirically, while condition (a) may be difficult to reach in this way.

Turning to the aggregation over commodities, we should begin by noting that what we are after is some aggregate commodity - e.g. consumer goods - that has been constructed as a weighted sum of a number of different goods. In particular, we will need both a satisfactory quantity index and a satisfactory price index since the aggregate commodity must have a price if we are to carry our micro-analysis through to the macro-level. Following our discussion of the last paragraph, we will be able to construct such an index (a) either when the changes in the relative prices within the composite commodity are irrelevant somewhow (b) or when the composite goods theorem (of Hicks (1946)) holds. With regard to (a) we note that in the (unlikely) event that commodities are either perfect complements in demand - like left shoes and right shoes - or perfect substitutes (in effect having linear indifference curves), then relative prices do not matter. The composite goods theorem, on the other hand, argues that commodities can be treated as if they were perfect substitutes if the relative prices of the components do not change, in practice. This, again, has an obvious empirical application; we next consider the details of the composite goods theorem, in view of its obvious application to inflation (if all prices rise in exact proportion, then the relative prices in the price index will not change).[18]

1.4.1 THE COMPOSITE GOODS THEOREM

The composite goods theorem provides the formal proof that constancy of relative prices is sufficient to establish the validity of the composite commodity as an economic entity. The validity is of interest because, once achieved, the composite commodity (an index number, formally) may be treated as if it were the direct provider of utilities (i.e. entered into the aggregate utility function) without fear of losing any of the richness of detail of the underlying microeconomics. It is one major step on the way from microeconomics to macroeconomics, and its importance is underscored because the theorem provides a direct empirical test - the constancy of relative prices or, equivalently, the proportionality of all absolute price changes - to use in establishing the viability of any potential aggregate.

The theorem also is known as Hicks's composite goods theorem, and this explains its pedigree, at least in so far as monetary-macro questions are concerned. Hicks (1946, p. 33) says,

> A collection of physical things can always be treated as if they were divisible into units of a single commodity so long as their relative prices can be assumed to be unchanged, in the particular problem in hand. So long as the prices of other consumption goods are assumed to be given, they can be lumped together into one commodity 'money' or 'purchasing power in general'.

Note, though, the inverted commas around "money"; as Samuelson (1947, p. 143) points out,

> It would seem that this involves rather a strained use of the term "money," and one almost certain to lead to confusion. Very properly when Hicks later comes to discuss monetary matters, he rejects this earlier notion.

This, of course, does not prevent us from aggregating "monies" by the rules about to be laid out.

Hicks presented a formal proof of his proposition employing six conditions on the "fundamental equation of value theory"; this standard expression divides the effects of a change in the price of good r on the quantity demanded of good s into an income effect $(-x_r(\partial x_s/\partial Y))$ and a substitution effect $(\mu(U_{rs}/U))$, as in Equation (1.62).[19]

$$\frac{\partial x_s}{\partial P_r} = -x_r\frac{\partial x_s}{\partial Y} + \mu\frac{U_{rs}}{U} \qquad r, s = 1, \ldots, n \qquad (1.62)$$

The six rules, then, consist of the usual ones that there is

(a) symmetry of substitution effects: $X'_{sr} = X'_{rs}$;
(b) negativity of own substitution effects: $X'_{rr} < 0$;
(c) a condition on the substitution effects: $\Sigma P_s X'_{rs} = 0$;

and three further propositions which impose restrictions on the substitution effects in the case of proportional changes in price.[20] In plain words, in the event that all price changes are in the same proportion, we will meet the necessary and sufficient conditions for the consumer's optimum, in terms of a composite commodity both before and after the (proportional) price change.

Patinkin (1965), in his restatement of the Hicks theorem, presents a useful discussion (but not a proof) of the theorem which helps to clarify what one must do to prove it. Thus, assume that there are three goods, whose quantities are q_1, q_2, and q_3, with prices P_1, P_2, and P_3. Consider an initial set of quantities (q_1^0, q_2^0) and define the expenditure on this initial set as in equation (1.63).

$$P_x = P_1 q_1^0 + P_2 q_2^0 \tag{1.63}$$

for any prices. As well, form a quantity index as in equation (1.64).

$$X = \frac{P_1 q_1 + P_2 q_2}{P_1 q_1^0 + P_2 q_2^0} \tag{1.64}$$

The problem is to show that for P_1/P_2 constant (i.e. for parallel shifts of the budget line between q_1 and q_2), X - the composite commodity - and q_3 have indifference curves between them of the usual sort (this is what Hicks's proof amounts to).

We may substitute (1.63) into (1.64) to obtain equation (1.65).

$$X = \frac{P_1}{P_x} q_1 + \frac{P_2}{P_x} q_2 \tag{1.65}$$

These, as well, are parallel lines in the q_1, q_2 dimension (shifting for dX) since the expression is homogeneous of degree zero in P_1, P_2 in this event. Clearly, as well, lower budget lines lie closer to the origin. If the original indifference curves between q_1 and q_2 have the usual properties, then they will be tangent to these "semi-budget" lines and will produce a locus of q_1/q_2. We need to establish that this locus is monotonically increasing (although not necessarily constant) for each level of the third good, q_3. This will establish that indifference curves drawn between X and q_3 are increasing, from left to right. As well, we need to establish the curvature of the indifference curves between X and q_3. This will require that given increases of consumption of the third good produce increasingly smaller decreases of consumption of the two goods in the aggregate. Patinkin draws his curves in just this fashion, and Hicks, in his last three conditions (not stated), puts restrictions on the curvature such that this result holds. Finally, note that a clear formal proof of the theorem is also available in the work of H.A.J. Green (1964).

1.4.2 AGGREGATION OF SPENDING

The foregoing establishes that if each economic agent is faced with a set of unvarying relative prices, then a composite commodity may be constructed and treated as if it were an entity in a macroeconomic analysis. We may, in a nutshell, speak of aggregate consumer demand, etc. We may, though, prefer to take a more direct approach, by-passing the (implicit) utility calculus (e.g.) and inquire as to the conditions under which we might aggregate individual (linear) spending functions (or demand for money functions, etc.).[21] Suppose that each spending unit has a linear demand function for "commodities", as in equation (1.66); here we arbitrarily designate a letter t for each observation (time or cross-section) on each unit's function.[22]

$$X_{it} = \beta_{oi} + \beta_{1i}Y_{it} + u_{it} \tag{1.66}$$

That is, let us not attempt any aggregation at the utility function level (e.g.) (but see the discussion in Chapter 4 on the production function), and, further, let us assume that each spending unit's function is of the same linear form and has the same arguments (Y, u, where u is a random error). We note that H.A.J. Green (1964) has proved that necessary and sufficient conditions for a consistent aggregation are that we have linear individual spending functions and identical individual propensities to spend.[23]

The aggregate version of equation (1.66), quite simply, is equation (1.67),

$$\sum_{i=1}^{N} X_{it} = \sum_{i=1}^{N} \beta_{oi} + \sum_{i=1}^{N} \beta_{1i}Y_{it} + \sum_{i=1}^{N} u_{it} \tag{1.67}$$

where N indicates either the number of individuals or, more relevantly, the number of households. We might first take the approach that if all of the micro-parameters of the individual functions (both the slopes and the constants) are assumed to be equal, we can obtain an unambiguous aggregate spending function; thus let

$$\beta_{0i} = \beta_{0j} = \beta_0$$

$$\beta_{1i} = \beta_{1j} = \beta_1$$

so that (1.67) becomes

$$\sum_{i=1}^{N} X_{it} = \beta_0 N + \beta_1 \sum_{i=1}^{N} Y_{it} + \sum_{i=1}^{N} u_{it} \qquad (1.68)$$

One could conceive of this equation as a regression equation using the sum of expenditures on the left and the sum of incomes on the right, over time, but if so, population growth, etc. (over time) will change both N and ΣY_{it} so that multicollinearity (and, hence, inefficient parameter estimates) between the constant and the independent variable will ensue. This also would affect a cross-section over regions, for example, since regions with larger populations will tend to have larger aggregate incomes. This problem is easily dealt with, though, by dividing equation (1.68) by N; the result is equation (1.69) in which a "number of households" or a population deflator is thereby justified in terms of its assistance with an aggregation problem.[24]

$$\frac{\sum_{i=1}^{N} X_{it}}{N} = \beta_0 + \beta_1 \frac{\sum_{i=1}^{N} Y_{it}}{N} + \frac{1}{N} \sum_{i=1}^{N} u_{it} \qquad (1.69)$$

This is a standard transformation of the data which, as one can readily see, has a straightforward rationale.

There are, though, at least three further problems to consider, even at this level.

(a) What happens if the individual errors in equation (1.69) are correlated?
(b) What happens (precisely) if individual micro-parameters are unequal?
(c) What happens if individual observations on income are unequal?

We can use the framework already presented to this point to deal with the first of these problems. Thus, let us suppose, on account of a war or a common fad, or some other general change in tastes, that the situation for the errors of equation (1.69) is

$$E(u_{it}) = 0 \qquad (1.70a)$$

$$var\ (u_{it}) = \sigma^2$$

$$cov\ (u_{it}, u_{jt}) = \rho\sigma^2 \text{ for } i \neq j \qquad (1.70b)$$

where a correlation (ρ) between errors has been introduced. Let us, then, aggregate the variance for equation (1.69) as

$$var\ (u) = E[(\frac{1}{N}\sum_{i=1}^{N} u_{it})^2 = \frac{1}{N^2}E[(\sum_{i=1}^{N} u_{it})^2] \qquad (1.71)$$

The error term, then, consists of two parts: a sum of individual variances all alike (by (1.70b)) and a sum of covariances all equal to $\rho\sigma^2$ by the same argument. Since there are N of the variances and $(N)(N - 1)$ distinct covariances, we have

$$var\ (u) = \frac{\sigma^2}{N} + \sigma^2\rho - \frac{\sigma^2}{N} \qquad (1.72)$$

and, we see, as $N \to \infty$, while both σ^2/N and $\rho\sigma^2/N \to 0$, $\rho\sigma^2$ is unaffected. In particular, for $0 < \rho < 1$, as one might reasonably expect for a consumption problem, the estimated aggregate variance will be $\rho\sigma^2$ (instead of σ^2) and, of course, will be understated (biased downward). The consequence is, even with all micro-parameters equal, we will tend to claim a significance which is not there. What one can do in this event is to calculate our original regression in double-logarithmic form, in which case the correlation (ρ) will be pulled into the constant. This is another popular transformation in empirical macroeconomics whose best rationale, again, may well be to deal with an aggregation problem. Note, though, that one should base any statistical tests of significance on the log-normal rather than the normal distribution, if this is the rationale behind the logarithmic transformation. There is, finally, an excellent discussion of problems (b) and (c) in Rowley and Trivedi (1975).

The foregoing has established that strong conditions are needed for successful aggregation; then, with (one hopes) suitable understatement, it is clear that the (statistical) aggregation conditions required to build a macro-relation from micro-perceptions are sufficiently unlikely so as to produce extreme caution in this area. That is, we required at various points in this section such things as perfect substitutes, unchanged relative prices, and an unchanged income distribution, and we made use of equal income and wealth and equal micro-parameters (in linear functions). We also found that deflation by population and transformation into logarithmic form would help with problems whose origins came from the aggregation. Even though this list is depressingly detailed, there is still another area of aggregation we have not touched on, and that is in the spending unit's "technology". In particular, there is technical progress in consumption, money-holding, and production, and consumers do not all use the same technology - and they might have the equivalent of "excess capacity" in their consumption process - so that there are other problems to consider (we normally discuss these only for the production function, in general). On the other hand, one can still safely employ microeconomics as a guide and an inspiration for macro-studies, and macroeconomics can proceed along its own path - following its own rules - so that appreciation of the many problems of aggregation should not and has not precluded the development of an effective and often useful sub-discipline in which one uses either analogies from the microeconomic sphere or the notion of a "representative economic agent", the latter, presumably, being thought of as having equal micro-parameters and not as an average. We will proceed, at any rate, into our functional studies with this as a provisional rationalization.

NOTES

1. Note that a further discussion appears in Section 2.6.
2. This creates severe problems for monetary policy since effective control in terms of an interest rate strategy (as is often done, for example, by the American Federal Reserve) requires that one know the relative value of these two terms in i. There is another "real" rate of interest in the literature calculated by subtracting the actual rate of inflation (over some period) from the nominal interest rate.

$$r_x = i - \dot{P}/P$$

This is an observable rate, since both sides of the equation can be calculated, but it is an *ex post* concept and as such is of little interest in macro-models. If, as is clearly untrue in general

$$\dot{P}/P = (\dot{P}/P)_e$$

then the two correspond. We notice frequent examples of negative real rates in the *ex post* sense, although we might not expect negative real rates *ex ante* since that amounts to asserting that lenders plan to give their money away. Inaccurate expectations (perhaps caused by erratic or nonsensical money policies), transactions costs, and (even) overall portfolio strategy would explain this divergence. It is often observed in practice. Later chapters take up all of these possibilities, and this important real/nominal distinction will frequently resurface in this book.

3. It would be stable in this case if, instead of equation (1.34), we had written

$$\frac{dq}{dt} = K_2(P_d - P_s)$$

where (e.g.) P_d is a "demand" price (a price read off the demand curve).

4. There are other basic points to make about disequilibrium macroeconomics, as well. For one thing, Grossman warns (1974), even accepting the Walrasian paradigm, as in equation (1.34), we need to define what we mean by quantity. What we usually say is quantity demanded and quantity supplied, but we should recognize that buyers may not be able to get the quantity demanded - they may have to take a lesser amount, the quantity *ordered* (or the quantity offered), which then becomes the disequilibrium constraint. Recognizing that orders may be less than demands, it is clear that actual amounts *bought* may be less than amounts demanded or ordered; inventories may absorb some of the imbalance. Any macro-sales data which is examined over the cycle may have the problem that disequilibrium may exist in any of these senses, and, clearly, the implications may be different (the disequilibrium between amount demanded and amount supplied is clearly not of the same implication as the disequilibrium between the amount produced and the amount consumed), but the data need to be interpreted one way or the other.

5. Patinkin (1965) argues that this is justified since firms will need to (e.g.) replenish part of any money balances lost on account of inflation. This can be justified either in terms of money in the production function or in terms of some "money requirements" function (see Chapter 4), although neither of those elements is in this problem explicitly.

6. One alternative is a non-Walrasian system in which case we have the situation in (a). Here multiple equilibria are possible: (b) shows the force of applying equation (1.48), but here taken as an equality rather than as an identity. We use the identity in the text because we will be working in disequilibrium positions (such as point α), and we

will need this leverage to control our system (as we shall point out, below).

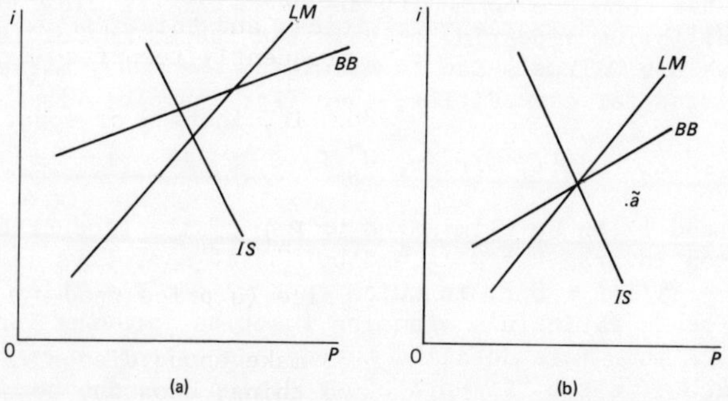

7. See Pesek and Saving (1957) as described in Chapter 2.
8. This appears in Clower (1965) and, of course, in Leijonhufvud (1968).
9. For the system

$$\frac{dp_i}{dt} = \sum_{j=1}^{n} K_{ij} X_i(P_1, \ldots, P_n) \qquad i = 1, \ldots, n$$

then for

$$K = \begin{vmatrix} K_{11} & \cdots & K_{1n} \\ \cdot & & \cdot \\ \cdot & & \cdot \\ \cdot & & \cdot \\ K_{n1} & \cdots & K_{nn} \end{vmatrix} \qquad A = \begin{vmatrix} a_{11} & \cdots & a_{1n} \\ \cdot & & \cdot \\ \cdot & & \cdot \\ \cdot & & \cdot \\ a_{n1} & & a_{nn} \end{vmatrix}$$

the system is stable if $|KA - zI| = 0$. The z are roots with negative real parts, and this being the case, we have

$$\prod_{i=1}^{n} z_i = |KA| = |K| \cdot |A| > 0 \text{ for } n = \text{even number of roots.}$$

This can provide a restriction to the system (i.e. if $|K| > 0$, then $|A| > 0$.
10. A recent paper looking into the stability of Tobin's reformulation is by I.M. McDonald (1980).
11. In this paper Tucker points out that while Patinkin does as much to advance the discussion of disequilibrium as

anyone, his system of structural equations, as it appears, for example, in equations (1.48) to (1.60), is not a disequilibrium system and is basically consistent with a model which has both the commodity and bond markets cleared with disequilibrium appearing only in the labour market (recall that we use Walras's Law to eliminate the money market). The demand for commodities, then (for example), is

$$c_d = c_d[i, W/P, \pi, M_0^H/P; 0, 0, L^* - L]$$

and π and L can be eliminated by use of the production function inverse $L = Q^{-1}y$ and by use of a profits identity $\pi = y - (W/P)L - B/P$, in which case we get something pretty close to Patinkin's spending function, proving Tucker's point. A much more detailed survey and extension of this approach - in the "fix-price" tradition - is by Muellbauer and Portes (1978). Their presentation shows how the holding of "buffer stocks" of money and inventories of goods helps smooth the transition implicit in persistent disequilibrium. A series of potential tests of whether or not a market is in disequilibrium is explained by Quandt (1978); some Monte Carlo experiments are included.

12. See below, in Chapter 2, for a discussion of how the Keynesian consumption function has been rationalized from a disequilibrium point of view. These spillovers have coefficients (as in equations (1.60) and (1.62)) which have some econometric potential, although no such studies appear to exist. Some of these questions are tackled in an empirical paper on the Dutch economy by Kuipers and Wilpstra (1977) in which both a theoretical and empirical preference for "loanable funds" is expressed; spillover coefficients are not estimated, however.
13. There is, of course, a big literature here, much of it highly technical, and not all of it clearly macroeconomic in design. Benassy (1975), Dreze (1975), and Varian (1977) have produced studies in which non-market clearing is employed to generate a kind of perpetual Keynesian disequilibrium; this is especially the case in Varian's paper. In contrast, Lorie (1978) shows that (in his case at least) a persistent underemployment equilibrium requires extremely pessimistic sales forecasts by business firms; indeed, Honkapohja and Ito (1979), who have written a number of papers on the subject, design a stochastic disequilibrium model in which Walrasian equilibria and Keynesian underemployment equilibria can coexist and coexist with rational expectations. Much of this material is surveyed in Grandmont (1977) and, especially, Drazen (1980a).
14. Among the empirical work we should note that there are

interesting studies discussed in both the investment and demand for money chapters, below; indeed, a number of estimation methods are mentioned there. A paper that does not fit into those topics but which contains interesting material on estimation is by Broer and Siebrand (1978) who propose a "compromise-transactions" approach, in which actual transactions are partly demand-determined and partly supply determined, with weights that depend on the "tension" between supply and demand. This deterministic framework contrasts with a stochastic method, in which this difference follows some distribution or, of course, to the completely deterministic "short side" approach (of Barro and Grossman, 1971). A study utilizing the basic Patinkin model, on the demand for factors of production, is by Nadiri and Rosen (1973). Nadiri and Rosen have a cost-minimization condition, a production function, and a system of porportionate adjustment equations, and achieve satisfactory results.

15. See, for example, Weintraub (1972).
16. See the survey by Laidler and Parkin (1975) which does not, however, dig deeply into the problems of this section.
17. The disaggregations most commonly have been over goods (e.g. breaking demand deposits into currency, demand deposits and time deposits) or over time (e.g. breaking the data into sub-periods); one does not often find the standard macro-concepts (e.g. aggregate consumer spending) broken down by personal economic agent, though.
18. The text has omitted the financial commodities. To begin with, if financial commodities are conceived of as the direct objects of utility (are inserted into utility functions), then the discussion of commodities just undertaken is directly relevant. But, as an alternative, one may wish to think of financial commodities as possessing "characteristics" - such as expected earnings, riskiness, and liquidity - and if this is the case, one must have (a) constant expectations of earnings, (b) equal variance (for risk), and (c) equal term-to-maturity (for liquidity) in order to obtain a consistent "over assets" aggregation. These characteristics, but not the aggregation problem, are further discussed in Chapter 3, on the demand for money.
19. Y is income, μ is the Lagrangean multiplier; and U is a determinant which describes all of the interaction in the utility function (U_i, U_{ij} are partial and cross-partial derivatives with respect to $r, s = 1, \ldots, n$); the determinant is

$$U = \begin{vmatrix} 0 & U_1 & \dots & U_n \\ U_1 & U_{11} & \dots & U_{1n} \\ \cdot & \cdot & & \cdot \\ \cdot & \cdot & & \cdot \\ \cdot & \cdot & & \cdot \\ U_n & U_{n1} & & U_{nn} \end{vmatrix}$$

U_{rs} is the appropriate co-factor.

20. According to Samuelson (1947, p. 143n), "All six of these rules are contained in the statement [that] $h'[X_{ij}]h$ is a non-positive-definite quadratic form of rank $(n - 1)$, which vanishes for values of h proportional to price, this being an immediate consequence of the primary conditions guaranteeing an extremum under constraint."
21. Note that the discussion of the construction of specific aggregates - e.g. the price level and national income - will be contained in the second volume of this study. So, too, will be the discussion of the actual empirical measures of money. There we will also take up questions relating to "ideal" price indices (e.g. the Divisia).
22. Based on the discussion in Cramer (1969).
23. If one is willing to impose other conditions, as in H.A. J. Green (1964), then other necessary and sufficient conditions hold. For example, we might, by analogy with the composite goods theorem, have equi-proportionate changes in income; in this case the micro-parameters may be unequal, assuming (still) the linear individual spending functions. Of course, if unemployment is expected to vary over the sample (a cyclical model, for example), this approach may well be very costly. There is, incidentally, abundant evidence that splitting income in various ways produces different (and, sometimes, significantly different) propensities to consume in linear aggregate consumption functions. See Ferber (1962) and Surrey (1970).
24. Note that if we deflate by the total population instead of the number of spending units - which, indeed, we usually do - then a further problem emerges. In this case, let $N = \lambda_t R$ where R represents population. Then, in equation (1.69), dividing by R will not completely solve the multicollinearity problem, as the following equation suggests.

$$\frac{\sum_{i=1}^{N} X_{it}}{R} = \lambda_t \beta_0 + \beta_1 \frac{\sum_{i=1}^{N} Y_{it}}{R} + \frac{1}{\lambda_t R} \sum_{i=1}^{N} u_{it}$$

Here λ_t, representing the variation in the size of households, may still be related to Σy_{it}.

2 The Consumption Function

2.1 INTRODUCTION

The study of the aggregate consumption function is one of the most important areas of macroeconomics, probably because of the interest given to it by the emphasis on the marginal propensity to consume in the multiplier and business cycle models of Keynes and the Keynesians and in the early growth models developed in the Keynesian tradition. This long tradition has produced a good deal of shifting about, as both technique and analysis have firmed up over the years, but it is interesting, nonetheless, that the classic studies (*e.g.*, Keynes's "General Theory") contain many of the elements of our recent theory, without many of the recent econometric refinements, to be sure. Thus there is a useful continuity to the consumption literature; on the other hand there are also a considerable number of provisional results, especially in the empirical area, and much has been made provisional in recent years on account of the "rational expectations" approach to the traditional problems.

At one time the basic macro-theories about the consumption function were grouped under the following headings: the absolute income hypothesis, the permanent income hypothesis, and the life-cycle hypothesis; but, in recent years, with the merging of the permanent income and life-cycle theories, and the disappearance of the "absolute" hypothesis except as a point of comparison, this design is not particularly relevant. What we can say is that the study of the consumption function has been gradually "complicated", especially with regard to its dynamics, and that while it is still useful to begin with simpler models and build up to the recent, more general, versions, it is still necessary to "digress" a good deal in order to capture all of the recent events. We will, then, start fairly traditionally - briefly discussing the absolute and relative hypotheses before tackling the recent and large "wealth-oriented" literature.

The design of this chapter is as follows. We will start with a short formal description of the absolute income hypothesis and the relative income hypothesis. We will mainly observe that Keynes has been misunderstood in the former and that the latter can be a very general (but possibly excessively micro) theory. Turning to the wealth-oriented theories, while we will show that both the permanent income and life-cycle theories spring from common perceptions, we will develop these theories in a slightly different way - the former being given a macro-statistical interpretation while the latter is often stated as the traditional dynamic consumption problem (often in a micro-inspired format). From that point we will consider a number of generalizations and extensions, usually of the life-cycle theory, involving wealth, liquid assets, the role of taxation, and, of course, rational expectations. We should also note that there will be a number of empirical surveys scattered about, both in the text itself and in the notes. Finally, as an important point on notation, the reader should note that most theories will be presented as if the variables consumption and income are measured in real terms (using c, y) whether or not the original papers actually did this. This is in keeping with modern practice (but when the price level is a separate variable we will not do this).

2.2 THE ABSOLUTE AND RELATIVE INCOME HYPOTHESES

Textbooks frequently attribute the absolute income hypothesis to Keynes in the "General Theory", and there is no doubt whatsoever that in that study he put forward a very simple relation between income and consumption, although there is also no doubt that he had much more than that to say on the consumption function - in particular in believing that interest rates, prices, and wealth would affect aggregate consumption. The absolute income hypothesis, pedigree aside, states that real consumption depends on real income and that the following restrictions hold:

(a) $0 < c_y < 1$ where $c_y = \partial c/\partial y$

(b) $c/y > c_y$

(c) $\partial c_y/\partial y < 0$

Keynes, and a number of other writers, mostly at the textbook level, have written a linear consumption function to represent the absolute income hypothesis:

$$c = \alpha + \beta_1 y \tag{2.1}$$

This equation does not actually meet condition (c) as it stands, but the addition of a term like $\beta_2 y^2$ would do the trick, if a mathematical form for the theory were desired.[1]

Setting aside, for the time being, any questions of what other variables might belong in the consumption function, we note that there are some very convincing cross-section empirical studies of equation (2.1) in the literature, in which all of the values needed to verify propositions (a) and (b) are achieved, although this is not really surprising. In particular, a combination of an absolute income equation along with demographic variables for age, sex, colour, location, occupation, and wealth of the head of the household certainly seems to hold its own compared to, for example, permanent income (which explains roughly the same pattern, albeit in different terms). But tests of time series of data have not been regarded as quite so favourable to the absolute income hypothesis. In particular, the simple linear model just given, although it provides an estimate of the propensity to consume we might even find plausible, also often has a serious amount of serial correlation in it, and when a trend variable is added, this trend variable is generally significant, suggesting the presence of omitted variables which are themselves correlated with "time". To be brief, the standard "absolute income" consumption function appears to have been shifting upward over time, producing an overestimate of the "true" propensity to consume; this, in turn, is related to a famous time series paradox which one no longer reads about.[2]

Finally, let us append a note on the relation of Keynes himself to the foregoing. In particular, the recent re-evaluation of Keynes's "General Theory" has stressed that both aspects of the modern "wealth hypothesis" - (a) the price-induced wealth effect, and (b) the interest-induced wealth effect - can be found there, even in the context of the short-run consumption function. Thus, says, Keynes, "Windfall changes in capital-values. . . should be classified amongst the major factors capable of causing short-period changes in the propensity to consume" (1936, pp. 92-3), and both the stream of expected returns and the interest rate (the two components of wealth) are mentioned as being important.[3] While Leijonhufvud (1968) is not actually certain of the role of the price-induced wealth effect in Keynes, Pesek and Saving (1967) certainly are; they cite the same passage from Keynes, as well as the following: "The consumption of the wealth-owning class may be extremely susceptible to unforeseen changes in the money-value of its wealth" (1936, p. 93), and since the mechanism here is still ambiguous (again, from Keynes), "in addition to this, as money-values fall, the stock of money will bear a higher proportion to the total wealth of the community" (1936, p. 93). But, on net, Pesek and Saving feel that Keynes "let wealth slip through his fingers by his failure to build it into his analysis". Perhaps, quoting Keynes on Pigou, this was on account of the "pitfalls of a pseudo-mathematical method", which led Keynes to lay down an equation (equation (2.1)), which represented only a small part of his thinking on the determinants of consumption.

We should also note a point to which we will return below, that Keynes espoused a "habit-persistence" version of the theory which could be tested with a distributed lag of past values of income. Consider the following quotation from page 97 of the "General Theory". "For a man's habitual standard of life usually has the first claim on his income, and he is apt to save the difference which discovers itself between his actual income and the expense of his habitual standard; or, if he does adjust his expenditure to changes in his income, he will over short periods do so imperfectly." Thus, without a doubt, many of the tests which reject or support the simple absolute income hypothesis in this vast literature do so not on behalf of Keynes himself but on behalf of a simple textbook version of his theory. Keynes's consumption function (e.g. equation (2.1)) is also likely to be "non-rational" as is clear from the literature on "rational expectations" discussed below, in Section 2.5. A disequilibrium interpretation has been given to this and is discussed at that point.

Perhaps the most obvious problem of the absolute hypothesis, aside from an obviously incomplete specification of the wealth-consumption relation, is that the summation over a heterogeneous population might introduce the problem of heteroscedasticity into the (frequent) regression results reported in this literature. Furthermore, there is another paradox to consider, for while the time series do not show proposition (b), the cross-section studies do. That is, in the cross-sections, the marginal propensity to consume often turns out to be smaller than the average propensity to consume. Returning to the heterogeneous population again, we note that the propensity to consume could differ regionally, by sex of household head, by race (or religion), by activity (farm versus manufacturing), and by the age of the head of the household (itself a factor in the life-cycle models (see below) to mention only some of the more obvious factors. As we will see, all of these (and more) appear to have some bearing on the consumption problem, especially on cross-section tests, where such factors are more easily identified.[4]

The relative income hypothesis of Duesenberry (1949) actually has two main strands to it, one directed toward the cross-section characteristics of a consuming population (as just described) and one directed toward the time series. With regard to the former, the broad argument is that the spending unit consumes according to its station in life; that is, it consumes at the average of its group, where location, age, race, and, of course, income might well be expected to dominate in the grouping. The groups could easily have different c/y, but when individuals are compared across groups, after adjusting for the group characteristics, the aggregate propensity to consume would be stable. In this view, then, the cross-section result that the marginal propensity is less than the average is essentially an anomalous result which occurs because the underlying data are not correctly adjusted for what are, loosely, sociological factors.

We should pause here to consider a small literature on the effect of changes in the personal distribution of income on the propensity to consume. Keynes seems to be arguing that a more equal distribution will also have a higher marginal propensity to consume, and while this is "obvious" to everyone it seems, it applies literally only to an individual (or to identical individuals), as Blinder (1975) shows. Part of the problem is that any actual redistribution is inevitably across non-homogeneous populations, and part is that in a life-cycle model (see section 2.3.1) the effect of wealth on the marginal propensity to consume is ambiguous. Blinder's empirical results generally show no effect (although a slight tendency for a "perverse" result is noted - and "explained" by recent changes in the composition of the labour force). On a cross-section of thirty-seven countries, Della Valle and Oguchi (1976) also found no distribution effects, but this result was challenged by Musgrove (1980) who used three parameters from the income distribution to the effect that more developed countries (where "supernumerary" income appears and where populations are more homogeneous) show some effect from the "asymmetry" parameter.[5]

Turning to the time series version of the relative income hypothesis, the argument is advanced that in this context - for the aggregate function - the bench-mark for the consumer is not a group income, but some previous income; in empirical studies, this previous income has been taken as the previous *peak* income, an average past income, or even the previous lowest income. Duesenberry, to test this proposition, used the following equation on US annual pre-World War II data:

$$\frac{s_t}{y_{dt}} = \beta\frac{y_{dt}}{y_d^*} - \alpha \qquad (2.2)$$

Here the dependent variable is the savings ratio, y_{dt} is disposable income, and y_d^* is previous peak disposable income. This appears to work well, and more provocatively, also provides an explanation of the Kuznets-Goldsmith paradox (see note 2). To see this, consider a variation on the model more in the spirit of equation (2.1):

$$c_t = \alpha + \beta_1 y_t + \beta_2 y_t^* \qquad (2.3)$$

where y_t^* is previous peak income. This is the ratchet model used on American data recently by Smyth and Jackson (1978). Note that (2.3) and (2.2) correspond perfectly (except for the constant in (2.3)) if the denominator for the dependent variable in equation (2.2) is taken to be y_{dt}^*, rather than actual disposable income. In any event by fitting (2.3) we introduce a shift parameter (y_t^*) which could explain the upward drift in the short-run consumption function with an economically-inspired variable. Note, in addition, that y_t^* would be expected to capture some of the trend effect, although there is an underlying non-linearity in the basic hypothesis which may well be poorly captured if equation (2.3) were tested as a simple linear function.

Duesenberry's model is also non-linear (see equation (2.4) below), and, somewhat surprisingly, a successful test of it may actually be consistent with the three propositions of the absolute income hypothesis. Thus, rewrite equation (2.2) as equation (2.4), where the non-linearity is apparent.

$$c_t = b_1 y_t + b_2\left(\frac{y_t^2}{y_t^*}\right) \qquad (2.4)$$

Then, for $1 > b_1 > 0$ and $b_2 < 0$, we would get proposition (a) for

$$b_1 > 2b_2\left(\frac{y_t}{y_t^*}\right)$$

which is the marginal propensity to consume in this model. For proposition (c) we would have

$$\frac{\partial\frac{\partial c}{\partial y}}{\partial y} = \frac{2b_2}{y_t^*}$$

which would be negative for $b_2 < 0$. For proposition (b), that the average propensity to consume is greater than the marginal propensity, we find that for b_2 negative, proposition (b) would hold:

$$\frac{c}{y} = b_1 + b_2\frac{y_t}{y_t^*} \qquad \frac{\partial c}{\partial y} = b_1 + 2b_2\frac{y_t}{y_t^*}$$

as one can see by comparing c/y and $\partial c/\partial y$ directly. Thus a successful test for the relative income model could then also support the absolute income hypothesis - at least for certain values of the parameters - and this might well establish that the former is a special case of the relative income hypothesis, at least in the form just laid out. It is a special case, to be explicit, because it holds for y_t^* constant; y_t^* is actually the additional variable provided by the relative income hypothesis.[6]

2.3 THE PERMANENT INCOME HYPOTHESIS

The relative income model can certainly deal with wealth in the aggregate consumption function, but not in a very satisfying way, in some respects. As one moves toward the more general models - in particular toward the permanent income and the life-cycle model - the distinguishing characteristic of the models is that the role of wealth (and, concomitantly, the dynamics) becomes increasingly complex. What might be suggested at this juncture is that these two major wealth theories - the permanent income and the life-cycle - are basically consistent with the absolute and the relative income hypotheses, but that separately they focus on different aspects of the wealth-consumption nexus. We will also develop the theme that the life-cycle model is a more tractable version of the permanent model, but first we will take up the more specific theory of Friedman) and some subsequent variations and extensions) for its considerable pedagogical value, for its careful attention to the micro-foundations of the problem, and for its interesting empirical implications. Before even that, however, it is necessary to state some generalizations about the role of wealth in the consumption problem.

2.3.1 WEALTH, INTEREST RATES, AND CONSUMPTION

Before discussing the main recent contributions to the macro-consumption literature, we should discuss the nature of the general model which underlies these presentations. Basically the analysis goes back at least to I. Fisher in 1930 (1965 reprint), but a useful starting point for the recent version appears to be the explanation of the Fisherian theory of saving in Friedman's Theory of the Consumption Function (1957). We will present a formal version here, with an illustration, to serve as the basis of much of our later work. Let the representative consumer (who will be treated as representing the aggregate consumer) have a dynamic utility function of

$$u = U(c_1, c_2) \tag{2.5}$$

where c_1 and c_2 represent his consumption in two periods (the present and one future period). Let him be constrained in the two periods by

$$\begin{aligned} c_1 &= y_1 - s_1 \\ c_2 &= y_2 + (1 + i)s_1 \end{aligned} \tag{2.6}$$

where s_1 represents his savings in period 1, and $(1 + i)s_1$ represents the value of his savings after one period.

To optimize, combine the constraints and form the Lagrangean given as equation (2.7):

$$s = U(c_1, c_2) - \lambda[c_2 - y_2 - y_1(1 + i) + c_1(1 + i)] \tag{2.7}$$

At the optimum, for c_1 and c_2 as choice variables, we have

$$\frac{\partial s}{\partial c_1} = U_1 - \lambda(1 + i) = 0 \tag{2.8}$$

$$\frac{\partial s}{\partial c_2} = U_2 - \lambda = 0 \tag{2.9}$$

and

$$\frac{\partial s}{\partial \lambda} = y_2 + y_1(1 + i) - c_1(1 + i) - c_2 = 0 \tag{2.10}$$

Eliminating λ between (2.8) and (2.9), we find that

$$-\frac{U_1}{U_2} = -(1 + i) \tag{2.11}$$

holds at the optimum. To see the situation graphically, consider Figure 2.1.

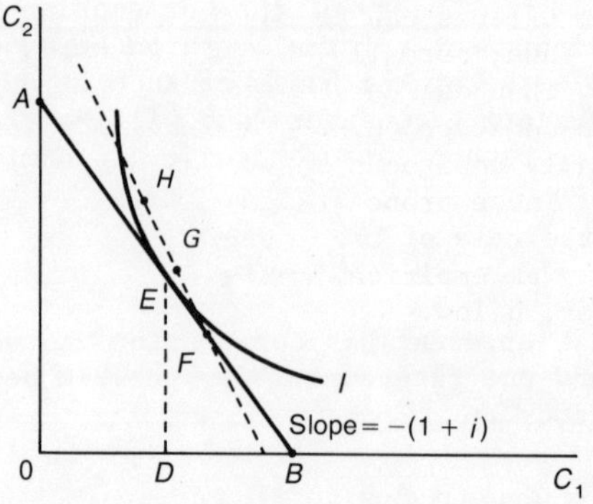

Figure 2.1 Optimal consumption in a two-period context

The comparative-equilibrium properties of this model are very straightforward, as a result of its simplicity. Clearly, an increase of income (y_1) will shift AB, the budget line, to the right, in a non-parallel fashion.[7] Here the effect on consumption in period 1 is ambiguous, clearly, in a theoretical sense (it depends on U_1/U_2 at the new optimum, and that can lie to the right or left of point D). To analyze an increase in wealth in period 1, let us define initial wealth as

$$W_1 = y_1 + \frac{y_2}{(1 + i)}$$

the present value of present and future income receipts. W_1 can increase because of a rise in any of its components (let us rule out the wealth effect of a change in the interest rate, for a moment); if both y_1 and y_2 rise, then, clearly, AB in Figure 2.1 will shift to the right. Again, however, the effect on c_1^* will be ambiguous in an *a priori* sense, as it was when y_1 changed. A change in "permanent" income, however defined, will also produce an ambiguous effect.[8]

Finally, consider the effect of a change in the interest rate. In particular, a rise in the interest rate will increase OA (see note 5), the former being an income adjustment and the latter a wealth adjustment on the budget line. Thus AB rotates to a steeper slope in the event of a rise in the interest rate. The new line, however, goes through point F in Figure 2.1, as represented by the dashed line, in which case we cannot assert that the new optimum (which may be at point G or at point H) produces a higher or lower first-period consumption (c_1).[9] Only when we know the magnitudes of the various effects can we say in which direction the effect will go. Thus, normally, an increase in income or wealth (when y changes) can be expected to produce a positive effect on consumption, but a change in the interest rate is generally ambiguous because it changes wealth and future income. These propositions state the empirical issues clearly, and the role of the interest rate is thereby seen to be basically an empirical one. We will expand this discussion further, below.

2.3.2 FRIEDMAN'S PERMANENT INCOME HYPOTHESIS

Friedman (1957) constructs his macro-consumption theory from micro-perceptions, but instead of depending on casual statements, he presents us with the formal aggregating equations, in effect. This is useful because it focuses attention on an important area of the theory which could produce problems. To begin with, we have two propositions, for the ith consumer, that both his income and his consumption can be divided into permanent (regular) and transitory (irregular) components:

$$y_i = y_{Pi} + y_{Ti} \qquad (2.12)$$

$$c_i = c_{Pi} + c_{Ti} \qquad (2.13)$$

In order to aggregate these individual components, we will assume that the distribution of income is identical across individuals; we will do this in terms of the mean and variance of a normal distribution of income. The aggregating conditions, then, are given by equations (2.14) and (2.15), for variances,

$$Var\ (y_{Pi}) = \sigma^2_{yP} \qquad (2.14)$$

$$Var\ (y_{Ti}) = \sigma^2_{yT} \qquad (2.15)$$

and equations (2.16) and (2.17) for the means.

$$E(y_{Pi}) = \mu_y \qquad (2.16)$$

$$E(y_{Ti}) = 0 \qquad (2.17)$$

The last two, formally, would require that any transitory income should have zero mean (that is, any perceived trend in it should be included in permanent income), if the data are time series. We can observe, though, that only positive transitory income data are utilized in the actual tests in the literature, and we can argue that this could tend to produce biased estimates of the propensity to consume this income. Finally, we assume an important aggregating condition for the covariation between permanent and transitory income as in equation (2.18).

$$covar\ (y_{Pi}, y_{Ti}) = 0 \tag{2.18}$$

That is, we assume that there is a zero correlation between permanent income and transitory income.

The foregoing are essentially theoretical restrictions argued, presumably, on the grounds of their plausibility (or necessity). At this point we can enter a more empirical restriction from Friedman's theory, that an individual's permanent consumption is proportional to his permanent income:

$$c_{Pi} = k_i y_{Pi}$$

or

$$c_P = ky_P \tag{2.19}$$

Then, it is a simple matter to achieve a satisfactory aggregation by assuming that all individuals have the same factor of proportionality; this is also expressed in equation (2.19). Note that k, while taken as a constant here, is actually written by Friedman as $k(i, w, u)$, where i is the interest rate; this is a function (we will continue this discussion below).

The foregoing theory - in the form of equation (2.19) and the earlier restrictions on the moments of the income distribution - results in an equation which is inherently untestable (2.19). This is because it relates two intrinsically unobservable variables (c_P and y_P). To deal with this problem, Friedman works in two stages. In the first stage he puts further restrictions on the underlying data (as we shall shortly describe) so as to have a "theory" in terms of actual consumption (c) and permanent income, as defined in his propositions (equations (2.12) to (2.19)). In the second stage he proposes a technique, using the past values of income, to estimate permanent (expected) income. To deal with the first stage, that of constructing a theory for actual consumption and permanent income, Friedman assumes that actual income and actual consumption are distributed jointly in terms of the bivariate normal distribution. This requires that we find the values of the five parameters of the bivariate normal $[E(c), E(y), V(c), V(y), cov\ (c, y)]$ in terms of observable variables or of the parameters of the distribution of permanent income.

To begin with, we may take equation (2.12) and calculate

$$E(y_i) = E(y_{Pi} + y_{Ti}) = E(y_{Pi}) + E(y_{Ti})$$

Then, since we have assumed values for these in equations (2.16) and (2.17), we know that $E(y_i) = \mu_y$ and $E(y_{Ti}) = 0$. Thus $E(y_i) = \mu_y$, which is observable. Of course, $E(\bar{c}_i)$ is directly observable and so is its variance, and thus we have the first three of our five parameters.

We may readily compute a variance for actual income as follows. Return to equation (2.12) and write out its variance as

$$var\ (y_i) = var\ (y_{Pi}) + var\ (y_{Ti}) + 2\ cov\ (y_{Pi}, y_{Ti})$$

Now $var\ (y_{Ti}) = \sigma^2_{yT}$ and $var\ (y_{Pi}) = \sigma^2_{yP}$. Thus, since the correlation between permanent income and transitory income is zero by assumption (in equation (2.18)), we have

$$var\ (y_i) = \sigma^2_{yP} + \sigma^2_{yT}$$

which has the required dimensions. In particular, knowledge of σ^2_y from the data and an estimate of σ^2_{yP} from our permanent income proxy (see below) enables us to deduce σ^2_{yT} from the result just given (we do not need a separate estimate).

To obtain the covariance between c_i and y_i, we can write out that expression as

$$cov\ (c_i, y_i) = E[(\bar{c} - c_i)(\bar{y} - y_i)]$$

From equations (2.12) and (2.13), this gives us

$$cov\ (c_i, y_i) = E[(\bar{c}_P + \bar{c}_T - c_{Pi} - c_{Ti})(\bar{y}_P + \bar{y}_T - y_{Pi} - y_{Ti})]$$

We may then reorganize the terms in the square brackets, in which case we have

$$E\{[(\bar{c}_P - c_{Pi}) + (\bar{c}_T - c_{Ti})][\bar{y}_P - y_{Pi}) + (\bar{y}_T - y_{Ti})]\}$$

and further, after multiplication, the expression for the covariance is seen to be the following collection of individual covariances:

$$E[(\bar{c}_P - c_{Pi})(\bar{y}_P - y_{Pi}) + (\bar{c}_T - c_{Ti})(\bar{y}_P - y_{Pi})$$
$$+ (\bar{c}_T - c_{Ti})(\bar{y}_T - y_{Ti}) + (\bar{c}_P - c_{Pi})(\bar{y}_T - y_{Ti})]$$

Now for the last three terms in this expression Friedman has made the following restrictions (stated in terms of assumptions about the correlation):

$$E(c_T, y_P) = 0 \quad \text{if } \rho_{cTyP} = 0$$
$$E(c_T, y_T) = 0 \quad \text{if } \rho_{cTyT} = 0$$
$$E(c_P, y_T) = 0 \quad \text{if } \rho_{cPyT} = 0$$

This leaves only $E(c_P, y_P)$ which, we can establish, is the term $k\sigma^2_{yP}$.[10] Although it cost us considerably in terms of the additional restrictions just named, we do have what we want, the desired parameter in an expression measured only in σ^2_{yP}.

The foregoing theory has certainly not been applauded in all corners, but it does have the following virtues:

(a) it focuses attention on an empirical issue, the measurement of permanent income;
(b) it lays bare the micro-foundations and statistical foundations of at least one standard macroeconomic paradigm;
(c) and it provides us with some derivative conditions - those on the correlations - which we may use to attempt to falsify the theory.

Indeed, it is clear from the voluminous empirical literature which followed (and preceded) Friedman that this is not perceived as an empty theory.

We should note, before going on, that Friedman actually proposed a more general form than that given in equation (2.19); in particular, his general function is

$$c_P = k(i, w, u)y_P \qquad (2.20)$$

In this equation the interest rate (i) represents the rate at which an individual can borrow on future earnings or lend to deficit households; quite possibly the higher the interest rate, the less incentive the consumer will have to consume in the present, but this statement is essentially not a theoretically derived one, as we have already pointed out. In addition, the individual will be able to borrow more easily if his wealth is in the form of non-human wealth; that is, the individual will find it hard to provide collateral drawn from his human wealth. To capture this influence on consumption, Friedman proposes the variable w, where w is the ratio of non-human wealth to permanent income. Presumably, the higher this ratio, the easier it is to borrow, and the more the consumer will actually borrow in order to consume in the present, *ceteris paribus*. Indeed, this variable is of some use in explaining differences in group consumption behaviour. A case in point is that of Blacks who might be expected to have lower non-human wealth as a percentage of their total wealth - and hence lower MPC out of their permanent income; this insight thus shows some considerable overlap between Friedman and Duesenberry, who also explicitly considers such a possibility in his relative income hypothesis. Finally, the third variable, u, is a "portmanteau" variable which, to Friedman, consists of all other relevant factors as they operate on the proportionality factor k; in a sense this device makes his theory more general, although the final result is also remarkably similar to both the relative income and the life-cycle hypotheses (as we shall see) in this particular form.

The principal way one might prefer to test the permanent income hypothesis directly is to compare its predictions with those of the obvious alternatives, but there are several problems which emerge immediately. The first of these is that the theories we have listed as alternatives have been shown to have considerable overlap. Indeed, we cannot compare y_p with y and with y/y^* as predictors of consumption both because each of these is merely one particular representation of the general theory proposed and because not only does y/y^* contain y (as we have seen), but so does y_p as usually calculated.

At this point we should also note that even though we have cast actual consumption (i.e. measured consumption) as the dependent variable in equation (2.20), we actually mean, following Friedman, that it is the flow of services from the using up of consumer goods rather than the actual purchases of consumer goods, per unit of time, that is the subject of our inquiry. This consideration, it would seem, underscores Friedman's preference for treating the purchase of a consumer durable as a form of saving. At the very least, at any event, one would expect the propensity to consume durables to differ from that for non-durables and in any test purporting to adhere to Friedman's rules, there would have to be some sort of adjustment to the data base to account for "saving" in the form of purchases of consumer durables. To repeat, durable consumer expenditures are not the complete using up of a consumer good and can be, indeed, a device for the straightening out of the stream of consumption (the actual use of the services provided by the consumer good) over time.

A more direct concern, though, is that if we accept Friedman's narrower hypothesis and attempt to test it directly, we must have a measure of the remaining unobservable variable, which is permanent income. Now "permanent" income is income which is expected to be earned or received regularly, and, presumably, it is composed of the systematic component of the income expected from both human and non-human activities. It is a forward-looking concept, and like much of modern expectations-oriented macroeconomic theory, provides us with a concept which is intrinsically not observable directly. The problem of finding a suitable proxy for an expected variable has, of course, produced a considerable literature, in which a number of particular measures have been proposed, analyzed, and then worked on the data. These measures, including that proposed by Friedman, generally utilize past observations of the actual income series (usually a weighted average) on the reasonable grounds that people will use their experiences with, for example, income to forecast its value in the future. Note, though, that while a particular device is always necessary to complete the testing of the theory, it is in general not part of the theory itself. In particular, rejection of Friedman's weighting scheme in favour of a rival scheme is not especially damaging to the general theory itself, at least as it has been described to this point. On the other hand, any direct test of the theory will necessarily (because of the unobservable permanent component in it) be the test of a joint hypothesis: this joint hypothesis is an aggregate consumption theory plus a particular expectations-generating mechanism. There is, of course, an infinity of these mechanisms (and quite a few of the basic theories for that matter). This problem is usually solved in a non-theoretical way (that is, the parameters of an arbitrary mechanism are estimated) although in recent years there has been some work on a theory of expectations (the most notable being the "rational expectations" approach, which we will return to, below, in this and other chapters). Note that so long as we do not put any limit on the proliferation of "expectations-generating mechanisms" then the permanent income hypothesis cannot be falsified; this may well seem to make it more of a "non-theory" even by Friedman's rules (see Pesek, 1979a).

One obvious way to begin to model the role of expectations is by means of distributed lag formulations of past incomes using, for example, the Koyck or Almon method. Furthermore.

results obtained this way can readily be compared with the absolute income hypothesis, although this comparison may seem a little simple-minded (at least it does to me). Estimations of these kinds of models, though, immediately run into a number of major difficulties. For one, you cannot distinguish "habit persistence" from "expected income" since both will be appropriately tested with past data. Indeed, the habit persistence theory, as we have argued, may certainly be taken as a form of the absolute income hypothesis; further, it is perhaps not unreasonable to argue that one's current income position relative to the past would be judged by a distributed lag - an average, after all - of past incomes to compare with present income (after adjusting for trend). For another, the Koyck lag, while giving one a neat structural form (if the weights decay), may run into trouble from serial correlation, affecting either the short-run or the long-run estimates of the propensity to consume. Finally, the estimates of the lag parameter (λ) may be affected by the choice of a reduced form or a structural estimation approach to the lags themselves. These matters are not only confused with reference to the three hypotheses discussed so far in this chapter, but also one should note that the life-cycle theory produces similar problems.[11]

Formally, then, let us assume that equation (2.21) represents the permanent income hypothesis,

$$c_t = k(i, w, u)W(\lambda L)y_t \qquad (2.21)$$

where the k function is that which we attributed to Friedman and $W(\lambda L)$ represents some arbitrary (or derived) weighting scheme for actual income (Y_t); a time-series context is assumed here, so that the variables also bear a time subscript (t). Note also that L is a "lag" operator.[12] The most often used weighting scheme is the Koyck. For this we have

$$W(\lambda L)_i = (1 - \lambda)\lambda^i L^i \qquad \text{for } i = 0, 1, 2, \ldots \qquad (2.22)$$

Since

$$W(\lambda L) = \frac{1 - \lambda}{1 - \lambda L}$$

when the right-hand term of equation (2.22) is summed (it is an infinite series which approaches zero as t approaches infinity assuming $\lambda < 1$), we can use this expression directly in our consumption function (equation (2.21)).[13] We assume $k(i, w, u) = k$ for simplicity, and the result is an expression for the permanent income consumption function as expressed in equation (2.23).

$$c_t = k\left(\frac{1 - \lambda}{1 - \lambda L}\right) y_t \tag{2.23}$$

which produces an estimating equation of

$$c_t = \lambda c_{t-1} + k(1 - \lambda) y_t + e_t \tag{2.24}$$

with an error term (e_t) tacked on arbitrarily. Here the specific Koyck weighting hypothesis is represented by the parameter λ, a parameter which is also justified by the "permanent" view that expected income calculations are based on (averages of) past incomes.

At this point we should note that this equation has a complication arising from the fact that it is a "reduced form" equation (with the consequence that ordinary least squares estimates of the coefficients are in general inconsistent). Equation (2.23), indeed, is the structural equation, and when an error (ε_t) is tacked on there, the correct interpretation of the error in equation (2.24) is

$$e_t = \varepsilon_t - \lambda \varepsilon_{t-1}$$

While the point at which the error term appears is often taken to be arbitrary, there are some real issues here, especially involving the estimates of the speed of adjustment and the short-run propensity to consume; we will return to these matters later in this chapter.

Friedman's approach to the problem of weighting past observations is to form a measure for permanent income as exhibited in equation (2.25).

$$y_p(t) = y_0 e^{\alpha t} + \int_{-\infty}^{t} \beta e^{\beta(T - t)} (y(T) - y_0 e^{\alpha T}) e^{\alpha(t - T)} dT \tag{2.25}$$

Here t represents the "present" and T the past observations on income. This is a trend adjusted weighted average (the trend rate of growth is α), written in continuous form[14] which introduces a weighting parameter, β. The weights are "trend weights" of

$$e^{\alpha(t - T)}$$

and "observation weights" of[15]

$$\beta e^{\beta(T - t)}$$

That is, in Friedman's scheme, at time t (the present), the first term represents the present point on the trend line, starting at y_0 (the initial value of income) while $y(T) - y_0 e^{\alpha T}$ represents each past observation's deviation (including $T - t$) from the trend line, multiplied by its appropriate weight $(\beta e^{\beta(T - t)})$. The last weight, $e^{\alpha(t - T)}$, which is applied to each deviation as a "trend weight", permits the trend in the data to have a different weighting scheme from the current level of income itself.

After some manipulation, which involves evaluating the integral at $t = T$, Friedman produces the following equation in observables.[16]

$$c(t) = k\beta \int_{-\infty}^{t} e^{(\beta - \alpha)(T - t)} y(T) dT \qquad (2.26)$$

Here the independent variable is a weighted average of past values of income. This version contains three parameters (k, β, and α) and is under-identified. Friedman proposes that the trend be calculated separately (this is estimated as equal to 0.02 in his series) and then β and k can be jointly determined in the regression of consumption on income. This, then, is the final result for the particular joint version of the permanent income hypothesis. Presumably for different times and certainly for differently measured dependent variables (or independent variables), different weights may well result (but this would not be a contradiction to the underlying theory in any sense). This technique has been used on the consumption function, of course, and, in addition, on other macroeconomic variables (money, prices, and interest rates). In most of these cases either the Koyck or the Friedman lag has often been judged to be appropriate, generally because the weighting scheme is thought to be monotonically declining. For investment spending, on the other hand, more complicated weighting schemes have been employed (see Chapter 5).

Now so long as one is talking about consumption in the sense of using up one's consumer assets, there is no real problem with Friedman's formulation, but if one looks at actual data, there is a potential "specification bias" in that actual consumption is often the purchase of consumer durables, some of which are intended to be consumed in future periods (as if they were personal investment expenditures). Thus a windfall in income that is totally unanticipated may prompt the spontaneous purchase of consumer durables (or storable non-durables), which is really not consumption in the sense of the "using up" of a consumer good; this would appear as consumption in the data if no adjustment were made on this account. Thus, following Darby (1974; see also Thurston, 1977, and Seater, 1980), if there is a suspicion that some of the consumption expenditures are really depositories of wealth for the reasons just given, we might well wish to explain actual total consumption as in equation (2.27).

$$c_t = k_1 + k_2 y_{Pt} + k_3 y_{Tt} + e_t \tag{2.27}$$

This can be explained as follows. In the event that c_t contains consumer "investment", then, since y_P alone will not explain it (it only explains consumption in the sense of the using up of the durables), it will appear in the residuals of the equation. Since this residual item then contains (new) wealth, it will be correlated with y_P (an alternative measure of wealth). Thus equation (2.27), without y_T, will show bias. If y_T is calculated by subtracting y_P from y - which is the usual method - then the resulting variable can be included as an argument in the consumption function, as it is in equation (2.27). Darby, indeed, finds that y_T is significant (when long lags occur) and its significance diminishes as one moves toward a measure of consumption more like the preferred theoretical construct (which is the using up of consumer goods).

The lag structure may also be too rigid in the Friedman or Koyck forms, and Friedman finds a seventeen-year lag which also seems too long; thus some effort has been directed toward using the more flexible schemes such as the Almon or Pascal lags. Both Mayer (1972) and Boughton (1976) have done this, with the latter finding a very short lag (within a year) using Pascal lags. Boughton also argues (a) that there is an unexplained non-proportionality in the US short-run consumption function, (b) that the functional forms might be different for the different types of consumer goods included in the aggregate, and (c) that there are omitted variables in the usual simple tests. Boughton finds that a "relative price" variable works (he subdivides consumption into three components) and that inflationary expectations and liquid assets are not important (although the latter just fails). Boughton feels that while his test meets the minimum conditions of the permanent income model, the short lags and the non-proportionality do not favour its general acceptance (indeed, actual income will do just as well). In this test, says Boughton, the other variables (especially relative prices and liquid assets) provide the cushion between income and consumption which the permanent income hypothesis (and the relative income and life-cycle hypotheses, for that matter) sought to provide.

Returning to the Koyck lag formulation, there are several other problems we should discuss here, so long as we are digging into econometric problems.

(a) There is the problem that the Koyck lag (or any lag for that matter), while giving one a structural form for estimating λ (if it is less than unity, it is a readily estimable structural parameter), may run into trouble from serial correlation, affecting either the short-run or the long-run estimates of the propensity to consume (and the mean lag), depending on how one estimates the model.

(b) The estimates of the propensity to consume may be affected by the choice of a "reduced form" or "structural form" estimating method either in the sense of the structure of adjustment (as in (a)) or in the sense of the structure of a larger econometric model of which the consumption function is but one equation.

With regard to (a), Zellner and Geisel (1970) have compared a general distributed lag model - of the Koyck form - under four assumptions about the error terms. The consumption function is

$$c_t = \lambda c_{t-1} + k(1-\lambda)y_t + u_t - \lambda u_{t-1} \qquad (2.28)$$

and the four assumptions are that

(1) $u_t - \lambda u_{t-1} = \varepsilon_t$ with ε_t normally distributed;

(2) u_t are normally distributed;

(3) $u_t = \rho u_{t-1} + \varepsilon_{3t}$ with ε_{3t} normally distributed; and

(4) $u_t - \lambda u_{t-1} = \rho(u_{t-1} - \lambda u_{t-2}) + \varepsilon_{4t}$ with ε_{4t} normally distributed.

Here (1) represents the usual procedure and (2)-(4) represent somewhat more realistic alternatives; indeed, both (3) and (4) allow for some "structural" auto-correlation in the residuals. Note that if any of (2)-(4) are appropriate, the estimators in (1) - the usual form - will be inconsistent. Zellner and Geisel use maximum likelihood and Bayesian methods on quarterly US data and conclude (mostly) in favour of model (1), but with an unstable short-run but not long-run propensity to consume. In a parallel test on the annual data of ten European countries, Klovland (1977) found that the "structural" model (3) generally worked best, although the estimates of the long-run propensity to consume were unaffected by the assumptions about the errors (the short-run were). The method was maximum likelihood and five theoretical cases were compared. An even more careful comparison of the various procedures (and, incidentally, the models) is by J.E.H. Davidson *et al.* (1978) utilizing British data (on a wider range of topics including seasonality and multicollinearity).

With regard to point (b) above, we have the problem that if the consumption function is one among a number of structural equations in the economic model (system), then a simultaneous-equations bias can exist. Thus if

$$c_t = \alpha + \beta y_t + u_t \tag{2.29}$$

then if $y_t = c_t + I_t$, one can write a reduced form of the system either as

$$y_t = \frac{\alpha}{1 - \beta} + \frac{1}{1 - \beta} I_t + \frac{u_t}{1 - \beta} \tag{2.30}$$

or, alternatively, as

$$c_t = \frac{\alpha}{1 - \beta} + \frac{\beta}{1 - \beta} I_t + \frac{u_t}{1 - \beta} \tag{2.31}$$

in the event that I_t is (assumed to be) exogeneous. (It is *real* investment expenditures.) In this event, we could obtain a consistent estimator of β and α if we fit, by ordinary least squares, either

$$c_t = \pi_0 + \pi_1 I_t + v_t \tag{2.32}$$

or

$$y_t = \pi_0 + \pi_2 I_t + v_t \tag{2.33}$$

and solved for the values of α and β from the estimates of π_0, π_1, and π_2 (by indirect least squares - see Cramer (1969)). If, instead, we attempt a direct estimate of equation (2.29) when $y_t = c_t + I_t$ is also true, then our estimate of β wil be biased. Indeed, in the limit,

$$plim\ \hat{\beta} = \beta + \frac{(1 - \beta)\sigma_u^2}{\sigma_I^2 + \sigma_u^2} \tag{2.34}$$

from which we see that the estimate will be too high (for $\beta < 1$); for the US annual deflated data for 1922-41 much used in this early literature this correction (by Wallis, 1973) produced a drop of about 0.06 (from 0.73 to 0.67) in the propensity to consume (see also Johnston, 1972). But in general we find surprisingly little interest in this problem in the macroeconomics literature (although at one time two-stage least squares tests were quite popular).

In the preceding discussion a proposition has been employed implicitly which can be formalized even more clearly; this concerns the popular "errors in variables" interpretation of the permanent income hypothesis. It is frequently asserted that the permanent income model is an error in variables problem and this, indeed, provides a clue as to how it might be distinguished from the absolute income hypothesis. First of all, let us write the absolute income hypothesis as

$$c = \beta y + \varepsilon \tag{2.35}$$

Then, assuming the correct model is the permanent income model, we can substitute to obtain

$$c = \beta(y_P + y_T) + \varepsilon \tag{2.36}$$

Here, of course, y_T is a type of "error" if y is actually used as the independent variable; in addition, by assumption y_T is randomly distributed with a zero mean. In this model, if

$$\rho_{yPyT} = \rho_{yP\varepsilon} = \rho_{yT\varepsilon} = 0$$

which we would argue from the permanent income hypothesis, then the

$$\text{prob. limit of } \hat{\beta} \text{ is } \beta\left(\frac{\sigma^2_{yP}}{\sigma^2_{yP} + \sigma^2_{yT}}\right) \tag{2.37}$$

that is, $\hat{\beta}$ is asymptotically biased (unless $\sigma^2_{yT} = 0$); indeed, the direction of the bias is clearly downward.[17] To put it another way, the propensity to consume will appear lower for certain types of spending units if they are approached by means of the absolute income hypothesis when there are actually substantial transitory elements in their income. There have been a number of direct empirical studies of this "errors in variables" model, mostly favourable to Friedman's hypothesis.[18]

There have also been numerous cross-section studies of the permanent income hypothesis, but this is not the place to launch a full-scale discussion. Briefly, though, disaggregation by farm-versus-city, Blacks-versus-Whites, age, variance of income, city size, educational level, occupation, housing expenditure, city type, personal insurance coverage, frequency of home ownership, family size, and city location have all been supported at one time or another.[19] These can usually be "explained" by the permanent income hypothesis - for example a farmer or a Black will have a larger percentage of transitory income in his total income and consequently a lower propensity to consume out of total income - but they nonetheless leave one uneasy about the stability of an aggregative theory, whatever its theoretical lineage. Looking back at our earlier work on aggregation, this is all too apparent, since many of the variables just mentioned are income distribution or wealth distribution proxies.

We conclude this sketchy (but one hopes representative) discussion of a very voluminous literature by evaluating what is perhaps the most fundamental empirical work on the permanent income hypothesis, that on the reaction of consumers to "windfalls" (that is, to positive transitory income). We may begin with reference to a paper by Friedman (1963) on the subject which establishes that we also have to clear up the theoretical and empirical issues relating to the "horizon" to which consumers hold their expectations. In particular, we can suppose that a consumer with a relatively distant horizon (in the sense of the average period of his calculations) will respond less to transitory changes in his present income than one with a relatively short horizon. To put it another way, if the consuming unit has a three-year horizon, then it could be argued that his personal rate of discount is approximately 33 1/3 per cent. That is, if r is an individual's rate of time preference, then $1/r = H$ defines his horizon.[20] We can obtain r from observing that

$$y_P = rW \tag{2.38}$$

where W is the consumer's wealth.[21] Then, since a windfall adds to wealth (dollar for dollar), there will be observable a spurious connection between a windfall (y_T) and actual consumption because of the correlation introduced between y_T and y_P. In the case of $k = 0.9$ and the 33 1/3 per cent discount rate, about \$.30 per dollar of windfall-oriented consumption would arise from this violation of the basic assumptions of the theory. For a longer horizon this bias would approach zero. Note, though, that the basic theory still holds, since it is a theory which is supposed to hold $\rho_{y_T y_P} = 0$ when actually tested.[22]

One must also consider a literature which relates the "length of horizon" question to the "proportionality" question. Friedman actually found in favour of a three-year horizon and proportionality, but the latter was questioned by Liviatan (1963) who used the "errors in variables" approach on data for which the horizon turned out to be at most two years (it was four to six months). Holbrook (1967), who notes that a second definition of the horizon is the length of time a factor must affect income before it is regarded as permanent, questions whether Friedman has really established a three-year horizon firmly (in a statistical sense). Indeed, Holbrook feels Friedman's tests - basically a test of $1/\beta$ - actually support a two-year horizon as much as they support a three-year horizon; of course, the shorter horizon rules against the permanent income hypothesis directly. A more direct test was launched by Landsberger (1971) as follows. Letting

$$C_t = \sum_{i=0}^{\infty} y_{t+1}(1 + r)^{-(i+1)} \tag{2.39}$$

where r is the discount factor, then the marginal propensity to consume transitory income received in time t is $\lambda/(1 + r)$ - the partial derivative of (2.39) with respect to y_t - and the marginal propensity to consume permanent income in period t (repeatedly discounted to infinity) is λ/r - from the total derivative of (2.39). The ratio of MP_P to $MP_T(-1)$ is $1/r$ and is, consequently, a measure of the horizon, as just described[23]; when it was estimated directly, Landsberger confirmed Friedman's results for a horizon of two and a half to three years. More recently, Bhalla (1979) looked at Indian rural data and used a procedure which corrects for joint "measurement" and "hypothesis" errors (recall that the permanent income hypothesis can be interpreted as an "errors in variables" problem which creates a nice mess if there are also measurement errors in variables). Bhalla finds an upper limit of three years and non-proportionality; a similar method used by Musgrove (1979) on South American data also finds non-proportionality, as does Attfield on British data (1977, 1980), although the required adjustment is small in the latter case.

Some of the more interesting evidence on the permanent income hypothesis comes from the direct windfall tests, which are themselves tests of the proposition that $\rho_{cPyT} = 0$. Basically, the procedure is a simple one: we identify a transitory component (generally positive) in an actual case and calculate the propensity to consume this windfall. If, for the consuming unit in question, the item is added directly into savings, then for $\beta = 4.0$ and $k = 0.88$ (Friedman's estimates), an unanticipated increase of a dollar will produce no more than \$.35 of actual consumption. This may fall as low as zero, depending on the underlying correlation between y_T and y_P (that is, on the consumer's rate of discount in this respect). Note, though, that an anticipated windfall is much more likely to produce a \$.35 reaction - indeed, earlier period's consumption may well be affected if it is possible to borrow ahead (as it often is, of course). Thus, a lot of attention in this literature has gone toward pruning out any anticipated windfalls.

An early study by Bodkin (1959) actually found a higher MPC out of transitory than out of regular income. Friedman argued that this was due to incorrect accounting for anticipations and wealth; Bodkin returned to the fray in a paper with Bird (1965) in which no clear difference between the propensities existed. Kreinen (1961) and Landsberger (1970), on Israeli data, found strong confirmation of the theory. Running the other way, L.R. Klein and Liviatan (1957) actually got an MPC greater than unity out of a category of income thought to be transitory; similar approaches by Reid (1962) and, recently, by I.A. Shapiro (1976), though, run in the direction suggested by Friedman. We should note that an overly large MPC out of transitory income, actually implying a positive role for fiscal and monetary policy, could be the result of imperfection in capital markets (you cannot borrow much on human capital) which, in effect, shortens the horizon; see Dolde (1978) and T. Russell (1974) for an explanation. At any rate, a broad conclusion one could offer is that while the permanent income hypothesis passes the windfall test, it fails the proportionality test. It is, nevertheless, a useful idea and is much used in macroeconomic modelling and in discussions of the effects of particular monetary and fiscal policies.

2.4 WEALTH AND THE CONSUMPTION FUNCTION

2.4.1 THE LIFE-CYCLE HYPOTHESIS

We have made a distinction between the absolute income hypothesis on the one hand and the relative and permanent hypotheses on the other hand and suggested that the permanent hypothesis actually involves a more explicit role for wealth than one generally finds in the relative hypothesis. Yet, we have also argued, Keynes himself included wealth in his discussion (and Duesenberry did in his) although both omitted wealth in their more exact formulations. Along these lines we should note that as we progress to more general models and tests, the role of wealth becomes more and more complicated. The life-cycle hypothesis is a case in point; indeed, as it has grown, it has developed from more specific early forms into a generalized dynamic consumption model. In the final analysis it has turned out to be a very flexible and useful model.

To begin, we should point out that there is a considerable overlap between the life-cycle model and Friedman's model which occurs over the underlying economic process which produces the calculation of permanent income. As we noted above Friedman presents a visualization of his permanent theory based on the Fisherian theory of interest. This was a two-period (1, 2) consumption model in which a consumer who expects to receive income over two periods may choose an optimal c_1, c_2 different from y_1, y_2 by borrowing or lending at the going interest rate. His motives, says Friedman, are (a) to straighten out his stream of consumption expenditures and /or (b) to earn interest. We may, then, also define the life-cycle hypothesis as a generalization of the Fisherian consumption model involving the age of the consuming unit as an additional influence on aggregate consumption. We will begin with an early version of the theory which basically concentrates on the age aspect before considering several more general formulations (see Modigliani and Brumberg (1954) in this and later sections of the chapter).

Putting aside some important questions concerning aggregation for the time being, let us begin with an intertemporal utility function for an individual as in

$$u = U(c_t, c_{t+1}, \ldots, c_L, a_{L+1}) \qquad (2.40)$$

where t is the current age of the head of the household, L is the lifetime (consisting of N working years and m retirement years) and a_{L+1} are bequests to one's heirs. Assume that the individual has a stock of present (non-human) assets (a_t) and expects with certainty to earn future labour incomes of y_i for $i = t, \ldots, N$ periods until his retirement. He would, thus, be constrained in his maximization of (2.40) by equation (2.41), his dynamic budget constraint.

$$a_t + \sum_{i=t}^{N} \frac{y_i}{(1+r)^{i+1-t}} = \frac{a_{L+1}}{(1+r)^{L+1-t}} + \sum_{i=t}^{L} \frac{c_i}{(1+r)^{i+1-t}} \qquad (2.41)$$

Note that all future incomes (sources) and uses (bequests and consumptions) appear in present value form; note, as well, that there are not interest-earning assets (a point of some concern if a generalization is desired).

This is a simple problem in consumer theory, and we can visualize the solution in the form of a set of first-order conditions as in equation (2.42), here taken at the maximum after setting up a Lagrangean expression, for each consuming unit:

$$\partial U/\partial c_i = \lambda/(1 + r)^{i + 1 - t} \qquad i = t, t + 1, \ldots, L$$
$$\partial U/\partial a_{L + 1} = \lambda/(1 + r)^{L + 1 - t} \qquad (2.42)$$
$$\partial U/\partial \lambda = [\ \cdot\ ]$$

In this problem the stream of consumption (c_i) and $a_{L + 1}$ are the choice variables. From this formulation we can calculate demand functions as in

$$c_{ij} = c_{ij}(a_{tj}, U_i, t, W_{tj}) \qquad (2.43)$$

where U_i as an argument represents taste factors associated with each future period and W_t is human wealth at age t (as in equation (2.41)). We include the age of the household as a separate variable, in addition to its role in a_t and W_t, and we could also include N if an abrupt shift in consumption is expected at retirement. We employ j here to emphasize that this formulation applies to the jth consumer - that is, that we have not aggregated as yet.

One way we might go on this problem is to calculate a set of second-order conditions and then, with suitable restrictions, turn out signs for equation (2.43); instead, Modigliani and Brumberg "trim" their general function until they get to a considerably simpler version of their basic model. To begin with, they assume that initial wealth is zero (no inheritance) and that final wealth is also zero (no bequests):

$$a_{1j} = 0$$
$$a_{L + 1, j} = 0$$

These simplifications are clearly unrealistic but reasonably innocuous in our context (we will discuss a literature which has grown up here later). This permits us to write

$$c_{ij} = C_{ij}(v_{tj}, t, U_i) \qquad (2.44)$$

where

$$v_{tj} = \sum_{i = 1}^{N} \frac{y_{itj}}{(1 + r)^{i + 1 - t}} + a_{tj} \qquad (2.45)$$

combines the two items of wealth; a_{tj} now consists of the self-accumulated wealth of a household of age t. Like Friedman, we may assume proportionality between the consumption of the jth unit and its wealth as in

$$c_{ij} = \gamma_{ij}(U_i, t)v_{tj} \tag{2.46}$$

here $\gamma_{ij}(U_i, t)$ still depends on the age of the household and its unspecified taste factors associated with each future period; indeed, it is very similar to Friedman's model (equation (2.20)) in that it has the rate of interest embodied in v_{tj}, the potential distinction between human and nonhuman wealth (again in v_{tj}) and a portmanteau concept (in the form of i which identifies taste factors associated with each future period). It also has a proposition from the relative income hypothesis in t, the age of the household.

Assuming that $r = 0$ and summing over the $N - t$ remaining work years for the consumer of age t (who receives y^e_{jt} for the rest of his working life), we obtain

$$v_{jt} = y_{jt} + (N - t)y^e_{jt} + a_{jt} \tag{2.47}$$

This then may be substituted into equation (2.46) to produce (after summing over all future periods (over i)):

$$c = \sum_{i=t}^{L} \bar{c}_{ij} = (y_{jt} + (N - t)y^e_t + a_{jt}) \sum_{i=t}^{L} \gamma_{ij}(i, t) \tag{2.48}$$

Assuming that $\gamma_{ij}(i, t)$ is a constant $(= \gamma_{ijt})$ and that γ is the same for each consumer (over j) and each future period (i), we have

$$\sum_{i=t}^{L} \gamma_t$$

which, when summed, equals $(L + 1 - t)\gamma_t$; this, in turn, is equal to unity. Defining $L_t = L + 1 - t$, we may, then, produce the final Modigliani and Brumberg function as

$$c = c(y, y^e, a, t) = \frac{1}{L_t}y_t + \left(\frac{N - t}{L_t}\right)y^e_t + \frac{1}{L_t}a_t \tag{2.49}$$

which is seen to depend on current income (y_t), permanent income (y^e_t), initial assets (a_t), and the age of the household (t). Note that the marginal propensity to consume in the model is

$$\frac{\partial c}{\partial y} = \frac{1}{L_t} + \left(\frac{N - t}{L_t}\right) \frac{\partial y_t^e}{\partial y_t} > 0$$

and tends to fall with increasing age (both $1/L_t$ and $(N - t)/L_t$ get smaller with age), given $\partial y_t^e/\partial y_t$.

In the original paper in which the life-cycle hypothesis appeared, Modigliani and Brumberg discussed empirical tests at great length, although they did not carry any out. They note that "A household whose current income unexpectedly rises above the previous 'accustomed' level . . . will save a proportion of its income larger than it was saving before the change and also larger than is presently saved by the permanent inhabitants of the income bracket into which the household now enters" (1954, p. 406). (This is interesting because it makes the life-cycle and permanent income theories sound very similar.) Indeed, in their comments on the empirical literature they clearly think that the data confirm the proposition just quoted. Modigliani and Brumberg also discuss other variables in their survey of the literature; these are assets, age, uncertainty, and the composition of wealth. With regard to assets, they point out that although $\partial c/\partial a > 0$, this is not necessarily a causal relation; that is, since in effect both c and a are choice variables, they both could be expected to vary with the income, expectations of income, and the age of the household. Finally, note that a simple linear function of y, y^e and age will not work as a test, since consumption is not a linear function of age.[24]

The life-cycle hypothesis in its broadest form, as for example in the original Modigliani-Brumberg paper, is clearly hard to distinguish from the broad form of the permanent income hypothesis. Actually, as we have already pointed out, both the life-cycle and the permanent income hypotheses are dynamic consumption problems and both emphasize the role of wealth in straightening out the discrepancies between the consumer's consumption plans and the consumer's expected stream of income (from all sources). The upshot is that many of the general tests described in earlier sections of this chapter which compare the relative value of a wealth formulation to that of a simple income or relative income formulation, are also germane to the topic of the life-cycle model. The results, quite simply, were (a) that many "relative" aspects do appear to matter; (b) that simple income, possibly surprisingly, often does as well as smoothed income; (c) that certain anomalies in the actual long-run behaviour of the average propensity to consume are effectively explained by the wealth model; (d) that "non-proportionality" exists between consumption and permanent income; and (e) that when there are significant transitory factors in income, the wealth model might well perform relatively better than its rivals.[25]

The specific contribution of the life-cycle theory is to involve the age of the household; some empirical work has been done on this. In an early paper, M. Fisher (1956) finds that s/y was very high for both the very young and those close to retirement (for the self-employed): the former is possibly unexpected, but less so when one reflects that the younger self-employed need to save to build up their capital as compared to those in their middle years. In another study Watts (1958) also finds that a classification by professions shows, for example, that households headed by young professionals (with the bulk of their income to come closer to retirement) do have higher c/y than those headed by young manual workers. Similarly, Stafford (1968) looked at the consumption patterns of one young group - graduate students - who may well expect higher income in the future. They turned out to have higher c/y out of "permanent income" - that is, out of regular income net of the spouse's (more transitory) income. Finally, since at least the narrow version of the life-cycle theory implies that all wealth is planned to be consumed over one's lifetime, Farrell (1959) looked at the asset distribution of older households and found that they held less than their fair share, as the theory predicts.

A more critical literature, even, is due to Thurow (1969). Thurow also uses the Fisherian theory, which is the basis of the life-cycle model, but points out that in its general form (e.g. equation (2.43) in the text) it is not obvious that the consumer's plan for consumption is either constant or gently rising. For one thing, the consumer's "time preference" (in λ) in (2.42) is involved in this decision although it pretty much drops out of the work leading to the final equation (2.49). While some of this also depends on what you consume (the young drink beer, the old medicine), it is arguable - and Thurow does some calculations to support that argument - that consumers would desire more in their youth than they are able to get given "imperfect" markets in human capital (and, conversely, less in old age). The disputes raised by the possibility of market imperfections are wide-ranging (see Motley and Morley, 1970; Daniere, 1975; and especially Heckman, 1974, who attributes the poor life-cycle prediction to a deliberate work-leisure decision by workers, rather than to a market imperfection). The impression one gets is that both the model and the many "tests" are at least suggestive of a reasonable proposition. This might be that consumers do form rough lifetime plans, but that their adherence to strict "rationality" - and their ability to follow their plans - may never be demonstrated to everyone's satisfaction.

There have also been some recent tests of the life-cycle model, usually in a modified version, and it is interesting to look at some of these. We will discuss a number of relevant studies of "rational expectations" below; these are, broadly, modifications of a life-cycle/permanent income framework, and so we will forbear here (typical is the basic paper by Hall, 1978). In a recent paper Drazen (1978b) notes that while the long-run savings ratio (s/y) is constant in the United States, this seems unreasonable in view of a number of "demographic" changes (such as in life expectancy, in the growth of social security relative to private pensions, and in the growth of human capital). He finds, using a life-cycle framework, that s/y - corrected for new human capital - has actually risen. Along the same lines White (1978) finds that a basic life-cycle model systematically underpredicts the savings ratio for the United States; that is, simulated values of the savings ratio are only about 60 per cent of the observed values. Even worse, White finds that adjustments to the assumptions of the model - such as an exponentially increasing income, a concept of family income, or an increasing pattern of consumption - generally produce a lower simulated s/y. In yet another paper Graham (1979) argues that while the life-cycle and permanent income theories imply that MPC (short run) < MPC (long run) - for a constant factor of proportionality (see above) - this result fails to hold at all times, at least when "short run" is defined as one business cycle and long run as an entire sample running over several business cycles. Graham suggests a model based on "household production theory".[26] This proposition, when combined with an income divided into "labour" and "non-labour" components (predicting an unchanged MPC - short run to long run - out of the latter) better explains the cycle-versus-long-run data just referred to. Even the elderly - who are supposed to dissave fairly rapidly - do not do so as quickly as the basic life-cycle model implies; this, at least, is the conclusion of Mirer (1979, 1980) whose regression results on US data support this conclusion. Perhaps doubts about the possibility of future social security payouts in the United States (as the system appears progressively nearer to collapse), doubts about the ability of the authorities to control the pace of inflation,[27] and, of course, doubts about the length of life, account for this. In any case, such factors do not really lead to rejection of the life-cycle hypothesis, but to the construction of a version of the theory which accounts for greater perceived risks at later ages.

2.4.2 WEALTH AND CONSUMPTION: SOME DIRECT MODELS

At this stage it is useful to go back a little in terms of the theoretical apparatus discussed and consider more direct formulations of the wealth hypothesis. One of the early studies incorporating wealth more explicitly into the underlying model is that of Ball and Drake (1964), in which the point of departure is the aggregate utility function

$$u = U(W, c) \tag{2.50}$$

Here wealth is an argument of the utility function on the grounds that it provides direct utility in satisfying a precautionary motive; that is, wealth is a "buffer stock" which helps the consumer stay on his desired consumption path (which is, then, unspecified). Assuming, then, that desired wealth is proportional to income (Ball and Drake assume equation (2.50) is homogeneous in wealth), we have

$$W_t^* = wy_t \tag{2.51}$$

Since $s_t = W_t - W_{t-1}$, we may argue that

$$s_t = b(W_t^* - W_{t-1}) \tag{2.52}$$

which is a partial adjustment formulation. Using equation (2.51), we than have that

$$s_t = bwy_t - bW_{t-1} \tag{2.53}$$

and, since $s_t = y_t - c_t$, we have a consumption function of the form

$$c_y = (1 - bw)y_t + bW_{t-1} \tag{2.54}$$

which has been estimated successfully (see Smyth and McMahon, 1972). This is surely the simplest wealth hypothesis possible.

There are some interesting empirical tests of the "direct wealth" hypothesis; indeed, Ball and Drake, Spiro (1962), and, of course, Ando and Modigliani (1963) all provide tests favouring the inclusion of wealth in the consumption function. Evans (1967) is critical of these studies, primarily on econometric grounds, and argues that no good case for this mechanism can be made. Arena (1964), in turn, considers a variation of the basic model. Instead of equation (2.51) he proposes $(W_t^* - W_t^{\ddagger})$ where W_t^* is desired target wealth and $W_t^{\ddagger}$ is "potential target wealth", defined as $W_t^{\ddagger} = a_{t-1} + G_t^e$, where G_t^e is expected capital gains. The equation estimated, then, is

$$c_t = \beta_1 + \beta_2 y_t + \beta_3 a_{t-1} + \beta_4 G_t + u_t \tag{2.55}$$

Bhatia (1972) then tested

$$c_t = k_1(1 - \alpha)y_t + k_2(1 - \alpha)G_t + \alpha(C_{t-1}) + u_t - \alpha u_{t-1} \tag{2.56}$$

and

$$c_t = ky_t^w + k\beta W_{t-1} + k\beta W(L)G_t \tag{2.57}$$

where (2.56) assumes that capital gains affect consumption through permanent income, while (2.57) follows if capital gains work through the wealth variable; $W(L)$ represents a distributed lag. Bhatia found in favour of (2.57), but McElroy and Poindexter argued that there was some double-counting between G_t and W_{t-1} (on account of the lags in $W(L)$); they favoured (2.56), in effect.

In a cross-section test, Friend and Lieberman (1975) also found strong evidence for a negative impact of capital gains on personal saving (between 2 and 4 per cent). They also found some evidence of an asset effect; but their equation (being cross-section) had age, family size, and occupational variables, but only occupation was ever statistically significant. Considerable disaggregation is also suggested in the work of Juster and Taylor (1975), who divide income into labour, property, and transfer (and include social security and tax payments).

In another version of the theory - and one using the dynamic consumption model more explicitly - we consider not wealth but deviations from desired wealth as the objective variable; this is the work of Deaton (1972). Let us begin with yet another version of the proportionality relation between desired (or optimal) aggregate consumption and income, in which y_p is permanent income.

$$c^* = \tilde{k}y_p \tag{2.58}$$

The tilde over k indicates that it is a random variable. In addition, let desired (or optimal) aggregate wealth be determined as in equation (2.59).

$$W^* = \tilde{m}y_p \tag{2.59}$$

$\tilde{m}$, then, is the ratio of desired non-human wealth to permanent income (whereby the theory is also seen to provide a variation on Friedman's w).

Assume, then, that all consumers face the same interest rate (it is compounded in y_p) and that the distributions of the random variables $\tilde{k}$ and $\tilde{m}$ are independent of the distribution of y_p. This implies that

$$\tilde{k} = \sum_i \bar{k}_i \frac{y_{pi}}{y_p} \tag{2.60}$$

where i identifies an age group and the interest rate affects both $\bar{k}_i$ and y_{pi}. Here the $\bar{k}_i$ is conceived of as "age group" means. The independence also permits us to write another aggregation as

$$\tilde{m} = \sum_i \bar{m}_i \frac{y_{pi}}{y_p} \tag{2.61}$$

We then need an explicit form for permanent income; let that be given by

$$y_p = \lambda y + (1 - \lambda)E^{-1}y_p \tag{2.62}$$

where E is a forward shift operator ($E^{-1} = L$, as the latter was defined earlier). We may also define permanent wealth as

$$W_p = \mu W + (1 - \mu)E^{-1}W_p \tag{2.63}$$

Turning to the optimization problem, Deaton works with a very specific utility function - a quadratic loss function - here presented as equation (2.64).

$$F = \alpha(c - \tilde{k}y_p)^2 + \beta(EW_p - \tilde{m}y_p)^2 \tag{2.64}$$

This function attributes aggregate disutility to the (squared) difference between desired and actual consumption and expected and desired wealth (recalling that (expected) permanent wealth is a decision variable). The budget constraint is

$$EW = (1 + \pi)^{-1}(y + W + R - c) \tag{2.65}$$

where π is the rate of inflation and EW is wealth expected at the end of the current period. This variable (EW) consists of y, W, and c, as well as capital gains or losses (R) all discounted by the rate of inflation $(1 + \pi)^{-1}$. Since W

is defined in equation (2.63), we may use this, after taking expectations, with equation (2.65) to produce

$$(1 + \pi)EW_p + \mu c = \mu(y + R + W) + (1 + \pi)(1 - \mu)W_p \tag{2.66}$$

We can then form the Lagrangean as

$$L = \alpha(c - \tilde{k}y_p)^2 + \beta(EW_p - \tilde{m}y_p)^2 + \lambda[(1 + \pi)EW_p + \mu c - \mu(y + R + W) - (1 + \pi)(1 - \mu)W_p] \tag{2.67}$$

The first-order conditions for this function are given as equations (2.68); in these expressions y_p and W_p are parameters and c and EW_p are choice variables,

$$\frac{\partial L}{\partial c} = 2\alpha(c - \tilde{k}y_p) + \lambda\mu = 0$$

$$\frac{\partial L}{\partial EW_p} = 2\beta(EW_p - \tilde{m}y_p) - \lambda(1 + \pi) = 0 \tag{2.68}$$

and $\partial L/\partial\lambda$. We may eliminate λ between these two expressions and EW_p between that result and a third expression for $\partial L/\partial\lambda$. Then, for $\sigma = \beta/\alpha$ and $\chi = \sigma\mu^2(1 + \pi)^{-2}$, we can derive the optimal consumption function as in equation (2.69).

$$c^{**} = \alpha_1 y_p + \alpha_2 W_p + \alpha_3(R + W + y) \tag{2.69}$$

where the α_i are written in terms of σ, $\tilde{k}$, $\tilde{m}$, and χ.[28]

This "generalized life-cycle model" shows that permanent income, permanent wealth, and total current resources $(R + W + y)$ are the direct influences on consumption (via α_1, α_2, and α_3) while income is only an incidental component of the last of these. Furthermore, this is a four parameter model (α_1, α_2, α_3, and λ), or, equivalently, $(\tilde{k} - \tilde{m})$, σ, μ, and λ, with π held fixed. Then, too, we have a measure, σ, of the importance attached to the relative uncertainty of the two permanent components ($\sigma = \beta/\alpha$, where β and α come from the loss function (equation (2.64)). Finally, we note that this model, while non-linear and still needing arbitrary lags for y_p and W_p (and an actual average value for π), can be directly estimated, as Deaton does; he finds that the adjustment for the taste for wealth does not add much to the test (σ turns out to be very small and $\tilde{k} - \sigma\tilde{m}$, the net marginal propensity to consume out of permanent income, comes out at 0.917).

This way of approaching things is bringing us closer to one of the more esoteric literatures in macroeconomics -

that on real balance and wealth effects - but for the moment we need to consider some basic material on a specific item of wealth - liquid assets. There are three broad roles for liquid assets in the literature, effectively bridging the gap between the "pure" wealth theories just discussed and wealth effect and real balance effect theories; these are

(a) liquid assets as providing a readily measurable concept of non-human wealth (perhaps serving as a proxy for the broader concept especially in the event that $L = kW$ for L defining liquid assets);
(b) liquid assets as providing a store of purchasing power for consumer durables; and
(c) liquid assets (especially money) providing a vehicle for real balance and for (other) wealth effects.

Let us consider (a) and (b) in this section and (c) in the next.

To begin with, there is an interesting result obtained by Zellner, Huang, and Chau (ZHC) in the context of a permanent income model (1965). ZHC begin with a consumption function written as

$$c_t = \beta y_t^e + \alpha(L_{t-1} - L_t^d) + \mu i_t + u_t \qquad (2.70)$$

Here the underlying model is similar in intent to the basic form of the well-known Patinkin model (as in Chapter 1) where

$$c = c(y, i, \frac{M_o}{P})$$

but instead of the level of money wealth, ZHC write the difference between desired liquid assets (L_t^d) and those held at the end of the previous period (L_{t-1}). α, by this interpretation, is an adjustment coefficient (assigned to unwanted balances of liquid assets); approximately, y_t^e represents the effect of the human component and L_t that of non-human omponents of wealth, but the latter is only applicable when an adjustment is required. To complete it, this model requires an expression for y_t^e, which is provided by equation (2.71), and a demand for liquid assets function, as provided by equation (2.72).

$$y_t^e = (1 - \lambda)(y_t + \lambda y_{t-1} + \lambda^2 y_{t-2} + \ldots + \lambda^n y_{t-n} + \ldots) \qquad (2.71)$$

$$L_t^d = \gamma y_t^e - \delta i_t \tag{2.72}$$

The former is appropriate for the Koyck transformation (if $\lambda < 1$), and the latter is the demand for liquid assets.

With these adjustments, an estimable consumption function given as equation (2.73) results.[29]

$$c_t = \lambda c_{t-1} + \alpha L_{t-1} - \alpha\lambda L_{t-2} + (\beta - \alpha\gamma)(1 - \lambda)y_t + (\mu + \alpha\delta)i_t - \lambda(\mu + \alpha\delta)i_{t-1} + u_t - \lambda u_{t-1} \tag{2.73}$$

This does not completely specify the structure; that is, while it has six variables and six coefficients (i.e. six unique parameters in the form of λ etc.), we have two additional restrictions because the coefficients on the first three terms are linearly related as are those on the first, fifth, and sixth terms. In the US study of ZHC the separate estimates (estimates made ignoring the implied restrictions) produced violations and so a non-linear method was adopted. This test obtained sizable values for α and statistically significant values for all of the coefficients, thus provisionally confirming the usefulness of this Friedman-style liquid assets approach to aggregate consumption; a British study by D. Fisher (1970) generally concurred.[30]

In addition to the paper just discussed, we have already noted (in this chapter) several other recent papers on the empirical results for liquid assets. Several of these referred to capital gains, and one, by Boughton (1976), explicitly tested for liquid assets. Boughton defines his liquid assets to be currency plus bank deposits (presumably M2), measured at the beginning of the period; his reason, that this concept provides a proxy for non-human wealth (rather than as an adjustment coefficient as in the ZHC model just discussed), is perhaps the usual one, although given the wide swings one observes in the various asset ratios (especially on quarterly or monthly data) it seems an unlikely proxy, to say the least. In any event, Boughton finds it marginally useful in his version of the permanent income model.

Somewhat more focus is given to these arguments with regard to the absolute-permanent-life-cycle debate in a recent paper by Pissarides (1978). Assuming that individuals can hold short-term assets (or borrow short term) and long-term assets, and assuming they wish to maximize $U(c_1, \ldots, c_T)$, then we can form the following Lagrangean expression to express the structure of the problem; here B_t represents the individual's overall budget constraint and a_t^0 his initial assets.

$$L = U(c_1, \ldots, c_T(+ \sum_{t=1}^{T} \lambda_t B_t + \sum_{t=M+1}^{T} \mu_t a_t^0 \qquad (2.74)$$

B_t, the variable of interest here, consists of (for each period)

total receipts of
  labour income
  maturing long-term assets
  sold long-term assets (sold at a penalty)
  net borrowing (short - or lending)
total payments for
  consumption
  purchase of long-term assets
  savings in short-term assets (or dissaving)

In this framework Pissarides obtains a variety of interesting results. For one thing, the wealth-holder's reactions to income and interest rate changes depend in part on his existing holdings of debt (in particular on the ratio of long-term to short-term debt). For another, Pissarides argues that both the permanent income and the life-cycle models - as adapted to his framework - show more influence from current income than do the more wealth-oriented theories discussed to this point. Finally, Pissarides points out that it is liquidity (not income) which should constrain the consumer in the Keynesian (absolute income) theory, since a consumer's first reaction to a change in income will be to run down his liquid assets. Note that "liquidity" consists of short assets, labour income, and maturing long-term assets (but not cash in this case). This work, it seems, provides a useful rationale for the surprisingly strong liquidity effects so often found in the empirical studies and for the strong role of current income; a study by Heller and Starr (1979) agrees.

With regard to the seasonal factor mentioned above, we should note that, in a consumption function aggregated to include both durables and non-durables, some confusion involving liquid assets might well result. In particular, if consumers use their liquid assets to store wealth for purchases of durables, then this is an additional factor (if liquid assets are lagged as they were in the ZHC study) suggesting that liquidity effects would be stronger on durable consumption than on non-durable consumption; indeed, this has tended to be the case (in ZHC and D. Fisher (1970)). But one should be careful here, since the quantity of liquid assets can be subject to sizeable transitory effects (perhaps on account of unanticipated inflation), and transitory effects on wealth may force adjustments among the other items of wealth (such as consumer durables) in the same direction as the effect on wealth, as suggested by standard portfolio theory. That is, an effect can be observed here not because it is a spurious effect but because of an incorrect aggregation (at least if one has adopted the permanent income model).

There is more work on "liquidity-and-consumption" which also brings us closer to the policy issues. Mishkin (1976), in one such, argues that monetary policy affects consumption in two ways not usually included in the standard discussions. These are that (a) it changes the prices of assets (especially common stocks) and (b) that it affects the cost and availability of credit, thus affecting the value of the consumer's debt. This last will directly affect the consumption of durables. Mishkin approaches the consumer as if he holds a portfolio of assets and consumer durables, and while the method lies outside this chapter (see chapter 3), the conclusions, at least, are not. Thus, if total portfolio wealth falls (for example, on account of (a)), then the consumption of durables will fall (and savings, to replenish their total, will rise); similarly, if the total of consumer debt or its cost rises, then consumption will be reduced. Mishkin finds some empirical support for these ideas, and, indeed, he finds some support in the work of others, in a separate note (1977). Another paper along similar lines involving the inflation-liquid assets nexus is by Howard (1978). Howard argues that inflation encourages the holding of real assets (some of which are durable consumer goods) and, by producing uncertainty and "pessimism", encourages saving. Additional effects are on the value of liquid assets (reducing s/y), and on the distribution of income (with an ambiguous effect). On net, he feels the effect will be positive for actual inflation and ambiguous for expected inflation (because some of the effects can be avoided). His single equation tests, using y_P, y_T, and liquid assets in addition to inflation and expected inflation (measured as a distributed lag of past inflation rates) provide some support for the inflation variables, particularly for the United States.

2.4.3 THE REAL BALANCE AND WEALTH EFFECTS

The foregoing propositions, especially the formal life-cycle and permanent income models, considered mainly the direct role of wealth (or its components) on consumption (usually in comparison with formulations in which only income appeared). There was, to be sure, some reference to liquid assets, liquid asset "effects", and the effect of capital gains, but what remains is a complicated and somewhat frustrating - but nevertheless important - literature which includes real balance (and wealth) effects. This literature is concerned with the influence which changes in the value of wealth (however induced) have on spending (or, narrowly, on consumption). There are various reasons one might be interested in this problem; these include (a) completing one's macroeconomic model, if the effects matter, (b) settling theoretical and empirical questions concerning the long-standing dispute between "Keynes and the Classics", and (c) establishing the magnitude of the effects of fiscal and monetary policies which alter private wealth (as all do, to some extent). The arguments concern such time-worn topics as the proper definition of wealth and the "transmission mechanism" of monetary and fiscal policy. We shall not be concerned with the latter in this discussion and shall only scratch at the surface of the other problems; there are surveys (see Modigliani, 1971; Meyer, 1974; D. Fisher, 1978, for various views).

The discussion here can usefully begin with the work of Pesek and Saving (1967) in which the position is taken that money (e.g currency and demand deposits) is actually net wealth to society (and so any changes in its total will affect consumption). In particular, they argue that "inside" money (money based on private debt, such as the demand deposits just mentioned) is actually net wealth; many economists, on the other hand, would argue that while "outside" money (e.g. currency issued by the government) is net wealth, the case for inside money in this role is not easy to establish. In any event, a protracted and continuing debate has ensued, with the issue somewhat quieted now, although a new outbreak can occur at any time.

Pesek and Saving were basically disputing some results generated by Gurley and Shaw in an earlier work (1960). Those authors had worked on the question of the neutrality of money and had argued, in the course of their presentation, that inside money (in their terminology the "indirect debt of financial intermediaries") is fundamentally different from outside money and that it is inappropriate to consolidate the inside sector (that is, to add together the financial and spending sectors) such that the demand and time deposit liabilities of commercial banks are netted out when compared to wealth-holders (the owners of the assets). By direct implication, Patinkin (1965) and other implicated Neoclassical economists were judged guilty of having had what Gurley and Shaw refer to as an inappropriate "net money" doctrine by their choice of analyzing the effect of monetary policy (e.g. open market operations) solely in terms of outside money. Indeed, Gurley and Shaw argued that a net money approach had a number of direct implications (compared to their "gross" money approach) such as that when outside money was dropped from the net money model, no money remained and the result was a barter economy in which the price level was indeterminate (a Say's Law economy, one might argue). In contrast, Gurley and Shaw argued, an inside money economy actually does have a determinate price level (etc.) and is not a barter system, *per se*, but, of course, to get this result, one must analyze the system from a gross money point of view.

Of more direct concern to our discussion of consumption is the argument of Gurley and Shaw that the familiar neutrality propositions of neoclassical monetary economics are not valid in a mixed inside-outside money economy, again with the implication that one has to approach the problem from their gross money point of view. In their words,

> a change in nominal inside money can have real effects when there is a combination of inside and outside money. When, on the other hand, the economy contains only inside or only outside money, a change in nominal money has no real effects. . . . Hence, by washing out inside money (and debt), net-money doctrine misses the effects on real behavior from a combination of inside and outside money. (1960, p. 144)

The policy implications are immediate, since the effect they have in mind is not limited to the short run. It also implies that an activist monetary policy has a role to play, of course, since real effects are seen to occur (at least if one takes their point of view).

Turning to Pesek and Saving, we note again that their principal arguments are that inside money is actually net wealth (a point subsequently disputed by Patinkin, 1969; Friedman and Schwartz, 1970; and Johnson, 1970, among others), and that Gurley and Shaw's point, that money is nonneutral in a mixed inside-outside money economy, is incorrect. First of all, Pesek and Saving distinguish between

(a) the price-induced wealth effect (of Patinkin or Pigou, 1947) and
(b) the interest-induced wealth effect (of Metzler, 1951).

The former arises from the inclusion of real balances in the optimizing problem (as, for example, arguments in production and utility functions), and the latter involves the revaluing of flows of desired services - especially the services of money - expected to be received over the life-time of a particular asset. The effects, in either case, are on consumption and investment (and on the supply and demand for bonds, money, and labour, in a more extended context), and the processes could be started up by (in either case) open market operations which would alter the price level and/or the interest rate.

The argument has gone on for some time now, but the following may well be the consensus. The neoclassical school (Patinkin, Friedman, Johnson) argue that inside money itself is not net wealth because "the origin of the net worth of the banking sector is not in the production of money *per se*, but in the monopoly rights which this sector has received" (Patinkin, 1969, p. 114). This view seems tenable in an economy in which money is produced costlessly and in which over-production (and an infinite price level, presumably) are prevented by requiring banks to take out charters which are then rationed. In this event, the market value of the monopoly rights or, equivalently, the market value of the firms that obtain them, will measure the value of the firm's product (money). But the essence of a modern inside-outside money economy is that it uses private resources to manufacture money; this argument is stated forcefully by Floyd and Hynes (1972). Indeed, the critics of Pesek and Saving seem to be involved in an argument which sounds as if an exchange of money for non-money, in a perfectly competitive economy, could be achieved without a gain in welfare. On this point, Buchanan warns the critics of Pesek and Saving that

> If pushed to their extreme limits, accounting conventions "prove" that gains from exchange are impossible . . . broadly speaking, this procedure is acceptable so long as all transactions are assumed to be made in full equilibrium where there are offsetting transfers of expected present values between contracting parties. The unique feature of the call-loan is that no such offsetting transfer takes place. (1969, p. 814)

In this event, the case when call-money is exchanged, one should think of a system, suggests Buchanan, in which the exact dollar liability of the commercial bank is replaced with the expected value of the call loan (the deposit). This expected value would then be expected to fluctuate with the probability of recall of the loan by the depositor. We note, though, that Pesek and Saving treat the deposit as a product (produced by the bank), carrying with it an "instant repurchase clause". This is not entirely semantics, then, since as a product it is more natural to think of money as providing direct utilities.

Pesek and Saving argue that the key issue in their debate concerns the fact that money (as they define it) does not pay interest; indeed, they argue, if a financial commodity pays interest, it is not money (or, rather, to the extent it pays interest, it is not money). Friedman and Schwartz, on the other hand, argue that this distinction is not an operational one, since interest-paying money is just providing joint services (and "the dollar of moneyness and the dollar of interest-payingness . . . cannot be added directly together" (1960, p. 116)) which are non-separable analytically (interest-paying-money has both characteristics at once, like a house offering both a view and a shelter). Indeed, Friedman and Schwartz conclude that the logic of Pesek and Saving's approach favours using high-powered money - that is, currency in the hands of the public plus commercial bank reserves held at the central banks - which are, conveniently, non-interest bearing in the United States, although this is not essential to their argument.

This entire argument actually involves the dynamic consumption function (since the real balance effect is most likely to be observed on consumption), rather than the (static) balance sheets of firms and individuals, and so it is interesting to spin out part of the argument of Saving (1970) in this paradigm. The starting point of Saving's approach is to deal with the dynamic consumption plan of a representative individual without inserting money directly into the utility function (this would beg the question); instead, it is argued, money serves the function of saving time in consumption. Assume that the individual maximizes an intertemporal utility function such as equation (2.75)

$$u = U(c_t, \ . \ . \ . \ , c_h, L_t, \ . \ . \ . \ , L_h) \qquad (2.75)$$

where h is the horizon (or expected life), c_t is the service flow from consumer goods during the current time period, and L_t is the proportion of total time given to leisure. Each time period, then, will be assumed to be divided up into working (W_t), transactions (T_t), and leisure (L_t) time, such that

$$W_t + T_t + L_t = 1 \qquad (2.76)$$

These are, of course, proportions. Further, the time spent in transactions can be reduced by holding more money (as in the inventory-theoretic model to be discussed in Chapter 3) and would be increased by consumption activity (consumer goods are presumably used up in one's leisure time); equation (2.77) represents these assumptions.

$$T_t = k(c_t, m_t) \qquad k_1 > 0 \qquad k_2 < 0 \tag{2.77}$$

Finally the consumer will have an initial fixed real wealth (a) and initial money balances (M/P) and will expect to earn (over the same horizon)

$$\sum_{i=t}^{h} \frac{y(w_i)}{(1+r)^{i-t}}$$

where $y(w_i)$ is the expected real income from work.

The consumer, in this exercise, is assumed to allocate his wealth, as just described, between money holding and consumption activities. Equation (2.78) describes his constraint formally.

$$W = \sum_{i=t}^{h} \frac{y(w_i)}{(1+r)^{i-t}} + \frac{M}{P} + a = \sum_{i=t}^{h} \frac{c_i}{(1+r)^{i-t}} + \sum_{i=t}^{h} \frac{rm_i}{(1+r)^{i-t}} \tag{2.78}$$

Here the cost of production of money is zero and money pays no interest. Note that the stock of real money balances (m_i) is converted to a service flow to put it into conformity with c_i, $y(w_i)$, etc. by the use of the premultiplied r; in this sense r is the best direct measure of the services which money provides (it is the opportunity cost of holding money) by the interest rate argument just considered. The interest rates in the denominators, of course, calculate present values (and incidentally convert all flows into stocks). The optimizing problem, then, is a simple one: subject to (2.76), (2.77), and (2.78), the consumer will maximize (2.75). The result is a stream of optimal real consumptions $(\hat{c}_t, \ldots, \hat{c}_h)$, a stream of optimal leisures $(\hat{L}_t, \ldots, \hat{L}_h)$, and, by (2.76) and (2.77), a stream of optimal real cash balances $(\hat{m}_t, \ldots, \hat{m}_h)$; these will each depend on income, the interest rate, and initial wealth.

To deal with the analytical questions in this section, Saving assumes that there are three types of agents (all individuals being consumers, ultimately), non-bank owners, bank owners, and banks. He then considers three cases: a (solely) outside money system, a (solely) inside money system, and a mixed system with a "repurchase agreement"; for the outside money economy he assumes that money is sold outright by a private producer (or a government which is owned by its citizens) who retains no liability. To provide formal proofs, all that needs to be done is to look at the constraint in equation (2.76) for each of the sectors, since an increase in wealth "normally" increases consumption; we could, that is, look for the effect of an increase in real balances on wealth with the understanding that a real balance (a type of wealth) effect on consumption will then follow. Saving then shows that the real balance effect for a purely inside money economy is identical to that for a purely outside money economy. Indeed, for a mixed economy, there is also no need to make the inside-outside distinction.

Saving goes on to consider several other cases in which the distinction between inside and outside money might be expected to matter; these results are as follows:

(a) When private money bears interest, there will be a difference between inside and outside money (when the price level changes) since the payment of interest will stand in lieu of the services of money presumably obtained above, whatever these services might be. In effect, changes in the interest rate will change the deposit-currency ratio (or other financial ratios) in this event, so that the various multipliers would not be constant (or even stable).

(b) When money costs resources to produce, banks cannot be described as they were in the foregoing. Nevertheless, the total effect of a change in real balances is the same, so long as the role of money is not altered (it saves time in transactions). That is, in the previous analysis a resource (time) was used anyway, so that all that is involved in introducing more resources (bank premises, etc.) is recasting the problem in marginal terms.

(c) If banks render services to customers, these services can be analyzed as alternatives to interest payments. In this event, as in (a), the inside real balance effect will differ from the outside real balance effect (which implies non-neutrality in this framework).

There have been further theoretical results in this literature, and there have also been empirical tests. The direct tests have generally involved either the RBE itself or tests of the existence of "money illusion". Patinkin himself (1965) discusses numerous studies of this sort, and there are results using the short-run consumption function of Zellner, Huang, and Chau (1965) - as contained in our discussion of liquid assets - where M/P or some other direct proxy involving money is employed, usually successfully.[31] Patinkin also accepts demand for money studies with real balance effects as relevant here since, in his theory, the effect should show up everywhere but in the bond market. There has been a dispute over what assets to include in the test, but at the risk of over-simplification (which we shall try to correct below), it seems fair to say that high-powered money (H), narrow money (in some models, at any rate), the monetary base, or the total of H plus government bonds in private hands would be acceptable, at least for those who have any faith in the hypothesis. There has also been a dispute as to whether the RBE is actually perverse, with a fall in the price level, by undermining the capital structure of business firms (by increasing the real value of their debt) actually inducing business failure and, consequently, imposing spreading losses on an economy (unemployment, etc.) which could outweigh the positive aspects of the real balance effect on consumption (see Brenner and Mishkin, 1979). This argument reminds one of the argument of Friedman and Schwartz (1963) that President Roosevelt's bank holiday had just such a perverse effect (4000 banks failed to reopen when the holiday was over, although not all failed). Apparently I. Fisher (1934) and Keynes (1936) also thought this case (the failure of business firms) an important one in the discussion of the RBE.

Dealing next with "money illusion", we note first a series of papers around some empirical work by Branson and Klevorick (1969) that suggests that there is substantial money illusion in the consumption function. Branson and Klevorick use a simple distributed lag function justified with reference to the life-cycle model; this is

$$\log c_t = \alpha_0 + \sum_{i=0}^{I} \beta_{1i} \log y_{t-i} + \sum_{j=0}^{J} \beta_{2j} \log W_{t-j} + \sum_{k=0}^{K} \beta_{3k} \log P_{t-k} + \epsilon_t \qquad (2.79)$$

Here they accept the hypothesis if $\sum_{k=0}^{K} \beta_{3k}$ is significantly positive (W is real consumer net worth and y is real labour income). This, indeed, is what they found. Cukierman (1972), further, pointed out that if consumers actually react to relative prices, since any change in P generally involves changes in relative prices, there could be some biases here; he makes the correction by using five indices (recall Boughton's test (1976) which successfully used three) to the effect that "the original conclusion [of Bransom and Klevorick] . . . is weakened but not altered". Another study by Craig (1974) strongly confirms the work by Bransom and Klevorick, this time adding a liquid assets variable. The major problem with this short literature is that the effect proxied by the price level may, in fact, be the result of some basic misrepresentation in the model; two thoughts leap to mind: aggregation bias produced by summing over individuals (van Daal, 1980, shows that there is an *a priori* case for this) and the use of a "non-rational" function when a rational expectations function is appropriate. In the latter case the use of the distributed lag on prices may be inadvertently introducing parts of the relevant information set actually used by consumers to set up their (rational) consumption plans. There are other studies, involving inflation, usually favouring the money illusion hypothesis.[32]

There are a number of related "wealth-oriented" matters which on the one hand utilize the life-cycle model and on the other involve the net wealth controversy: these are questions of whether government bonds are net wealth, whether or not social security is net wealth, and, finally, on the effect of taxes on aggregate saving (some of this latter is discussed below, in the section on interest rates). The Pesek-Saving literature has produced considerable agreement on whether high-powered money (H) and currency (C) are net wealth (they usually are) but not on whether inside money is. With regard to bonds, usually inside bonds are ruled out, but whether we should drop outside (government) bonds is still arguable. With regard to H and C, if individuals are to perceive changes in them as net wealth, it is argued, then they have to perceive the changes as permanent and not liable to be "paid off" by some future tax[33]; by extension, as Barro (1974) points out, government bonds will be perceived as net wealth only if their value exceeds the capitalized value of the implied stream of future tax liabilities. Of course, a bond issue goes with an expansionary fiscal policy, and so it is interesting to note that the potential effects here seem small and rely on such devices as imperfect capital markets (and monopoly power); furthermore, Barro applies the argument to social security, which if unfunded, is merely a transfer from young to old which can be expected to be repeated for each generation once the system has stabilized.

Underlying the Barro result is the idea that if there are intergenerational transfers in the system - put there by government policy - that rational individuals (and the collection of individuals) will arrange their bequests so as to cancel out these effects. For example, if the expected transfer is from one's children to oneself, then individuals will save more in order to increase the value of their bequest to their children; see the discussion of Blinder (1976).[34] Indeed, various studies have shown that the elderly - after retirement - actually increase their savings (e.g. Mirer, 1980, and the references cited there) although whether this is an intergenerational transfer (a bequest), the result of diminished productivity in individual consumption functions (age = tired), a remarkably slow reaction to unanticipatd gains, or a reaction to increased uncertainty is hard to say on the evidence. Barro, thus, sees the extent of "tax discounting" as critical to whether bonds are net wealth or not (he argues that generational effects do not provide wealth effects on account of the overlapping nature of generations - so that the representative individual acts as if his life is infinite); a version of this using IS/LM is available by Bruce (1977). The empirical literature seems to run in favour of "tax discounting" and against the "net wealth" hypothesis, for government bonds at least.[35]

With regard to the social security question the first fact of interest is that an individual unit pays taxes in youth, which are transferred back to it, plus interest, when it retires; it is a supplement to private pensions, and if it is actuarally solid, it should have no effect on savings or on wealth so long as it is neither better nor worse than the private plan - and the private plan is funded (the government plan is not funded, but it has a tax system to back it up). Of course, if social security lowers the age of retirement (Feldstein, 1974), this may reduce private saving (by reducing the production of incomes) although this may well be a once-for-all intergenerational impact resulting from the start-up of the system. With overlapping generations and a fully implemented system (all workers contributing from their jobs) not expected to change markedly in the future, the effect on saving may well be minimal. Feldstein, indeed, produced empirical results which suggested a strong downward impact on saving, and Munnell (1974) concurred, but in recent papers by Barro (1978) and Leimer and Lesnoy (1980) this finding is disputed. The latter study, in fact, claims that a data error in the original Feldstein paper produced the result.[36]

2.5 RATIONAL EXPECTATIONS AND THE CONSUMPTION FUNCTION

Our work to this point has emphasized a number of problems which the basic consumption-income (or wealth) model has. One of these was that the use of current income, whether by itself in the absolute income hypothesis or as one of a series of incomes (mostly lagged) in a proxy for expected income introduced bias into a regression of consumption on income because of mutual endogeneity. The appropriate estimating technique is then two-stage least squares. A second major problem emerged, above, when it was argued (by Darby (1972), for example) that to avoid the bias coming from an incorrect specification in the permanent income model - incorrect because the correct model is possibly an "errors-in-variables" model - one should introduce both permanent and transitory income into the regression model as independent variables. Neither of these two approaches is entirely satisfactory though, the first because the theoretical problem behind the "errors-in-variables" is not resolved, and the second because of "mutual endogeneity"; but more interestingly, putting the two ideas together leads one quite naturally into considering how one might justify a purely errors-in-variables approach, along the lines of the "rational expectations hypothesis". We will follow the work of Hall (1978) before tacking on some more recent material.

By "rational expectations" we mean that any economic agent who needs to form an accurate expectation about an economic variable in order to reach his optimal position does so with all the relevant information available at the time he forms his expectation. If, for example, one is planning an investment in the stock market, then, if it is true that stocks tend to follow the earnings of corporations in the long run, it would be rational - if one were considering an investment in a particular stock - to obtain all of the information one can on the probability of that firm achieving various levels of earnings.[37] If all investors form their expectations about future events in this way - if all judge solely in terms of expected earnings and filter the stock of available information about the company in such a way as to retain only that relevant for accurate earnings projections - and if there are a large number of investors doing this, then it follows that at any moment the market price of that firm's stock will embody (be determined by) those expectations. In all likelihood, that is to say, the price of the stock will reflect the average market view of the firm's potential, so far as the currently available information goes. Only surprises to investors (or, in our example, information available to insiders, and the like) will cause the price to deviate from the path dictated by expected earnings; in the language of the market, in the short run stock prices will follow a random walk, where tomorrow's expected price is today's price plaus a random number:

$$E(P_{t+1}) = P_t + \varepsilon_{t+1}$$

In the long run they will follow earnings.

There have been a number of application of this proposition outside of the area of financial economics - such as to the demand for investment goods, to the demand for money, and to the debate over the effect of monetary policy - and, as noted already, there is an application to the permanent income/life-cycle consumption model by Hall, that goes as follows. Assume a standard and simple life-cycle model of the following general form:

$$\text{Max } E_t \sum_{j=0}^{T-t} (1+\delta)^{-j} u(c_{t+j}) \tag{2.80}$$

subject to

$$\sum_{j=0}^{T-t} (1+r)^{-j} (c_{t+j} - y_{t+j}) = A_t \tag{2.81}$$

Here E_t represents expectations in t, conditional on all information available at that time; δ is the rate of time preference; A_t are all non-human assets; and y_t represents earnings that are stochastic (and are known in period t when the optimal consumption is chosen).

It follows, if the consumer maximizes his expected utility by picking c_t for each period, that

$$E_t u'(c_{t+1}) = \left(\frac{1+\delta}{1+r}\right) u'(c_t) \tag{2.82}$$

Thus, the only information which could help in predicting future consumption (c_{t+1}), when one is predicting from period t, is c_t; y_t and A_t are actually irrelevant, given c_t. Furthermore, if the utility function is assumed to be quadratic, then the consumption function is

$$c_{t+1} = \alpha + \beta c_t - u_{t+1} \tag{2.83}$$

In an empirical test equation (2.83) represents a very basic consumption function indeed. In fact (see note 38), we would expect α to be near zero ($r = \delta$) and β to be near unity in such a test (if they were not, we could fairly call the process a "biased random walk"). With regard to other influences - policy and (other) exogenous shocks, for example - these are either transitory (in which case they are impounded in u_t) or permanent. If the latter are expected, they are impounded in c_{t-1}; if they are unexpected (i.e. unpredictable), they are impounded in u_t. Thus, to affect consumption in a macro-policy design, one has first to affect permanent income; a policy perceived to be a transitory policy will have no effect. Indeed, since consumption in equation (2.83) depends only on exogenous (u_t) or predetermined (c_{t-1}) variables, it should be treated in other equations as an exogenous variable. This, as Hall points out, has implications for macro-model building, especially that of forecasting models. But Hall's tests do not actually provide very strong support for his hypothesis.

Rational expectations will be wrong - or at least appear to be wrong - if consumers are constrained from achieving their optimum, if they use some other method of forecasting which cannot be considered rational, or if they are really responding in the way "habit persistence" suggests. "Adaptive expectations" - such as in the Koyck or Friedman lags - may be rational, of course, but if the method leads to systematic errors (the Koyck lag underpredicts when there is a trend in the data), then this is a non-rational procedure in effect.[39] With regard to habit persistence, Bilson and Glassman (1979) construct a test which distinguishes between habit persistence and forecasting lags. Basically, they show that consumption changes should respond to unanticipated changes in income (and that these should depend on unanticipated changes in the process which generates income). In this framework they show that this is a reasonable model and that it outperforms an adaptive expectations model based on habit persistence, on the data. They do report some "under reaction" though which may be evidence of irrationality (or a lot of other things). In a follow-up paper on "cross-country" data, Bilson (1980) argues that since consumers in this theory will react sharply to unanticipated changes in income, a correct conclusion from a permanent income-rational expectations model may well be that fiscal or monetary policy has a large effect on consumption (recall spring, 1980!) and not the small effect Friedman anticipated (by using adaptive expectations rather than rational expectations). This effect is in the simple income-expenditure model (of Keynes) and not the real world, though (the model has rigid prices and wages and elastic aggregate supply). His tests for three countries (USA, UK, and Germany) show some support for the basic theory, but, at this reading, seem to be provisional because of data and other problems.

In some ways, more obvious empirical contradictions to the rational expectations theory would be expected to come from the successful use of lagged income, the constant (α) in equation (2.83), and other lagged variables; indeed, both lagged income and lagged stock market prices (this providing a kind of permanent shock?) also work, implying problems for the theory (Hall thinks it is due to slow adjustment). Sargent (1978) tried a different approach - that of separating the forecasting equation from the consumption function itself - which involved stating some across-equation constraints on the coefficients (income, for example, appears in both parts). Testing these restrictions, Barro (1977) rejected them, in effect rejecting the rational expectations framework.

Above we mentioned that the Keynesian consumption function is "non-rational" in that it includes the level of current income among the list of arguments. But this actually can be justified in terms of quantity (or liquidity) constraints as, for example, discussed in Chapter 1. In particular, the Clower "dual-decision" framework (1965) as modified by Barro and Grossman (1971) has been invoked in this context (see, for example, Leijonhufvud, 1968), and it also seems to fit nicely into the rational expectations model just described. But there is a theoretical problem with both the Clower and Barro-Grossman approach as described by Mackay and Weber (1977). This is that both of these frameworks require (for the individual) that the actual constrained quantities and not current income should be entered in the consumption function; then, in the event that different consumptions are weakly separable (so that the inability to sell any income-generating factor has only a simple income effect) the Keynesian theory could be deduced from either the Clower or Barro-Grossman (disequilibrium) framework. This may seem an unreasonable restriction, although we should note (as described in Chapters 1 and 4 in more detail) that weak separability between consumptions is a minimum condition for the existence of the aggregate consumption function (although this is not discussed in the Mackay-Weber paper).

Along different lines, exceptions will come - and macro-policy will have a hold on short-run consumption - to the extent that permanent surprises to "calculating" consumers are engineered by the monetary authorities. Of course, this is a short-run game, since consumers will be including the authorities in their "permanent" calculations whenever the authorities are at all consistent, but it does suggest a way to apply the theory to recent consumption experiences.

To begin with, note that the expected wealth of the consumer consists of his human wealth and his non-human wealth; furthermore, note that both are discounted by the interest rate. As a proxy for surprises in the calculation of permanent income, a calculation of transitory income (all income not explained by $y_t = a + \beta_1 c_t + \beta_2 y_{t-1}$) would be appropriate; call it y_T. As a proxy for surprises in the calculation of the interest rate, one might use the residuals from a regression of

$$\left(\frac{\Delta P}{P}\right)_t = \alpha + \left(\frac{\Delta P}{P}\right)_{t-1} + u_{1t}$$

which identify the monetary-induced surprises in the nominal interest rate in each period (call it $(P/P)_T$).[40] Finally, to identify "permanent" and unexpected effects on his non-human wealth, we might use a policy reaction function, such as

$$m_t = \alpha + \beta_1 m_{t-1} + \beta_1 U_t + \beta_3 (\Delta P/P)_t + \beta_4 B_t + u_{2t} \qquad (2.84)$$

to identify the systematic component of monetary policy and then use the unexplained part of the money stock (m_T) as the proxy for surprises in the calculation of non-human wealth. Note that U is unemployment (or employment) and B represents the balance of payments, and that all three contemporaneous variables are monetary-policy "objectives" in this almost certainly non-rational reaction function.[41] The consumption function which results, then, is

$$c_t = \alpha + \beta_1 c_{t-1} + \beta_2 y_{Tt} + \beta_3 m_{Tt} + \beta_4 (\Delta P/P)_{Tt} + u_{3t} \qquad (2.85)$$

and to the extent that β_2, β_3, β_4 are significant, we would have located a possible policy effect on consumption. This test has not been carried out.

2.6 INTEREST RATES AND CONSUMPTION

This section summarizes some work on the role of interest rates as an influence on aggregate consumption. Usually the context of these studies is the life-cycle model when that basic model is suitably amended to include that influence. To begin with, we should note that a considerable theoretical effort has been directed toward this problem. While Modigliani/Ando/Brumberg basically avoided these issues by holding the interest rate constant, the consumers' wealth does figure in both their versions of the life-cycle model and in the permanent income models; since the interest rate also figures somewhere in the wealth calculation, the interest effect is included, although it is often not analyzed. The empirical literature, in turn, has produced both positive and negative effects, with the latter dominating (although frequently the interest elasticity has been low and the effect has often been non-significant statistically). The basic theoretical problem, as discussed above, is that a change in the interest rate produces income, substitution, and wealth effects, and these need not run in the same direction.

To deal with these complexities, a variety of specialized results have been constructed which, taken as a whole, cancel out somewhat (although by weight of numbers, a negative interest rate effect dominates). Thus, Yaari (1964) constructed a model in which terminal wealth (bequests) were added to the life-cycle model, with all assets being interest-bearing notes. Yaari's model does not distinguish between the value of assets and their earning power; but, even so, a rise in the interest rate may or may not depress consumption in all periods, and only in the case in which it also depresses bequests is it certain to reduce current consumption. Furthermore, since saving is done for two reasons (for straightening out consumption and for bequests), the analytical symmetry between current consumption and current saving is broken.

In another paper, also in the life-cycle model, Heien (1972) specifies a multi-period CES utility function which produces a non-linear consumption function.

$$c_t = \gamma_t + \{ \sum_{i=t}^{n-1} [\delta^i (1 + r_t)^i]^\sigma (1 + r_t)^{-i} \}^{-1} W \qquad (2.86)$$

where n is the planning horizon, γ_t is "supernumerary consumption" in the current period, and σ is the constant elasticity of substitution.[42] The interest rate effect here enters as a discount factor $(1 + r_t)^{-i}$, as an earnings-augmenting factor, and in W (which is the present value of wealth), but if the function is Cobb-Douglas $(\sigma = 1)$, then equation (2.86) collapses to

$$c_t = \gamma_t + (\sum_{i=t}^{n-1} \delta^i)^{-1} W$$

and it only has the interest rate included in wealth. Heien's tests, then, show σ to be greater than unity, so the more complicated equation (2.86) seems relevant. In that equation there is not necessarily a positive or a negative role for the interest rate, and, in any event, one would not directly test for the interest rate effect there; on the other hand, Heien was able to show that if $\sigma > 1$ its coefficient would be positive. σ, again, is the constant elasticity of substitution between consumptions of different periods (and σ greater than unity implies the elastic rather than the inelastic).

The empirical work on this question has not been particularly voluminous, no doubt partly because the profession prefers to generate "tests" from strong *a priori* positions. We noted above that the "horizon" and the "rate of discount" are coincident phenomena ($H = 1/r$), but not only is the rate of discount a constant in such cases, it is also unbelievably high (estimates are from 33 1/3 per cent *up*), at least if we wish to treat it as "the" interest rate. To get around this, clearly, one must at least separate "time perference" from "opportunity cost", and it is presumably in this spirit that Wright (1967) proposed to estimate

$$c = \alpha + \beta_1 w^* + \beta_2 r \tag{2.87}$$

an equation derived from taking the total derivative of a standard life-cycle model. w^*, here, is the sum of current net worth, the present values of expected labour income, and the present value of expected property income (this last measures the income effect of a change in the interest rate). By this interpretation, β_2 is the substitution effect since income and (some) wealth effects of a change in the interest rate are already measured. After employing a "permanent" measure for expected income (combining labour and property), Wright exhibits significantly negative coefficients for β_2.

Weber (1970), on the other hand, finds a positive effect of the interest rate on consumption. Using a CES utility function and the life-cycle model, Weber derives a "representative" consumer's consumption function of

$$c_t = g(r, t) v_t \tag{2.88}$$

where v_t is discounted human plus initial non-human wealth and

$$g(r, t) = \{ \sum_{j = t}^{L - 1} [(1 + \gamma)(1 + r)^{-\beta_1}]^{\sigma(j - t)} \}^{-1}$$

Here $\sigma = 1/(1 + \beta)$ is the partial intertemporal elasticity of substitution of consumption, and γ is the rate of time preference. Note that the Modigliani-Brumberg model has $r = \gamma = 0$, as noted above. More importantly for this section, a change in the interest rate affects v_i and $g(r, i)$; in the latter case it is seen to affect the propensity to consume. To deal with the interest rate, Weber suggests that the consumer uses the market rate only as a guide to his interest rate expectations; he proposes using

$$r = \theta_1 + \theta_2 r_m$$

where r_m is the market rate and θ_1 is a kind of "risk premium"; this is then substituted into equation (2.88) to produce his estimating equation, the messy

$$c_t = \sum_{j=t}^{L-1} \{[(1+\gamma)(1+\theta_1+\theta_2 r_m)^{-\beta}]^{\sigma(j-t)}\}^{-1}$$

$$[w_t + y_t \sum_{J=t}^{L-e-1} (\frac{1+\varepsilon}{1+\theta_1+\theta_2 r_m})^t] + u_t \qquad (2.89)$$

Here ε is a parameter from the weighting function used on expected income (e.g the Koyck) and e is the age of the representative consumer. There are some econometric problems because the numerous parameters are not identified, but it turns out to be possible to obtain the sign of the interest rate effect empirically (positive), as well as the value of $\sigma(= 1/2)$. This is done by using the estimated values of the parameters in (2.89) in its reduced form. The original study was on annual data, and when it was extended to quarterly data, there were some surprises (σ was unaffected), one of which was that some interest rates did not matter. This difficulty was partially resolved by using a short and a long rate - although without any reference to term structure theory - where a negative effect from the short rate was dominated by a positive effect from the long rate.[43] Note that this is a "gross" interest rate effect obtained by using a specific functional form for consumption and is not necessarily a contradiction to Wright's negative result (for the substitution effect).

The implication, to this point, is that there are effects of interest rates on consumption, but their sign is not clear, and that is about as far as one can go. Recently, though, Boskin (1978) has challenged our complacency on these issues by arguing that the negative interest elasticity (on consumption) is a firm and sizeable result and, furthermore, that it is sizeable enough to cause tax policy to affect economic welfare drastically. Considering first the evidence, Boskin finds that a real interest rate has the expected negative effect (and, when added, the inflation rate does, too). Now this real rate can be thought of as influenced by tax policy (via a production function). In particular, new saving adds to wealth by increasing income, but it is taxed and thus the real rate of return is lower than it otherwise would be. Thus, an increase in income taxes will lower the real rate of return on capital and, since the effect on savings of an increase in the interest rate is positive (as an empirical fact)[44], lower real savings. Boskin does some thumbnail-type calculations which produce enormous welfare losses.

We should, then, pursue the nominal/real interest rate distinction further here, particularly when the consumption function also includes "inflation" or "real balance" terms. In Chapter 1 we noted that the *ex ante* real interest rate $[r = i - (\dot{P}/P)_e]$ is the appropriate variable for the consumption function, but we have made no mention of this so far in Chapter 2 and have reported results for all sorts of empirical studies in which only the nominal interest rate was employed. Part of this lack of concern is empirical - much of the data being drawn from periods of time in which $(\dot{P}/P)_e$ may well be low in value and, even, constant - but any data set which includes data from the 1970s and later could be expected to be influenced by variable inflationary expectations. Even so, not a lot of work has been done on this problem, but one recent paper, by Pesando and Yatchew (1977) on Canadian data on the demand for consumer durables has tackled some of the complexities. The model employed is the Hamburger (1967) macro-model, itself similar in spirit to the Zellner, Huang, and Chau model (1965); the difficult problem of finding the *ex ante* price expectations in order to measure the real and nominal components of the interest rate is done using the "rational expectations" method. This involves generating expected inflation rates (and interest rates) from past inflation rates and deducting these from nominal interest rates; this is, consequently, a "reduced form" approach, since it does not look to what those price expectations are based on. Pesando and Yatchew, on the quarterly Canadian data (1961 through 1971) found that there was no real difference in the "magnitude" of the nominal versus the real rate but that the real rate was statistically significant, while the nominal was not. This is not a strong result, though, since neither the coefficients nor the standard errors (or any other coefficients in the equations) could be shown to be unlike each other, statistically; no doubt this is due to their choice of a data period for which inflation rates were not very high (a surprising choice for a paper published in 1977).

Finally, we might consider an attempt to combine the "interest-induced wealth effect" and the "real-nominal" distinction, motivated by some empirical findings which otherwise might seem hard to explain (Zwick, 1974). The empirical findings are two: (a) a monetary injection tends to be followed by a cycle (down and then up) in the real interest rate - this is called "snap-back" and can be explained with reference to lags - and (b) nominal interest rates do not appear to reflect fully inflationary expectations - which could be because the method of calculation of the expected variables (r and $(\dot{P}/P)_e$) is incorrect. With regard to (a), what Zwick suggests is that both of these can be explained as resulting from the operation of an interest-induced wealth effect; in particular, following a monetary injection which shifts the LM curve to the right and lowers the interest rate, *if* the IS curve is induced to shift upward by a wealth effect (recall that there is some support for this in the empirical literature), then the interest rate goes through a cycle. Actually, what happens in Zwick's model is a rotation of the IS curve (which just modifies the interest rate impact of a monetary injection) as Meyer and Yawitz (1977) point out; furthermore, in practice, the monetary injection will also tend to produce some inflation which could shift the LM curve backward (by reducing the real value of fixed nominal money balances) and, even shift the IS (and LM) curve back on account of either money illusion or a price-induced wealth effect.[45] The combination of these effects is probably ambiguous, and a monstrous empirical problem remains, involving, among other things[46], the proper definition of private wealth.[47]

When there is a single interest rate in the dynamic consumption problem, then, in effect, all bonds (all financial commodities, really) are conceived of as aggregated into one total. In this event, while one cannot always obtain results, the general expectation is that an increase in the interest rate would decrease consumption in the present period. When, however, the possibility emerges of holding bonds of differing maturity, then (a) it is not so obvious that the simple result can be obtained, and (b) there is the likelihood that short-rate effects will differ from long-rate effects, opening up (unfortunately) all sorts of possibilities to the wealth-holder. To generalize things, in this event, it becomes necessary to introduce a stochastic framework, since the shorter security, presumably, can be renegotiated and, if it is, will be renegotiated at a rate of interest which generally cannot be known in advance. More importantly, this term structure context raises an issue we have so far neglected (for the one interest rate model). In particular, if we run an empirical test for a consumption function with only one rate - let us say a short rate - then we could get either a positive sign for the interest elasticity of the consumption function or a negative sign depending on how the long rate reacts. For example, if the long rate rises more than the short rate, so that distant consumptions are more readily achieved, then a general shift toward current consumption may occur, leaving a coincident rise in the short rate and a rise in current consumption, rather than the fall one might expect. Let us attempt to generalize the dynamic-consumption-term structure problem which we must solve if we are to obtain any theoretical results here.

The originating paper in the formal part of this literature is by Stiglitz (1970). Stiglitz proposed to answer the question of why individuals hold short-term bonds; his reason is that in so doing they thereby avoid uncertainty in their consumption streams; we follow the work of Bernstein and D. Fisher (1978) for much of the following. Let us define a three-period horizon for a representative individual who can be assumed to be constrained by the following relation in the first period,

$$C_1 + S_1 = W_1 \tag{2.90}$$

where

$$S_1 = B_{S1} + B_{L1} \tag{2.91}$$

and by

$$C_2 + \frac{C_3}{(1 + r_{S2})} = W \tag{2.92}$$

in his second and third (final or end) period, where W is his second and third period wealth, evaluated at period 2 and r_{S2} is a future one period rate. The latter, of course, is stochastic if the optimization is viewed from the first period.

Stiglitz, to simplify his arithmetic, assumes that initial wealth (W_1) is fixed and implicitly assumes that $S_1 = \overline{S}_1$ is given; these assumption imply that C_1 is also exogenous and thus that the optimizing problem should be written in terms of equation (2.93).

$$u = U(C_2, C_3) \tag{2.93}$$

The procedure, then, is to maximize (2.93) subject to (2.92) and here W is defined as in (2.94).

$$W = \overline{S}_1[b_{S1}(1 + r_{S1}) + (1 - b_{S1})\frac{(1 + R_{L1})}{(1 + r_{S2})}] \qquad (2.94)$$

Here we show how wealth grows either by investment in b_{S1} $(= B_{S1}/\overline{S}_1)$ or in the long-term bond $[b_{L1} = B_{L1}/\overline{S}_1 = (1 - b_{S1})]$ in the initial period. Note that $(1 + R_{L1})$ is a compound consisting of an implicit forward rate (ρ_t) for each of the two periods $(1 + \rho_1)(1 + \rho_2)$.[48]

To solve the optimization problem for C_2 and C_3, from the point of view of the second period, we maximize (2.93), subject to (2.94). In this context W is given, and consequently our necessary and sufficient condition for an optimum is merely

$$U_2 = U_3(1 + r_{S2}) \qquad (2.95)$$

This would produce two consumption functions for our representative consumer of the general form of

$$C_2^* = h_{C2}(r_{S1}, r_{S2}, R_{L1}, \overline{S}_1) \qquad (2.96)$$

and

$$C_3^* = (W - h_{C2})(1 + r_{S2}) \qquad (2.97)$$

These can be solved for interest rate effects, but as this is not the most general case studied here, we will forbear for the moment.

The simple problem we have set ourselves is not yet complete because the representative consumer has not yet found his optimal portfolio $(= b_{S1}^*)$; that is, his problem of dividing his initial wealth between (fixed) first-period consumption, short-term bonds, and long-term bonds in order to achieve his optimal consumption stream, remains to be solved. To do this, we must operate in an uncertain environment (we are back in period 1), and so we now maximize

$$E[U(C_2^*, C_3^*)] \qquad (2.98)$$

where b_{S1} is the control variable, subject to the optimization already determined for C_2 and C_3 in the non-stochastic framework. Approximately, what we are doing is solving the problem in two stages - a stochastic and a non-stochastic - first obtaining the future consumption demands as if the future had already arrived (that is, assuming the consumer has a definite plan) and then solving the entire problem in a stochastic framework in which the present decision (the value of b^*_{S1}) is taken. This is a general approach.

We may substitute (2.96) and (2.97) into (2.98) in which case we have

$$E[U(h_{C2}, (W - h_{C2})(1 + r_{S2}))] \tag{2.99}$$

The necessary condition for a maximum, then, is

$$E[\frac{\partial U}{\partial C_2}\frac{\partial C_2}{\partial b_{S1}} + \frac{\partial U}{\partial C_3}\frac{\partial C_3}{\partial b_{S1}}] = 0$$

then, recalling that $U_2 = \partial U/\partial C_2$ and $U_3 = \partial U/\partial C_3$, we have that at the optimum,

$$E\{(U_2 - (1 + r_{S2})U_3)\frac{\partial C_2}{\partial b_{S1}} + U_3\overline{S}_1, [(1 + r_{S1})(1 + r_{S2}) - (1 + R_{L1})]\} = 0 \tag{2.100}$$

Now $\overline{S}_1$ is fixed (and can be ignored), and by equation (2.95) the first term is zero. Thus, at the optimum (since $U_2 - (1 + r_{S2})U_3 = 0$), we have

$$E\{U_3[(1 + r_{S1})(1 + r_{S2}) - (1 + R_{L1})]\} = 0 \tag{2.101}$$

This expression contains a familiar term structure term, although it is worth underscoring that r_{S2} is not a forward rate, but a future one. Then, if the household is risk-neutral, so that we can carry the expectations operator inside the expression, our optimal condition becomes

$$(1 + r_{S1})E(1 + r_{S2}) = (1 + R_{L1}) \tag{2.102}$$

That is, if all individuals were risk-neutral and in equilibrium, then, in a dynamic consumption framework the expected yield curve would be flat. This result obtains no matter what the desired consumption profile might be, so long as risk-neutral consumers are price-takers in bond markets. Of course, whether or not actual yield curves are flat is another matter; they would be if $E(r_{S2}) = r_{S2}$ or if the forward rate $\rho_t = E(r_{S2})$, but these equivalent expressions are only one possibility for the relation between expected and actual interest rates. Note that in the absence of uncertainty

$$(1 + r_{S1})(1 + r_{S2}) = (1 + R_{L1})$$

holds so that in equilibrium, long and short securities are perfect substitutes. But it takes a dynamic consumption/uncertainty case to show how that result lacks generality.

Turning to the more general problem in which first-period consumption is variable, we note, from the outset, that the arithmetic is necessarily more complicated in view of having two control variables in the first period or "portfolio choice" part of the problem. Let us write beginning of period constraints for the three periods as follows:

$$C_1 + B_{S1} + B_{L1} = W_1 \quad (2.103)$$

$$C_2 + B_{S2} = W_2 + (1 + r_{S1})B_{S1} \quad (2.104)$$

$$C_3 = W_3 + (1 + r_{S2})B_{S2} + (1 + R_{L1})B_{L1} \quad (2.105)$$

Here we again have fixed initial wealth and (again) assume that the long-term bond is not sold in the second period but held until the (beginning of the) third period and then cashed in (at $1 + R_{L1}$). Since B_{S2}, the one-period bond purchased in the second period, appears in both (2.104) and (2.105), we may collapse these expressions to yield

$$C_2 + \frac{C_3}{(1 + r_{S2})} = W_2 + \frac{W_3}{(1 + r_{S2})} + (1 + r_{S1})B_{S1} + \frac{(1 + R_{L1})}{(1 + r_{S2})}B_{L1} \quad (2.106)$$

Our choice problem, then, is to maximize the expected utility for the three periods by choosing C_1^*, C_2^*, C_3^*, and b_{S1}^* (or C_2^*, C_3^*, b_{S1}^*, and b_{S2}^*), subject to (2.106) for the second and third periods and (2.96) for the first period. Our only stochastic variable, as before, is r_{S2}. Again, we can optimize in two stages such that first we will maximize (2.93), subject to (2.106). The first-order conditions which directly result are

$$U_2 - \lambda = 0 \quad (2.107)$$

$$U_3 - \frac{\lambda}{(1 + r_{S2})} = 0 \quad (2.108)$$

and

$$-C_2 - \frac{C_3}{(1 + r_{S2})} + W_2 + \frac{W_3}{(1 + r_{S2})} + (1 + r_{S1})B_{S1}$$

$$+ \frac{(1 + R_{L1})}{(1 + r_{S2})}B_{L1} = 0 \qquad (2.109)$$

These can be solved for demand functions for C_2 and C_3 as in

$$C_2^* = h_{C2}(r_{S1}, r_{S2}, R_{L1}, B_{S1}, B_{L1}, W_2, W_3) \qquad (2.110)$$

$$C_3^* = h_{C3}(r_{S1}, r_{S2}, R_{L1}, B_{S1}, B_{L1}, W_2, W_3) \qquad (2.111)$$

Again, we have the optimal condition that $U_2 = U_3(1 + r_{S2})$.

There are various ways one might go to try to provide useful comparative equilibrium results for (2.110) and (2.111) and for C_1^* (in a second stage of solution). A strong restriction on the utility function (making it homogeneous of degree $1 - \beta$ with $\beta > 0$) enables one to sign

$$\frac{\partial C_2^*}{\partial r_{S1}}, \frac{\partial C_2^*}{\partial R_{L1}}, \frac{\partial C_3^*}{\partial r_{S1}}, \frac{\partial C_3^*}{\partial R_{L1}}$$

which are all positive, but even with this restriction it still proves impossible to determine any effects on C_1^*, from any variables, and so this analysis confirms that the interest rate effect on consumption is an empirical matter. Stiglitz was not really interested in results on consumption, but, roughly, with an additive utility function ($u = U(C_1) + (1 - \theta)U(C_2)$, where θ is the rate of time preference) he obtains results similar to those stated above (for C_2^* and C_3^*, in effect). Green (1971) has provided the "general equilibrium" solution for Stiglitz's problem by permitting C_1 to vary (as described earlier in this section); he also considers the use of two other specializations of the utility function, a quadratic function and a logarithmic function. Green, also, is not interested in the consumption function; even so, even with increasing absolute risk aversion (in both functions), only some positive wealth effects (on first-period consumption and saving) are obtainable, barring any further specializations (about expected interest rates, for example).

The results of this section, thus, imply that more than one interest rate may well influence current consumption but that in a term structure context it is not possible to sign these effects; in Chapter 3 we will argue that the more specific models of the demand for money (the mean-variance and the inventory-theoretic models) actually produce expected signs for the term structure, and so, by analogy, one might well expect the multiple interest rate conclusions to carry over for similar assumptions. Of course, these paradigms do not contain consumption (it is, in effect, solved for in a first stage), and when the dynamic consumption framework is applied to the demand for money problem (in a term structure context), the same indeterminancy of sign returns. But for the demand for money there is actually some successful empirical work (see below) which suggests that empirical work on this problem in the context of the consumption function may well have some pay-off. Little exists, though, except for the work of Weber, referred to above.

NOTES

1. We come especially close to identifying Keynes with the absolute income hypothesis if we argue that he held proposition (c), although we will also, below, wish to emphasize other aspects of his theory which give it a distinctly modern tone. There is, however, a quarrel with this argument, raised, for example, by D. Ott, A. Ott, and Yoo (1975), that Keynes in the "General Theory" never actually held proposition (c), that the marginal propensity to consume declines at higher levels of income. He did, though, as the following quotations should confirm:

   > Furthermore, if we are considering changes of a substantial amount, we have to allow for a progressive change in the marginal propensity to consume, as the position of the margin is gradually shifted; and hence in the multiplier.

   In particular,

   > it is probable that there will be, as a rule, a tendency for it to diminish as employment increases; when real income increases, that is to say, the community will wish to consume a gradually diminishing proportion of it. (p. 120)

   Note that the last clause, by itself, might be read as proposition (b) if it were not taken in this context (as it should be), since Keynes is explicitly referring to the *marginal* propensity to consume. Keynes, on the next page, gives his reasons (essentially redistribution effects) which also make it clear that he is referring to the *marginal* propensity to consume.

2. A literature generated first by Kuznets (1946) and added to by Goldsmith (1955) has argued that long-run consumption functions do not show the declining average propensity to consume that the theory requires (conditions (a) and (b)) as the level of income has steadily risen over time in, for example, the United States. But this famous paradox, that "short-run" (i.e. ten-year period) results differ from "long-run" (i.e. the whole long-run of data) results, is actually not as telling as it might seem for a simple reason already pointed out in our discussion of the trend variable. In particular, when one looks at the ratio of average income to average consumption, he is not looking at c/y but $\overline{c}/\overline{y}$; c/y will fall for propositions (a) and (b) simultaneously holding in the simple linear model. To put the point another way, consider a regression of equation (2.1), which must pass through the point of the means of the two data serios $(\overline{c}, \overline{y})$; this being the case, the following relationship must hold at the mean: $\overline{c} = a + b\overline{y}$, where a and b are estimated coefficients. Rewriting this, we have

$$\frac{\overline{c}}{\overline{y}} = \frac{a}{\overline{y}} + b$$

We note that having the left-hand term constant (as Kuznets and Goldsmith found) is perfectly consistent with a and b having the appropriate values for propositions (a) and (b). What might be happening, in effect, is that a is rising as fast as $\overline{y}$ over the period in question (or, rather, we can offer that interpretation), and if this is the case, their results could even be taken as supportive of the hypothesis rather than as damaging. Note, as well, that the result that a trend term enters successfully, scaling up a with $\overline{y}$, actually explains the phenomenon and could leave the paradox as little more than the proposition that some trend related omitted variables (such as shifts in consumption or changes in consumption technologies) are relevant, a fact which Keynes, if not the writers of the textbook literature, would (and did) readily admit about this simplest of theories. One should note that the permanent income hypothesis also provides an explanation of this paradox, where the cross-section is a transitory result (see below).

3. One view taken is that the wealth effect does not matter

because the interest rate is irrelevant; in this connection one should underscore (a) that Keynes advanced the theory of the liquidity trap (in which the interest rate does not change), and (b) that Keynes felt that the "long-term rate" ("the" interest rate in Keynes) was relatively inflexible in the short run. This would leave only changes in the stream of expected returns to provide a push here, in the short run. We are thinking of $W = R/r$, where R is a typical element in a perpetual (for simplicity) stream of returns.

4. We should mention here a brief literature which shows that advertising affects aggregate consumption. The studies are by Schmalensee (1972), Taylor and Weiserbs (1972), and Parsons, Schultz, and Pilon (1979), and all find a positive effect in rather simple models.
5. There is also an empirical paper on the effect of changes in the functional distribution of income on the Canadian consumption function by Park (1974); Park divides income into labour and property and finds the propensity to consume the latter zero (in effect, the variable, measured as a "permanent" variable, does not work). There is, however, no theoretical work in the paper so it is not possible to judge just what structure this reduced form is supposed to represent.
6. We will provide some empirical documentation below. For the moment we should note that Duesenberry identified increased urbanization and the increase of "contractual" savings as potentially interesting factors. In contrast, Tobin (1951) found that for some cross-sections of farmers, races, and cities, these "grouping" variables did not provide much assistance to the theory. Tobin, incidentally, related the time series constancy of $\overline{c}/\overline{y}$ to increased deficit financing by the household (Duesenberry mentions this, as well). Tobin did find that Blacks had a lower propensity to consume than Whites, but this could also be explained in terms of relative wealth rather than relative income. There have been many other variables which have worked at times, and there are numerous surveys of this material, as we shall see.
7. Since $\overline{OA} = y_2 + (1 + i)y_1$ and $\overline{OB} = y_1 + y_2/(1 + i)$, the intercept $\overline{OA}$ moves out further than $\overline{OB}$.
8. As in D. Ott, A. Ott, and Yoo (1975), we may define permanent income as expected income ($= y_2$ in this problem), as steady state (or long-run) income (where $y_1 = y_2$), or as the amount the consumer can use up without reducing his wealth (this is $iy_1 + iy_2/(1 + i)$ in our problem). The last-named is in accordance with Friedman's theory, in all likelihood.

9. A new budget line with the old values of consumption (c_1^*, c_2^*) is

$$c_2^* = y_2 + (y_1 - c_1^*) + (y_1 - c_1^*)i_2$$

It clearly cannot go through

$$c_2^* = y_2 + (y_1 - c_1^*) + (y_1 - c_1^*)i_1$$

and, indeed, has to lie to the right of the point c_1^*, c_2^* for $i_2 > i_1$
10. This follows directly from equation (2.19) since c_P and y_P are then seen to be perfectly correlated. Note that not all versions of the theory have $\rho_{cTyT} = 0$, and Friedman himself is not always clear on this point, although in his conclusion (p. 222) he states this clearly enough. Thus an argument between Holmes (1974) and Laumas (1969), in which Laumas tests this relation (and finds against Friedman) and Holmes claims that Friedman does not impose this condition, must be judged in Laumas's favour. But Holmes does make several valid points about Laumas's tests, and, one notes, Holmes assumes that income and consumption are *each* normally distributed rather than bivariate-normally distributed. This, of course, cuts out the covariance and the need to impose $\rho_{cTyT} = 0$; as noted, we prefer here to take Friedman's theory in a different sense. For a test which does impose this condition and uses it to separate out "permanent income error" from "estimation error", see Musgrove (1979); the former error arises when one selects a particular weighting scheme for y_P.
11. For example, Modigliani and Brumberg (1954) note that Keynes's theory could be tested (on account of his reference to "sticky" consumer adjustments) with a distributed lag; they also note

> In our model [the life-cycle], on the other hand, savings tend to go up either because the new level of income is regarded as (partly or wholly) transitory or, to the extent that it is regarded as permanent, because the initial asset holdings are now out of line with the revised outlook. If the outlook has improved, assets are too low to enable the household to live for the rest of its expected life on a scale commensurate with the new level of income. (p. 407)

This use of Friedman's terminology is the first use in the aggregate context (it is based on some earlier work of Friedman's (and is so referred to). But the important point is the verbalization of a high-degree of overlap between the theoretical perceptions (as opposed to the specific, and less general, equations actually tested).

12. $Ly_t = y_{t-1}$, $L^2y_t = y_{t-2}$, . . . , $L^ny_t = y_{t-n}$.

13. The Koyck series has an average lag of $\lambda/(1 - \lambda)$ and a variance of lag of $\lambda/(1 - \lambda)^2$. These are produced by taking $dW(\lambda L)/dL$ and $d^2W(\lambda L)/dL^2$ evaluated at $L = 1$. The term $(1 - \lambda)$ in equation (2.22) normalizes the weights (makes them sum to unity).

14. This being the case, since the data are discrete, an approximation must be made. See Mayer (1972, pp. 362-4).

15. The weights of $\beta e^{\beta(t - t)}$ sum to unity, since the expression $\int_{-\infty}^{t}\beta e^{\beta(T - t)}$ evaluated at t (the present is $(1/\beta)\beta e^{\beta(T - t)} = (\beta/\beta)e^0 = 1$. The leading β, thus, normalizes the weights.

16. We may pull out the term $y_0e^{\alpha t}$ from the integral in equation (2.25); this produces

$$-\int_{-\infty}^{t}\beta y_0 e^{\beta T - \beta t + \alpha t} + \beta \int_{-\infty}^{t} e^{(\beta - \alpha)(T - t)} y(T)dT$$

The first part of this is just a constant, and evaluated at $T = t$, it produces

$$-\int_{-\infty}^{t} y_0 e^{\alpha t}$$

which cancels with the first part of equation (2.25). This leaves

$$y(t) = \beta \int_{-\infty}^{t} e^{(\beta - \alpha)(T - t)} y(T)dT$$

A discrete analogue of this continuous time formula is

$$y_{Pt} = \frac{\beta}{\beta - \alpha}k \sum_{i=0}^{\infty} (1 - b)^i y_{t-i}$$

where $b = 1 - e^{-(\beta - \alpha)}$.

17. We may also see the bias directly in terms of the income elasticity of consumption, and this gives us a clear proof of the proposition; this, in fact, is the examination of the proportionality hypothesis ($\varepsilon_{yc} = 1$) in much the way Friedman looked at the data. Define

$$\varepsilon_{yc} = \frac{\overline{y}}{\overline{c}}\frac{dc}{dy} = \frac{\overline{y}}{\overline{c}}\frac{\Sigma c^* y^*}{\Sigma y^{*2}}$$

where $\overline{c}$, $\overline{y}$ are sample means and c^*, y^* are deviations from those means. (We follow the discussion in Cramer, 1969.) We may write the following expression for the probability limit of (a) as

(b) $$P \lim \varepsilon_{yc} = P \lim \frac{\bar{y}}{\bar{c}} \, P \lim \frac{\Sigma c^* y^*}{\Sigma y^{*2}}$$

Upon directly substituting our expected values from the permanent income hypothesis (see above), the following derivations hold:

$$P \lim \frac{\bar{y}}{\bar{c}} = \frac{\mu_y}{k\mu_y} = \frac{1}{k}$$

$$P \lim \frac{\Sigma c^* y^*}{\Sigma y^{*2}} = \frac{P \lim (1/n)\ c^* y^*}{P \lim (1/n)\ y^{*2}} = \frac{k\sigma^2_{yP}}{\sigma^2_{yP} + \sigma^2_{yT}}$$

Thus

(c) $$P \lim \varepsilon_{yc} = \frac{\sigma^2_{yP}}{\sigma^2_{yP} + \sigma^2_{yT}}$$

with the elasticity different from unity to the extent of bias (the "error" term σ^2_{yT}).

18. These studies are by J.L. Simon and Aigner (1970) and Holbrook and Stafford (1971), and the latter, particularly, produces an estimate of bias. See also an earlier study by Eisner (1958). Recently, in two studies on British cross-section data, Attfield (1976, 1977) finds that *if* one assumes away errors of measurement, then the critical assumption of $\rho_{yTyP} = 0$ is violated. When errors in variables are assumed to exist, Attfield (1980) finds that while the interaction is reduced, it is still there. Of course, violation of this assumption in no way damages Friedman's argument (his condition must be met on the actual data used), but the failure of conventional measures of permanent income to meet the condition is certainly a problem. Two notes are in order, though: Attfield measures permanent income directly ($y_P = \alpha' W + U_1$, where W is a vector of all those (exogenous) variables (age etc. which determine permanent income)) and the magnitude of the interaction is not large (i.e. the maximum adjustment to the marginal propensity to consume permanent income is not large).
19. Compare Friedman (1957) and Mayer (1972) especially.
20. The time horizon can also refer to the entire length of the planning period (seventeen years in Friedman's time series study), although that is not the meaning here.
21. Note that we are not necessarily consuming all of wealth

- that is, $k >/< 1$ are all possible - just stating how quickly changes in wealth will be absorbed into the consumption plan. Note that the 33 1/3 per cent rate, while used here as the rate at which transitory income becomes permanent, is really used as a subjective rate of discount in Friedman's model. Thus, $C + ky_p$ implies $C = krW$ or $C/r = kW$ where r is now employed in its discounting (of consumption) form. To put it another way, if you consume 33 1/3 per cent of new wealth, you are implicitly valuing present consumption highly. Note that a high rate here is plausible in view of the high interest rates consumers seem willing to pay on installment contracts (often well over 18 per cent). Note that Friedman actually estimated a $\beta = 0.4$, which gives a horizon of 2.5 years. The explanation given here is from his paper which explains the concept of the horizon.

In a Canadian study, Clark (1973) reiterates Friedman's experiment on Canadian data. She gets a comparable value for β (0.45 instead of 0.40) when the function is tested without an intercept, but a value reaching 0.62 (implying even faster adjustment) when an intercept is included (the horizon in this case is 1.6 years). Her major point, though, is that the horizon is different from the demand for money; when that function is approached by Friedman's method, a β of 0.22 (a horizon of 4.5 years) is obtained.

22. A given fiscal policy would tend to have a sharper effect - or to have to be maintained for a shorter period of time - if the horizon is shorter. Others who supported the short horizon view are Wright (1969) and Mayer (1972). But see below, on rational expectations, for a different conclusion.

23. The estimating equation is $c_t = \beta_1 + \beta_2 y_{Tt} + \beta_3 y_{Pt} + \beta_4 y_{PPt} + U_t$ where y_{Pt} is lump sums and y_{PP} is "other windfalls".

$1/r$ is estimated from $\hat{\beta}_2/\hat{\beta}_3 - 1$. The "instrumental variables" method of estimation was employed. Another test by Mohabbat and Simos (1977) who used direct estimates of wealth strongly confirmed Friedman's results.

24. This is because $\partial c_t/\partial a_t = 1/L_t$ and L_t, of course, varies with age and expected life.

25. In later papers Ando and Modigliani (1960, 1963, 1964) do carry out original tests. They actually suggest that

$$c_t = \beta_1 y_t + \beta_2 y_t^e + \beta_3 a_{t-1}$$

is a fair representation of their theory. Since each of the coefficients for β_1, β_2, β_3 depends on L and t (the age of the household), sufficiency of aggregation also requires that the age structure of the population be constant. They propose several tests of this equation of

$$c_t = \alpha_1 y_t + \alpha_2 a_{t-1}$$

versus

$$c_t = \alpha_1 y_t + \alpha_2 \frac{L_t}{E_t} y_t + \alpha_3 a_{t-1}$$

where L_t/E_t is designed to adjust for the different income expectations of working and unemployed workers (E_t is the number of workers in production). These adjustments produce only marginal gains over simpler forms.

26. This is mostly a microeconomic literature which is drawn from that on "human capital". The individual, in this case, rents part of his human capital and uses the remainder (and other resources) to produce more human capital.

27. The data themselves, reflecting adjustments on account of expected inflation, may contain a spurious element (see Jump, 1980).

28. $\alpha_1 = (\tilde{k} - \sigma\tilde{m})(1 + x)^{-1}$; $\alpha_2 = \sigma\mu(1 - \mu)[(1 + x)(1 + \pi)]^{-1}$; $\alpha_3 = x(1 + x)^{-1}$

29. ZHC argue that equation (2.73) is implied from an underlying model in which expectations are revised as in

$$y^e_t - y^e_{t-1} = (1 - \lambda)(y_t - y^e_{t-1})$$

As an alternative, they propose

$$y^e_t - y^e_{t-1} = (1 - \lambda)(y_t - y^e_{t-1}) + \sigma y^e_{t-1}$$

which incorporates a trend adjustment in expectations. This produces

$$y^e_t = (1 - \lambda)[y_t + (\lambda + \sigma)y_{t-1} + \dots + (\lambda + \sigma)^n y_{t-n} + \dots]$$

which, when transformed, yields a consumption function in the same form as equation (2.73), but with a different interpretation of the coefficients

$$c_t = (\lambda + \sigma)c_{t-1} + \alpha L_{t-1} - \alpha(\lambda + \sigma)L_{t-2} + (\beta - \alpha\gamma)(1 - \lambda)y_t + u_t - (\lambda + \sigma)u_{t-1}$$

ZHC also consider the problem of the induced serial correlation in equation (2.73). They assume, in particular, that

$$v_t = \rho v_{t-1} + e_t$$

where $v_t = u_t - \lambda u_{t-1}$, in which case we obtain

$$c_t = (\lambda + \rho)c_{t-1} - \rho\lambda c_{t-2} + \alpha(L_{t-1} - \lambda L_{t-2}) - \rho\alpha(L_{t-2} - \lambda L_{t-3}) + \alpha\delta(i_t - \lambda i_{t-1}) - \rho\alpha\delta(i_{t-1} - \lambda i_{t-2}) + (\beta - \alpha\gamma)(1 - \lambda)(y_t - \rho y_{t-1}) + e_t$$

This model, for which $\mu = 0$ (see equation 2.70) seems to work well in ZHC's actual tests on the US data.

30. In the British study it was proposed to use $(M_{t-1} - M_t^d)$ in place of $L_{t-1} - L_t^d)$ on the grounds that since some sort of exogenous or unexpected change in wealth has to occur to motivate this difference, the most likely effect would be that from monetary policy. In this case, as well, the test is in a form which gets pretty close to the Patinkin model, although the motivation was more along the lines of Pesek and Saving (1967); see below. In any event, comparable coefficients were produced. Note that this argument is similar to that for "rational expectations", as described below. In another paper Hamburger (1967) used an approach which is very similar to ZHC's in an attempt to see if monetary quantities and/or interest rates influence consumption; Hamburger looked at two classes of durable goods and included relative price and depreciation terms. He found that the interest rate did have an influence (negative) but that the monetary aggregates did not; this was on quarterly US data 1953 - 64.
31. We discussed a British test by D. Fisher (1970) above; a Canadian study by Tanner (1970) is discussed below.
32. Juster and Taylor (1975) justify their successful use of price expectations in an aggregate savings model in terms of a money-illusion effect, an intertemporal substitution effect, and an uncertainty effect. The latter results because inflation (expected to occur with uncertain impact) will make real wage expectations uncertain (and hence induce more saving). Both the level of and the variance of expected price changes were significant in their tests. There are two earlier papers by Juster and Wachtel (1972a, 1972b) to the same effect and a study by Deaton (1977) which is more in keeping with the rational expectations approach - that it is unexpected inflation which produces

the higher s/y one has observed. On all of these, Jump (1980) suggests that spurious elements in the data, arising from the effect of inflation on interest rates and on various tax bases, could easily have produced a spurious rise in s/y (and, even, in some of its presumed "causes").

33. A study by Tanner (1970) on Canadian data finds no distinction on the inside-outside basis (both currency and bank money showed an effect) and no effect from broader measures using (outside) government debt. He concluded that the tax consequences of the debt issue were apparently foreseen, which is one possible interpretation. Another, of course, is the "interest-payingness" of the various measures. Indeed, here, as elsewhere, one can argue that insufficient attention has been paid to the aggregation of the various items (they are merely summed as if they have constant and unitary prices). See Pesek (1979b) and the discussion of the definition of money in Chapter 3.
34. As Drazen (1978a) points out, the argument does not hold if there are negative transfers (the "parents" use bonds to transfer resources from their "children" to themselves), and it also does not hold if "parents" transfer positive resources to their "children" by means of expenditures on education (human capital). Given the considerable magnitude of the latter, this finding restores the potential of the bond-induced wealth effect.
35. Barro's work runs against the net wealth hypothesis. Tanner (1970) found almost perfect discounting on Canadian data, and Kochin (1974), working with US data and the permanent income model, also found tax discounting. Tanner (1979) also uses the US data and arrives at the same conclusion. Note, also, the discussion of both theoretical and empirical work earlier in this chapter which implies that a liquidity constraint on the young is part of the problem.
36. Feldstein (1981) also updates his work, finding a small but significant effect.
37. Information is not free, of course, so the statement in this paragraph should be read as qualified in this sense.
38. The constant in equation (2.83) is $\alpha = c[(r - \delta)/(1 + r)]$. The CES function for (2.84) is $u(c_t) = c_t \exp (\sigma - 1)/\sigma$.
39. Consumers might also have a problem that faces economists; this is that they have to use a proxy (such as a weighted average of past incomes) in the absence of better information about future income. Arak (1978), though, argues that such a measure is not optimal if past consumption is part of the information set (because, along with past incomes, it provides a better measure of past sav-

ing). Arak shows that such is, indeed, the case.
40. We are using $i = r + (\Delta P/P)_e$ and proxying $(\Delta P/P)_e$ by the function just described.
41. A simple rational function would be $M_t = \alpha + \beta M_{t-1} + u_t$.
42. The utility function is

$$u = \sum_{i=0}^{n-1} \delta^i (c_i - \gamma_i)^\rho$$

where the σ^i are the subjective discount factors. Supernumerary consumption is consumption above the minimum needed for subsistence. $\sigma = 1/(1 - \rho)$ is the constant elasticity of substitution (= 1 in the Cobb-Douglas case). Heien was interested in demographic effects, too, especially increases in the median age of the population (which he found to be a significant factor (1948-65)). Using a similar model on Canadian data, Denton and Spencer (1974) do not find either household or age-distribution effects important (they also do a cross-country test on OECD data, to the same effect). Both papers use the life-cycle model; the idea for "supernumerary" or "uncommitted" income (in Denton and Spencer) comes from Goldberger (1967).
43. The interest rate equation then becomes $r = \theta_1 + \theta_2 r_{m1} + \theta_3 r_{m2}$ which, of course, is an explicit term structure. See the Heller and Khan (1979) study of the demand for money for a similar procedure. Weber extended the study further (1975) in the direction of considering both durables and non-durables, relative prices, and inflation rates. The interest rate effect was still positive; the relative price (of durables/non-durables) worked; but the inflation rate did not.
44. We have, of course, made this a general argument - that the effect is ambiguous, theoretically. For a paper directed to Boskin's argument, see Feldstein (1978).
45. There are quite a few other ways in which government policy may affect s/y (or consumption). For a comprehensive survey see von Furstenberg and Malkiel (1977). Some of the topics discussed there appear in parts of this and other chapters and some in the second volume of this survey (when fiscal policy is discussed).
46. With regard to the incomplete adjustment of the nominal interest rate to changes in inflationary expectations, Zwick argues that since the interest-induced wealth effect causes the nominal rate to adjust only slowly (it takes up some of the adjustment, in a temporary way, itself), then

the nominal rate may well *lag* (and incompletely adjust to changes in) the expected inflation rate.

47. There are other papers. In one, Nagatani (1972) incorporates exogenous risk premiums (in order to introduce an element of uncertainty) into the problem; this risk premium is added to the market interest rate which is why we consider it here. In an extension, Bowden (1974) endogenizes the risk premium (that is, obtains these after formalizing the effect of risk on the utility function). Indeed, if the individual is risk averse in his early years (and has a low wealth), his propensity to consume is clearly less than in his middle years when his risk aversion is low (and his wealth is high). Then, in later years he becomes more risk averse (as his wealth decreases). One can also predict higher savings accounts in young consuming units, shifting to equities, and then back to savings accounts, as the consuming unit passes through middle into later years. None of this seems unreasonable, in any event, although it remains to be implemented empirically.

48. Stiglitz makes a three-period problem look like a two-period problem by fixing first-period consumption, and equation (2.96) shows the effect of this, since $(1 + R_{L1})/(1 + r_{S2})$ is a single-period rate of interest. Note that this expression is similar to the well-known Hicks (1946) formula as employed by Meiselman (1962); this is

$$1 + r_n = \frac{(1 + R_n)^n}{(1 + R_{n-1})^{n-1}}$$

where r_n is a forward rate and R_n is an observed yield. r_{S2} in the above is not a forward rate but a future rate; that is, it does not exist until period 2 arrives; r_n (in effect) exists at period 1, and it is a theoretical construct, rather than a market rate.

3 The Demand for Money

3.1 INTRODUCTION

Quite possibly the most disputed area in macroeconomics is that which bears directly or indirectly on the demand for money. This has long been the case, as even a casual glance at the history of economic thought will bear out, but lately, no doubt on account of the persistent and variable inflation we have observed in recent years, interest seems to have been revived, that is, if the recent outpouring of literature on the subject has any significant bearing on the underlying problems (of unemployment and, especially, inflation). The demand for money is involved in these issues in two major ways: (a) it is quite possibly the object of monetary policy to influence it, and (2) it is a key function in all models of the economy, whether they be large or small. The latter point hardly needs elaboration, since we have already taken the consumption function in this spirit, but we should explain the unique policy attention. This, briefly, arises from the possibility that if a simple and stable demand for money exists then an activist monetary policy can gain a simple and direct leverage on both monetary and real variables in the economy. We will not be interested in the direct policy issues here although we will attempt a summary of where we stand on the stability debate; instead, we will concentrate on the traditional literature in a fashion parallel to our discussions in Chapter 2.

We will begin, then, with a very general summary of the various models. This done, we will enter into a discussion of some important definitional issues in the demand for money before turning to the main theoretical approaches to the subject. As we proceed, we will carry along the results of empirical studies (mostly) in the footnotes; at the end of the chapter though, we will hazard a summary of what the growing empirical record might be telling us.

One traditional approach to the subject - an approach we

will adopt when convenient - is to undertake to make as precise a distinction between the "asset" demand for money (of such apparently disparate points of view as those of Keynes (1936) and Friedman (1956)) and the transactions theory of the demand for money (of such apparently disparate points of view as those of I. Fisher (1963) and Baumol (1952)). In the transactions approach (see Section 3.5), the Fisherian proposal is to suppose that individuals hold a fixed proportion of the expected money value of their transactions in the form of money. If individual demands are then aggregated, one might expect an aggregate proportionality between the quantity of money demanded and the total value of transactions in the economy. This proportionality might then be redefined if another variable (income) is substituted for transactions, and it might well be itself variable if interest rates (let us say as an opportunity cost factor) affect money holding. In Baumol's approach to the transactions demand (see Section 3.5.1), explicit transactions costs are introduced - in the form of the sum of (a) penalty or brokerage costs attached to converting other assets to cash and (b) interest earnings foregone by holding non-interest-bearing cash - and both a direct proportionality between the quantity of money demanded and transactions (or, by some writers, income) and an inverse proportionality with the interest rate are established. This work has been significantly upgraded in recent years as, for example, by Niehans (1978); we will continue the discussion below.

In the asset theory of Keynes, as generalized by the mean-variance model of Tobin (1958) - which is discussed in Section 3.4 - money is held as one among a portfolio of assets distinguished by their expected average returns and the expected variances of their (expected) returns. In this case even non-interest-bearing cash logically could be included in the portfolio because of its unique services, its "liquidity", and its low variance of return. A rise in the interest rate on an alternative would (*ceteris paribus*) make cash holding less attractive, and an increase in the volume (or frequency) of transactions, or an increase in wealth (or, even, income) of the wealth-holding unit would tend to inspire an increase in cash holding. Finally, in the asset theory of Friedman (see Section 3.3.3), the consumer is presumed to possess five major stores of value (cash, bonds, equities, physical capital, and human capital) and to adjust his holdings in the same manner as the mean-variance model implies in accordance with changes in the rates of return on the various components of capital and in his income and wealth.

Both of these broad theories, the asset theory or the

transactions theory, generally imply in the aggregate a negative effect on the demand for money from an interest rate variable and a positive effect from an income, wealth, or transactions variable (it does matter, as we shall see, which of these "scale variables" is used). The empirical debate has been something like a civil war (we say this because, for one thing, both Keynes and Friedman postulated "asset-style" theories, at least if we take their basic theoretical constructs in the way just described), and it has not produced as much consensus as one might have expected from the volume of work carried out. Part of the problem has been that the demand for money has appeared (at least until just after 1971) to be a stable function of a few key variables (income or permanent income and the interest rate)[1], and all of the four basic theories just described include an income/interest rate formulation. The difference, then, lies not so much in the general formulation (that is, in the model itself and in its implied and stated theoretical characteristics) or even in the empirical record, but more in the details of the formulation. What we are saying, then, and it is an important point of departure for both the theoretical and the empirical work discussed below, is that a model-oriented approach which pays particular attention to the characteristics of the model will be more revealing than (for example) a Keynes-versus-the-Classics approach. In addition, such an approach will enable us to sidestep some of the difficult doctrinal issues, although we will not want to do that entirely, if only because there are clearly some real issues involved in these debates. The models we propose to discuss, then, are

(a) general equilibrium,
(b) mean variance,
(c) transactions (e.g. inventory-theoretic), and
(d) dynamic consumption (in passing).

But we will begin with some important preliminary issues on the definition of money which should also help to clarify the entire literature on the demand for money.

3.2 THE DEFINITION OF MONEY

There is both a microeconomic and a macroeconomic literature on the topic of the definition of money with the former cast in terms of "functions" or characteristics and the latter dominated by disputes over the ideal level of aggregation to assume, but we will spend most of our time here on the macroeconomic issues, although a word on the "uses of money" is necessary to get things going.[2] Money, traditionally, is defined by its characteristics; these are its character of being able to serve as a medium of exchange, a store of value, and a unit of account, and these concepts are approached primarily by means of a microeconomic discussion. As a medium of exchange, money serves to bring down net transactions costs; as an asset which is readily and cheaply exchangeable (that is to say, "liquid"), it is a useful store of value; and, finally, in a monetary economy, accounts will normally be kept in monetary units, to the considerable advantage of economic agents. Money, less traditionally, may be viewed as an asset, and it might be asked why people hold it, rather than holding other more lucrative-appearing assets. The answer, following Keynes for example, is that money holding satisfies transactions, precautionary, and speculative motives, with the first two roughly coincident with the medium of exchange and store of value characteristics and the last - the speculative demand - a Keynesian wrinkle which we will come back to in this chapter (and will forbear to discuss further for the moment).

3.2.1 *A PRIORI* APPROACHES

Much macroeconomic work, as we shall see below, takes an essentially empirical and thus eclectic approach to the problem of the definition of money, but there is an interesting body of literature that attempts an *a priori* macro-approach based (loosely) on the "medium of exchange" concept. By far the most comprehensive of these efforts is that of Pesek and Saving (1967), as already discussed in Chapter 2. Money, it can be recalled, was then sharply contrasted with private debt; indeed, the contrast is clearly defined in an empirical sense in that debt pays interest while money does not. With regard to outside money - for example, currency issued by a government - so long as the public disregards any implied liability for the part of the stock issued by the government (fiat money) - and so long as it is considered an economic good - then outside money is properly net wealth to society. Approximately, it is held because it is perceived, at the margin, to provide services equal to its market value. These services are those of a medium of exchange, primarily, although clearly some scope exists for a store of value function too, so there is no need to be dogmatic about it. With regard to whether inside money - for example, commercial bank demand deposits - ought also to be conceived of as net wealth, a furious debate has raged. The following seems to be the consensus, although not all would agree (see the references in Chapter 2).

(a) If, in an inside money economy, monopoly exists in the banking sector, then open market operations will produce changes in net wealth (if only because they change the value of the monopoly).
(b) If private deposit-issuing institutions can, in fact (whether monopoly or not), ignore the liability aspect of their deposits, then, in a largely book-keeping sense, inside money is properly net wealth to society.

The former case suggests that we must measure the degree of monopoly in the banking sector, to evaluate this source of a wealth effect, and the latter suggests that we must measure the probability (risk) of a bank having a significant change in its deposits. Even at this level, it seems, there are interesting empirical problems.

As a "store of value", money clearly is of special interest to the economist. While it is obviously its long history as a medium of exchange that is at the root of its store of value function, it is also true that to store one's wealth in the form of money normally does not require the wealth holder to have any special information about how financial markets work; this is in contrast to the problems of storing one's wealth in stocks or bonds, for example. Of course, one surrenders something in the form of interest payments if his wealth is held as non-interest-bearing money, and this, indeed, is one reason why the financial markets are induced to produce close money substitutes such as the interest-bearing time deposit (or, these days, interest-bearing checking accounts or checkable savings accounts).

The biggest problem with the store of value approach is that as an asset (as, that is to say, a store of value) money can most readily be merged with other similar financial assets in private portfolios to such an extent that a close substitutability may often be observed. This implies, in turn, that to "define" money - that is, to distinguish money from other assets - one must somehow measure the degree of substitutability among financial assets which actually appear to be pretty similar. This is not a simple task, partly because there are many unobservable or controlled rates of return in this sector, and it has produced a considerable and largely inconclusive literature which has been surveyed on a number of occasions.[3]

An alternative approach to the problem which has been suggested is to try to identify and compare the "liquidity" of the various financial assets; this, in turn, requires that we somehow define liquidity itself, and this turns out to raise further ambiguities (although the work itself is in very common use in monetary and financial analysis). To identify the liquidity of an asset, indeed, the following have been proposed:

(a) a relatively narrow spread between bid and ask prices,
(b) a relatively broad market (that is, one with numerous buyers and sellers),
(c) a relatively stable price,
(d) relatively low transactions costs, and
(e) a relatively short term to maturity of the asset in question.

While all of these are measurable to some extent, they are not going to be the same for all assets. Thus, for one example, certain time deposits cost a lot to convert to cash, in terms of surrendered interest, but they can become converted at a fixed price; then, for another example, certain mutual funds sell "liquid" assets which one can convert to cash costlessly if necessary, but this is done at a variable price depending on what stands behind the liquid assets. Thus, an empirical dimension remains which has certainly not been fully explored.

3.2.2 MACRO-EMPIRICAL DEFINITIONS

A point of principle which one should again underscore about the construction of aggregates, whether they be monetary or not, is that one's purpose in aggregating is usually to attain simplicity, while, ideally, employing microeconomic perceptions in the macroeconomic context. Indeed, a successful aggregation makes the subsequent theory and empirical work both easier and less expensive (in, for example, computer time) to carry out. The saving in cost or effort, however, is offset by the simple fact that every aggregation necessarily suppresses some information, and it is a question of judgment, with an empirical side to it, as to which level of aggregation is best under the particular circumstances of any given problem. In macroeconomics we refer to these "commodity" aggregations, if they meet the substitutability condition discussed in Chapter 2 as "definitions", and the discussion of the aggregation problem and the definition of money problem merge at this point. In truth, there is a strong empirical flavour to this literature, something that it has in common with macroeconomics in general. The empirics are relevant, to repeat the point, because there is information (of potential relevance) which ought, in some way, to be compared with the simplicity (presumably) achieved by combining the variables in a particular way.

An emerging literature, prompted partly by recent institutional changes in the United States, has tackled this question in the terms of Chapter 1; see, especially, the paper by Barnett, Offenbacher, and Spindt (1981) and the references summarized there. We generally add together components of the "capital certain" sector - demand deposits, time deposits, NOW accounts, etc. - to produce our monetary definitions (M1, M2, etc.), but this does not produce a satisfactory aggregate except under very unlikely conditions. While the items usually included are often "fixed price" by law, and thus are eligible for the composite goods theorem, it is actually the flow of services of a durable good which is relevant here, and the necessary close substitution for the composite goods theorem is not a matter of record, for the simple sums (see below). We may aggregate monies, then, if we know the "user cost function" - see Donovan (1978) - and when we do, an index number approach is the best to take. One can choose among fixed weight, variable weight, and Divisa-type indices, with the latter having the advantage that they are "parameter free", and hence one need not estimate the parameters of the aggregating function. Indeed, Barnett and Spindt (1979) have shown that the velocity of money is a well-behaved function of interest rates and, indeed, that the apparent recent shifts of the US demand for money (see below) disappear when "Divisia aggregates" are employed. This topic is continued below, in Section 3.6.5 on empirical studies of aggregation.

Returning to general issues, the most obvious gain of an aggregation, perhaps, is in the simplicity of theoretical effort, and it is this aspect which not only motivates much of macroeconomics but has produced a research strategy in Keynes's "General Theory" which, on the one hand, produced the desired economy and, on the other, generated a dispute as to how closely the subsequent Keynesian economists followed Keynes's approach; we follow Leijonhufvud here (1968). Standard macroeconomic theory generally deals with five aggregates: consumer goods, producer goods, labour services, money, and bonds; yet, at the same time the same theory usually contains only three relative prices (the price level, the wage rate, and the interest rate). The unique quantities of these five commodities can be determined along with only three relative prices, in general, only if one of the goods is irrelevant, which is not an interesting case, or if one of the goods is absorbed into another (that is, is aggregated) so that only four goods remain. Three prices would then be sufficient, if an overall constraint (such as Walras's Law) is also applied. Indeed, Leijonhufvud feels there is a difference between the two Keynesian schools, in that Keynes aggregates capital goods (or their financial manifestations, equities) with bonds, to produce consumer goods, non-money assets, labour services, and money as his four goods, while Keynesians combine consumer goods and investment goods to produce commodities, labour services, bonds, and money as theirs.

This aggregative structure produces differing emphases, of course, since the functions studied will differ, but it also produces differences of detail which directly affect the demand for money function. In particular, the representative interest rate in the demand for money implied by the aggregate structure differs between the two "schools". Keynes, for one, chooses a long-term rate to stand for the yield on non-money assets on the grounds that it represents, directly, the yield on the conglomerate long-term asset; in this context it represents the return on one of the alternatives to holding money. Further, Keynes would seem to prefer a very broad definition of money and quite possibly one which is broader than that used by the Keynesians. The Keynesians, in their turn, would gather all bonds together (as the natural antithesis of money) and represent the conglomerate by the yield on the shortest asset in the collection, the Treasury Bill yield. This is because the shortest bond may well be the closest substitute for money and thus would dominate the longer-term assets in the portfolio at least with regard to the demand for money. This establishes a clear theoretical and empirical difference between these two non-monetarist approaches.

The monetarists also have a macro-definition literature, and this is an almost entirely empirical one, although it has nothing (directly) to do with substitutability. Friedman and Schwartz (1970) have argued that one should define money according to whichever definition (that is, aggregation) is the most convenient for a particular purpose (such as studying the demand for money). Indeed, the writings of Friedman and others make it clear that to them there is no separate issue of the definition of money - it is a question of what seems to work well, with the context (estimation, forecasting, etc.) determining what the appropriate aggregation should be. Indeed, the monetarists have recommended that the best definition should correspond to the underlying tasks which money performs[4], to the stability of the demand for money in empirical tests[5], or to the measure of "moneyness" which most effectively predicts changes in money national income.[6]

In conclusion we should note that in the following pages evidence will be presented which bears considerably on the definition problem (since it clearly involves trying different definitions in the context of a demand for money formulation). The following points should be made here as a summary of what is to come, in passing, on the empirical definition problem:

(a) The aggregation of currency and demand deposits seems a reasonably effective one, except in times of very unusual strain in monetary markets (such as during a currency panic) or when substantial institutional changes are in progress (as in the United States with the arrival of automatic transfer and the payment of interest on demand deposits).
(b) The aggregation of individual and business demand functions may well be a shaky one in view of at least some evidence which suggests that

   (i) businesses hold different types of monetary assets, for example, holding more Treasury Bills (as a percentage of their total financial assets), repurchase agreements, and Eurodollars;
   (ii) businesses may well respond more quickly to financial influences; and
   (iii) businesses may respond to different financial variables, in particular to short-term interest rates rather than to long, and to sales rather than income or wealth.

(c) The aggregation of narrow money and time deposits (= broad money), while sometimes seeming to provide a stable measure, does not always do so. This seems primarily to have to do with the fact that time deposits are permanent savings for many, and, if they are not, they are held for down-payments on consumer durables and the like. This last is a transactions motive, to be sure, but a transactions motive with a different time dimension (and a "lumpiness").
(d) The evidence on the broader measures of money, which include financial intermediary deposits and large size certificates of deposit, is hopelessly ambiguous, with some research finding stability and some instability.

These points are offered without documentation here, but we will describe some evidence, as it unfolds, in the following sections. Note, though, that recent innovations with regard to interest payments on demand deposits and permitting checkable savings deposits imply that we may well have to go to a broader measure of moneyness than has heretofore seemed to be preferable.

3.3 THE GENERAL EQUILIBRIUM AND MONETARIST APPROACHES TO THE DEMAND FOR MONEY

The main formal model of the demand for money in existence prior to Keynes is one we might call a "neoclassical-classical" formulation in which the demand for money is used as the central relationship in the quantity theory of money. In this view money (a) is employed in transactions as a medium of exchange and (b) serves as a store of value; in addition, in this framework a strict proportionality is sometimes assumed, in which money is argued to be held at a level strictly proportional to the money value of transactions (or of income). Keynes's insistence on the role of speculative factors in the demand for money, and the subsequent emergence of mean-variance and inventory-theoretic models which motivate money holding in some specific ways, have put this older theory at a practical disadvantage, but a modern resurgence, based on some interesting theoretical work by Patinkin and buttressed by a considerable amount of empirical work, has produced a neoclassical-monetarist version of the older theory which compares favourably with the Keynesian inspired approaches in some respects. Thus it is (a) because it has enjoyed some success on the data and (b) because it raises interesting questions of some use in our survey of macroeconomic theory that we begin with what we provisionally identify as the neoclassical general equilibrium approach to the demand for money. We will also attempt to show how a monetarist model can be built up from this general equilibrium framework, following Patinkin's line.

Let us assume that there are n goods in an exchange economy with the supplies of these goods $(\overline{S}_i, i = 1, \ldots, n)$ fixed in quantity (we assume that is to say, the absence of production). The utility functions of individuals, we will argue, will contain the stocks of consumer goods, arbitrarily, but will not contain money[7]; this, in turn, implies that money must enter the problem, if it is to do so in a meaningful way, in a constraint of some kind, since its role at the consumer's optimum is undefined as things stand. Each individual will be thought of as supplied with an initial supply of commodities and money ($\overline{S}_{ij}$ where the nth good is money (arbitrarily) with a price (arbitrarily) of unity ($P_n \equiv 1$); in turn, each consumer will have a series of demand functions which, when aggregated across individuals, yield the following excess demand functions for each of the j commodities.[8]

$$X_j(P_1, \ldots, P_{n-1}) \equiv D_j(P_1, \ldots, P_{n-1}) - \bar{S}_j$$
$$j = 1, \ldots, n - 1 \qquad (3.1)$$

Putting aside the excess demand for money for the moment, let us assume that all funds in the economy must be spent on commodities so that there is never an excess demand for the n goods taken as a whole; formally, this can be stated as

$$P_n X_n(P_1, \ldots, P_{n-1}) + \sum_{j=1}^{n-1} P_j X_j(P_1, \ldots, P_{n-1}) \equiv 0 \qquad (3.2)$$

which we can, conventionally, label as a formal version of Walras's Law (note that $P_n \equiv 1$). Finally, define equilibrium in the $n - 1$ commodity markets in terms of equation (3.3); this, simply, says that overall equilibrium is achieved when all commodity markets are in equilibrium.

$$X_j(P_1, \ldots, P_{n-1}) = 0 \qquad j = 1, \ldots, n - 1 \qquad (3.3)$$

From our formulation of the problem it should be clear that the excess demand for money (and, given the supply of money, the demand for money) is actually defined as a very general function in equation (3.2); indeed, there it clearly depends on the $n - 1$ individual prices and, through the constraints underlying consumer choice, on initial stocks of commodities and money (see note 9). This function is uninteresting though, since money is just like the $n - 1$ commodities in its characteristics, and so the classical theorists have produced a less general demand for money function by any one of the following means: these are to use a proportionality constraint, to assume a homogeneity condition, or to utilize Say's Law. These are all of some interest, but we will go into detail only about the proportionality constraint here, since it is tied up with the quantity theory of money and since it produces a widely employed demand for money function (in macro-studies).

Let equations (3.2) and (3.3) represent the system of excess demand relations for all of the goods in the economy, and also assume that each of k individuals holds a stock of money balances which is strictly proportional (α_i) to the sum of money value of his actual expenditures; this, then, implies (for the S_{ji} referring to the equilibrium purchases of commodities) that

$$\mathcal{D}_{in} \equiv \alpha_i \sum_{j=1}^{n-1} P_j S_{ji} \qquad i = 1, \ldots, k$$

and, in the aggregate (summing over i):

$$\mathcal{D}_n \equiv \alpha \sum_{j=1}^{n-1} P_j \overline{S}_j \tag{3.4}$$

Then, since $X_n \equiv \mathcal{D}_n - \overline{S}_n$, we have a defined excess demand for money in this model, as given by equation (3.5).

$$X_n \equiv \alpha \sum_{j=1}^{n-1} P_j \overline{S}_j - \overline{S}_n$$

$$\equiv X_n(P_1, \ldots, P_{n-1}, \overline{S}_i; \alpha) \qquad i = 1, \ldots, n \tag{3.5}$$

That is, the aggregate excess demand for money depends on the $n - 1$ prices, the proportionality factor, and the initial endowments of commodities and money, and it does so in a very specific way, as examination of the two parts of equation (3.5) show.[9] Furthermore, this model contains a basic classical result. On the one hand, the excess demand for money function just stated is non-homogeneous since a doubling of prices in equation (3.5), *ceteris paribus*, will cause a positive excess demand for money. On the other hand, a doubling of prices and initial money balances will leave the excess demand unchanged; this further result was of special interest to classical economists because it gave a condition for monetary neutrality and implied, even, that actually doubling the quantity of outside money might also double prices under real-world conditions.

We may proceed from equation (3.4), the demand for money, to a more familiar notation by replacing each of the P_j with an average, the price level (P), and by summing so that

$$\mathcal{D}_n \equiv \alpha P \sum_{j=1}^{n-1} \overline{S}_j$$

Next we may sum all commodities (which are now in real terms) to produce S. This leaves us with equation (3.6),

$$M_d \equiv \alpha PS \tag{3.6}$$

which is, then, our implied aggregate relation between the

demand for money and spending. At equilibrium, where $M_s = M_d$, we may employ an insight like $MV = PT$ (where T replaces S and $V = 1/\alpha$) in this classical framework; the key role of the demand for money (and of the proportionality constraint) is then clear from this derivation of an aggregate relationship between the variables.

Turning to a macro-version of the argument, we also return to the general equilibrium macroeconomic model of Chapter 1. This was a short-run model in which stocks of consumer goods, bonds, investment goods, labour, and money were traded, and the price level, the wage rate, the interest rate, and the level of income (taken as a stock, generally) were determined simultaneously. This model could easily represent neoclassical and Keynesian results, as we demonstrated, and it is partly in this spirit that we consider a version of the model which is consistent with the neoclassical world in order to explore further the nature of the demand for money.

The demand for money in our earlier model appeared as equation (1.13), and our version here, similar to that of Patinkin (1965), appears as equation (3.7).

$$\frac{M_d}{P} = L\left(y,\ i,\ \frac{M_0}{P}\right) \tag{3.7}$$

The variables are easily rationalized, at least with regard to real income (y) or the interest rate (i), since whether we impose a proportionality, rank assets by their liquidity, formally model transactions costs, or insert money into an aggregate utility function, we might expect $L_1 > 0$ and $L_2 < 0$, generally. With regard to M_0/P, the real value of initial money balances, so long as these are net wealth, as they are if (a) only outside money is included in M_0 or (b) we accept the Pesek and Saving "net wealth" argument, M_0/P joins real income in the constraint, as it did in the microeconomic version of the theory we just discussed. Finally, we could even argue that M_0/P could appear in equation (3.7) as a proxy for the real value of all non-human private wealth, although for this proxy we may well prefer a more inclusive (that is to say, a broader) measure of total non-human wealth.

Let us, then, derive the properties of an aggregate demand for money from a general equilibrium macroeconomic framework in which Walras's Law is assumed to hold, pretty much as these properties were deduced under the various micro-constraints earlier in this section. Note, firstly, that equation (3.7) has no *a priori* signs attached to it. Indeed, what we are going to do in this section is show that if we assume a certain pattern of signs for the other relations in a general macroeconomic model, then, if we also assume Walras's Law, the properties of the demand for money are defined in this case.

Assume, then, that we have three markets: a commodities (consumption and investment), a bond, and a money market. Let us also assume that the commodities market has a consumption function and an investment function, but let us aggregate them, as we did to produce equation (1.37), so that the IS curve appears as

$$y_f = F(y_f, i, \frac{M_0}{P}) \qquad F_1 > 0, F_2 < 0, F_3 > 0 \qquad (3.8)$$

where y_f represents full-employment real income. For the bond market, then, we will use equation (1.43), the net bond demand function, here repeated as equation (3.9).

$$B(y_f, \frac{1}{i}, \frac{M_0}{P}) = 0 \qquad B_1 \gtrless 0, B_2 < 0, B_3 > 0 \qquad (3.9)$$

Similarly, assuming that the nominal supply of money is fixed (at M_0), we may express the LM curve as

$$\frac{M_0}{P} = L(y_f, i, \frac{M_0}{P}) \qquad (3.10)$$

which equates the real supply of money M_0/P with the demand given as equation (3.7).

There are only two endogenous variables in the problem - the interest rate (i) and the price level (P) - so without some further restriction we may well not have a unique solution (having only two endogenous variables and three equilibrium conditions). This restriction is a macroeconomic version of Walras's Law, and the form it takes here is given by equation (3.11), here taken as an identity.[10]

$$\frac{M_0}{P} - L(y_f, i, \frac{M_0}{P}) \equiv [F(y_f, i, \frac{M_0}{P}) - y_f] + B(y_f, \frac{1}{i}, \frac{M_0}{P}) \qquad (3.11)$$

Putting M_0/P on the right, and switching signs, we obtain the implicitly defined demand for money function. Its properties, as we shall see, are derived from the statements on slopes already made.

There are three variables of interest to us in this derived function, the price level (P), the level of full employment income (y_f), and the interest rate (i). When the former is changed, equation (3.12) results.

$$L_3\frac{\partial\frac{M_0}{P}}{\partial P} \equiv \frac{\partial\frac{M_0}{P}}{\partial P} - F_3\frac{\partial\frac{M_0}{P}}{\partial P} - B_3\frac{\partial\frac{M_0}{P}}{\partial P} \qquad (3.12)$$

Now in this expression $\partial(M_0/P)/\partial P$ is common to each term and can be removed; this leaves

$$L_3 \equiv 1 - F_3 - B_3 \qquad (3.13)$$

In this case we see that if $F_3 + B_3 < 1$, the "real balance effect on the demand for money" is defined to be positive.

Turning to real income, we note that, again, a similarly simple relation holds:

$$L_1 \equiv 1 - F_1 - B_1 \qquad (3.14)$$

If the two marginal propensities (F_1 and B_1) are less than unity in their total, then L_1 is again defined to be positive. Note, as well, that the magnitude of L_1 could be small since a gain in real income may go mostly to commodities (F_1 itself near unity) rather than money. Of course, the income elasticity is not affected by these comments (which are meant to suggest a possible simultaneous equations bias) which refer to slopes and not elasticities (although elasticities are sometimes low in empirical studies). Finally, we may calculate the defined interest rate effect on the demand for money. This is given as

$$\frac{\partial L}{\partial i} \equiv -\frac{\partial F}{\partial i} - \frac{\partial B}{\partial i}$$

Since $\partial F/\partial i < 0$ and $\partial B/\partial i > 0$. we see that this effect is an ambiguous one. To put it another way, we would expect $\partial L/\partial i$ to be negative (from the bond market influence alone) modified by the effect of the interest rate on spending. To Keynes (one might argue) that latter effect would be zero, and thus the liquidity preference function is defined as a negative relation deriving from the bond market.

The net result, then, of this application of Walras's Law in a simple macro-world is a defined (or equilibrium) demand for money function of a conventional form (so long as the other functions are defined previously). This lesson is not designed to imply that the demand for money is redundant, but to provide a macroeconomic counterpart of the micro-general equilibrium model and to illustrate the implication of the adoption of Walras's Law along with a full set of constraints on the signs on the remaining $n - 1$ equations in the model. Of course, the demand for money laid out here is also an interesting one in its own right, and its actual properties can be further investigated by empirical means.

A more formal neoclassical theory has been constructed along the lines of the neoclassical investment function by Motley (1969); roughly, it treats money as an alternative to consumption in a dynamic consumption problem in continuous time. Assume the following dynamic utility function

$$u = \int_0^\infty \lambda(t) U[x(t), m(t), t]dt \tag{3.15}$$

where $\lambda(t)$ represents time preference and $x(t)$ is consumption (it is the stock of consumer goods, assumed to be proportional to the flow of services). Assume, also, a resource constraint of

$$\int_0^\infty e^{-it}[Y(t) - p(t)c(t) - \dot{M}(t)]dt = 0 \tag{3.16}$$

where $Y(t)$ is nominal labour (and bond) income, $c(t)$ is the gross purchase of consumer goods (in real terms) and $\dot{M}(t)$ is the rate of change of nominal money balances ($= dM/dt$). $c(t)$, then, is related to $x(t)$ by

$$c(t) = \dot{x}(t) + \delta x(t) \tag{3.17}$$

where δ is the rate of depreciation of consumer goods. Forming the Lagrangean for this system, we have

$$L = \int_0^\infty \lambda(t) U[x(t), m(t), t]dt + k_0(\int_0^\infty e^{-it}[Y(t) - p(t)c(t) - \dot{M}(t)]dt + k_1[c(t) - \dot{x}(t) - \delta x(t)] \tag{3.18}$$

This, for the choice variables $c(t)$, $x(t)$, and $m(t)$, produces the following first order conditions:

$$\frac{\partial L}{\partial c(t)} = -k_0 e^{-it} p(t) + k_1(t) = 0 \tag{3.19}$$

$$\frac{\partial L}{\partial x(t)} = \lambda(t) U_x(t) - k_1(t)\delta + \frac{d}{dt}k_1(t) = 0 \tag{3.20}$$

where

$$U_x(t) = \frac{\partial U[\ ]}{\partial x(t)}$$

$$\frac{\partial L}{\partial m(t)} = \lambda(t)\frac{U_m(t)}{p(t)} + \frac{d}{dt}k_1e^{-it} = 0 \qquad (3.21)$$

where

$$U_m(t) = \frac{\partial U[\ \ ]}{\partial m(t)}$$

and terms for k_0 and k_1. Eliminating k_1 between (3.19) and (3.20) and carrying out the differentiation of d/dt, we obtain

$$\lambda(t)U_x(t) = k_0e^{-it}p(t)[\delta + i - \frac{\dot{p}(t)}{p(t)}] \qquad (3.22)$$

where

$$\dot{p}(t) = \frac{dp(t)}{dt}$$

Rearranging (3.21), we obtain

$$\lambda(t)U_m(t) = k_0e^{-it}p(t)i \qquad (3.23)$$

such that (3.22) and (3.23) represent the marginal utility conditions at the optimum. These, along with the budget constraint are sufficient to establish a demand for money *functional* of the following form

$$M(o) = f[W(o),\ i(t),\ i'(t),\ p(t)] \qquad (3.24)$$

where $W(o)$ is initial wealth (and includes the time path of income and initial money balances). This is also seen to depend on the time path of the interest rate and prices and on $i'(t)$, which is $p(t)[\delta + i - \dot{p}(t)/p(t)]$, the "user cost of consumption services" from equation (3.22).

Such a framework is certainly hard to approach empirically, but it is not impossible. Noticing that we have derived a demand for money from the same sort of programme in which consumption (of a durable good) or investment can be derived, we note that the presence of consumption as a choice variable and of permanent income implies that both the demand for money and the consumption function will be approachable by the same measure of permanent income - with, in effect, the same lags. One actually finds the principal empirical tests of this idea on the Canadian data, with Clark (1973) finding different lags while Kohli (1978) could not support this idea on quarterly data. But in neither case was there a theoretical inspiration for this approach; thus G. Fisher and McAleer (1979) adapted Motley's model (in effect) in which money is included in the dynamic utility function and then employed the durable extended linear expenditure system (of Dixon and Lluch, 1977) on the Canadian data. They found a sharp break in 1967 (there was a Bank Act in 1967) but, more importantly, a single equation alternative performed surprisingly well (although it utilized the lagged dependent variable to do so) in comparison with the expenditure system. On the whole it was a draw, but, one might surmise, incorporation of "rational expectations" into the linear expenditure approach may well break the tie; there are other studies.[11]

3.3.1 MONETARIST MODELS OF THE DEMAND FOR MONEY

The foregoing are essentially neoclassical formulations, with simple homogeneity properties or simple constraints, and it seems fair to attach the growing monetarist theoretical literature here. Foremost among the monetarist models, of course, is Friedman's famous restatement of the quantity theory of money as a theory of the demand for money (1956); his version of the demand for money appears as equation (3.25).

$$M_d = f\left(P,\ i_b - \frac{1}{i_b}\frac{di_b}{dt},\ r_e + \left(\frac{\dot{P}}{P}\right)_e - \frac{1}{r_e}\frac{dr_e}{dt},\ \left(\frac{\dot{P}}{P}\right)_e,\ w,\ \frac{Y}{i},\ u\right) \qquad (3.25)$$

Here we consider money as among five potential stores of value: money (P), bonds $(i_b - (1/i_b)di_b/dt)$, equities $(r_e + (\dot{P}/P)_e - (1/i_b)di_b/dt)$, physical goods $((\dot{P}/P)_e)$, and human and non-human capital (w and Y/i); u is a taste factor. Presumably a rise in the price level will increase nominal money holding, while an increase in the expected inflation rate $((\dot{P}/P)_e)$ would reduce money holding in favour of physical goods. Y/i is the discounted (by i) value of a stream of perpetual income (Y) and would be expected to have a positive influence, while an increase in w, which is also the ratio of non-human wealth to human wealth and is included here as an additional variable because non-human wealth is more liquid than human wealth, may reduce the need to hold money balances (although, in truth, it might also indicate an increased "taste" for liquid assets). Note that permanent income (as defined in Chapter 2) would be an appropriate proxy for Y/i in this model.

With regard to the alternative securities in equation (3.25), there are two, bonds and equities. i_b is the nominal rate of interest on bonds where, as in Chapter 1, the typical bond is assumed to be a perpetuity paying $1 a year; the term modifying this represents the expected percentage rate of change in the value of the bond (where $1/i_b$ represents the price of the bond). In this expression, as the interest rate changes, the value of the bond changes and is properly deducted or added to the interest earnings to get the overall earnings. Equities, too, have a perpetual real dividend (r_e) and a capital gains component, and so are treated in the same fashion. Note that the term $(\dot{P}/P)_e$ puts this real rate in a nominal form and can be rationalized by the observation that only nominal interest rates matter for the demand for money (as discussed in Chapter 1).

The Friedman equation is somewhat complicated in appearance, but it is a general portfolio-choice framework nonetheless. It may also be simplified strategically - as, for example, by Meltzer (1963a) - in which case an appropriate final demand for money equation might be that given as equation (3.26).

$$M_d = g(i)W_n \tag{3.26}$$

Then, if we define the unspecified function $g(i)$ to be equal to the exponential i^b, we obtain, in logarithmic form, equation (3.27)

$$\log M = b \log i + c \log W_n \tag{3.27}$$

where c is expected to be equal to unity. This, of course, is the basic demand for money equation which most of the numerous empirical studies of the demand for money have used (whether they have a Keynesian inspiration or a neoclassical-monetarist one similar to Friedman's), although with different measures for i and W_n. This may be somewhat disconcerting to those brought up on the Keynes-versus-the-Classics debate, so it is necessary to point out that there is little dispute over the general formulation (although there is, still, over the magnitude of the effects).

To deal with the expected inflation rate $(\dot{P}/P)_e$ in equation (3.25), the basic monetarist paper is that of Cagan (1956), where the context is that of hyperinflation; in this event the rate of expected inflation may well dominate the other variables. Cagan, like Meltzer, adjusted the basic Friedman equation. Thus, with the assumption that (3.25) is homogeneous in P and Y, we have the result that the demand for money function can be written in real terms with real income as an argument.

$$\frac{M_d}{P} = f(i_b,\ i_e,\ (\dot{P}/P)_e;\ w,\ Y/P;\ u) \tag{3.28}$$

It is this demand function, where the expected rate of change of prices is included, that is considered relevant under the condition of rapid inflation. Cagan, in order to test the hypothesis that $(\dot{P}/P)_e$ dominates in hyperinflation, makes two assumptions:

(a) that desired real cash balances are equal to actual real cash balances at all times and
(b) that the expected rate of change of prices depends on the actual rate of change of prices.

The former lets us read all observations as if they were on the demand curve (i.e. we can substitute $\dot{M}$ for M_d), and the latter allows us to measure $(\dot{P}/P)_e$ as a function of the observable past actual rates of inflation.

Cagan proposes an error-learning model to deal with the expected rate of change of prices; thus, for E equal to the expected rate of inflation, equation (3.29) argues that this is revised in accordance with past forecasting errors in the actual rate of inflation.

$$\frac{dE}{dt} = \gamma[(\frac{\dot{P}}{P})_a - (\frac{\dot{P}}{P})_e] \tag{3.29}$$

Thus, in equation (3.29) γ shows the speed of adjustment to inflation expectations $(\dot{P}/P)_e$ to realities $(\dot{P}/P)_a$. This leaves the problem of measuring $(\dot{P}/P)_e$ which Cagan does by assuming the simple permanent income style measure which we discussed in Chapter 2; we may accordingly describe this as "permanent prices" and put it in the form of Friedman's equation here.

$$P_p(t) = \beta\int_{-\infty}^{t} e^{(\beta - \alpha)(T - t)} P(T)\,dT \tag{3.30}$$

Note that t refers to the present.

Cagan, then, in the hyperinflation case, directly substitutes his measure of $(\dot{P}/P)_e$ into equation (3.28) as its only explanatory variable (on the grounds that in the case of very rapid inflation the other terms would be dominated). In this event the effect of inflation on the demand for money is still a complicated one since it contains the direct hypothesis $(\partial f/\partial(\dot{P}/P)_e)$, the partial adjustment hypothesis (which involves γ), and the specialization of the expectations mechanism (which involves α and β). Cagan did not really adopt a strong *a priori* view, of course, and, while he reported considerable success with his estimating equation in terms of the stability of his results on hyperinflation, a considerable number of doubts have emerged, either in terms of the omitted variables or in terms of the specific mechanism of expectations-formation.[12]

An interesting extension of the foregoing model is due to Jacobs (1975), who notes that in effect the inflation rate in Cagan's model is entirely exogenous, whereas in his view it should be partly endogenized. To see how this can be effected, we can rewrite Cagan's model in a linear form:

$$M_d = -\delta - \mu\left(\frac{\dot{P}}{P}\right)_e \tag{3.31}$$

where μ depends on α, β, and γ, as described earlier. This, with equation (3.29), implies that if $(\dot{P}/P)_e$ depends entirely on past changes in the money stock, then, since M is exogenously determined (in Cagan's monetarist model), so is $(\dot{P}/P)_e$. This, indeed, would be consistent with a "rational expectations" approach to the demand for money in which the money stock plays just such a role.[13] The equation at the root, of course, is $\dot{P}/P = g(\dot{M}/M)$. Instead of Cagan's approach, though, suppose that actual changes in the money stock (dM/dt) also depend on an adjustment relation as in equation (3.32) where M_d refers to desired money balances and M are actual balances.

$$\frac{dM}{dt} = \pi(M_d - M) \tag{3.32}$$

This formulation, in effect, argues that since the absorbed money balances (πM_d) will not produce inflation, that an equation such as equation (3.33) might be adopted for the determination of the actual role of inflation.

$$\frac{\dot{P}}{P} = \frac{\dot{M}}{M} + \pi(M_d - M) \tag{3.33}$$

This, as noted, partly endogenizes the actual inflation rate (it depends on M_d) and consequently implies that Cagan's model might be misspecified in equation (3.30), actually relating two (partly) mutually dependent variables. Of course, it is a question of fact as to whether π is non-zero (presumably in a rational expectations approach it would be zero).

A natural extension of the foregoing is to cast the probblem in terms of rational expectations, as described in our discussion of the consumption function in Section 2.6. Sargent and Wallace (1973) noted that if Cagan's adaptive scheme is "rational", then his estimator of α is not statistically consistent; Cagan's argument that the rate of production of money was way too rapid was based on this statistic; this over-production, of course, was "irrational" of the creators of money. Part of the problem is the single-equation approach, and so in a first paper on the problem Sargent (1977) uses a simple simultaneous equations model to produce a consistent estimator. Sargent shows that an implication of the assumption that Cagan's adaptive expectations are rational is that the rate of money creation equals the expected rate of inflation plus a random term; this is in accordance with the often-heard view that (e.g.) the German monetary authorities were merely responding to inflation (trying to hold the real value of money constant). In any event inflation and money creation in Sargent's paper form a bivariate stochastic process; this is then used to produce an estimator for a bias, but on the usual actual data the confidence intervals are so wide that α is not different from zero (in the case of one Hungarian inflation Cagan's charge that money was "over-supplied" was rejected). In a follow-up paper, Salemi and Sargent (1979) used a vector autoregressive procedure which produced estimates of α. Salemi and Sargent generally support Cagan (in sign) although, once again, the confidence bands are very wide around the estimates. Note, finally, that further study of the German hyperinflation is by Frenkel (1977) and others, and is discussed in Section 3.7 on the "open economy".

Turning to rational expectations in the non-rapid-inflation case, we find a very slim literature indeed, although activity is certainly likely to grow in this area. Noting that a rational expectations demand for money is not really consistent with certain money supply rules (for example, the rule $M_t = M_{t-1} + a$ which has all price changes totally unexpected - it is a Patinkin-style model), Bomhoff (1980) suggests a demand for money of the form:

$$\log M_t = -d + \log \Delta P_t + (1 - \beta_1) \log \Delta y^e_t + \beta_2(\log \Delta y - \log \Delta y^e)_t - \beta_3 \Delta i_t + a_t \qquad (3.34)$$

with d a constant and a_t a shock. Note that future changes in income and prices are assumed to be predictable in this framework, but those in interest rates are not. The term log ΔP_t makes the function homogeneous in the price level; the term $(1 - \beta_1) \log \Delta y^e_t$ reflects expectations concerning the behaviour of velocity (this will change, reflecting a non-unitary income elasticity of the demand for money and technological change in the money industry); and $\beta_2(\log \Delta y - \log \Delta y^e)_t$ reflects the difference between the desired and actual money stock (assumed to be related solely to income). As noted, future changes in (nominal) interest rates are unpredictable (but see the notes on Bomhoff's empirics, in Section 3.7.

3.4 THE MEAN-VARIANCE APPROACH TO THE DEMAND FOR MONEY

Let us take the view that money is one among a number of assets and that the wealth holder makes his choices among these assets on the basis of their economic characteristics. Let us suppose that the characteristics of most interest to the wealth holder are the expected return on each asset (which provides utility) and the expected variation in the price of each asset (which provides disutility to the risk-averse investor).[14] The wealth holder can then be presumed to combine his assets into various potential portfolios and to pick the best of these portfolios, the best being the one which maximizes his expected utility. What we have said amounts to the assumption that the representative wealth holder will maximize a utility function like equation (3.35)

$$U = U(E, \sigma^2) \qquad U_1 > 0, \; U_2 < 0 \tag{3.35}$$

where E is the expected return on the portfolio and σ^2 is its expected variance. Note that the assumption $\partial U/\partial E = U_1 > 0$ and $\partial U/\partial \sigma^2 = U_2 < 0$ have already been justified.

We could proceed to develop a picture of mean-variance space at this point and show the nature of the asset choice problem there, but it is convenient, instead, to specialize the utility function and to derive some more exact results. Thus, assume that utilities are generated by equation (3.36).

$$U = a - ce^{-b\pi} \tag{3.36}$$

where a, b, c are positive constants and π represents the earnings of the portfolio; this function appears in Freund (1956). Equation (3.36) actually is consistent with equation (3.35), although it is written only in π (i.e. in actual earnings), and this can be seen by noting that

$$\frac{\partial U}{\partial \pi} = bce^{-b\pi} > 0$$

while

$$\frac{\partial^2 U}{\partial \pi^2} = - b^2 c e^{-b\pi} < 0$$

where the latter is the analogous concept to the variance (or risk) in this equation.

Our problem, though, is one in expected utilities, and so we will maximize equation (3.37) instead of the certainty version just given as equation (3.36).

$$E(U) = a - cE[e^{-b\pi}] \tag{3.37}$$

For the expectations on the right we will assume that the random variable (π) is normally distributed, so that it can be represented by two parameters, the mean and the variance of the distribution of π. In this case we can replace the expectation on the right-hand side of equation (3.37) with the probability derived from the normal distribution. This gives equation (3.38).

$$E(U) = a - ce^{-(b)(\mu_\pi - \frac{b}{2}\sigma^2_\pi)} \tag{3.38}$$

To find the maximum of this function, we note that anything which maximizes the spread between the return (π) and the risk (σ^2) will make the term ce as small as possible. For any positive a this will lead to the maximization of expected utility. Thus we may work with the simpler function given as equation (3.39) as our objective function in what follows.

$$W = \mu_\pi - \frac{b}{2}\sigma^2_\pi \tag{3.39}$$

Finally, we note that for equation (3.39) the conditions that $\partial E(u)/\partial \mu_\pi > 0$ and that $\partial E(u)/\partial \sigma^2_\pi < 0$ are upheld, as formerly required for actual utility in equation (3.35).

Now let us switch to matrix notation for ease of application. Let $\tilde{v}$ be a vector (n x 1) of sums invested in assets including money, and $\tilde{m}$ be an associated vector of actual yields. Thus the actual yield of the portfolio (π) is given by the following inner product:

$$\pi = \tilde{m}'\tilde{v} \tag{3.40}$$

When one constructs a portfolio, one naturally does so not with the actual yields of equation (3.40) but with expected yields. To work in this direction, we can write actual yields in a stochastic form as the sum of expected returns ($\tilde{m}^*$) plus an error term ($\tilde{\xi}$), where the error term represents a vector of forecasting errors; this results in equation (3.41) in which, to anticipate, the mean of the forecasting errors will be assumed to be zero.

$$\tilde{m} = \tilde{m}^* + \tilde{\xi} \tag{3.41}$$

We may now combine (3.40) and (3.41) to obtain equation (3.42).

$$\pi = (\tilde{m}^* + \tilde{\xi})'\tilde{v} = \tilde{m}^{*\prime}\tilde{v} + \tilde{\xi}'v \tag{3.42}$$

This expression relates the actual return of the portfolio to the expected return plus the forecasting error. Since $E(\pi)$ defines expected returns, we can also write equation (3.43), which makes use of the already stated assumption that the mean forecasting error is zero.

$$\mu_\pi = E(\pi) = \tilde{m}^{*\prime}\tilde{v} \tag{3.43}$$

This gives us μ_π for use in equation (3.39). Needless to say, of course, $\tilde{m}^{*\prime}$ is a vector of expected yields and will not be directly observable; we will comment further on this problem.

The variance of the yield (σ_π^2) is the other parameter that we require for equation (3.39). One way we might define this variance is

$$\sigma_\pi^2 = E[(\pi - E(\pi))^2] \tag{3.44}$$

We may directly rewrite the term within the square brackets in equation (3.44) in terms of equations (3.42) and (3.43) to obtain equation (3.45).

$$\sigma_\pi^2 = E\{[(\tilde{m}^{*\prime}\tilde{v} + \tilde{\xi}'\tilde{v}) - \tilde{m}^{*\prime}\tilde{v}]^2\} = E[(\tilde{\xi}'\tilde{v})^2] \tag{3.45}$$

We are thus seen to be asserting the reasonable proposition that actual variations in earnings come from forecasting errors entirely. Note now that $\tilde{v}$ is $(n \times 1)$; $\tilde{\xi}'$ is $(1 \times n)$ since $\tilde{\xi}$ is $(n \times 1)$, with the consequence that $\tilde{\xi}'\tilde{v}$ is a scalar (or, rather, an inner product); thus we can write $(\tilde{\xi}'\tilde{v}) = (\tilde{\xi}'\tilde{v})'$. Since this is so, we may write out the square in equation (3.45) as another equivalent scalar, $v'\tilde{\xi}\tilde{\xi}'v$. When we take the expectations, we get another form for equation (3.45) which is more convenient:

$$\sigma_\pi^2 = \tilde{v}'E(\tilde{\xi}\tilde{\xi}')\tilde{v} = \tilde{v}'S\tilde{v} \tag{3.46}$$

Here we find the variance in our problem really consists of a weighted expression - with the amounts invested $(\tilde{v})$ providing the weights - in the variance-covariance matrix of forecasting errors (S).

Let us assume in what follows that the representative wealth holder in question is restricted to holding only a certain set of types of assets and holds positive quantities of each; in particular, we may be looking at final wealth holders' collection of cash, bonds, and equities. The result is a budget constraint of the following form,

$$\tilde{v}'\tilde{\iota} + F = 0 \tag{3.47}$$

where F consists of any non-relevant assets and all balancing items in the portfolio (e.g. capital assets) and $\tilde{\iota}$ is the unit vector of suitable length, introduced here merely to effect the sum required. The combination of equations (3.39), (3.43), and (3.46) yields a new statement for the objective function as in equation (3.48).

$$\theta = \tilde{m}^{*\prime}\tilde{v} - \frac{b}{2}\tilde{v}'S\tilde{v} \tag{3.48}$$

It is this specific function that the wealth holding unit will be assumed to maximize in what follows.

The maximizing problem we have set ourselves is, given $\tilde{m}^*$, S, and F, choose $\tilde{v}$ such that equation (3.48) is maximized subject to (3.47). To solve the problem we form the Lagrangean expression (noting that it is a stochastic formulation) as follows:

$$L = \tilde{m}^{*\prime}\tilde{v} - \frac{b}{2}\tilde{v}'S\tilde{v} + \lambda(\tilde{v}'\tilde{\iota} + F) \tag{3.49}$$

where λ is the Lagrangean multiplier. We can then state the first-order conditions for a maximum as in equations (3.50).

$$\begin{aligned} \frac{\partial L}{\partial v} &= \tilde{m}^* - bS\tilde{v} + \lambda\tilde{\iota} = 0 \\ \frac{\partial L}{\partial \lambda} &= \tilde{v}'\tilde{\iota} + F = 0 \end{aligned} \tag{3.50}$$

Assuming that the second-order conditions are also met, we can write our stable solution vector for $\tilde{v}$ and λ as equation (3.51).

$$\begin{bmatrix} \tilde{v} \\ \\ \lambda \end{bmatrix} = \begin{bmatrix} bS & -\tilde{\iota} \\ \\ -\tilde{\iota}' & 0 \end{bmatrix}^{-1} \begin{bmatrix} \tilde{m}^* \\ \\ F \end{bmatrix} \tag{3.51}$$

The coefficient matrix in this expression may then be inverted to yield the demand functions for assets (including money) as in equation (3.52).

$$\tilde{v} = \frac{1}{b}\left[S^{-1} - \frac{S^{-1}\tilde{i}\tilde{i}'S^{-1}}{\tilde{i}'S^{-1}\tilde{i}}\right]\tilde{m}^* - \left[\frac{S^{-1}\tilde{i}}{\tilde{i}'S^{-1}\tilde{i}}\right]F \qquad (3.52)$$

These functions are related, in the sense of consumer theory, and a proper estimation of any function will include these (essentially simultaneous equations) relations as restrictions.[15] These imply, among other things, that one should distinguish, whenever one considers the demand for an asset (e.g. money), (a) scale effects (from F), (b) "own rate effects" from the diagonal of equation (3.52), which are positive (as an *a priori* matter), and (c) "cross-rate" effects from the off-diagonal terms in (3.52). These can bear negative (substitute) or positive (complement) signs. We note that this general framework implies that more than one interest rate is appropriate in the demand for money, depending, of course, on the facts (that is, on whether or not collections of other assets are close enough substitutes or complements to be picked up by empirical means).

3.4.1 SIMULTANEOUS EQUATION STUDIES OF THE DEMAND FOR MONEY

Explicit use of the generalized mean-variance model on the problem of the demand for money is actually quite rare, but there is an interesting and growing literature on the simultaneous asset equations approach, utilizing a "demand systems approach" based, sometimes loosely, on consumer theory. The premier study here is by Feige (1964) who used a demand system approach to estimate cross-elasticities; he suggested that demand deposits may well be the complements of savings and loan deposits, and in later work (1974) he continued to regard weak substitution (at most) among the liquid assets as the likely result (see also, Feige and Swamy, 1974, and Feige and Pearce, 1977).[16]

Weak substitution - or, often, failure to establish signs - might suggest that single equation methods would be adequate, but these early results have certainly not gone unchallenged in a still-growing literature. Lee (1966, 1972) adjusted Feige's data and arrived at the opposite conclusion on substitutability, and Chetty (1969) formulated an explicit "direct utility of money" approach deriving the demand functions for liquid assets directly. His approach was to take the following generalized CES (constant elasticity of substitution) utility function

$$u = (\beta_0 S_0^{-\rho_0} + \beta_1 X_1^{-\rho_1} + \ldots + \beta_n X_n^{-\rho_n})^{-\frac{1}{\rho_0}} \tag{3.53}$$

and impose a budget constraint of

$$W = \sum_{i=0}^{n} \frac{X_i}{1 + r_i} \tag{3.54}$$

in order to derive the demand functions for the various liquid assets.[17] His empirical results supported Feige. Moroney and Wilbratte (1976) also used a direct approach, but their appeal was to "duality theory"; they maximized wealth

$$W = \sum_{i=0}^{n} (1 + r_i)X_i \tag{3.55}$$

subject to a transactions constraint

$$T = f(X_0, X_1, \ldots, X_n) \tag{3.56}$$

mainly in order to avoid the estimation of demand functions in which there exist a number of potentially collinear (exogenous) interest rates. They found close substitution among financial assets.[18]

The work just described has been further extended by Donovan (1978) on Canadian data. Donovan redefines the budget constraint so that the wealth holder is constrained by the amount he wishes to allocate among his liquid assets (and not by total wealth); the rental prices used in his constraint are also different, involving own interest rates and the price level. Utilizing a flexible-form indirect utility function of

$$g(v) = \sum_{i=1}^{n} \sum_{j=1}^{n} \beta_{ij} V_i^{-\frac{1}{2}} V_j^{-\frac{1}{2}} + \sum_{i=1}^{n} \alpha_i \log \frac{V_i}{V_i^*} \tag{3.57}$$

where $V = r/y$ is a vector, $\beta_{ij} = \beta_{ji}$, and $\Sigma\alpha_i = 0$. V_i^* is normalized, and r represents a vector of the rental prices already referred to. This function places no restrictions on the magnitude of sign of the substitution effects (although they must be symmetric), although $\Sigma\alpha_i = 0$ represents a testable homotheticity condition. Unfortunately, the empirical tests do not include currency and demand deposits, so that savings deposits must be interpreted as money in this study;

even so, most relations for most years showed complementarity rather than substitution, so that this general study also provides support for Feige's conclusion.

There is also a well-known literature on the proper use of the wealth constraint; this discussion was initiated by Brainard and Tobin (1968). Brainard and Tobin argued for the use of a simultaneous equations framework for the analysis of financial markets, involving both real and financial variables (in both static and dynamic formulations). Current income is one way the real impinges on the financial and so does a measure of the marginal efficiency of capital; furthermore, the demand functions must be consistent with the balance sheet constraint (net worth). The demand functions for the i assets in their approach (see Ladenson, 1971, and Clinton, 1973b) are of the form

$$M^*_{it} = \beta_i W_i + \sum_{k=1}^{K} \beta_{ik} X_{kt} W_t \tag{3.58}$$

where the X_{kt} are the explanatory variables (especially income and interest rates). What the simultaneous equations approach does is to allow the investigators to impose an overall constraint such that

$$\Sigma M^*_{it} = W_t$$

i.e. that asset demands equal wealth. This enables one to avoid the problem that single equation estimates (when summed) may produce inconsistent results if unconstrained (a pitfall!). Brainard and Tobin are also concerned that the wealth constraint be applied out of equilibrium (in dynamic problems), and so they specify a simultaneous stock adjustment model with differences between desired and actual stocks depending on all (other) asset stock disequilibria (as discussed in Chapter 1). The imposition of the overall wealth constraint then affects the estimates of the stock adjustment coefficients, again suggesting a way in which single equation studies may have gone wrong. But this framework separates the portfolio allocation decision from the savings-consumption decision and thus is not completely general (another pitfall!).[19]

There is a recent study of the mean-variance model described in the previous section, utilizing British data on capital-certain assets; this is by Townend (1972). There were severe problems with the ordinary least squares estimates (a "stacking" procedure was employed), but when lags were introduced, a reasonable number of expected signs were achieved. On the other hand, when the roots of the equations were examined, the result in equilibria proved to be unstable; autocorrelation was conjectured to be the culprit in this case. On the whole, interest elasticities and cross-elasticities obtained in this study were low.[20] There is also a mean-variance study on US data by Gramlich and Hulett (1972) who were concerned with the supply and demand for savings deposits. Their procedure is almost exactly the same as that outlined in our theoretical discussion of the mean-variance model, and they estimate an equation similar to equation (3.52) with numerous restrictions (and adjustments) and with some attempt to bring in the supply side (in the form of, for example, interest rate ceilings). They find low substitution, generally, somewhat to their surprise (but this study did not include cash). There are also some recent studies using the Divisia index number approach under study by the Board of Governors of the Federal Reserve System. The studies currently available are by Barnett and Spindt (1979) and Offenbacher (1980a); the latter uses a trans-log model and finds the substitution between currency and demand deposits to be quite low.

Finally, while it goes somewhat beyond the scope of this chapter, we should note that "simultaneous equation" in the heading of this section also can refer to the supply of funds or to the behaviour of other suppliers of financial instruments, when relevant. The Gramlich and Hulett study just referred to did include supply functions for assets; there is also a voluminous literature on money supply theory which we will forbear to discuss here, saving it for the forthcoming policy study. This leaves a demand-oriented literature which is largely empirical in its focus. Typical papers are by Teigen (1964), Gibson (1972, 1976), B. Klein (1974) and Spitzer (1977). But since the actual demand hypothesis in these studies is generally either very simple or discussed elsewhere in this chapter, we will not discuss these papers here, beyond noting that the careful modelling of money and asset supplies has important implications for empirical work on the demand for money, particularly in the face of (recent) technological changes in financial markets.

3.4.2 A MEAN-VARIANCE MODEL OF THE DEMAND FOR MONEY

Let us begin by characterizing the problem in the following manner; we follow the work of Bernstein and D. Fisher (1981). We wish here to examine a term structure of interest rates demand for money problem from the point of view of the mean-variance model in order to provide a portfolio rationale for the appearance of the term structure of interest rates in the demand for money; we are also interested in generating comparative equilibrium results (when possible) and advice as to how to formulate empirical work. Tobin (1958) and others have used the mean-variance model to generalize the Keynesian speculative demand for money, and Bierwag and Grove (1967) have used it to deal with bond holding; the present discussion combines these approaches and carries the analysis a little further. We note that recent empirical work - motivated by the inventory model (see below) - has found a term structure strengthening the role of interest rates in the demand for money.[21]

The introduction of money into a bond-holding problem - differentiated by term to maturity - brings up several problems immediately. For one thing, money does provide services (such as the saving of transactions time) and as such can be assigned a rate of return (that is, an implicit interest rate). In a term structure context, where future expected rates of interest (including that on money) are relevant to current money holding, this implies a (further) stochastic element to the portfolio problem. Secondly, we should note that a mean-variance solution can be thought of as the second of a two-stage problem; in the first stage a dynamic consumption-saving decision is made, and in the second stage a portfolio problem is solved. We certainly do not need to produce a solution for the larger problem here, the solution for which would be empirically uninteresting anyway (see Chapter 2), but we can certainly boost the role of money in the present framework. This will be done by assuming that money is valued (a) for itself, differing in this respect from other financial commodities, (b) for what it can add in the way of liquidity (to satisfy a liquidity preference), and (c) not solely for what it can add to future consumption. Money, then, will bear an explicit interest rate and be entered into the utility function, in what follows, in both present and future periods.

Suppose an individual has a planning horizon for T periods, and in period 1 the investor can hold wealth in the form of money or a bond maturing in T periods. From the outset we should point out that making money pay interest does not reduce the generality of our results. To be held at all, money must do something, and, clearly, that "something" can be represented by an implicit yield if, as in some cases, an explicit yield is illegal (and, of course, if money yields utility directly). Next, in period 2 the investor has the money from period 1 with its accumulated interest and may or may not sell the bond purchased in period 1; with this accumulation new money balances can be obtained or a bond with maturity $T - 1$ shorter can be purchased. Hence in any period t, money or a bond with maturity equal to the remaining time of the planning horizon $T - t + 1$ are the commodities which may be purchased with the money balances (including interest) from $t - 1$ and the proceeds from bonds (not already sold) with terms to maturity ranging from T to $T - t + 2$. In order to focus on the demand for money and to be able to derive the most specific properties concerning this demand, we assume that $T = 3$, which is the minimal number of periods for a well-defined term structure problem.

In the first problem the investor can hold either money or a long-term bond, as described in equation (3.59); $\overline{S}_1$ is fixed initial wealth.

$$M_1 + B_{L1} = \overline{S}_1 \tag{3.59}$$

Money, as noted before, pays interest, and so does the long-term bond, but for convenience we will assume that the latter is held for two periods (and the interest payment is made at the end of the second period); this matters, though, as we shall describe, below. In addition, in the second period, the investor may hold money balances for one further period (M_2) or may purchase a short-term bond (B_{s2}) to be redeemed in period (3). The constraint appears as equation (3.60).

$$M_2 + B_{s2} = M_1(1 + r_{m1}) \tag{3.60}$$

Notice that we have distinguished money from short-term bonds and short-term bonds from long-term bonds in accordance with their term to maturity and not in accordance with their payment of interest.

For the third period, all assets are cashed in and terminal wealth is held in the form of money; thus, for period 3 the appropriate constraint is given by

$$M_3 = M_2(1 + r_{m2}) + B_{s2}(1 + r_{s2}) + B_{L1}(1 + R_{L1}) \tag{3.61}$$

We may, then, combine equations (3.59), (3.60), and (3.61) - also making a minor adjustment in notation for $m_t = M_t/\overline{S}_1$ - and the result is the single constraint given as equation (3.62).

$$m_3 = m_1[(1 + r_{m1})(1 + r_{s2}) - (1 + R_{L1})] + m_2(r_{s2} - r_{m2}) + (1 + R_{L1}) \tag{3.62}$$

In order to determine the expected return and variance of

the portfolio, we note that the return on the portfolio (R_p) is $R_p = m_3 - 1$. In this event the expected return is

$$E(R_p) = m_1[(1 + r_{m1})(1 + E(r_{s2})) - (1 + R_{L1})] - m_2E(r_{s2} - r_{m2}) + R_{L1} \tag{3.63}$$

a result which reflects the fact that only second-period bond and money interest rates are uncertain and that there are two second-period rates - one for money and one for bonds. In equation (3.63), then, there exists an expected term structure - $[(1 + r_{m1})(1 + E(R_{s2})) - (1 + R_{L1})]$ - in which the expected component is a future bond rate. In addition, the difference between the expected second-period rates on bonds and money reflects the fact that the larger this difference (if positive) the more a given position in money $(m_2 > 0)$ will cost in terms of expected return on the portfolio.

The variance on the portfolio can be calculated directly and is

$$V(R_p) = (m_1(1 + r_{m1}) - m_2)^2\sigma_r^2 + m_2^2\sigma_m^2 + 2(m_1(1 + r_{m1}) - m_2)m_2\sigma_{rm} \tag{3.64}$$

where $V(r_{s2}) = \sigma_r^2$, $V(r_{m2}) = \sigma_m^2$, $C(r_{s2}, r_{m2}) = \sigma_{rm}$, with r_{s2} and r_{m2} assumed to be normally distributed.

Money is in the problem as an interest-paying asset, and this is enough to give it a unique role to play in view of its shorter term to maturity, but we have found that it is possible to solve a more general problem, in which both m_1 and m_2 appear in the utility function, therefore providing implicit services in addition to their interest rates. This more closely captures the role of money in an economy such as that of the United States, particularly where broader measures of money, including interest-bearing time deposits, are analyzed. Equation (3.65), then, is the utility function and is assumed to be twice continuously differentiable;

$$U = U(E(R_p), V(R_p), m_1, m_2) \tag{3.65}$$

here we assume that $\partial U/\partial E = U_e > 0$, $\partial U/\partial m_1 = U_1 > 0$, and $\partial U/\partial m_2 - U_2 > 0$. Equation (3.65) defines the preferences for the investor such that return, risk, and liquidity provide the motivation for portfolio selection. Thus equation (3.65) is maximized with respect to m_1 and m_2, subject to equations (3.63) and (3.64). Clearly, once m_1 and m_2 are determined, the remaining choices for b_{L1}, b_{s2}, and m_3 are simply residual. Note, though, that we are assuming that the long-term bond is not cashed in at the end of the first period, and so this complication - involving a further stochastic element - is avoided at the cost of some desirable generality.[22]

The first-order conditions for an interior solution with m_1 and m_2 both positive are

$$\frac{\partial U}{\partial m_1} = U_E[(1 + r_{m1})(1 + E(r_{s2})) - (1 + R_{L1})] + U_v[2(m_1(1 + r_{m1}) - m_2)(1 + r_{m1})\sigma_r^2 + 2(1 + r_{m1})m_2\sigma_{rm}] + U_1 = 0 \qquad (3.66)$$

$$\frac{\partial U}{\partial m_2} = - U_E E(r_{s2} - r_{m2}) + U_v[- 2\sigma_r^2(m_1(1 + r_{m1}) - m_2) + 2m_2\sigma_m^2 + 2\sigma_{rm}(m_1(1 + r_{m1}) - m_2) - 2m_2\sigma_{rm}] + U_2 = 0 \qquad (3.67)$$

These equations have some interesting properties; we assume $U_{11} < 0$ and $U_{11}U_{22} - U_{12}^2 > 0$ as second-order conditions. We have assumed that U_E, U_1, U_2 are all positive; then, in the event that $U_v = 0$, which is the (strong) assumption of risk neutrality, we can see from equation (3.66) that $(1 + r_{m1})(1 + E(r_{s2})) - (1 + R_{L1}) < 0$. That is, even if the gross long-term rate is greater than the short rates (as compounded), the investor will hold money because money provides desired liquidity in period 1 $(U_1 > 0)$. This seems an important property to have in one's model. In addition, even though the expected short-term rate on bonds exceeds the expected rate on money, the investor will demand second-period money balances. The difference in the expected second-period rates is equal to the rate of substitution between liquidity (U_2) and return (U_e); again, inclusion of m_2 in the utility function provides this generality. Finally, notice that if the investor is satiated (at the margin) with liquidity in period 1 $(U_1 = 0)$, and $U_v = 0$, as before, then $T^* = (1 + r_{m1})(1 + E(r_{s2})) - (1 + R_{L1}) = 0$; further, if satiation occurs in the second period, then the implication is that $E(r_{s2}) = E(r_{m2})$ - that is, no basis exists for contrasting expected interest rates at the margin. Indeed, we can directly see that short-term rates must rise relative to the gross long-term rate, and the expected rate on money must increase relative to the expected rate on bonds as the investor moves from non-satiated to satiated equilibrium.

Returning to our system of equations in (3.66) and (3.67),

we may directly solve for desired first- and second-period money holdings. These solutions appear as equations (3.68) and (3.69), where

$$T^* = [(1 + r_{m1})(1 + E(r_{s2})) - (1 + R_{L1})]$$

$$T = [(1 + r_{m1})(1 + E(r_{m2})) - (1 + R_{L1})]$$

we can refer to T^* as an "expected bond rate term structure" (a "cross" term structure in our problem) and to T as an "expected money rate term structure" (an "own" term structure in our problem).

$$m_1 = \frac{\xi_1(\sigma_r^2 + \sigma_m^2 - 2\sigma_{rm})}{(1 + r_{m1})^2 H} + \frac{\xi_2(\sigma_r^2 - \sigma_{rm})}{(1 + r_{m1})H} + \frac{\rho[T(\sigma_r^2 - \sigma_{rm}) + T^*(\sigma_m^2 - \sigma_{rm})]}{(1 + r_{m1})^2 H} \quad (3.68)$$

$$m_2 = \frac{\xi_1(\sigma_r^2 - \sigma_{rm})}{(1 + r_{m1})H} + \frac{\xi_2\sigma_r^2}{H} + \frac{\rho[T\sigma_r^2 - T^*\sigma_{rm}]}{(1 + r_{m1})H} \quad (3.69)$$

Here $H = [\sigma_r^2\sigma_m^2 - \sigma_{rm}]$ will be assumed to be positive[23], and the other parameters are $\rho = -U_E/2U_v$, which is the inverse of the usual measure of absolute risk aversion, and $\xi_j = -U_j/2U_v$, which is a measure of absolute liquidity preference in period $j (j = 1, 2)$.

Thus, the demand for money (m_1 or m_2) depends on the degree of risk aversion and liquidity preference of the investor, along with the variances and covariance of the uncertain interest rates and the "own" and "cross" expected term structures. Indeed, there is more than one term structure in each of the two demand for money functions - and each of these refers to a different financial commodity. Moreover, equations (3.68) and (3.69) are non-linear in the individual interest rates but yet are linear in the own and cross-expected term structures. Hence the mean-variance paradigm provides a rationale for putting many interest rates in the demand for money, but in this case these interest rates must enter in a specific fashion so that the demand function is linear in the expected term structures. Let us now consider the properties of these functions, briefly.

The independent variables in this problem are the long-term rate (R_{L1}), the own rate on money (r_{m1}), the expected money rate $(E(r_{m2}))$, and the expected bond rate $(E(r_{s2}))$; these, we will argue, are minimum elements in the demand for money (along with initial savings, wealth, or income).[24] We will assume, conventionally, that $\rho > 0$ and that ξ_1, ξ_2 are also positive. These assumptions are the usual ones and imply risk aversion (for ρ) and liquidity preference (for ξ_1 and ξ_2). Under these conditions, and with some further constraints on certain elasticities (those between interest rates and the terms ρ, ξ_1, ξ_2), we can show that

(a) the expected coefficient of the long-term rate is negative,
(b) the expected coefficient of the own rate is positive,
(c) the expected coefficients for the two expected interest rates are both positive, and
(d) the expected coefficients for T, T^*, ρ are positive

for the demand for money balances in the first period. Indeed, these results are available in the Bernstein-Fisher paper for m_1, m_2 and for one- and two-period holding periods for the long-term bond. Thus, the pay-off is an exact equation (equation (3.68)) to estimate (it is discussed below) and some sign expectations for interest rates in the demand for money, the latter derived from a basic optimization model of a representative wealth holder.

3.4.3 SOME FURTHER EMPIRICAL NOTES ON THE MEAN-VARIANCE MODEL

The foregoing models imply that one can capture the essence of the mean-variance model if one performs empirical tests in which across-equation constraints are applied (as in, for example, the work on financial intermediaries already referred to) *or* by direct estimation of equations like (3.68). In equation (3.68) the ρ, and σ^2, ξ_1, and ξ_2 variables are parameters, and the interest rates are variables - so that a regression of M on i and Y is certainly appropriate for a simple mean-variance test - but these parameters also may vary (they represent, after all, expected values) in which case econometric problems may appear. To see that such may well have been the case in recent years, we note that a number of studies have included variance terms (of σ_i^2 and of $\dot{P}/P$) and have invoked the mean-variance model in support of the approach. Furthermore, these terms have sometimes been successful.

In one such study on quarterly US data, Slovin, Sushka,

and Hill (1978) predict the existence of a positive effect from bond rate variability - and they obtain it in their tests. Their equation had two interest rates in it, as well,

(a) the commercial paper rate (which they felt would be relevant for large wealth holders) and
(b) the deposit rate for S & Ls (which they felt would be appropriate for small savers).

Both had negative signs, and it was the variance of the commercial paper rate which produced the positive sign. In a somewhat parallel (and earlier) paper, Artis and Lewis (1976), in a framework in which an own rate on money and a long-term rate were included, invoked the portfolio model to justify inclusion of the "standard deviation of the logarithmic first differences" of the long-term rate. This had a positive sign and was generally significant. But such results are still relatively infrequent in the literature. Finally, Bernstein and Fisher (1982) have successfully tested a simplified version of equation (3.68) on British data, using what are assumed to be expected rates derived from the term structure of interest rates itself, in the manner of Hicks (1946) or Meiselman (1962).

3.5 TRANSACTIONS COSTS AND THE DEMAND FOR MONEY

In this section we will discuss a sample of theoretical and empirical results bearing on the role of money in reducing the costs of carrying out transactions in goods, financial, and input markets. While much of this work is in terms of the popular inventory-theoretic model, as extended, a growing and more important part is in terms of general transactions paradigms (e.g. Saving, 1971, and Niehans, 1978), and so, once again, it is efficient to begin with the early special cases and to end up with the generalizations. Actually, much of the work in this section is devoted to making more precise what we mean by the "medium of exchange" function of money. That is, money is given a role to play in a world where there exist frictions in trading, frictions which produce transactions costs (associated with resource costs of various sorts). The demand for money, then, arises as part of the natural solution of a problem in which an economy economizes on its scarce resources. In particular, as a medium of exchange, certain forms of money permit exchange to be conducted more efficiently (at a saving of resources), and as units of account the same forms lower accounting costs generally. It will be this perception which motivates much of the following although, to be sure, in the aggregative framework adopted here, some (essentially) microeconomic studies of (especially) the transactions and precautionary demand will not be appropriate.

3.5.1 THE INVENTORY-THEORETIC MODEL

The inventory-theoretic model (IT model), as applied to the demand for money, is a popular model, certainly - because of its ease of manipulation and, no doubt, because it has had some empirical success - but it is also a relatively exact model, so that one pays a high price, in terms of imposing *a priori* values on the coefficients of the model, in exchange for these advantages. The point of departure for this model is to frame the problem of money holding not as that of maximizing expected utility but as that of avoiding some undesired result by holding optimal quantities of some liquid assets in one's portfolio. In the case of money holding, then, the undesired results follow directly from running out of money; in actual studies they are either definite (penalty costs or foregone interest are examples of definite costs) or indefinite (such as the embarrassment of running out of cash). The problem to which we address ourselves in this section, in particular, is that of managing an asset collection when one (or more) of the assets is subject to a stochastic drain and there are some explicit penalty costs (perhaps in the form of costs of disposing of the assets) associated with the running out of them. Provided we specify an equation for the relative penalties associated with the running out of each of the assets, this model could be just as general as the mean-variance model; this is done in a paper by Gray and Parkin (1973) and in one by Santomero (1974). But in our discussion of the demand for money in this section we will generally consider only a two-asset model. The result will be an *a priori* demand for money with properties which differ from those of the mean-variance and monetarist models mainly because the operating rules are different.

The standard result in this area is from Baumol's paper (1952) which offers the often-used square root formula; there is a parallel paper by Tobin (1956). The motivation Baumol provided was that of an inventory control problem. The general idea, then, is to impose a cost of liquidating one's inventory of liquid non-cash assets (which earn an interest rate of i) in addition to the interest cost foregone by holding non-interest-bearing money; the former cost is met by assuming that each withdrawal of M dollars from the bank requires the payment of a brokerage fee (b). In commonsense terms, these could be justified in terms of the cost of making trips to the bank or, even, the time used up in converting one's assets into cash; they could also be explicit brokerage fees or "substantial penalties for early withdrawal". If we assume that an individual pays out T dollars per unit of time, then T/M represents the velocity of cash - that is, the number of times cash must be raised - and $b(T/M)$ the money cost of these trips. The individual's average cash holding over the interval of time in question will be $M/2$, and the cost of these holdings is $i(M/2)$ where, as noted, i represents the interest earnings foregone by holding cash. Thus, the total costs of "liquidity" will be the sum of the two components, as given by equation (3.70).

$$\frac{bT}{M} + \frac{iM}{2} = C \tag{3.70}$$

The foregoing is actually an individual choice problem where the size of M, the cash balance, is the decision variable. The problem is to choose M, given T, b, and i, such that (3.70) is minimized; the derivative of (3.70) is (3.71),

$$\frac{dC}{dM} = -\frac{bT}{M^2} + \frac{i}{2} \tag{3.71}$$

and when this is solved at the minimum, we obtain the well-known square root formula for the transactions demand for money:

$$M^* = \left(\frac{2bT}{i}\right)^{\frac{1}{2}} \tag{3.72}$$

The function just described can be directly analyzed; thus, if one takes the log of the function, he obtains

$$\log M^* = \frac{1}{2}\log T + \frac{1}{2}\log b + \frac{1}{2}\log 2 - \frac{1}{2}\log i \tag{3.73}$$

Then, since the elasticity of M with respect to T is given by

$$\frac{\partial \log M^*}{\partial \log T}$$

we obtain the direct result that this elasticity is equal to 1/2. This result, which implies that a 100 per cent increase in transactions results in a 50 per cent increase in cash holdings, is often referred to as the case of "economies of scale" in the demand for cash balances. It is the direct result of the choice of a specific functional form (equation (3.70)) and will clearly differ for different versions of the inventory control problem. Further, taken literally, the theory implies that when the demand for money is estimated, if the theory is to be carried along, the restriction that this elasticity is 1/2 should be imposed on the estimating procedure; indeed, all of the coefficients in equation (3.73) are known in advance, and so there is little to do except to look for omitted variables (i.e. to look at $\bar{R}^2$), at least if the approach is taken that the coefficients should be constrained to their *a priori* values. This cannot be done, of course, by regression methods unless other non-fixed variables are present. Finally, with regard to the other variables in equation (3.73), we note that the penalty cost has an expected positive sign - that is, an increase in the expected penalty cost (which is that of converting bonds to cash in this case) will induce more cash holding - and that the predicted sign for the interest rate is negative, on the opportunity cost grounds specified explicitly in equation (3.70).[25]

3.5.2 SOME BASIC EXTENSIONS OF THE INVENTORY MODEL

In this section we will take up a number of extensions and qualifications of the inventory model from the much larger (and growing) set in the literature. These concern problems arising from its assumptions - (a) that the model is micro-oriented and may present problems in aggregation and (b) that the description of the cash flow of the individual (he has none in the model just discussed) could be improved - and extensions. The latter involve the role of the wage rate in the demand for money; an interesting result, based on some recent work by Friedman, which provides a term structure framework that is parallel to that generated in the mean-variance model discussed above; and some work incorporating the inventory model with the mean-variance model or with "utility theory" and introducing relative prices and inflation rates into the model. In a final section (3.5.3) we will discuss some generalizations of the broader transactions framework (in which the inventory model is considered to be a special case).

The basic IT model presents a version of cash adjustment which is both extremely simple and extremely rigid. In this problem the individual gradually runs down his initial money balance at a steady rate until it is totally gone; he then replenishes it entirely and runs it down again, at the same rate. While the steady rate of individual or even aggregate disbursement is not unreasonable, the micro-version of the theory produces sharp discontinuities in holding, which seem unreasonable in the aggregate (where individual discontinuities might reasonably be expected to average out. With regard to the problem of aggregation in the inventory model, a basic result is by Barro (1976). Barro adopts a variation of the Baumol model similar to that of Tobin; here the individual can hold two assets, savings (S) and money (M), and chooses his number of trips (n) to the bank per fixed time period (t). If the individual is faced with an interest rate on savings (i_s) and money (i_m) and receives an amount of income (X) at the beginning of the period, then for b defining his transactions costs per trip, his net revenue function is

$$\pi = \overline{S}i_s t + \overline{M}i_m t - nb \qquad (3.74)$$

where $\overline{S}$ and $\overline{M}$ are average holdings of the two assets. If the individual spends at a constant rate (y), then, if he uses up his income entirely over t, this rate is $y = x/t$. We may substitute this value into (3.74) to obtain

$$\pi = \frac{1}{2}yi_s t^2 - \overline{M}(i_s - i_m)t - nb \qquad (3.75)$$

In this framework Barro (that is, Tobin) shows that transfers between money and savings will occur evenly over the period; indeed, they will occur at the points t/n. That is, if t is thirty days and if one takes three trips to the bank, then t/n is ten days, the average number of days per conversion. The size of the balance is determined by the rate at which the individual uses up his case (the rate is y), so the money transferred each time is $M = y(t/n)$ and the average money balance is

$$\overline{M} = \frac{yt}{2n} \qquad (3.76)$$

We may substitute this last expression into equation (3.75) to obtain

$$\pi = \frac{yt^2}{2n}i_s - \frac{1}{2}\frac{yt}{n}(i_s - i_m) - nb \qquad (3.77)$$

and this is then maximized by choosing n, the number of trips to the bank. The result of the optimization (one simply differentiates and then evaluates the resulting expression at the maximum) is

$$n^* = t[y(i_s - i_m)/2b]^{\frac{1}{2}} \qquad (3.78)$$

By substituting this optimal number of trips to the bank in-

in equation (3.76), we then obtain the demand for money

$$M^* = \frac{yt}{2n^*} = [yb/2(i_s - i_m)]^{\frac{1}{2}} \tag{3.79}$$

Here the familiar elasticities are obtained, clearly.

Note n^* in this framework is not an integral number, and so a different solution (n) will exist if an integer-constrained solution is desired for the individual (you cannot take a half of a trip to the bank). That is, while n^* may well be expected to be near n, it is actually an all-or-none decision to go to the bank, and consequently the individual unit may well differ from an aggregate unit - for an individual a step-function might well capture the all-or-none aspect, while for the aggregate a continuous function is undoubtedly appropriate. Barro, then, aggregates from the micro step-functions, using parameters from the income distribution (in the United States) assuming that all individuals face the same i_m, i_s, b, and t so that only income differs among individuals. The result, which is algebraicly complex, is that the exact values of the Baumol-Tobin elasticities for the effects of changes, in income, interest rates, and transactions on the demand for money, hold in the aggregate if the average number of trips to the bank (to convert one's savings to cash) over the interval is more than 1½. On the other hand, if $\bar{n}$ is less than that, then the micro-inspired Baumol-Tobin formula would actually tend to understate the income elasticity and over-state the interest elasticity. Barro notes that this average may well be considerably smaller than 1½ , but, of course, whether it is or is not is clearly an empirical issue.

With regard to the second of our major adjustments - the cash flow problem - we should note that Baumol in his original paper actually does produce a cash flow solution, which runs as follows (for some of this we will follow the presentation of Brunner and Meltzer (1967). Assume, then, that the firm (or individual) generates a cash flow from the sale of its products and uses up this cash flow on payments for inputs, investments on securities (S), and residual money balances (R). If T is the gross money (receipts less immediate purchases) available from the business, then $R = T - S$ is the money left over after the investments are undertaken. R/T represents the ratio of the residual balances to the original money balances; at an even rate of disbursement, R/T represents a fraction of the time between receipts which can be covered by the money balance. R/T, of course, is equal to $(T - S)/T$. The average money balance over that time period is $(T - S)/2$, and this average is worth $i(T - S)/2$ times the length of the period covered $(T - S)/T$. If there is a cost

(b_d) for depositing money - a service charge - in the savings account, this can be tacked on to our expression to obtain

$$i\left(\frac{T - S}{2}\right)\left(\frac{T - S}{T}\right) + b_d S$$

If it runs out of money during the period, the firm will have to sell (or withdraw) from its S account; this produces an additional cost of

$$\left(\frac{C}{2}\right) i \left(\frac{S}{T}\right) + b_w S$$

where $C/2$ is the average amount withdrawn, i represents the interest earnings, and S/T is the length of the period one can cover after the initial balances (R) are used up. We add a term to measure the cost of the withdrawal, assuming all funds are planned to be withdrawn eventually.

To optimize, we sum the last two expressions and partially differentiate with respect to S, the amount of funds invested (making this, in effect, a portfolio problem). At the optimum, then, we obtain

$$R = C + \frac{T(b_d + b_w)}{i} \qquad (3.80)$$

where $R = T - S$, as already noted. C, in this expression, is also a choice variable, and if we invoke our square root rule for this (that is, substitute in equation (3.72)), we obtain a cash flow version of the demand for optimal residual balances of

$$R = (2bT/i)^{\frac{1}{2}} + \frac{T(b_w + b_d)}{i} \qquad (3.81)$$

To get from R and C to observed money balances (M), Brunner and Meltzer argue that during a part $((I - T)/T)$ of the transactions period, firms (or, for that matter, individuals) hold average balances of $R/2$ and that during the remainder (I/T) they hold $C/2$. The average optimal money holding for the entire period, then, must be

$$M = \left(\frac{R}{2}\right)\left(\frac{T - I}{T}\right) + \left(\frac{C}{2}\right)\left(\frac{I}{T}\right)$$

After substituting for R $(= T - I)$ from equation (3.81), they obtain

$$M = (bT/2i)^{\frac{1}{2}}\left(1 + \frac{b_w + b_d}{i}\right) + \frac{T}{2}\left(\frac{b_w + b_d}{i}\right)^2 \qquad (3.82)$$

Brunner and Meltzer, then, calculate the transactions elasticity for this function, and, directly, it turns out to be close to unity, for large values of T. This, they feel, is a quantity theory of money result, although, as it turns out, their formulation also implies a relatively large interest elasticity under these conditions.[26]

Moving further into the literature on the firms' demand for money, we may consider even more general formulations, in which a stochastic cash flow is included in the inventory model. In the best known of these, Miller and Orr (1966, 1968), and Orr (1971) concentrate on a two asset problem in which cash is non-interest-bearing. Thus, let p be the probability of the cash balance increasing by m dollars during an hour (an hour = $1/t$) and $q = 1 - p$ be the probability of its decreasing by the same amount in the same period of time. Then, assuming a Bernoulli process, over n days the distribution of changes in cash balances will have a mean and a variance as given by equation (3.83).

$$\begin{aligned} \mu_n &= ntm(p - q) \\ \mu_n^2 &= 4ntpqm^2 \end{aligned} \qquad (3.83)$$

a distribution which approaches the normal distribution as n increases.

Miller and Orr assume that $p = q = 1/2$, in which case $\mu_n = 0$ and $\sigma_n^2 = nm^2t$; furthermore, they assume the usual cost-minimizing objective for the money-holding unit. Then, the expected cost $(E(C))$ per day (T) of managing the portfolio of stocks (earning an average of i) and money is given by equation (3.84),

$$E(C) = \gamma\frac{E(N)}{T} + iE(M) \qquad (3.84)$$

where γ represents the cost per transfer, $E(N)/T$ is the number of portfolio transfers per day, and $E(M)$ is the average daily cash balance of the representative money-holding unit. This framework does not as yet contain choice variables; thus, let the money-holding unit purchase securities in the amount $(h - z)$ whenever h, the upper limit of desired cash balances, is reached. Then, whenever the lower limit (0) is reached, let it sell z worth of securities to replenish its cash balances. The limit h and the balance z, then, are the decision variables, and one must find expressions for equation (3.84) in terms of these choice variables; equation (3.84) can then be minimized.

Considering the term $E(N)/T$ first, we note that it is the expected number of transfers of funds per day (times a cost factor i). This is equal - assuming a Bernoulli random walk between 0 and h - to

$$\left(\frac{1}{z(h - z)}\right)(t)M^2$$

where the first part of the expression is the duration of each step in the Bernoulli process and t and M^2 convert the steps to days and dollar amounts (it is M^2 because both z and h need to be converted). Miller and Orr also derive the second part of this expression, which is the average cash balance times the interest rate (i); under the assumed condition it is

$$i\left(\frac{h + z}{3}\right)$$

and the expression for equation (3.81) is then

$$E(C) = \frac{\gamma m^2 t}{zZ} + \frac{i(Z + 2z)}{3} \qquad (3.85)$$

where $Z = h - z$. This is the kind of specific result one expects in this literature. The first-order conditions can then be calculated directly, for z and Z; they are

$$\frac{\partial E(C)}{\partial z} = -\frac{\gamma M^2 t}{z^2 Z} + \frac{2i}{3} = 0$$

$$\frac{\partial E(C)}{\partial Z} = -\frac{\gamma M^2 t}{Z^2 z} + \frac{i}{3} = 0$$

This, when solved, produces optimal values for the decision parameters of

$$z^* = \left(\frac{3\gamma M^2 t}{4i}\right)^{1/3} \qquad (3.86)$$

and

$$h^* = 3z^* \qquad (3.87)$$

This solution implies that the typical firm will - under the assumed conditions - set the lower point (z^*) well below the mid-point of the range over which cash balances fluctuate (since $z^* = (1/3)h^*$). It also implies that firms will run off assets frequently (in small lots) compared to their sales, since the frequency of such transactions is greater the closer z^* is to zero.

The representative firm's (individual's) demand for money which results from this exercise can, of course, be derived directly from equation (3.86); it is

$$M^* = \frac{4}{3}\left(\frac{3\gamma}{4i}\sigma^2\right)^{1/3} \tag{3.88}$$

where we employ the fact that $\sigma^2 = m^2 t = \sigma_n^2/n$. The parameters here have the usual signs, of course, with the negative elasticity of the interest rate to be noted especially. We are not able to deduce a scale elasticity directly, though, because σ^2, the variance of the cash balance, is not directly related to the volume of sales. This, in a sense, is reasonable, since this result makes it clear that it all depends on the type, size, and typical style of transactions of the business firm. Thus, Miller and Orr conclude that this elasticity could range from the case of economies of scale to that of diseconomies of scale without altering any of the assumptions of their model. This finding has a somewhat wider empirical range than some of the other results in the literature discussed so far in this section.[27] Note that the (implicit) discussion of the firm's demand for money is continued in Section 3.6.5, in Section 4.5 where money as a factor of production is considered, and in Section 5.4 where money holding is included in a standard neoclassical investment function.

The foregoing introduces a stochastic flow of funds into the transactions model, and it is natural to adapt this framework to the case in which the rate of return is stochastic; what results is an interesting transactions cost/mean variance model of the demand for money which is the work of Buiter and Armstrong (1978). Beginning with the total return of

$$R = \frac{r(Y - D)}{2} - c\frac{Y}{D} \tag{3.89}$$

where D is deposits, Y is income or wealth, and c is the brokerage cost, then with r stochastic (with distribution (μ_r, σ_r)), the mean and the standard deviation of total return are

$$\mu_R = [(Y - D)/2]\mu_r - c\frac{Y}{D} \tag{3.90}$$

$$\sigma_R = [(Y - D)/2]\sigma_r \tag{3.91}$$

Adopting the following quadratic utility function with a maximum of R^*

$$U = b(R - R^*)^2 \qquad b < 0,\ R^* > -c \tag{3.92}$$

and maximizing expected utility (the indifference curves are

$E(u) = b[(\mu_R - R^*)^2 + \sigma_R^2] = k)$, the first order condition is

$$-2c^2Y^2D^{-3} + (\mu_r cY^2 - 2R^*cY)D^{-2}$$
$$+ R^*\mu_R - \frac{1}{2}(Y - D)(\mu_r^2 + \sigma_r^2) = 0 \qquad (3.93)$$

The average demand for money, then, is

$$\frac{D}{2} = f(Y, \mu_r, \sigma_r^2, c) \qquad (3.94)$$

which is the combined mean-variance/transactions cost form. The derivations $d(D/L)dx$, with x denoting the arguments of equation (3.94), are generally ambiguous in sign unless R^* has a sufficiently high value (it is the satiation level of total return required by the adoption of the quadratic) in which case the derivatives have the expected signs. Income elasticity is also derived in the Buiter-Armstrong study and could show a value greater than unity, a result which one commonly gets with the more general models.[28]

Yet another use of the IT model is that of Grossman and Policano (1975) and Policano and Choi (1978). In the first of these papers, the authors look at two types of money balances - those held in proportion to present expenditures (M_w) and those held in proportion to future purchases (M_v) - and then derive exact results for the influence of changes in expected inflation. In particular, an increase in expected inflation will decrease working balances (M_w), since the consumer buys "now" in these circumstances, and also will reduce (M_v), since the consumer will need to hold smaller balances for future expenditures (these will be expected to be smaller if the goods are purchased "now"). In the second paper the authors use the same IT model but combine it with a utility maximization approach. Quite simply, the household maximizes

$$U(X_1, X_2)$$

subject to

$$Y - C - \sum_{j=1}^{2} P_j X_j = 0$$

where C is the cost of inventory management (this defines the role of money). This framework permits an analysis of the influence of changes in relative prices on the demand for money; the result, of course, depends on the direction of change of commodity demands in each of the two periods studied (as one might have expected, based on the results obtained in the 1975 paper just described).

Turning to another kind of extension of the IT model then, we first consider a paper by Karni (1973) in which the distribution of income enters the problem. Thus, assume that disposable income and the value of transactions are related by equation (3.95),

$$T = ay \tag{3.95}$$

and, further, that income is divided between labour income (time worked times the real wage) and other income (PI).

$$y = T_w w + PI \tag{3.96}$$

This implies that

$$T = a(PI + T_w w) \tag{3.97}$$

Assuming that the demand for money is

$$m^* = (bT/2i)^{\frac{1}{2}} \tag{3.98}$$

Karni generates exact results for the demand for money after explicitly defining b, the brokerage cost; thus let

$$b = \tilde{P}'\tilde{x} + T_e w \tag{3.99}$$

where $\tilde{P}'\tilde{x}$ represents a sum of quantities of transactions goods times the associated prices (both are vectors) where the goods are such as trade documents, transportation, etc. Substituting (3.99) and (3.97) into (3.98), we obtain the demand for money in this model as

$$m^* = [(\tilde{P}'\tilde{x} + T_e w)a(PI + T_w w)/2i]^{\frac{1}{2}} \tag{3.100}$$

From this we can directly calculate the elasticities for the various independent variables as follows:

$$\varepsilon_{mw} = \frac{1}{2}(2 - \frac{P'x}{b} - \frac{PI}{y}) = \frac{1}{2}(1 - S_x + S_w)$$

$$\varepsilon_{mT_w} = \frac{1}{2}(1 - \frac{PI}{y}) = \frac{1}{2}(S_w)$$

$$\varepsilon_{mPI} = \frac{1}{2}(\frac{PI}{y}) = \frac{1}{2}(1 - S_w)$$

$$\varepsilon_{mi} = -\frac{1}{2}S_w$$

Here $S_x = \tilde{P}'\tilde{x}/b$ and S_w is the share of personal income going to wage earners.

Then, if we pick some exact (or known) value of S_x and S_w, the two parameters, exact results will follow. For example, if $S_x = 0.5$ and $S_w = 0.7$, we get

$$\varepsilon_{mT_w} = 0.35; \ \varepsilon_{mPI} = 0.15; \ \varepsilon_{mi} = -0.35; \ \varepsilon_{mw} = 0.6$$

These are, of course, values which have the expected signs, as well. We note, though, that the elasticity for the real wage is remarkably strong here, at 0.6. This approach justifies an empirical demand for money function of the general form of

$$m = \alpha + \beta_1(S_w)PI + \beta_2(S_w)i + \beta_3(S_w)T_w + \beta_4(S_x, S_w)w$$

which is essentially a variable coefficients model (unless S_w and S_x are taken as constants, in which case, as in earlier forms of the model, the coefficients are known without the need for a direct empirical test). Even so, this model serves to justify the use of the wage rate in the demand for money, and certain empirical results certainly can be rationalized in this fashion.[29]

Finally, we note that there is an IT-inspired version of the term structure/demand for money problem which has been worked out by Friedman (1977). In a context in which there is a single bond (a perpetuity) and non-interest-bearing cash, in which an investor can deal in a futures market in a perpetuity (in which there exist transactions costs) in order to line up the maturity of his obligations with his preferred holding period for the perpetuity, Friedman generates results comparable to those reported above, for the mean-variance/demand for money/term structure model. Thus, when every rate increases - that is, when the entire term structure shifts upward - then $\partial M/\partial i < 0$. This, of course, is the analogous result to the usual single interest rate effect. When the tilt of the term structure changes, Friedman obtained results exactly like those described above for the mean-variance model. Thus, Friedman finds that when the short rate falls and/or the long rate rises, then the demand for money is reduced. In terms of the mean-variance model described above, where

$$T = (1 + i_{s1})(1 + E(i_{s2})) - (1 + R_1)$$

this implies a decrease in T. That result, too, was for a reduction in money holding, so the two models dovetail on this important point.

There is an empirical test by Heller and Khan (1978) of Friedman's proposal - which is simultaneously a test of the mean-variance model since no theoretical constraints from the IT model were imposed. Heller and Khan estimated (by regression) a simple term structure (yield on a quadratic of maturity) and then used the parameters directly in the demand for money. The terms were significant (and negative), and the formulation appeared to be stable. This procedure has an econometric problem, since the estimated coefficients of the quadratic approximating function are not "fixed in repeated samples", suggesting that (at the least) a stochastic regressors approach may have been more appropriate. In any event, this work was extended by Allen and Hafer (1980) who updated the (American) data and used a cubic approximating equation, obtaining more accurate forecasting and stability; a British test of the quadratic form by Bernstein and Fisher (1982) obtained the expected signs, but illustrated instability.

3.5.3 SOME SPECIFIC RESULTS FOR TRANSACTIONS COSTS

In this section we will discuss some results for the broader class of transactions costs models in which the inventory-theoretic model is but a special case (a specialization, in effect, of the transactions process) if, indeed, it enters the discussion at all. The first result is that of Saving (1971) who discusses the case of the consumer. Supposing that the consumer maximizes an inter-temporal utility function in which the rates of consumption of goods and services and leisure time are the arguments,

$$u = U(c_t, L_t) \qquad t = 0, \dots, h \tag{3.101}$$

and h is the horizon, Saving supposes that he is constrained by his dynamic income profile

$$y_t = F(W_t, t) \tag{3.102}$$

where t is included as an argument to represent the time path itself, and W_t represents the time the consumer actually spends on income-generating activities. In this more general framework, then, there are three additional constraints, one of these is for his allocation of time (T_t is transactions time),

$$L_t + W_t + T_t = 1 \tag{3.103}$$

and one is a production function for transactions time

$$T_t = G(y_t, c_t, \bar{y}_t, \bar{c}_t, \bar{m}_t^k) \tag{3.104}$$

in which $G_1 > 0$ and $G_2 > 0$ represent the fact that the flow activities of income-earning and consumption activity use up time, and G_3, G_4, $G_5^k < 0$ define the roles in the model of the stocks of income, consumer goods, and the various forms of money possible (k = currency, demand deposits, etc.) in economizing on transaction time. At this critical point, then, we find a crucial and simple stock flow distinction to be part of the problem of specifying the role of money in a dynamic context. The last constraint in the problem, then, is a general dynamic budget constraint in which bonds (b) also appear and in which there are explicit storage costs (δ_i) for each of the stocks.

$$\sum_{t=0}^{h} \left(\frac{1}{1+r}\right)^t y_t + b_0 + M_0 = \sum_{t=0}^{h} \left(\frac{1}{1+r}\right)^t [c_t + r(\bar{y}_t + \bar{c}_t + \sum_k \bar{m}_t^k) + \delta_{\bar{y}}\bar{y}_t + \delta_{\bar{c}}\bar{c}_t + \sum_k \delta_{\bar{m}(k)}\bar{m}_t^k \tag{3.105}$$

There are also real interest-earnings foregone in the holding of stocks of consumer goods, income, or money (in its various forms). Note that the coefficient for $\bar{m}_t$ could include the rate of inflation. Saving, here, has a complicated problem which he resolves by picking optimal values of c_t and L_t and then optimizing with regard to m_t^k alone. The result is a set of demand for money functions of the general form of equation (3.106).

$$\bar{m}_t^k = \gamma^k(\hat{C}_t, \hat{L}_t. r. \delta_{\bar{y}}, \delta_{\bar{c}}, \delta_{\bar{m}(k)}, t) \tag{3.106}$$

Then, for the wage rate measuring the value of leisure time and the inflation rate representing $\delta_{\bar{m}(k)}$, one gets a "transactions cost" version of the demand for money when money has a storage cost and saves time in transactions and one has to forgo interest if he holds money.

In a second paper, Saving (1972) extends the general transactions-cost analysis to the case of the business firm. Here the firm has a production function of

$$x_t = \phi(v_{it}) \tag{3.107}$$

for $i = 1, \ldots, n$ inputs (not including money), and the transactions cost function depends on the number and on the size of transactions:

$$T_t = G(P_t x_t, \Sigma w_{it} v_{it}, \overline{x}_t, \overline{v}_t, \overline{M}_{ct}, \overline{M}_{dt}) \qquad (3.108)$$

Here $P_t x_t$ and $\Sigma w_{it} v_{it}$ compare to y_t and c_t in equation (3.104) - the case of the consumer - and $\overline{x}_t$, v, $\overline{M}_{ct}$, and $\overline{M}_{dt}$ represent the average sizes of the holdings of the illiquid real stocks of commodities (x_t) and inputs (v_t) and the liquid assets (currency and demand deposits). The signs expected are $G_1, G_2 > 0$ and G_3, G_4, G_5, and $G_6 < 0$ with the last two reflecting the productivity of money in saving resources normally devoted to vigilance concerning the firm's cash flow. Saving, conventionally, assumes that the firm maximizes the present value of the time profile of its profits; this function is

$$PV\pi = \sum_{t=0}^{h} \left(\frac{1}{1+r}\right)^t \{P_t x_t - [\phi(x_t) + T_t + \gamma_t]\} \qquad (3.109)$$

where $\phi(x_t)$ is a cost function and γ_t represents, as in equation (3.105) the storage costs of holding the four stocks in equation (3.108).

$$\gamma_t = (r + \delta_{\overline{x}})\overline{x}_t + (r + \delta_{\overline{v}})\overline{v}_t + (r + \delta_{\overline{M}c})\overline{M}_{ct} + (r + \delta_{\overline{M}d})\overline{M}_{dt} \qquad (3.110)$$

The rate of inflation could be included in the δ_i in this case.

After optimizing, Saving obtains a general transactions form of the demand for money as illustrated in equation (3.111).

$$\overline{M}_k^* = H_k(P, r, \delta_{\overline{x}}, \delta_{\overline{v}}, \delta_{\overline{M}c}, \delta_{\overline{M}d}) \qquad (3.111)$$

Here k identifies whether it is the demand for currency or the demand for demand deposits. While the specific assumptions on the form and derivatives of the function underlying this result are sufficient to produce some explicit comparative-equilibrium results for the arguments of (3.111), only the own cost can be signed in this framework; it is negative, of course. Even so, this general transactions cost-storage cost framework has a considerable amount of intuitive appeal and does isolate some of the aspects of the role of money which a general transactions model can provide.[30]

More recently, Niehans (1978) has produced a more general solution for the stock-flow problem taken up by Saving. While Niehans claims a general solution to the problem of integrating "value" theory and the theory of money (not a topic of concern for this book) by means of a careful specification of the transactions constraint, his actual contribution seems to lie in the area of using an appropriate mathematical technique (dynamic non-linear programming with linear constraints) and in the patience with which he sets up his model (it is solved in the stationary state); we will discuss the work in his Chapter 4. The consumer, then, maximizes

$$u = U(x_1, \ldots, x_t, \ldots, x_h) \qquad (3.112)$$
$$t = 1, \ldots, h$$

where h is the horizon. There are, then, three constraints; the first is for commodities (stock = S^g) for day t. As is usual for the transactions models, the constraints contain most of the interesting details.

$$S^g_{t+1} - S^g_t = (\overline{x}_t - x_t) + (z^g_t - y^g_t) - \gamma S^g_t$$
$$- c^t(z^g_t + y^g_t) - c^b(z^b_t + y^b_t) \qquad (3.113)$$

Here the one period change in commodity stocks depends on the fixed endowment supply $(\overline{x})$ versus the demand (x) for commodities, on the difference between purchases (z^g) and sales (y^g) of commodities, on storage costs (γ) for commodities, and on transactions (brokerage costs) in commodities and bond markets. The second constraint refers to changes in bond stocks

$$S^b_{t+1} - S^b_t = z^b_t - y^b_t$$

which are merely the differences between those bought and sold, and the third is for money stocks.

$$S^m_{t+1} - S^m_t = P^g_t(y^g_t - z^g_t) + P^b_t(y^b_t - z^b_t) + rS^b_t$$
$$+ \rho S^m_t - T_t \qquad (3.114)$$

Here we convert to money terms via p^g and P^b, r is the coupon on bonds, ρ is an own interest rate on money, and T_t is a lump sum tax payment (Niehans has the government as the only supplier of money). The result, after solution of the problem, is a demand for money of

$$S_t^{*m} = S_t^{*m}(\bar{x}, P^g, P^b, T, r, \rho, \gamma, c^g, c^b) \qquad (3.115)$$

where $\bar{x}$, P^g, P^b, T are vectors over time. Note that there is no direct non-commodity wealth effect in (3.113) since $\bar{x}$ contains only initial commodity stocks and the remaining variables are prices (as in Saving's model). Even so, this is the most general solution yet produced on the theoretical demand for money (with P^g, P^b not solved for in a two-stage procedure) and contains two further important insights:[31]

(a) The price level has to do with the flow demand for money and the interest rate with the stock demand for money.
(b) Money, even in satiation, has a role to play in lowering transactions costs over time (there is no "diamonds-water" paradox), and the intuition of Pesek and Saving (1967) on net wealth is confirmed.

Turning to the small empirical literature on this subject, we note several direct methods of approach. One of these, clearly, is to use a wage proxy for transactions costs - as in a Dutton and Gramm (1973) and the Karni papers already referred to - but there also exists some scope for even more direct tests. In one such study, Meyer and Neri (1975) associated the transactions motive with the level of expected income and the asset approach with permanent income. While they realize that permanent income dominates actual income in the demand for money (see below), they argue that when the transactions motive is formulated in terms of expected income rather than actual income, the transactions theory does as well as the permanent income theory.[32]

Then there is the matter of a direct proxy for transactions. As we have already pointed out, one can include income in the demand for money as a proxy for wealth in an asset theory, in its own right in a flow-oriented general equilibrium theory, or as a proxy for the volume of transactions. In the latter case, though, income may not be especially appropriate - particularly if it is not proportional to transactions or if the proportionality is unstable, and so it is just as well to conclude by noting that in a recent paper Lieberman (1977) finds, for the US data, that the difference this proxy makes may well be considerable.[33] Of course, the money value of transactions is much greater than is the value of income, but the more important problem concerns the empirical performance of the two variables in demand for money functions. Thus, while Lieberman finds that variations in income and variations in transactions (measured by bank debits) correlate poorly, the more important point is that the demand for money with a bank debit proxy (for transactions) has "economies of scale" compared to one in which an income proxy is used. Even more importantly, perhaps, when a trend variable is included in the bank debit version to measure technological progress, the speed of adjustment is such that essentially 100 per cent occurs within a year (using a simple lag formulation); this removes a result for the demand for money which many researchers have found anomalous, which is that the speed of adjustment in income-proxy models has seemed excessively long. We note, as well, that the rate of technological change in the demand for money is 1.3 per cent per year (see note 53). This variable was insignificant in the test with the income proxy.[34]

3.6 EMPIRICALLY-ORIENTED RESULTS FOR THE DEMAND FOR MONEY

In this section we will undertake a brief review of a series of theoretical results which have been generated in an empirical context; we will also append some empirical notes on these and earlier models. It is an important part of the style of the demand for money literature to produce theory along with an empirical test (or illustration); in addition, we should note that there is a certain looseness about the empirical record so that a good part of the empirical material is actually consistent with any of the general paradigms so far discussed in this chapter. Indeed, much of the empirical work begins with an already "specified" demand for money function and seeks to establish certain regularities within that context. The establishment of these regularities, then, involves questions of

(a) variables: income, wealth, prices, the wage rate, population, the rate of inflation, the short-term interest rate, the long-term interest rate, and the normal (or the expected) interest rate;
(b) functions: short run, long run, additive, multiplicative, and generalized; and
(c) aggregations: narrow money, broad money, private versus business deposits, and temporal;

and with regard to all of these general areas,

(d) related questions of the relative stability of the various formulations.

Finally, we should note that some considerable interest still exists over how to represent Keynesian or monetarist positions with regard to these topics.

There are so many possibilities in the list just given that empirical work on the demand for money is necessarily piecemeal. There are, consequently, an enormous number of studies to look at, and they are all different: they exclude some of the areas just identified; they run over different time periods, one to another; and they use data from different countries. Space limitations, therefore, require that the material in this chapter not be even a close substitute for the recently published surveys on these topics[35], and we also will not repeat our earlier empirical notes in this chapter, except in the event that clarity seems to require it. As noted, we will be concentrating on the theoretical models, and the empirical notes will be largely designed to complete the story. In this spirit, there will generally be no reference to "money supply theory" - although such reference is certainly relevant to empirical work on the demand for money. Indeed, some of the empirical results on the demand for money do appear to differ, depending on how the supply is (or more usually is not) modelled, and this needs to be recognized at the outset. Some reference will be made to this as we proceed, but most of the story will be told in the second volume of this survey, where policy issues motivate the discussion.

3.6.1 INCOME

With regard to income or wealth (or, for that matter, permanent income) the general impression one gets from the *a priori* literature is that wealth or a wealth proxy such as permanent income might well be expected to work better than income in the demand for money. This proposition has certainly received some strong early support in the empirical literature, although exact comparisons were not always the rule. The story begins with Friedman (1959) although his interest was more in explaining an empirical conflict in the behaviour of velocity than with many of the fine points in the demand for money. The empirical irregularity is that income velocity rises during cyclical (short-run) expansions but falls during secular (long-run) expansions and conversely for contractions. Briefly, Friedman argues that the secular picture is correct but that the cyclical pattern for velocity is obscured because there are substantial transitory changes in income during the cycle. He then estimated a demand for money function (without an interest rate in it) which had a permanent-income elasticity of 1.81.

The earliest "Keynesian" test in the literature was published almost immediately after Friedman's paper. In this study, Bronfenbrenner and Mayer (1960), including an interest rate, judged that the short run (that is, a function with a lagged dependent variable) demand for idle balances was more responsive to a wealth than an income variable. This line of attack was pursued by Laidler (1966), who confirmed that for a variety of functions (all "long run"), where an interest rate was included, the permanent income variable out-performed the level of income. Bronfenbrenner and Mayer's result, for a short-run function, basically contradicts Friedman and was the topic of a direct comparison by Chow (1966). Chow argued that the short-run demand would be expected to show a relative dominance for income while the long-run function would favour permanent income; this result was marginally confirmed on US data and later was studied on British data, Canadian data, and again on US data, using basically the same methodology.[36] These results are suggestive, at most, although one can still observe a mild preference for permanent income over the level in this literature; the question of the role of wealth has not received much study, however.[37]

The fundamental difficulty in the foregoing is that the problem of the role of income is mixed up with the problem of the partial adjustment of economic stocks (such as money and bonds) toward their desired levels. In particular, a model may include the lagged dependent variable in order to capture directly the partial adjustment aspect, but it may also include it as the result of the application of the Koyck transformation, itself used to convert the unobservable permanent income into observables (current income in this case). These two disparate motives produce essentially identical estimating equations. A number of recent attacks have been mounted against these problems of which we will briefly consider two.

In one of these, Darby (1972) argues that transitory money balances may be treated as a shock absorber; he proposes that

$$\frac{dM_{Tt}}{dt} = \beta_1 S_{Tt} + \beta_2 M_{Tt} \qquad (3.116)$$

that is, that β_1 describes how transitory savings provide cash while β_2 (< 0) describes how transitory money balances are used up over time (as the stock is adjusted toward the desired level). Then, since

$$M_t = M_{Tt} + M_{Pt}$$

where P signifies permanent money balances, and

$$S_{Tt} = y_{Tt} - C_{Tt}$$

with $E(C_{Tt}) = 0$ by assumption, we have (directly) that

$$M_t = \beta_1 y_{Tt} + (1 + \beta_2)M_{t-1} + M_{Pt} - (1 + \beta_2)M_{Pt-1} \quad (3.117)$$

Assuming that

$$M_{Pt} = \beta_3 + \beta_4 y_{Pt} + \beta_5 i_{Lt} + \beta_6 i_{St} + \beta_7 i_{mt}$$

where i_m is the own interest rate on money and L, S identify long and short term rates, we have the following estimable demand for money.

$$\begin{aligned} M_t = &- \beta_2\beta_3 + \beta_1 y_{Tt} + (1 + \beta_2)M_{t-1} + \beta_4 y_{Pt} \\ &- (1 + \beta_2)\beta_4 y_{Pt-1} + \beta_5 i_{Lt} - (1 + \beta_2)\beta_5 i_{Lt-1} \\ &+ \beta_6 i_{St} - (1 + \beta_2)\beta_6 i_{St-1} + \beta_7 i_{mt} \\ &- (1 + \beta_2)\beta_7 i_{mt-1} + u_t \end{aligned} \quad (3.118)$$

This is, after all, a conventional demand for money function except that it focuses on y_T and y_P.

Darby's model has lagged values in the independent variables - and the dependent variable - on account of transitory cash flows and lags in the adjustment of desired to actual money balances. While the equation tested closely resembles a Koyck-transformed equation, there is certainly a different interpretation put on the coefficients - and there are different variables. In any event, Darby estimates y_P directly from past income data (and $y_T = y - y_P$) and finds that not only are the interest rates consistent with his expectations (i_m had a positive coefficient) but also that there is a fairly slow response of desired to actual transitory money balances. This result, which also supports the idea that both partial adjustment and permanent-income figure importantly in the demand for money, has been challenged in a study by Santomero and Seater (1978) who construct a theory of partial adjustment (with the adjustment itself depending on interest rates). They find that the partial adjustment hypothesis itself provides a significant but small (that is, quick) effect on the US data, while the observed effect of money on income and the lagged money stock ought to be interpreted as confirmation of the strong role of permanent income on the demand for money rather than as due to the effect of partial adjustment. In this respect they take issue with the earlier work of Goldfeld (1973) who had argued the case for the level of income over permanent income in the demand for money; we will return to his study below.

Before we leave the question of the role of income, we should briefly return to the "economies of scale" question which arises from the juxtaposition of Friedman's view that money is a luxury good (he produced a permanent-income elasticity of 1.81) with the expectation of the basic Baumol-Tobin model that the transactions elasticity should be 0.5. With 1.0 representing the division between economies and diseconomies of scale, a neat empirical distinction can be drawn; indeed, it is one which may throw some light on the appropriateness of the inventory-theoretic model, if all goes well. The facts, though, indicate otherwise. An enormous amount of evidence has been produced (in every empirical and theoretical study on the demand for money a role has been given to transactions, income, or wealth), but the results cover the range from a negative income elasticity (we are, after all, testing a "reduced form" equation) to Friedman's value of 1.81. Laidler (1977) who seems to have turned over more of this evidence than anyone else, recently concluded that results favouring economies of scale dominate in advanced economies, but, one should note, sub-periods of this data, and many individual studies, indicate that one cannot reject out of hand the proposition that the scale elasticity (at least for permanent income) may well be around unity (or a little less). Perhaps it can be left that the role of income-wealth-transactions-partial adjustment needs to be tidied up further before this issue - which involves an exact value rather than merely a sign - can be resolved.

3.6.2 INTEREST RATES

There are four general types of empirical questions with regard to interest rates as follows:

(1) Which interest rate (if any) belongs in the demand for money - a long one or a short one?

(2) Where do we stand on the use of an "own" rate of interest?
(3) Do multiple interest rates affect the demand for money?
(4) Is there a liquidity trap?

For Question (1), since Laidler's early study (1966), at least one interest rate has been in common use, and when only one is used, it is usually, but not always, a short-term rate. Furthermore, we have already assessed question (3) to a great extent, and so a few words in review should suffice as a reminder here. The most relevant observation is that the empirical evidence is now strongly in favour of the view that more than one interest rate will enter the demand for money. Furthermore, there is a strong consensus that an own rate (with a positive sign) plus several short-term rates (with, quite possibly, negative signs) may well be a successful formulation. Less clearly, perhaps, a formal term structure version has received some support with an own rate, a short rate, and a long rate showing up either directly or indirectly. One suspects that there will be more work on this problem in the near future.

With regard to the own rate - question (2) - a number of recent studies warrant some separate discussion. The basic problem, of course, is that institutional constraints on the payment of interest on demand deposits (this kind of regulation is not restricted to the United States) has necessitated the calculation of implicit rates of interest (that is, yields) on currency and demand deposits. The earliest measures simply calculated a negative own rate by employing the service charges of banks, with some success.[38] While bank service charges are clearly one aspect of money holding, they are, after all, only part of the story. Thus, more recently, Klein (1974) calculates i_m as a weighted average

$$i_m = \left(\frac{C}{M}\right) i_c + \left(\frac{D}{M}\right) i_d$$

where i_c is the rate of return on currency - assumed to be zero - and i_d is the interest rate on bank deposits. For narrow money, this return is

$$i_m = i_s\left(\frac{DD - R_{dd}}{M_1}\right)$$

where DD are demand deposits and R_{dd} are reserves held against demand deposits (the reserves of member banks of the Federal Reserve System pay no interest in the United States) and for broad money (old M2) it is

$$i_{m2} = i_s(1 - \frac{H}{M2})$$

where $H = C + R$. Note that i_s - an observed short-term rate - is used here because the true marginal return is not observed. Klein argues for the appropriateness of this measure on the grounds that competition will force commercial banks to find ways to compensate depositors for their foregone interest (so that $(i_m)M = i_s(M - H)$). If this were a valid "own" rate, then, it would have a positive sign in a demand for money function, and this Klein finds, although this certainly cannot be taken as strong evidence of its validity.[39]

Becker (1975), who also does not consider the problem of the yield on currency, approaches the rate of return on demand deposits by calculating the difference between the aggregate non-interest cost of Federal Reserve member banks per dollar of demand deposits and service charges and fees per dollar of demand deposits; this variable seems to work well with the currency-deposit ratio as the dependent variable.[40] In an earlier paper, Barro and Santomero (1972) use a "remission rate" (on service charges) paid to large customers - who qualified for this because they held "compensating balances" - as a measure of the marginal rate of return. This worked in their study, but in a careful paper by Santomero and Seater (1978), while the three measures were not highly correlated, none worked with the expected sign. Perhaps, as Boyd (1976) points out, this is either because the actual options open to both banks and their customers are considerably more complicated than these measures can comprehend or because at least part of the variable in question - the size of the deposit or the size of the compensating balance - is demand determined (as is the currency-deposit ratio).

With regard to multiple interest rates, the reader should look back to Section 3.4 and to the empirical notes there, attached to various simultaneous-equation frameworks. There are, in addition, a small number of direct studies, generally of the single equation variety, where the theoretical structure is often not specified. Of these, easily the most ambitious are two studies by Hamburger (1969, 1977). In the first of his papers, Hamburger has as many as *five* interest rates (for the United States) although no results are achieved in which all five are statistically significant. Possibly the most relevant test here for the mean-variance model is a test in which an "own yield" on money has a positive coefficient, while an accompanying short rate has a negative sign. For the UK data, Hamburger uses three interest rates, but in this case the short rate does not enter while the yield on shares (common stocks) does and so does the Euro-dollar rate. Goldfeld, in an important study (1973) of US data, also uses two interest rates, but in this case only a short-term rate is statistically significant. On UK data, Crouch (1967) uses two short-term rates, one of which has a positive coefficient which might represent an own rate. Finally, in a Canadian study modelled on the Goldfeld approach, W.H. White (1976) uses two interest rates on the grounds that the "company sector" might respond to a short rate and the "personal sector" to a long rate but backs off when the shorter rate comes up with a positive sign, because of a (possibly unjustified) concern over multi-collinearity.

This leaves the theoretical question of Keynes's liquidity trap, a question which has a curious hold on the profession - curious because both its theoretical and empirical validity have been hard to establish and because it is, in any event, somewhat of a theoretical anomaly, at least as it was conceived by Keynes. The point of departure for the problem, as discussed earlier, was the formulation by Keynes of a speculation-based relation between the demand for money and the interest rate based on "differences of opinion" between individual investors. The rationale aside, the empirical questions which emerge are two:

(1) Do speculative influences (however justified) from bond and stock markets influence the demand for money, and, if so,
(2) is their presence strong enough to impart a substantial interest elasticity to the demand for money?

The bulk of the literature, both theoretical and empirical, concentrates on (2) although, to be sure, any failure to establish (1) implies that a search for (2) is fruitless.

With regard to the existence of speculative forces, the tests concern attempts to measure "normal" interest rates or to locate the influence of "error-learning" types of adjustment in the demand for money; the tests are inconclusive, on the whole.[41] With regard to the liquidity trap, though, one can come somewhat closer to a successful test. The basic paper is that of Pifer (1969), who offers the following demand for money function.

$$M_t = b_1(i_t - i_{min})_t^{b_2} Y_t^{b_3} e^{u_t} \qquad (3.119)$$

This, when transformed logarithmically, has four parameters (b_1, b_2, b_3, and i_{min}) and only two independent variables (plus a constant), and, consequently, a non-linear (maximum-likelihood) approach is adopted in which (in effect) various i_{min} are tried in order to find the one which maximizes R^2. The result, for the annual US data, was an i_{min} of around 2.06; this was not well-determined, though, and it remained for Eisner (1971) to straighten out what appear to have been basically computational errors.[42] After this was done, the test was pronounced a success (in favour of the existence of an i_{min}). Note that this test establishes that there is a lower asymptote - toward which the interest rate would move if it were pushed down far enough. No direct observations in the liquidity trap are needed here (only sufficient curvature) in order for a successful test to result.[43]

Tests of the functional form of the demand for money have not been especially common, and when they appear, it is usually in connection with the stability of the demand for money (see below) or with regard to the liquidity trap formulation of Pifer and his successors. Recent papers by Mills (1975, 1978) go a long way toward clarifying the issues involved. Employing a Box-and-Cox "generalized functional form", Mills writes the demand for money as

$$\frac{M_t^\lambda - 1}{\lambda} = \alpha_0 + \alpha_1 \frac{Y_t^\lambda - 1}{\lambda} + \alpha_2 \frac{i_t^\lambda - 1}{\lambda} + \alpha_3 \frac{M_{t-1}^\lambda - 1}{\lambda} \quad (3.120)$$

Then, when $\lambda = 0$, so that, for example

$$\lim_{\lambda \to 0} \frac{M^\lambda - 1}{\lambda} = \log M$$

we get the following demand for money,

$$\log M_t = \alpha_0 + \alpha_1 \log Y_t + \alpha_2 \log i_t + \alpha_3 \log M_{t-1} \quad (3.121)$$

whereas if $\lambda = 1$, we get

$$M_t = \alpha_4 + \alpha_1 Y_t + \alpha_2 i_t + \alpha_3 M_{t-1} \quad (3.122)$$

where $\alpha_4 = 1 + \alpha_0 - \alpha_1 - \alpha_2 - \alpha_3$. The important point in this derivation is the fact that the parameter λ, for any value it takes, defines a different function. Thus, (3.121) is the standard log form, while (3.122) is the standard linear form of the demand for money. Most important, though, is the flexibility this approach - when estimated by maximum likelihood methods - gives one in separating questions of functional form (those representing λ) from structural form (those representing a_i) when either the stability of the demand for money or the role of the choice of functional form is in question.

There is, then, further work on equation (3.120) in which each coefficient is permitted its own functional form; this is by Spitzer (1976).

$$\frac{M_t^{\lambda_0} - 1}{\lambda_0} = \alpha_0 + \alpha_1 \frac{y_t^{\lambda_1} - 1}{\lambda_1} + \alpha_2 \frac{(i - i_{min})^{\lambda_2} - 1}{\lambda_2} \qquad (3.123)$$

For this formulation, Pifer's test is equivalent to $\lambda_0 = \lambda_1 = \lambda_2 = 0$ (we would still use the non-linear maximum likelihood approach here). With this even more general approach Spitzer argues that there is evidence on the same US data of a "trap" but that the value of i_{min} increases along with the generality of the function. Indeed, while he finds the most generalized function works best, it turns out to be only marginally better than Pifer's formulation, which is thereby supported by this test. Spitzer (1977) also tests a simultaneous equations model (using the same methodology on money demand and money supply). This produced lower estimates of the level of the "trap" and significant variations in some of the other parameters of the model; the model also fitted better. Finally, we note a study by Boyes (1978) which corrects for some remaining specification bias in the single equation tests and (still) concludes in favour of the possibility of an asymptotic liquidity trap.

3.6.3 THE PRICE LEVEL AND THE RATE OF INFLATION

With regard to the price level, there are two questions usually raised:

(a) should a separate price level variable be included in the demand for money - with a free coefficient - on the grounds that some money illusion may exist, or
(b) should one assume the absence of money illusion and deflate all nominal variables by the price level?

These are, of course, related questions (although the literature generally discusses one or the other); in any event, we really have a small amount of evidence on (a), although most of it suggests that only a marginal gain would occur. With regard to the deflation problem, we note that there is actually an *a priori* argument - the monetarist view that nominal M is determined by conditions of supply and real M

by conditions of demand - which suggests that demand for money functions fitted in real terms will work better. But practice still varies considerably, although most recent efforts tent to fit the function in real terms; even so, as Jacobs (1974, p. 1235) has argued, "Our theoretical model indicated that three common methods of defining the aggregate money demand function - deflating the aggregate data by population and prices, deflating by prices only, or using nominal data undeflated by population or prices - are mathematically equivalent when the data are dominated by a time trend." This leaves the issue pretty much unresolved since a time trend is generally present.[44]

There is another issue with regard to the price level, as argued in a recent paper by Hafer and Hein (1980), following the lead of Goldfeld (1973). The typical (short-run) demand for money function estimated is

$$\log m_t = f(\log i_t, \log y_t, \log m_{t-1}) \qquad (3.124)$$

and is based on a *real* adjustment mechanism of

$$\log m_t - \log m_{t-1} = \lambda(\log m_t^* - \log m_{t-1})$$

where $m_t = M_t/P_t$, etc. But money stock adjustments to price level changes take time, and so it might be that the nominal form

$$\log M_t - \log M_{t-1} = \lambda(\log M_t^* - \log M_{t-1})$$

is the correct adjustment mechanism. When equation (3.124) is adjusted for this possibility, the amended version is

$$\log m_t = f'(\log i_t, \log y_t, \log \frac{M_{t-1}}{P_t}) \qquad (3.125)$$

so that the effect of the adjustment is to deflate the lagged variable by current rather than lagged prices. Goldfeld (1975) earlier found little effect here (but preferred nominal adjustment slightly); this finding was repeated by Hafer and Hein who also dealt with a troublesome instability in recent US data (see below) by using a log-first difference formulation of the model.

There is a related question (as it turns out), involving the direction of causality between the variables in the basic demand for money function. In Laidler's recent survey some concern was expressed over this problem, and a recent paper by Mehra (1978) and a survey by Moore (1979) have brought this matter up yet again.[45] The problem is a basic one, of course: can we write $M = g(Y, i)$ as our demand for money if M is the primary influence on nominal income as the monetarist analysis (and evidence) seems to indicate? That is, if Y is determined by M (and other variables), how can we avoid bias in estimates of the demand for money which (incorrectly) assume that Y is exogenous? Indeed, more provocatively, how is it that two-stage and simultaneous equations tests do not produce evidence of misspecification, when monetarist successes with "multiplier" studies indicate that this evidence should be present?[46] The answer may be that the results for stability of the money multiplier ($Y = f(M)$) are derived using nominal variables (correctly) and imply that an estimate of $M = f(Y)$ would be incorrect if done in nominal form (even if P were included as an explanatory variable) while estimates of $m = g(y)$ in real terms are also correct. While Mehra (1978), who derives these results, concentrates on the econometrics of this relation, one can also recall the monetarist view that the nominal quantity of money is (or should be) explained as determined by the authorities (or, at least, by forces exogenous to the standard macro-economy) while the real quantity is demand-determined.

The remaining variable of interest, then, is the inflation rate, or its variance. The most obvious case in which such a variable might appear is that of rapid inflation or hyperinflation, situations which have existed primarily in underdeveloped countries. In this case, as a glance at the definition of the nominal (observed) interest rate suggests,

$$i = r + \left(\frac{\Delta P}{P}\right)_e$$

one would anticipate that the expected (or even actual) rate of inflation would be a dominant variable in the demand for money. Indeed, a voluminous empirical record already referred to suggests that this is so (see note 12). With regard to the variance of inflation, though, and with regard to the variability of the coefficient of expectations in the Cagan model described above, a recent debate has appeared, to a somewhat uncertain conclusion, the principal problem being that a theoretical case is not easy to establish.[47]

With regard to developed countries a long-standing interest in the inflation rate has recently surfaced with some successful empirical work, although the theoretical foundations are not always made explicit. The problem is that there seems to be some uncertainty as to whether to use i or r (and $\Delta P/P$) and, indeed, just what the rationale is. Some of the successful attempts actually use i and $\Delta P/P$ (as a proxy for $(\Delta P/P)_e$)[48] even though this seems illogical in view of the proposition that money demand, taken by itself, is generally thought to be a function of i and not r, as such (see the discussion in Chapter 1). A reason why $\Delta P/P$ may work along with i in empirical studies is advanced by Donovan (1978) in a study referred to above. This is that money - a durable good - is in competition in wealth holder's portfolios with other real (durable) assets for which r is appropriate; a single equation test, then, may well pick up this effect. This is a relative price change between real and money assets which comes about because one reacts to inflation and one does not. Consideration of this factor might suggest the inclusion of common stocks in simultaneous equation "liquid asset" portfolio studies. A variation on this theme is suggested by W.H. White (1978) who argues that during inflation, the stock of real financial assets falls relative to real assets and thus wealth holders find their financial assets below desired levels. This produces a kind of real-balance effect as wealth holders try to rebuild their liquid assets by increasing their savings. These conjectures, incidentally, accord well with recent events in developed countries, in which consumption fell sharply (and liquid asset balances recovered in real terms) following high and (apparently) unanticipated inflation rates.

3.6.4 STABILITY

One of the underlying issues not discussed so far in this chapter concerns the stability of the demand for money, especially in recent years. While a string of monetarist-inspired results seems to have come down strongly on the side of stability, at least for developed countries[49], numerous contradictions have appeared; indeed, in recent years some solid evidence of instability has been produced in various contexts. A major part of the problem is directly involved in the discussion of this section, as it turns out, for one of the consequences of having the "wrong" model (for example, by omitting relevant variables) is the appearance of instability when different periods of time are compared or when forecasting is attempted. Indeed, the inflation rate and the variance of the inflation rate are certainly part of this problem, at least on recent estimates, and so are recent changes in the characteristics of financial entities.

To begin with, we might note that some earlier studies have been found wanting in terms of their stability. Thus, Eisner (1963) had some doubts about the stability of the demand for money in Bronfenbrenner and Mayer's (1960) early Keynesian-style study, and Courchene and Shapiro (1974) found that Meltzer's (1963a) basic monetarist-style test did not pass a simple Chow test.

With regard to more recent US studies we note that opinion is still divided over the stability question. Slovin and Sushka (1975) have argued that a relaxation of Regulation Q in the United States in 1962 - in favour of sharply higher maximum interest rates on time and savings deposits - in effect made savings more attractive relative to currency and deposits and reduced the demand for narrow money on a once-for-all basis. More generally, using a technique which permits one to search for instability without having to know exactly where to look (Slovin and Sushka, in effect, suspected that a break would occur in 1962), Laumas and Mehra (1976) studied the behaviour of the parameters of a standard demand for money function (in real and nominal terms, with and without lagged adjustment, and for various measures of income and various interest rates); looking for permanent changes in the coefficients, they found that partial adjustment is required to stabilize the demand for real balances and that it does not matter which measure of income (permanent or total) is used. Indeed, in their study, the demands for M1 and M2 are both stable.[50] On the other hand, on recent monthly data, Mullineaux (1977) finds that a disaggregation down to the demand for currency is necessary to find a stable function. In contrast, Hamburger (1977) argues that the problem is more one of inadequate specification; there are other papers[51], and there are studies on British, Canadian, Australian, Norwegian, and Indian data.[52] On the whole, this seems an open question although this work - taken as a whole - seems to confirm the need to complicate the demand for money if stability is to be achieved. We note, though, that recent financial innovations seem certain to present severe problems in the estimation of the demand for money[53] and may force one to retreat to simpler relationships, such as that between prices and the monetary base.

3.6.5 AGGREGATIONS

We have already discussed the commodity aggregations (M1 versus M2, etc.) at numerous points in this chapter so we will forbear to go into those variables further. This leaves two aggregation questions which have only partially been treated, that of the "temporal" aggregation and that of the aggregation of business and personal demands for money. With regard to the temporal aggregation, we note that this has been done in quite a simple manner usually and generally has been limited to the use of explicit measures of permanent income or to the use of the Koyck transformation. Both of these produce estimates of the independent variables (income, prices, interest rates) with monotonically declining weights assigned to the past values of these variables. The (temporally) aggregated variable then achieved is a defensible concept, of course, and, in view of the lack of a theory, is about as far as one can go if one believes that the past either influences or guides the present decision-maker but is, nevertheless, completely hazy about the exact form of that influence or guide. From this point of view we generally find that permanent measures frequently provide gains - although small ones often - in estimates of the demand for money.

Using these simple models, then, as much of the literature does, there seems to exist a fairly wide range in the findings over the length of the lag in the demand for money function, with Gibson (1972) on US data being the shortest, perhaps, and Goodhart and Crockett (1970) producing the longest (on British data); note, in reference to our discussion of stability, that recent estimates have tended to favour a short lag. There is a policy problem here, as well, for a long lag implies an important slippage in monetary policy; if the lag is itself unstable as well, we have further policy problems. The normal method of estimating this lag, by using the least squares estimate of the coefficient on the lagged value of the dependent variable, tends to produce an over-stated lag if there is positive serial correlation in the underlying model, as noted by Griliches (1961). If one first removes the serial correlation from the data, then some resolution can be achieved; this is often done in this literature and has been referred to at several points in this chapter. Actually, a prior problem - discussed by Thomas (1975) and implicit in some of the papers already referred to - is that the use of quarterly or annual data (viewed as an aggregation over monthly data), when the correct aggregation is monthly, produces an upward bias in the estimates of the length of the lag which is, of course, most severe for annual data.[54]

At this point a number of studies have brought in the flexible Almon (1965) lag technique, first employed on the investment function (it is described more fully in Chapter 5). Dickson and Starleaf (1972) on "quarterly" US data (1952-69) found the total lag to be much shorter than for the "annual" data studies (for narrow money); time deposits, further, were found to have a longer lag than narrow money and to respond to different variables, casting some further doubts on the usefulness of the broad definition of money for that period. Goldfeld (1973) reported similar results.

Shapiro, in a parallel study (1973), fitted an equation in first differences on quarterly US data and found a rather rapid response, regardless of the definition of money used. Shapiro found a lag of money to income which was 75 per cent complete after eighteen months. Of course, eighteen months is a long time, and the monetarist concern with the potential problems of such a lag in the conduct of monetary policy still seems valid, even on Shapiro's results.

Goldfeld's work (1973) on the post-war US quarterly data provides a benchmark because of his thoroughness. First of all, Goldfeld underscores a point we might accept after considering the functional form debate, that the lag on interest rates would not be expected to be the same as that on income (or wealth); the simple Koyck procedure treats both alike. Furthermore, Goldfeld proposes a rationale for lagged adjustment which is different from the usual lag of actual to desired balances: ". . . the adjustment can be conceived as a slow response of desired stock itself to actual current values of income and interest rates, rather than a gradual shift in money holdings to meet a promptly adopted new level of desired holdings" (1973, p. 599). This produces an equation of the same general form as the short-run models described above, but in his case the adjustment parameter comes from an equation showing how expectations are revised, such as equations (3.126) and (3.127).

$$y_t^e - y_{t-1}^e = \gamma(y_t - y_{t-1}^e) \qquad (3.126)$$

$$i_t^e - i_{t-1}^e = \delta(i_t - i_{t-1}^e) \qquad (3.127)$$

Thus, rather than

$$m_t = a_0 + a_1 y_t + a_2 i_t + a_3 m_{t-1} \qquad (3.128)$$

the estimating equation we would derive from his case is in the form of equation (3.129) after substitution in of $m_t = a + bi^e + cy^e$, with a Koyck model for the lags.

$$m_t = a_0 + a_1 y_t + a_2 y_{t-1} + a_3 i_t + a_4 i_{t-1} + a_5 m_{t-1} + a_6 m_{t-2} + u_t \qquad (3.129)$$

The form of this equation is just like that used in many empirical tests referred to above, but here the coefficients have different interpretations (that is, represent a different structure), the adjustment coefficients are interpreted differently (as rates of revision of expectations rather than as actual adjustments), and the error terms will, also, have a different form.[55]

Our second topic in this section concerns the aggregation of the "personal" and the business demands for money. Reasons vary for considering the business firm as a special case - indeed, there may well be some empirical differences - and there are three major possibilities: (1) businesses might be thought to have a different structure to their demand (for example, money might be best viewed as a factor of production, a concept which has no direct analogue in consumer theory unless a "consumption technology" is specified); (2) businesses may face a different economic environment (for example, their cash flow may be so variable that its variance is relevant); and (3) businesses may respond differently to the same independent variables as do individuals (for example, they may achieve their optimum portfolio of financial assets more quickly). The first two involve the *a priori* structure, while the latter seems essentially an empirical matter; all, of course, have empirical implications.

We will discuss in Chapter 4 the possibility of including real balances in the production function, and so we will not take up that question for the moment. On the other hand, there is an intriguing bit of literature going back to Keynes (1937) who proposed something now called the "finance motive" for holding money; this is a function not of actual activity but of expected activity. Davidson (1973) has revived this proposition recently and proposes the following "disaggregated" demand for money, reflecting consumers (C) and firms (I),

$$M^* = \alpha C^* + \beta I^* \tag{3.130}$$

Here the asterisk identifies an expected variable. If C^* and I^* are defined as equations (3.131) and (3.132),

$$C^* = a_1 + a_2 Y - a_3 i \tag{3.131}$$

$$I^* = b_1 - b_2 i \tag{3.132}$$

then we get a "quasi-reduced form" demand for money which is given as

$$M^* = (\alpha a_1 + \beta b_1) + \alpha a_2 Y - (\alpha a_3 + \beta b_2) i \tag{3.133}$$

Here we see a standard model but with quite a different interpretation given to the coefficients.[56]

With regard to the empirical results, we note that direct

comparisons are actually not very frequent, although recently there has been some interest (and some data). Price (1972), on the British data, found that when the individual (as opposed to the business) demand for money is tested, it turns out to be relatively slow in its response to interest rates. Price also noted that the aggregation of business and private demand appeared to be involved with the choice of independent variables; indeed, firms responded to the short-term interest rate, while individuals responded to the long-term rate, and the income elasticity of the personal demand was around 2.0 while that for businesses was less than unity (but the business function did not fit well). Much of this was confirmed by an American by Hoffman (1979) on disaggregated data for the Southeastern United States (the interest rate result is the reverse of Price's finding). For the United States, Meltzer (1963b), and later Brunner and Meltzer (1967), also found evidence of only mild economies of scale for business firms using sales as the scale variable. Wilbratte (1975) found the US business demand for money (M1) unstable and found sharp differences in terms of the household demand in terms of the significance and magnitude of the interest rate (non-significant) and income variables. We should also refer to a recent study by Laumas (1977) who uses the same methodology to identify instability as employed in the Laumas-Mehra paper discussed earlier in this chapter. Laumas employs a measure of broad money which includes time deposits, US government securities, state and local debt, and commercial paper and uses sales as the scale variable. In this case, the broad measure of money is stable, while M1 is not. With regard to the interest rate it appears that it is not significant in either case (M1 or the measure of broad money).[57] On Israeli data, though, Ungar and Zilberfarb (1980) find the business demand for money stable, find no economies of scale, and find strong interest rate effects. They used the ratio of firm wealth to firm sales to control for firm size and used firm specific dummies in a technique known as the "least squares dummy technique". Returning to US data, then, we note a paper by Katzimbris and Miller (1980) who find that including a size distribution variable reduces scale elasticity (although they were not able to establish an *a priori* case for this) in the Baumol-Tobin framework.

Disaggregation by sector is also suggested by Tinsley and Garrett (with Friar)(1978). They observe that problems in the stability of the demand for money may well be related to the development of certain liquid assets ("immediately available funds") widely used these days by business firms and by their implicit impact on the transactions demand for money. Their empirical work features an Edgeworthian model of the precautionary demand for money. An earlier British study using the same methodology is by Gray and Parkin (1973) where the business/personal question is not discussed. One should note that since 1978 the personal sector also has had an increasing access to liquid funds (let us call them "almost immediately available funds"), and so further warnings about the dangers of using monetary aggregates as targets or indicators in monetary policy can be issued. Of course, this is now well-known and is much discussed in the policy literature, particularly at the popular level.

Finally, we may return to the "demand systems" approach since it also answers questions concerning aggregation. We referred, in our discussion in Section 3.2.2, to some recent work on monetary aggregation being done at the Board of Governors of the Federal Reserve. This work suggests that the strong substitution necessary to justify simple sum aggregations (e.g. $M1 = C + D$) is not supported by the results of consumer demand system tests, and a Divisia index number approach to measuring monetary quantities is recommended (and used in a few instances). A paper in that series by Offenbacher (1980b) is germane to the earlier topic and to the business-personal question. Offenbacher uses the Rotterdam differential demand equation model - a general demand system approach - which requires user costs in the event that durable goods, such as the various types of money, are included. The "own" rates used on fourteen categories (there was some further simplification) of liquid assets (up to Savings and Loan RPs) were generally observed market rates, and some items were arbitrarily assigned to business (RPs) or consumers (currency), while data were available to disaggregate demand deposits (and several other categories) between the two sectors. The results were again in favour of very low substitution - and thus were basically against using the simple sum approach - and in the business sector there was no discernible substitutability at all. This leaves the possibility of applying Divisia aggregation to this problem and further reopens the question of the aggregation of business and private money demands until, at least, the Divisia model has been checked out. That is, the failures noted repeatedly above were all based on simple sum aggregations (to produce M1, M2, M3) and did not take advantage of the possibility of forming an aggregate in a different (Divisia) and more logical way, everything considered.

3.7 THE OPEN ECONOMY

Many of the issues concerning the open economy - where the degree of openness might be defined in terms of both the percentage of GNP which is traded and the volume of the flows of liquid and non-liquid capital - are (monetary) policy issues and not in the domain of this study. But there have been a few recent direct empirical studies on the demand for money of an open economy, and so some comments can be offered. The most obvious thing to do - to "open up" a domestic demand for money - is to include foreign assets in the potential portfolio of domestic wealth holders. Thus, an additional interest rate or so, livened up with data from before and after the ending of "fully" fixed exchange rates (1971-3), represents one (essentially) empirical approach to the problem. As the following brief survey indicates, one can also find studies offering simultaneous equations tests of the demand for money (on "currency substitution" mainly), on rational expectations, and, even, on the role of the demand for money in the "monetary approach" to the balance of payments.[58]

In a fixed exchange rate system, to begin with a policy issue, any attempt to control the domestic economy by means of the traditional methods of monetary control can be undermined by capital flows which will tend to affect the monetary base. For example, when foreign interest rates rise relative to domestic rates, both domestic and foreign-based wealth holders will tend to switch from domestic to foreign assets, an action which suggests that the monetary base will fall. In a flexible exchange rate system, while the policy issue is changed, wealth holders will still respond to foreign interest rates, so there is still a reason to study the demand for money as a function of interest rates, including foreign interest rates in this case. While one may well expect the demand for money to differ from a fixed to a flexible exchange rate system, this is far from inevitable; indeed, an interesting study on Canadian data by Gregory and McAleer (1980) finds no important differences across regimes. They used a single equation format (they had a supply of money in the problem) and tested for "endogeneity switches" across regimes (among other things). A single equation demand for money tested by ordinary least squares showed no simultaneous equations bias across regimes.[59]

We remarked above that simultaneous equations studies of the demand for money dovetail with the literature on "currency substitution", and so this is the place to return to that topic. To begin with, there is the problem that with the likelihood of increased risks associated with fluctuating exchange rates there will be both direct and indirect negative effects on the domestic demand for money. For the direct effect, as suggested by the literature on "currency substitution", domestic money holders may increase their holdings of foreign currencies in order to "spread the risk".[60] For another (indirect), the increased cost of foreign trade associated with less stable exchange rates (if such occur) could induce less money holding, at least if trade itself declines faster than costs increase. Actually, as discussed by Girton and Roper (1981), the degree of currency substitution itself incluences the stability of the exchange rate. In a world where the currencies are exogenously supplied, the greater the currency substitution, the wider the potential fluctuations in the exchange rate, with perfect currency substitution implying perfectly indeterminant exchange rates. In a world where currencies are endogenously supplied, however, stronger currency substitution is associated with smaller fluctuations in exchange rates. Girton and Roper conclude that one of the implications of their study is that a fixed money growth rule (of the monetarists, for example) may well lead to a depreciating and inferior currency if there are competitively produced close substitutes.

An empirical study roughly sympathetic to the issues just raised is by Bomhoff (1980), who employs rational expectations on the following function for Dutch data (see Section 3.3.2 for a discussion of the model).

$$\log \Delta M_t = \log \Delta P_t + \beta_1 \log \Delta y_t + \beta_2 r_{1t} - \beta_3 \Delta r_{2t} - \beta_4 \Delta FP_t \qquad (3.134)$$

Here FP is the forward premium (variously, with the mark and the dollar), r_1 is an "own rate" and r_2 a "cross rate" of interest (they are combined in estimation). The expected signs were achieved in this study, with the forward premium used to capture the influence of changes in the ratio of the forward to the spot rate (negative). The theoretical argument behind the use of the forward premium is not as clear as one might hope here because there are at least two reasons advanced in the literature as to why one might turn up something with this variable: (1) the forward premium may be a proxy for expected inflation as in Frenkel (1977); or (2) the premium may measure the substitution between domestic and foreign money, again as considered by Frenkel; of course the two may act in concert. That is, the first case is substitution between goods and money and the second between monies; a third approach (see Abel *et al.*, 1979) combines these, assuming substitution both with goods and external assets. Indeed, in the third case, two measures are needed: expected inflation (in the Abel *et al.* study the actual rate of inflation was used) and the forward premium. The authors of that study reported some success with the German data.

The most direct purely empirical paper is by Hamburger (1977) whose penchant for including multiple interest rates in the demand for money has already been noted. For Germany, using the narrow money stock, Hamburger compares a short-term domestic interest rate, an equity yield (measured by the dividend/price ratio), and the "covered yield on short-term foreign assets". While the equity yield proved unsuccessful, the foreign rate proved just as successful as the domestic rate (and it was estimated in the context of a demand function which proved to be stable). For the UK, again on narrow money, the best performance was obtained in a formulation which had the equity yield and the uncovered rate on three-month Euro-dollar deposits; indeed, when a domestic interest rate was included, it was not significant. These results, while certainly empirical in their orientation, do suggest that the performance of the UK demand for money (for which frequent allegations of instability have been voiced) may well be improved by broadening the context to that of the open economy.

With regard to measures of income, Bomberger and Makinen (1977) have pointed out that in an open economy it is possible that the influence of the interest rate on the demand for money may be different in sign, depending on which income proxy is used; the choices are "production" or "expenditure" proxies, with the two differing to the extent that the balance of trade is not zero (actually, why not broaden the issue to include the entire current account, that is, to include the financing of net capital flows?). The problem, in a nutshell, is that foreign traders need to hold inventories of money and that these money requirements may be larger or smaller than purely domestic needs. Expenditures, then, being $C + I + G +$ imports, could exceed a production proxy for income and, say Bomberger and Makinen, the LM curve could slope negatively (Levin, 1974); the crucial empirical distinction is whether with the production proxy the demand for money has a positive slope while with the expenditures proxy it is negative. They found, for twelve countries, the expenditures variable produced a better fit, but only in one case (UK) was there a positive interest rate for the production proxy. Of course, there is much more detailed work on the interest rate, and so this very provisional literature should be dovetailed with that of the previous paragraph for a more convincing result.[61]

NOTES

1. See Laidler (1977) and D. Fisher (1978).
2. See, especially Brunner and Meltzer (1971).
3. See M. Friedman and Schwartz (1970) and Feige and Pearce (1977).
4. Hulett (1971) phrases the solution in such a way that the dependent variable (money) will be defined if the appropriate variables (e.g. wealth in a portfolio model) perform successfully in the test of the demand for money.
5. M. Friedman and Schwartz (1970), Laidler (1969a).
6. For example, Laumas (1968) fit $\Delta Y = \alpha + \beta_1 \Delta M + \beta_2 \Delta S_1 + \beta_3 \Delta S_2 + \beta_4 \Delta S_3$ where S_1 was time deposits, S_2 was S_1 plus Mutual Savings Bank shares and Post Office savings, and S_3 was S_2 plus Savings and Loan deposits. He found that relative moneyness (money "services" national income) declines in the order $S_1 > S_2 > S_3$. This is not unexpected, possibly, but it is certainly no coincidence that something like an inverted demand for money was just expressed (in the form $\Delta Y = f(\Delta M)$); it is also no coincidence that this equation is very much like a monetary multiplier (M. Friedman and Meiselman, 1963) or a monetary indicator (Keran, 1970). It is no coincidence because, one might argue, many monetarists do not see a separate question of the problem of the definition of money, separate, that is to say, from the problem of the stability of the demand for money (or of the relation between money and national income).
7. We should, of course, enter the flow of services from the commodities, but we are actually taking a stock approach to the problem here, to be consistent with what comes later in this section.
8. We arbitrarily refer to the collection of $n - 1$ items as *commodities* and the collection of n items as *goods* (commodities plus money), although the text should be clear enough without this device.
9. Perhaps another derivation, due to Lloyd (1968) will illustrate this argument more concisely. Let

$$u = U(S_1, \ldots, S_n)$$

represent an aggregate utility function, and

$$\sum_{i=1}^{n-1} P_i S_i + S_n = M + Y$$

represent the budget constraint, where Y is initial "income" (a stock) and M is initial money balances. The proportionality constraint, then, is such that the final money balance S_n (= D_n in equilibrium) is proportional to expenditures, as in

$$\text{(c)} \qquad S_n = k \sum_{i=1}^{n-1} S_i P_i$$

Using (b) and (c) without (a), we can derive

$$\text{(d)} \qquad S_n = \frac{k}{1 + k}(M + Y)$$

which shows the demand for money to be proportional to initial money balances and income (really wealth) at equilibrium (where $S_n = D_n$).

10. If we relax this to an equality, i.e. a proposition only holding at equilibrium, then the following propositions about the demand for money hold only at equilibrium. The difference is that one market is eliminated (let it be the money market) for all equilibrium and disequilibrium experiments, if equation (3.11) holds. If it is eliminated, then, for all practical purposes, its functions are defined implicitly by the remaining relations. This is how we proceed in what follows here, although we do not need to take this approach, as noted.
11. The Fisher and McAleer paper is actually only one of the more recent of a set of essentially microeconomic studies of the demand for money which include Phlips (1978) and Saito (1977). These papers have in common the linear expenditure system approach.
12. We will not discuss the literature on hyperinflations or underdeveloped countries further, so a brief annotated bibliography might be helpful. Cagan found that the lag in price expectations tends to shorten as inflation rates get higher and claimed that his function was stable in his tests. In a follow-up volume of studies edited by Meiselman (1970) several other factors were added; thus Deaver (1970) included real income in his Chilean test successfully and found that it was in a measured rather than a permanent form. Diz (1970), analyzing the Argentinean data, added the variance of the inflation rate successfully and also found permanent income dominated measured income.

These studies, says Dutton (1971), may well be misspecified, however, in that the simple monotonic weights may well be inappropriate in the case of the wildly fluctuating inflation rates observed in these cases. In contrast,

Vogel (1974) in a recent paper found that a monetarist model fitted reasonably well over a sample of sixteen Latin-American countries. Finally, we note that there have been several successful attempts to locate a real rate of interest (since $i = r + (\dot{P}/P)_e$) rather than an expected rate of inflation; these are by Frenkel (1977, 1979), Frenkel and Rodriguez (1975), and Corbo (1974). Frenkel (1977, 1979) uses the foreign exchange market, and the first Frenkel paper fits into our discussion of the open economy and is discussed below, briefly.

13. See Sargent and Wallace (1973) and Black (1974).
14. We note, in passing, a large literature on the limitations of the mean-variance model. See, for example, Samuelson (1970), D. Fisher (1978) for this and other works. The analysis of the rest of this section is due to Parkin (1970) and Parkin, Gray, and Barrett (1970).
15. The restrictions are

    (a) the entire first matrix in (3.52) is symmetric, since S and S^{-1} are symmetric;
    (b) the first matrix has non-negative diagonal terms representing "own effects";
    (c) the row sums of this matrix are zero; to see, post-multiply by $\tilde{i}$;
    (d) the column sums of the second matrix in (3.52) are unity; to see, pre-multiply by $\tilde{i}'$.

16. Two recent papers which agree with Feige and Pearce, roughly, are by Edwards (1972), who uses a cross-section test, and O'Brien (1974), who found low substitutability, although that between demand and time deposits was relatively high.
17. But he ignored (3.54) in his derivation of these functions, and, in addition, (3.54) is a definition of wealth which includes usage on activities other than liquid asset holding; see Donovan (1978), whose paper on Canadian data is discussed below. A study using the Chetty approach on Canadian data is by Short and Villanueva (1977). They favoured a narrow definition of money, on the evidence of substitution (and stability).
18. They claimed that duality implies that the system (3.53) and (3.54) produces identical derived demand functions to (3.55) and (3.56) if the two use identical parametric forms. This is not so unless one minimizes (3.55), and this is because the second-order conditions are the same in the two models; see Donovan (1978)
19. Recent work toward an "integrated model" is by Purvis (1978); see also G. Smith (1975) for a clarification of

the Ladenson-Clinton debate.

20. Townend's work on the UK personal sector was extended by Bhattacharyya (1979) who also studied capital-certain assets. Bhattacharyya found that substitution estimates varied considerably over time, depending on model characteristics and, even, political factors. He used, among others, a "joint non-linear estimation" technique.
21. There are some problems with the mean-variance model, as a model of the demand for money. See the surveys in D. Fisher (1978), Nagatani (1978), and Baron (1978). One major problem is that a quadratic utility function must be used, but the quadratic implies that upward and downward changes in risk and return are equally desirable; in addition, it implies reduced absolute and relative risk aversion as wealth (or income) increases, whereas one might well expect wealthier individuals to become less risk averse, especially at very high levels of wealth. Let absolute risk aversion be defined as

$$R_A(W) = -\frac{U''(W)}{U'(W)}$$

and relative risk aversion as

$$R_B(W) = -\frac{WU''(W)}{U'(W)}$$

These are standard measures (U' and U'' are the first and second derivatives of the utility function with respect to wealth). For the quadratic $U(W) = a + bW + cW^2$, $R_A(W)$ yields

$$\frac{1}{-\frac{b}{2c} - W}$$

which for $c < 0$ (diminishing marginal utility of wealth) increases as W grows. As noted, this may seem unreasonable.

22. Where $\beta = 1$ for a two-period holding period and $\beta = 0$ for a one-period holding period (of the long-term bond), equation (3.65) could be written as

$$u = U[\beta E(R_p) + (1 - \beta)E(R_p),\ \beta V(R_p) + (1 - \beta)V(R_p),\ m_1,\ m_2]$$

and parallel results worked out for the two cases. This is done in Bernstein and D. Fisher (1981).

23. σ may be positive, but not so positive that it dominates

either σ_m^2 or σ_r^2. We need this assumption for the theoretical distinctions to be noted below. On the whole we are encouraged to think that our restriction is not an unreasonable one according to at least some of the work described in Section 3.4.1, especially that of Feige (1969), who found at most a "mild substitution" between money and other financial assets (i.e., a small positive value for σ_{rm}).

24. We will not analyze $\overline{S}$, here, as an influence, but we note that (3.58) and (3.59) are homogeneous in this variable (which we called "fixed" initial wealth). Our investor is a myopic individual who resolves his portfolio problem each period; his fixed initial wealth thus changes each period. The individual chooses his wealth, by varying M_1, M_2, etc., but receives surprises each period which show up in $\overline{S}$. Thus *permanent* wealth or permanent income are not appropriate variables for these functions, and *total* wealth is (since it includes the transitory component).

25. One finds little comment in the literature on the question raised in this paragraph, but see below, for the discussion of a recent paper by Barro (1976) which argues, in effect, that the rigidity of the model applies only to the individual money-holding unit so that when one looks at an aggregate, a genuine empirical question exists. With regard to the interest rate, we should note that this use of the interest rate does not bear directly on the speculative demand of Keynes. Since the framework is essentially Keynesian here, yet another difference - the choice of model - exists between (some) Keynesians and Keynes. On the other hand, the inventory model provides an easy rationale for the precautionary demand for money since money holding here is essentially motivated with reference to avoiding some unpleasant or expensive outcome. Several studies have followed this line of attack successfully: Gray and Parkin (1973), Santomero (1974), Weinrobe (1972), Whalen (1966), and Cropper (1976). See, also, the discussion of inventories in Chapter 5.

26. For small values of T, the elasticity approaches 1/2. Ahmad (1977) claims that if the unitary income elasticity is a quantity theory result, then a large interest elasticity is a Keynesian result. This view resurfaces from time to time, and it certainly has a firm hold on the textbook literature, if nowhere else. In addition, comparison of M. Friedman's work and that of the Keynesians leads one in this direction, although, at least, recent work of the monetarists (e.g. M. Friedman, 1970, and Laidler (1977)) certainly does not seem overly concerned with

either the interest rate or the income issue in these terms. I am here assuming that monetarists generally hold to the quantity theory of money in some form - see Mayer (1978).

27. There is also further work in this area, the most notable of which is that of Frost (1970) and Miller and Orr (1966, 1968). The latter argue that a long-term interest rate is relevant for the firm's demand for money, on the grounds that it is a major item in the cost of capital (for investment in fixed capital). Akerlof and Milbourne (1978) note that Miller and Orr, whose model is time-independent as well as "threshold" monitoring, really imply a zero income elasticity if applied to the quantity theory of money problem. They introduce time-dependence (in the spirit of I. Fisher) and conclude that the income elasticity is zero in this even more general framework. Several later papers pursue this topic, with the emphasis on rationalizing the low income elasticities one often finds (Akerlof, 1979, and Akerlof and Milbourne, (1980).

28. For a generalization of the transactions cost/mean-variance problem not involving the demand for money explicitly, see Mayshar (1979). For a recent survey of the business demand literature, emphasizing some micro-aspects in general, see D. Fisher (1978) or Katsimbris and Miller (1980); the latter look for the effects of differences in firm size, finding some in their empirical work (on the economies of scale) but not in their theory (using the Baumol-Tobin model).

29. Karni has two papers on the US and UK data which show a high and significant value for the wage elasticity (1974, 1975). There are also some successful results in the more general transactions framework based on a paper by Saving (1971); these are by Dutton and Gramm (1973) and show a strong wage rate effect. A paper which extends the Baumol-Tobin and Miller-Orr models and introduces parameters from the personal distribution of income (because of aggregation) is by Chant (1976). This puts distribution parameters in the adjustment parameters in the standard (distributed lag) demand for money.

30. In a recent paper Saving (1976) shows that the inventory model is a special case of the transactions model (as just outlined). This he does by having consumers maximize $u = U(C)_t$ subject to

$$\sum_{t=0}^{h} (1+i)^{-t}\{Y_t - [T_{bt} + T_{gt} + (1+\delta_{\overline{M}})\overline{M}_t + (1+\delta_{\overline{C}})\overline{K}_t]\}$$

where T_{bt} and T_{gt} represent the transactions cost functions in the bonds and goods markets (they are written in terms of the number of trips to the bank, the transactions costs per period in each market, income, initial money balances, and consumption so that they contain all of the elements of the inventory model). With specific linear functions for T_{bt} and T_{gt}, Saving is able to obtain optimal money expressions from which the square root rule can be obtained by direct simplification.

31. In a paper of the same vintage, Clower and Howitt (1978) argue that a general transactions model should have total costs (C) which consist of

(a) Holding costs equal to
waiting costs $\rho(\overline{D} + \overline{S} + \overline{M})$
storage costs $\beta S + \alpha D + \gamma M$

(b) Trading costs equal to
set-up costs $ay/D + by/S$
bunching costs $f(S, D, m)$

Here $\overline{S}$ are stocks of consumer goods, ρ is time preference, m identifies the gap between purchases and sales (in time) and thus money does not directly enter into trading costs (although its demand can be derived from solution of the stock flow problem identified by (a) and (b)).

The simple inventory model of Baumol just has storage costs (the interest rate) and set-up costs (converting bonds to money). Saving's model has all but the bunching costs (but it does have a variable expenditure date, and, in an extension in the same paper, it has a variable income date). In the production function literature representative contributions are by Dutton, Rozek, and Wu (1974) and Dutton, Gramm, and McDonald (1974). In the former the firm maximizes

$$\pi = P\phi_1(L, K, m) - wL - (i + \delta)qK - \phi_2(M)$$

where the production function (ϕ_1) includes real money balances and a transactions cost function (ϕ_2) is included. In the latter, the production function is

$$x_t = \phi(L_t, K_t)$$

and the cost function is

$$T_t = T(x_t, L_t, K_t, m_t)$$

and explicit results are obtained for the parameters after

these functions are specialized by

$$x = AL^{\gamma}K^{\beta}$$

and

$$T = e^{\alpha_1 x + \alpha_2 L + \alpha_3 K - \alpha_4 m}$$

The positive sign for wealth and the negative sign for the interest rate are obtained in this paper as an *a priori* result.

32. Meyer and Neri use

$$y_t^e - y_t = \lambda(y_t^n - y_t)$$

where n designates "normal" income (which is measured by a Cagan-Friedman permanent measure). If $\lambda = 0$, then

$$y_t^e = y_t$$

and the transactions approach is supported; if $\lambda = 1$, then

$$y_t^e = y_t^n$$

and the permanent hypothesis is supported. In the tests, λ comes out generally less than unity, so, at least, the transactions approach makes a contribution; indeed, in several cases it is not significantly different from 0.5. Parenthetically (see the next section) we should note that Meyer and Neri found short lags for the demand for money. A recent paper by Gupta (1980) questioned their specification (they had only one interest rate) and re-estimated, to the effect that $\lambda = 0$ (i.e. in favour of the transactions motive).

33. In an earlier paper, Enzler, Johnson, and Paulus (1976) argued that a marginal but interesting gain (especially in the ability of the standard model to predict) came from the use of a proxy for transactions costs based partly on bank debits.

Lieberman's model, incidentally, is

$$\left(\frac{M}{P}\right)_t = ke^{rt}D_t^{\beta_1}i_t^{\beta_2}e^{u_t}$$

34. Lieberman did a considerable number of experiments which included econometric variations and stability tests as well as the use of other variables (wealth, permanent in-

come, and a dummy variable for the introduction of the large-sized certificate of deposit in the United States). None of these adjustments affected his general conclusions in favour of his transactions proxy. It should be pointed out that Meyer and Neri explicitly rejected the bank debits proxy on the grounds that it was highly correlated with current income (and, as well, hard to interpret). Lieberman also compared M1, M2, and M3 in a separate paper (1979), employing the same approach.

35. See Laidler (1977), D. Fisher (1978), and Havrilesky and Boorman (1980).

36. See D. Fisher (1968, 1970), Clark (1973), and Goldfeld (1973). In a recent paper, Lieberman (1980) revives the Chow model, correcting the original data for institutional changes in 1933 and correcting the estimation procedure for serial correlation. He finds in favour of the transactions model over the "asset or utility demand" model - i.e. he finds against wealth and permanent income. See also note 32 for a parallel literature.

37. As noted earlier, the Patinkin model implies that there may well be a real balance/wealth effect in the demand for money (as well as in the consumption function, as discussed in Chapter 2). Bronfenbrenner and Mayer (1960) and others have occasionally included a wealth variable, usually on *ad hoc* grounds, but poor data on wealth (especially quarterly data) have held activity down in this sector. There are, though, several empirical studies, two on British data by D. Fisher (1970, 1975), using money balances as the wealth proxy and one on US data by Butkiewicz (1979), using the monetary base and the real value of the public debt. Both studies turn up a significantly positive effect for real balances.

38. There are numerous studies following this line. The earliest, perhaps, was by Feige (1964). An interesting variation is by Klein and Murphy (1971) who calculate

$$i_m = \frac{C_0 - S}{D}$$

where C_0 are total operating costs attributed to demand deposits and S refers to service charge revenues.

39. See also Marwah (1976) for some problems attendant on using i_s as a proxy for the marginal return on M1 and M2. In a recent paper Carlson and Frew (1980) argue convincingly that the positive sign for i_m in $M = a + b_1 y + b_2 i_s + b_3 i_m$ may well be the result of the high degree of collinearity between i_s and i_m (since $i_m = (1 - H/M) i_s$) in the event that i_m is also correlated with M. Indeed, if i_s

has a negative elasticity with M, then i_m will have a positive elasticity, irrespective of its value as a proxy for the implicit services of money. The answer is to provide new information in either i_m or i_s as Darby does (1972).

40. Startz (1979) calculates implicit interest rates utilizing the Functional Cost Analysis Program of the Federal Reserve. The result is a rate which appears to be about half that which would result in the absence of prohibitions on interest payments. This appears to be due to the basic economic waste which is the result of the use of a barter system. In another paper, Frodin and Startz (1979) look at the effect on the demand for M1 of the NOW account experiment in New England. They find this effect producing as much as a 38 per cent increase in the individual demand (after removing the business demand). They use an implicit interest rate of zero on this test on account of some back-of-the-envelope calculations which reduce a measured implicit interest rate of 4.18 per cent on NOW accounts to no more than 0.5 per cent. The NOW interest rate was 5 per cent at this time. All of this has considerable policy significance in the United States as (in 1981) NOW accounts go nationwide.

41. Feige (1967) found a "permanent" interest rate (in the style of Friedman-Cagan) worked better than a simple interest rate (but its elasticity was still low); also, on the US data, Crouch (1971) found no evidence of a "normal" rate. In contrast, Courchene and Kelly (1971) found a normal rate on Canadian data, and D. Fisher (1973) found some success for an "error-learning" mechanism on British data. This last was in contrast to some work on the US data by Starleaf and Reimer (1967).

42. Eisner also dealt with a problem Pifer had in estimating for a trap with $i - i_{min}$ as the dependent variable. This specification, motivated by the thought that the aggregate stock of money is exogenous, provides a non-constant variance of the regression (*a priori*) from test to test since i_{min} is varied, and so a Box-and-Cox procedure was employed. We will return to the exogeneity question, below.

43. There exists empirical work on the 1930s in the United States - a period in which interest rates may well have been low enough to provide a direct test of the liquidity trap; we refer only to recent studies. A paper by Gandolfi and Lothian (1976) argued that the interest elasticity may well have decreased then and, in any event, was quite low during the Depression. A corroboration by Scadding also exists (1977).

44. With regard to the population deflation, again practice varies - and a small literature exists. We should note

again the general argument advanced in Chapter 1 which was that deflation by population would tend to remove a potential multi-collinearity between the constant term and the income term in a regression. Authors who have recently claimed that population deflation is important empirically include Laidler and Parkin (1970) who reworked a paper by D. Fisher (1968), claiming that the earlier results overstated the fit of the equation. Jacobs, though, claims that the two results are the same when allowance is made for the time trend. Jacobs also reworks a study for Norway by Syring (1966) to the same effect, as well as offering some similar conclusions for the dispute between Meltzer and M. Friedman (the latter deflated by population). Those papers are Meltzer (1963a) and M. Friedman (1959).

45. See Laidler (1977), Kavanagh and Walters (1966), and the "liquidity trap" papers of Pifer (1969) and Eisner (1971). Eisner claimed it actually made no difference which way it was estimated.

46. The empirical literature on simultaneous equations approaches is actually quite voluminous, and this brief statement is certainly not meant to do it justice. Demand for money functions (e.g. Goldfeld, 1973) are embedded in small- and large-scale econometric models, and certainly information about the function can be gleaned from these studies. We have referred to portfolio models of various sorts (see Feige and Pearce, 1977) and to tests with the linear expenditure system (see G. Fisher and McAleer, 1979) but have neglected one of the mainstream literatures which has worked on the problem by specifying a money supply function in addition to a money demand function. Teigen (1964) introduced this topic with the function

$$\frac{M}{M^*} = (i - i_d)$$

where M^* is the maximum money stock (based on actual reserves) and i_d is the (Federal Reserve's) discount rate. Gibson (1972) proposed a more general function

$$M^s = f(R, i, i_d)$$

and found a strong income response in the demand for money and a very short lag (such findings are rare); there was also an exchange in 1967 in *Econometrica* in Teigen's favour. The simultaneous equation approach has also been used by Spitzer (1977), who tied it to his general functional form approach (see above); Valentine (1977a), who worked with Australian data (finding that he did not need the supply side), and Wong (1977) who found "credit constraint" variables dominating the inflation rate in a number of underdeveloped countries (of course, in these cases there were no short-term interest rates available).

47. An increase in expected price variation may increase precautionary holdings (bad times are coming!) but at the same time decrease holdings of assets (e.g.) denominated in nominal terms. This is, therefore, an empirical question, at least when put this way. Eden (1976) argues that the appearance of the (expected) variance of inflation rather than the expected real rate of return on money, which should be used, actually biases the results. The latter is a broader concept which includes the variance of the rate of inflation. With regard to the coefficient of expectations itself, Khan, in several papers (1977a, 1977-b) has argued that individuals will adjust to inflation more rapidly at higher rates of inflation so that the coefficient of expectations (in Cagan's model) would itself vary positively with the rate of inflation (Cagan realized that this was a problem); Khan achieved some empirical success on several cases of rapid inflation. Klein (1977) used a "moving average deviation from a moving trend" to find a positive effect on M_d, while Blejer (1979), using an alternative measure, found a negative effect on some recent South American data (where variances are much larger than in the United States).

48. While M. Friedman and Schwartz (1963) could report in 1963 that no one had isolated an inflation effect, A. Shapiro (1973) found an influence on the US data. Shapiro's model was

$$\Delta M_t = a + \sum_{j=0}^{n} b_j y_{t-j} + \sum_{j=0}^{m} c_j i_{t-j} + \sum_{j=0}^{v} d_j \left(\frac{\Delta \dot{P}}{P}\right)_{t-j}$$

Here i is a nominal interest rate, and an Almon format was employed (all of the independent variables are thus "permanent" variables); indeed, the variance of inflation term $(\dot{P} = dP/dt)$ had a negative sign, when the effects were summed. Similarly, on the French data Melitz (1976) asked whether i or permanent prices worked better. Here inflation out-performed the interest rate in an economy in which inflation did not exceed 7 per cent per year; an earlier interpretation of the same data by Grandmont (1973), however, provides a direct contradiction to Melitz, from a more general dynamic model. On Norwegian data, Isachsen (1976) corrected two earlier studies by Syring (1966) and Teigen (1971) and introduced the rate of inflation, with a significantly negative coefficient. There were other adjustments, and two-stage and simulation experiments were produced. There was a suggestion of instability (but see the study by Klovland, 1978).

49. See Laidler (1977) and D. Fisher (1978).

50. Laumas has two further papers on stability (1977, 1979). In the first of these, business firms are examined and found to have an unstable demand for M1 while a broad measure, including liquid assets, is stable (with evidence of economies of scale). The estimation was by the varying parameter technique of Cooley and Prescott (1973), and when the same method was applied to the household demand for M1, in the second paper, this variable was again unstable while broader measures were not. There is another Laumas and Mehra paper on US annual data (1977), employing the same technique and again concluding that without lagged adjustment M1 and M2 have unstable demand functions (but otherwise they are generally stable).

51. A study by Enzler, Johnson, and Paulus (1976) showed that the demand for demand deposits was hard to estimate in the post-1973 period, and a parallel study by L. Meyer (1976) showed that the M1 function performed less well than M2 and M3 after 1970. Hamburger (1977) argues that the demand for money ought to be estimated in the context of a multi-dimensional portfolio framework (he opts for the addition of both an equity yield and a long-term rate). This adjustment appears to improve the stability of the demand for narrow money. More recently, Hafer and Hein (1979), using the Brown-Durbin-Evans test, report favourably on the question, concluding that long-term policy based on a stable demand for money will be better than has been recently claimed. They refer to the Enzler, Johnson, and Paulus study and to one by Goldfeld (1976). Hein (1980) also notes that dynamic forecasting methods may have produced the impression of a more or less continuous downward drift in the US demand for money when, in fact, there were only three major shifts (in 1974, 1975, and 1978); otherwise a standard M1 function forecasted successfully. Garcia and Pak (1979) have located the instability problem in the Goldfeld study as lying in the demand deposit equation and, in particular, in the business demand for demand deposits; they suggest including "immediately available funds" (overnight money in the federal funds market) in the definition to stabilize the function.

52. On the British data, involving the more rapid inflation of recent years, Hacche (1974) found evidence of the instability of the British demand for money which was subsequently contradicted by Artis and Lewis (1976) who em-

ployed the standard deviation of alternative returns and an own rate of return to achieve the stabilization. A more recent study by Rowan and J. Miller (1979) also finds stability (once the change in the financial structure in 1971 is accounted for) for a standard M1 function, with partial adjustment and an expected price deflator. A partly parallel test, using the Cooley-Prescott technique (see note 47) is by G. Laumas (1978) who also finds stability for M1 (around the 1971 data break).

On the Canadian data, Clinton (1973a) used an "own" rate of interest on data up to 1970 and found a narrow measure stable while a broad measure was not; this was reestimated and extended into the rapid inflation period (to 1975) by D. Foot (1977) to the same effect. With regard to price expectations, however, L. Smith and Winder (1971) found these to be significant in the earlier period, throwing some doubt on the Clinton and Foot models (since they did not include this variable). Rausser and P. Laumas (1976) used the Cooley-Prescott (1973) approach on the quarterly data to 1971 and found exactly the opposite result to that of Clinton. Using the Brown, Durbin, and Evans (1975) method of dealing with serial correlation in stability tests, Cameron (1976) finds the demand for narrow money to be "more stable" than that for broad money; there are also some structural breaks in some of the functions. Finally, Poloz (1979), also using the Brown, Durbin, and Evans methodology, found the demand for M1 to be stable (1952-77).

For the Australian data, Valentine (1977b) successfully incorporated a price expectations term in a recent test. Valentine also found that a measure of money which included "unused overdraft facilities" marginally improves the results. In a parallel paper Pagan (1977) takes issue with three unpublished Australian studies which claim instability. Again, price expectations are involved in the story.

For the Indian data, P. Laumas (1978), again using the Cooley-Prescott approach, finds both M1 and M2 stable. For the Norwegian data, Klovland (1978) uses a portfolio model on the stability question for the 1925-37 period; the demand for money function was widely believed to be unstable then, but Klovland could not confirm this. Indeed, the interest elasticity of the function actually declined in the 1930s.

53. Frodin and Startz (1979) looked at the effect of NOW accounts on the demand for money in New England and found, at most, a 10 per cent increase in the demand for money, spread out over time considerably. A NOW account is an

interest-bearing checking account. The NOW system went nationwide for banks and savings banks on 1 January 1981, and all sorts of dire predictions have been made, although the Frodin and Startz study is certainly not pessimistic (at least if estimating the demand for money is one's concern).

54. Actually, as an Australian study shows, when the underlying serial correlation is positive, the estimated lag tends to decrease with aggregation, and when it is negative, it increases with aggregation; this result was obtained on Australian by Ganjarerndee (1972).

55. Recent work by Cameron (1979) on the Canadian demand for money uses the Brown, Durbin, and Evans (1975) "recursive residuals" approach on Canadian data. This is, in effect, a temporal aggregation procedure designed to shed light on the stability question (see note 49).

56. Note, though, that (3.130) is the demand for money, while (3.133) shows the net effect of the consumption and investment functions as they operate through the demand for money (hence "quasi-reduced form"). Note that the positive effect of Y on M^* and the negative effect of i comes not from "transactions motive" or "opportunity cost" but solely from (3.131) and (3.133). α and β only modify these effects. The reader should also refer to a paper by Meyer and Neri (1975) who feel that the finance motive is important and justify their transactions approach in those terms. In a recent paper P. Smith (1979) criticizes this literature for lumping together the "transactions" and "finance" demand, where the latter is the credit required in the interval between planning and execution (Keynes, 1937). Smith suggests the function

$$M_d = \beta_1(i, Y) + \beta_2(i, Y^* - Y)$$

where Y^* is planned expenditure and Y is actual expenditure. Note that finance balances appear in both terms, with β_2 picking up "excess finance balances". There are no empirical results in this study.

57. We should also refer here to a literature on "compensating balances" in which the possibility is raised that firms are required by banks to hold larger balances than they would otherwise (in terms of their transactions demand), in return for other services (stand-by credit etc.). Narrowly, this is an attack on a purely transactions model, and Sprenkle (1969) says there is a problem, and Orr (1974) denies it. Broadly, in terms of this section, such considerations cast doubt on aggregations across individuals and businesses, since the former may escape

such pressures. It is not clear that the business firm cannot bargain away the constraint (so they do not pay for services they do not want), and this is provisionally confirmed by Campbell and Brendsel (1977) who find the constraint inoperative in the aggregate.

58. The demand for money figures in the monetary approach in the following sense. Define the balance of payments as

$$(X_g - M_g) + (X_s - M_s) + (X_m - M_m) \equiv 0$$

here g represents goods, s capital and m money; X is exports, and M is imports and all variables are in the flow dimension. Then, as Johnson (1977) argues, a faster growth of real income may actually tend to "improve" a country's balance of payments (given the money stock) by increasing the demand for money. In this event M may rise (or X_m fall), and thus equilibrium could reguire X_g and/or X_s to increase (this is called an "improvement" in the balance of payments literature).

59. There is a lot more to this topic than these brief notes can convey. The Girton and Roper paper has a summary of the literature and a bibliography, and Miles (1978) provides an empirical test for Canada (he found that foreign currency was a substitute for domestic currency in periods of floating rates). See also a paper by Sargen (1977) who also tests Canadian data (along with German and British data) to roughly the same effect as Gregory and McAleer.

60. See Girton and Roper (1980), Miles (1978), and, especially, Akhtar and Putnam (1980). The latter conduct a demand for money test on German data, using the variance of the spot rate to measure foreign exchange risk in a standard single equation demand for money. The term had a negative sign which was marginally significant.

61. Tower (1975) considers whether the exchange rate affects the demand for money and concludes that it depends on the income elasticity of the demand for money; thus, if the income elasticity is greater than 1, devaluation will tend to shift the demand downward (and vice versa). This result is not obtained from a general model and is not subjected to empirical tests and so is very provisional; even so, Tower concludes that the nominal demand for money may well depend on the interest rate and both nominal income and nominal expenditures.

4 The Production Function

4.1 INTRODUCTION

This chapter is somewhat different from those which have gone before primarily in paying a good deal more attention to the problems inherent in choosing specific functional forms to represent the production structure. We have, of course, discussed a number of particular functions elsewhere - the linear, the quadratic, the logarithmic, and even the CES - but the list of functions whose properties are well understood is more extensive than those just mentioned and, even for those just listed, detailed comparisons have not been made to this point. Normally, we might consider the study of production after we have studied investment, on the grounds that the latter is part of aggregate demand (two components of which we have already considered in Chapters 2 and 3) while the former is a key concept in aggregate supply. This procedure is not optimal in this study primarily because we use specific functional forms for the production function in our study of investment; that is, the production function (as it is studied here) is one input into an aggregate investment function. There are, of course, other inputs into the investment function - such as a specification of the cost of capital and of tax laws - which are also studied later. Of course, we do not mean to ignore the simultaneous equation nature of the production process either, so it is more a matter of logical order as designed in this study than a matter of principle. We should note, though, that all we have to say on the topic of "aggregate supply" is contained in Chapter 1.[1]

The study of production has a number of important direct and indirect implications of interest to the macro-theorist. We may be interested in the structure of aggregate production itself and that has to go down as our main interest, of course. In addition, we have noted that a production function is an input into the study of aggregate investment, and it is clear that the choice of specification of production influences the nature of the investment function. We have also noted that the study of functional form is more detailed in this literature and that this is an area which is of broad interest, beyond production studies. We have not noted, but it is nevertheless of considerable interest, that we normally take the aggregate production function as the link between the input markets (capital and labour) and the commodities markets (consumption, investment, and the demand for money) so that it has a key role in any generalization of the economy. Then, too, partly as a result of the specificity mentioned above, the aggregate production function serves as a basic input into macro-growth theory, at least if one wants to concentrate on issues concerning technical progress or of the effects of growth on the quantity and quality of the factors of production. Finally, we note that we can work on the topic of the functional distribution of income by means of a production specification since one can work back to the distribution of the proceeds of production from the production function itself; indeed, the choice of specific production functions (along with input assumptions) provides specific results for the macro-distribution problem.

There is another feature of the literature on the aggregate production function, and that is that it is transparently micro-economic in its orientation, and this fact makes this chapter a little unusual for a macro-study. For one thing, we will be looking at evidence which is often fairly disaggregated, and we will be using a methodology (profit-maximizing, for example) which may well seem micro-inspired. In view of this, we will also add some material to our discussion of aggregation in Chapter 1, focusing here on problems which are more specific to production studies. In particular, we will note a strong thread running through the literature which argues that the aggregation of micro-production functions is unsafe because the individual decision units have (for example) different capacity utilizations, different production techniques, or, even, different motives; in this event, it seems, we may have to study the "aggregate" function in a (somewhat) disaggregated context, the amount of disaggregation depending, of course, on the circumstances. Things may not be as bad as all that, of course, and it may be possible to work with a single (specialized) production function over some important data spaces; further, of course, much of the macroeconomic literature does not specialize the production function but instead merely assumes its existence, in effect ducking the question of aggregation which one must face when he turns to the data. This seems to leave the question of the aggregate function as an empirical matter while, at the same time, permitting us to undertake to produce theoretical results of broad interest from what are essentially "representative" technologies.

In the following pages we will present our results in a fairly standard way. In the remainder of this first section we will define our terms - mainly the production function itself and the elasticity of substitution. In Section 4.2, then, we will present results for the Cobb-Douglas (CD), constant elasticity of substitution (CES), and variable elasticity of substitution (VES) functions, deriving their basic properties and some results for the functional distribution of income in addition to describing some of the more compelling empirical results. In Section 4.3 we return to the aggregation problem in terms of a theorem on "weak separability" where the discussion is related to Section 4.2. In Section 4.4 we present a discussion of the flexible Translog (TL) production function and show some of the recent results for this general entry in the production function sweepstakes. We will also briefly discuss a growing literature on flexible functional forms at this point. In Section 4.5 we append some interesting proposals for including money in the production problem - or, for that matter, in the investment problem - without inserting it directly into the production function as an input in its own right.

4.1.1 DEFINITIONS

Generally speaking, when we specify a production function, we are interested in defining a formal link between inputs and final outputs. This link will provide specific parameters when the production function is specialized, but, of more immediate importance to a macro-theorist, it will give scope to the following areas of interest:

(a) the influence of technology on output;
(b) the determination of the shares of the proceeds of production going to the various factors (i.e. the determination of the functional distribution of income);
(c) the determination of the equilibrium (aggregate) prices and quantities of the various factors of production; and
(d) the aggregate supply function.

Indeed, when we specialize the production function, we will obtain specific answers to questions (a) and (b) which will differ, of course, depending on the specialization chosen. For (c) and (d), on the other hand, we are often less interested in particular functional forms and more likely to work with a general function.[2] Let us begin with a generalization before considering, in Sections 4.2 and 4.4, the four leading specializations (and some of their variations and implications).

The basic production model is as follows. Suppose that a vector of real aggregate output (x) is produced in equation (4.1), where the $V_i (i = 1, \ldots, k)$ are the k inputs (factors of production) to the production process, themselves measured in the appropriate real terms,

$$x = \phi(V_1, \ldots, V_k) \tag{4.1}$$

Let us assume the existence of an aggregate firm, then, whose objective is to maximize profits. Let profits be defined as in equation (4.2)

$$\pi = P_x x - \sum_{i=1}^{k} P_i V_i \tag{4.2}$$

where P is the price level of output (for the vector x), and the P_i are the factor prices. We will assume that all of the prices are given to the aggregate firm (i.e. we will assume that the aggregate firm is a price-taker). Substituting equation (4.1) directly into equation (4.2), we obtain equation (4.3).

$$\pi = P_x[\phi(V_1, \ldots, V_k)] - \sum_{i=1}^{k} P_i V_i \tag{4.3}$$

Here we would locate the maximum, for the choice variables, V_i, if the following set of maximizing conditions holds (this is, of course, a direct calculation).

$$\frac{\partial\phi}{\partial V_i} = \frac{P_i}{P_x} \qquad i = 1, \ldots, k \tag{4.4}$$

Each of these is the proposition that the marginal physical product of a factor is equal to the ratio of that factor price to the overall price level (the aggregate firm produces everything).

Note that we can now proceed directly to the empirical work on the production function by giving ϕ a specific functional form. That is, if ϕ were Cobb-Douglas, then we can readily compute $\partial\phi/\partial V_i$, and directly estimable equations will then result. (We would estimate (4.1) and (4.4) with suitable error terms attached.) This, indeed, describes much of the empirical work in the following sections as we move from simple to more and more complex (and usually more general) production functions. Of course, when we select a particular function, we carry along a set of general conditions (quasi-concavity, monotonicity) and a set of more specific conditions (e.g. homotheticity) which in principle any data that we approach should possess. Methods of screening the data for exceptions do exist and are discussed by (e.g.) Hanoch and Rothschild (1972) and more recently by Diewert and Parkan (1979). The latter design linear programming tests to determine if technologies are quasi-concave or concave, non-decreasing, and linear homogenous without recourse to specific functional forms (e.g. the Cobb-Douglas). These are referred to in the literature as "non-parametric" tests. Finally, and of some potential importance in future work, we should note that the use of an inputs-outputs approach, as discussed in the remainder of this chapter, is not our only strategy, and we could adopt a "characteristics" (inputs)-outputs approach in the event that the characteristics are less numerous and more homogeneous than the inputs. This approach, which has been suggested by Archibald and Rosenbluth (1978) has not been implemented although it obviously could help in the ongoing search for a stable aggregate function.

For purposes of discussion in this chapter we will consider functions in use in industry-wide (two-digit) studies as the least aggregate acceptable in a macroeconomic context. In addition, we will devote most of our attention to topics (a) and (b) in the list given above, with the former now requiring a further taxonomy (and some discussion) in order to make the following work comprehensible. In particular, when we discuss technical change, we will be interested in how it affects a specific production function (i.e. a specific technology) in four basic ways; these are [3]:

(1) the efficiency of the various technologies, where the efficiency is measured by the marginal product $\partial X/\partial V_i$;
(2) the "economies of scale" of the various technologies, where economies of scale are measured by the degree of homogeneity of the production function;
(3) the "factor intensity" of the various technologies, where factor intensity is measured by (e.g.) the capital-labour ratio; and
(4) the "elasticity of substitution" (σ) between any two inputs, where the elasticity of substitution is the proportionate increase in V_i/V_j associated with the

proportionate change in the marginal rate of substitution (MPP_{Vi}/MPP_{Vj}) between the two factors.

In the sections which follow, then, as we develop more and more complex production functions, we will refer to these topics.

Finally, let us provide several alternative formulas for the elasticity of substitution; here the partial derivative is used to remind the reader that more than two factors can be involved in the calculation.

$$\frac{\partial \log \frac{V_i}{V_j}}{\partial \log \left(\frac{MPP_{Vj}}{MPP_{Vi}}\right)} = \frac{\partial \log \frac{V_i}{V_j}}{\partial \log \left(\frac{P_{Vj}}{P_{Vi}}\right)} \tag{4.5}$$

Here the second form recognizes that in competitive equilibrium the ratios of the marginal physical products of factors to their relative prices are equal (that is, $MPP_{Vi}/P_{Vi} = MPP_{Vj}/P_{Vj}$).[4]

4.2 THREE PRODUCTION FUNCTIONS: CD, CES, VES

4.2.1 THE COBB-DOUGLAS PRODUCTION FUNCTION

Equation (4.6) represents a general statistical version of the Cobb-Douglas (CD) production function, where L and K now identify labour and capital inputs, and t is a time subscript.

$$x_t = AV^{\alpha}_{Lt}V^{\beta}_{Kt}e^{u_t} \tag{4.6}$$

This can be written and directly tested in a logarithmic form, in which case we have

$$\log x_t = \log A + \alpha \log V_{Lt} + \beta \log V_{Kt} + u_t \tag{4.7}$$

Indeed, it was estimated directly in an early Cobb-Douglas paper (1928).

Equation (4.7) has, among its properties, that it is homogeneous of degree $\alpha + \beta$. If we also assume that $\alpha + \beta = 1$ (i. e. that equation (4.7) is linear-homogeneous), we might test

$$\log \left(\frac{x_t}{V_{kt}}\right) = \log A + \alpha \log \left(\frac{V_{Lt}}{V_{Kt}}\right) + u_t \tag{4.8}$$

where the capital efficiency (x_t/V_{Kt}) of the technology is written as a linear function of its labour intensity (labour per unit of capital).[5] That is, for $\alpha > 0$, output per unit of capital will be higher if the amount of labour per unit of capital also rises. This, of course, occurs because the marginal product of labour $(= \alpha x/L)$ is always positive in this function for $\alpha > 0$.

The CD model, even in its constant returns to scale form $(\alpha + \beta = 1)$ has scope for a variable efficiency (x/V_i) or a variable factor intensity (V_j/V_i) although, as we have just pointed out, the relation between the two has a specific form (in equation (4.8)). In addition, it has the possibility of an easy extension to a multi-factor framework, simply by multiplying the new factors into equation (4.6), as seems relevant. Furthermore, there is the possibility of representing technical change in a number of ways:

(1) in A, as $A(t)$ for example, much in the fashion the constant in the consumption function was scaled up; or
(2) in an additional variable multiplied in such as $e^{\gamma t}$, where t represents (proxies) "disembodied" technological change and γ is a parameter.

As well, we can represent "embodied" technical progress in the sense of identifying the influence of a change in the quality of the inputs, in the form

$$V_{it} = V_{io}e^{\delta t}$$

Indeed, we can identify changes in both quality (δ) and quantity (r) in a factor in the form

$$V_{it} = V_{io}e^{(r + \delta)t}$$

But both of these expressions are explicitly dynamic, and the appropriate framework is one of (e.g.) "neoclassical growth" in view of the fact that r and δ are rates of growth.

Despite these considerable virtues, which relate to points (a) and (1), (2), (3) in the taxonomy we have laid out for this chapter, the CD model does not deal in a totally satisfying way with (b) or with (4) since the elasticity of substitution in the model is equal to unity, and the share going to each factor is constant.[6] Thus, retrieving our formula for the elasticity of substitution in the form

$$\sigma = d \log (V_K/V_L)/d \log (P_L/P_K) \tag{4.9}$$

we may employ the Cobb-Douglas model to find an exact expression for the numerator; this turns out to be equal to $d \log (P_L/P_K)$ so that in this case $\sigma = 1$, as asserted.[7] This result holds regardless of the values of α and β but is often disliked in the theoretical literature (and often rejected in the empirical literature in favour of $\sigma < 1$), and this has helped to spur interest in alternative specifications of the aggregate technology with more flexibility in this respect.

The next theoretical topic with regard to the CD function concerns the theory of the "functional" distribution of income implicit in this choice of functional form. A two-factor distribution is given by

$$1 = \frac{P_K V_K}{Y} + \frac{P_L V_L}{Y} = S_K + S_L$$

where Y is the nominal income split between the factors and the S_i are the percentage shares. At the optimum we have the condition from equation (4.4) that

$$\frac{\partial \phi}{\partial V_i} = \frac{P_i}{P_X}$$

We have also pointed out that for the CD function the marginal product $(\partial \phi / \partial V_L)$ of labour (e.g.) is $\alpha (X/V_L)$; these facts, along with the proposition that $Y = P_X X$, imply that

$$\frac{P_L V_L}{Y} = \frac{P_L (P_X \alpha X / P_L)}{Y} = \alpha$$

so that the elasticity (α) is equal to the share. Similarly, the share going to capital (see equation (4.6)) is β. This raises a logical problem when $\alpha + \beta \neq 1$, since, when $\alpha + \beta > 1$, the same principle implies an "overpayment" (which is impossible). Thus, the constant returns $(\alpha + \beta = 1)$ case is necessary at least if we wish to retain the assumption of a perfectly competitive equilibrium and if we wish to have a straight-forward aggregation.

Finally, let us note several results which frequently appear in the textbook literature and which have implications for the estimation of the CD model, as we shall see. We have a production function $X = AL^{\alpha}K^{\beta}$ and two marginal productivity conditions $\partial X/\partial L = W/P_X$ and $\partial X/\partial K = r/P_X$ where P_X is the product price. If we were to substitute the last two expressions into the production function (after calculating them), we would then obtain the associated *cost function* for the CD case.

$$C = r\left(\frac{\alpha + \beta}{\beta}\right)\left[\left(\frac{\beta W}{\alpha r}\right)\frac{x}{A}\right]^{1/(\alpha + \beta)} \tag{4.10}$$

By equating $\partial C/\partial x$ to P_x, we then can obtain the supply function (under competitive conditions) which we can write as

$$x = A^{\frac{1}{1-\alpha-\beta}}\left(\frac{\alpha}{W}\right)^{\frac{\alpha}{1-\alpha-\beta}}\left(\frac{\beta}{r}\right)^{\frac{\beta}{1-\alpha-\beta}}P_x^{\frac{\alpha+\beta}{1-\alpha-\beta}} \tag{4.11}$$

This function, in the event that we are speaking of the aggregate firm, is then the aggregate supply function, although no parameters from the labour supply function are present. It is infinitely elastic if $\alpha + \beta = 1$, the constant returns case.[8]

The CD function has done surprisingly well in a variety of empirical contexts, compared even to the "flexible functional form" TL model (see below). There are numerous surveys of this literature available[9], so we will content ourselves here with some rather general comments on what appear to be basic papers; there will also be a number of empirical notes scattered at later points in this chapter, as direct comparisons between functional forms become possible. The basic test, of course, is the direct one of equation (4.6); indeed, a term for technical progress $e^{\gamma t}$ is often added in as well. A direct variation which is also popular is given as equation (4.12).

$$\log \frac{x_t}{V_{kt}} = \log A + (\alpha + \beta - 1)\log V_{kt} + \alpha \log \frac{V_{Lt}}{V_{Kt}} + u_t \tag{4.12}$$

This permits the constancy of returns to scale to be an open question.

There are also other direct estimates of the CD function, for example by Bodkin and Klein (1967) using linear and nonlinear (because of additive errors) single and simultaneous equations models. This battery of tests was on the US time series data, 1909 - 49, with real private non-farm GNP as the "output variable".[10] The results, which included a trend variable, were in unconstrained and constrained ($\alpha + \beta = 1$) forms. In the unconstrained form Bodkin and Klein always obtained increasing returns to scale ($\alpha + \beta$ ranged from 1.202 to 1.465, the latter estimate coming from a simultaneeous/non-linear version).[11]

The problem of simultaneity in the production model has also received considerable attention in the literature. In an important early paper, Marschak and Andrews (1944) followed the framework laid out in equations (4.1) and (4.4) and proposed that each of these expressions be written in logarithmic form with an error term attached so that we have (for the two input case),

$$\log x_i - \alpha \log L_i - \beta \log K_i = \log A + u_{1i} \tag{4.13}$$

$$\log x_i - \log L_i = \log (WR_1/\rho\alpha) + u_{2i} \tag{4.14}$$

$$\log x_i - \log K_i = \log (rR_2/\rho\beta) + u_{3i} \tag{4.15}$$

Here we have included terms R_1 and R_2, as suggested by Hoch (1958), in order to capture the possibility that the aggregate firm does not achieve its optimum (does not, because of institutional constraints, etc., satisfy the first-order conditions exactly). Note that the index i represents the data space (say two-digit industries or a time series) and the u_{ji} are random errors attached by the econometrician to represent (a) for u_{2i}, u_{3i} failures to adjust the inputs properly and (b) for u_{1i} failure to exploit the technology fully (and luck). The latter implies that we should set up the problem not as the deterministic one of maximizing profits since the stochastic element here will certainly be known to exist by the (aggregate) firm.[12]

There are also a number of important cross-sectional CD studies in the literature. In one instance there is a study by Hildebrand and Liu (1965) who abandoned the assumption of perfect competition generally employed and worked in a disaggregated (fifteen sector) cross-section context for the 1957 US data. They find returns to scale increasing in most cases (and a significant "technology-output elasticity" in all cases). Similarly Griliches (1967b) looked at the 1958 US Census of Manufacturing with a CD function with measures of capital and labour quality as in

$$x = A(LZ_1)^{\alpha}(KZ_2)^{\beta}e^{u} \tag{4.16}$$

where Z_1 is the quality variable for labour and Z_2 the quality variable for capital. By means of ordinary least squares Griliches found capital and labour coefficients consistent with the long-run shares data, but with increasing returns to scale. The quality of labour variables (e.g. education expenditures by state) were significant with the expected signs. Griliches also tested to see if a CES function might be preferable and concluded against that function.[13]

4.2.2 THE CES PRODUCTION FUNCTION

Among the properties of the CD production function are the unitary elasticity of substitution and the associated constancy of the relative shares of the factors of production. The former is an unlikely property for disaggregated data, as we shall see, and the latter is certainly implausible over cyclical data (although it may be satisfactory over some long runs of data); indeed, on the cyclical data both a counter-cyclical and a cyclical pattern have been claimed to represent the behaviour of the share of labour. To modify the CD function, Arrow *et al.* (1961) proposed a constant elasticity of substitution (CES) production function of the general form of equation (4.17)

$$x = A(\alpha L^{-\rho} + \beta K^{-\rho})^{-1/\rho} \quad (4.17)$$

which has a constant, but not necessarily unitary elasticity of substitution, and a non-constant distribution of income among the factors of production. It also contains the CD function as a special case. Let us investigate its properties in the more general form of equation (4.18).

$$x = A[\alpha L^{-\rho} + \beta K^{-\rho}]^{-\varepsilon/\rho} \quad (4.18)$$

Equation (4.18) has five parameters (A, α, β, ρ, and ε) while the equivalent CD has three. Here A represents the total efficiency of production; α and β represent the distribution or intensity in the sense of attributing to each factor its contribution to output (and we can, of course, take $\beta = 1 - \alpha$); ε is the degree of homogeneity (reflecting returns to scale) which is often taken to be unitary in theoretical exercises using the function; and ρ represents the elasticity of substitution (the elasticity of substitution (σ) is $1/(1 + \rho)$). Then, to demonstrate the economies of scale of the function, let both factors change by λ in equation (4.18) such that

$$x(\lambda) = A[\alpha\lambda^{-\rho}L^{-\rho} + \beta\lambda^{-\rho}K^{-\rho}]^{-\varepsilon/\rho}$$

Factoring out λ, we obtain

$$x(\lambda) = \lambda^{\varepsilon}A[\alpha L^{-\rho} + \beta K^{-\rho}]^{-\varepsilon/\rho}$$

showing that, indeed, the CES function has homogeneity of

degree ε.

Because we need the marginal products of the CES function for both theoretical and empirical purposes in this section, we will calculate these directly from equation (4.18). Thus

$$\frac{\partial x}{\partial L} = \alpha\varepsilon A^{1 - (\frac{\rho + \varepsilon}{\varepsilon})} \left(\frac{x^{\frac{\rho + \varepsilon}{\varepsilon}}}{L^{1 + \rho}}\right) \tag{4.19}$$

and for capital we have

$$\frac{\partial x}{\partial K} = \beta\varepsilon A^{1 - (\frac{\rho + \varepsilon}{\varepsilon})} \left(\frac{x^{\frac{\rho + \varepsilon}{\varepsilon}}}{K^{1 + \rho}}\right) \tag{4.20}$$

which clearly differ only by the distribution parameters α and β. Thus for A, α, and β positive, these functions are positive as one might desire for a neoclassical production function. Differentiating a second time by the input, we see that the resulting functions are negative so that we also have diminishing marginal productivity, again as a neoclassical framework would seem to require.

The next step is to deduce the (constant) elasticity of substitution for this model. Using the first version of the definition in equation (4.5), we have

$$\sigma = \frac{d\ \ell og\ (\frac{K}{L})}{d\ \ell og\ (\frac{MPP_L}{MPP_K})} = \frac{d\ \ell og\ \frac{K}{L}}{\frac{\alpha}{\beta}\ d\ \ell og\ (\frac{K^{1 + \rho}}{L^{1 + \rho}})}$$

$$= \frac{d\ \ell og\ \frac{K}{L}}{(1 + \rho)\ d\ \ell og\ \frac{K}{L}} = \frac{1}{1 + \rho} \tag{4.21}$$

This is the formula we noted above, and it provides the link between the CD and the CES models. Thus, for $\rho = 0$ and $\varepsilon = 1$ we have $\sigma = 1$ (which was our result for the CD function), and the expressions for the marginal products collapse (in the limit) into the form of those given for the CD function. For $\rho = \infty$, the function collapses to the "fixed coefficients" production function.

The parameter A in the CES model performs the same function (that of identifying "total factor" productivity) in the CES function as it does in the CD and need not be discussed further here. On the other hand, the distribution parameters α and β have become important in both theoretical and empirical work, and so we will continue on this topic. Recalling that the CD model had a constant distribution of income, we now inquire into that relation for the CES; our distribution formulas, under competitive conditions (when the entire output (= X here) is distributed to the factors), are

$$S_L = (MPP_L)\frac{L}{X}$$

$$S_K = (MPP_K)\frac{K}{X}$$

and combined with the expressions taken from the CES model, this produces the relation

$$\frac{S_L}{S_K} = \frac{\alpha}{\beta}\left(\frac{K}{L}\right)^{\rho} \tag{4.22}$$

Here the relative shares functions is seen to be a nonlinear function of the capital-labour ratio (it is, though, linear in the logs). Note that if $\rho = 0$ (and thus $\sigma = 1$), the relative distribution is again a constant (= β/α) as in the CD case. In general, then, a rise in the capital-labour ratio, for $\rho > 0$ (and therefore $\sigma < 1$), will imply an increase in the relative share of labour (on account of the relatively rapid fall of the marginal productivity of capital). Note, especially, that $\rho > 0$ is not inevitable, although it may well be the most likely aggregate result on the basis of an empirical literature which has most frequently found $\sigma < 1$.[14] We should also note, with reference to this discussion of distribution and to that both above (for the CD) and below (for the VES and TL), that linking the distribution of income to technology in this (neoclassical) way requires both that the aggregate technology chosen be realistic and that (e.g.) the marginal product of capital be a unique inverse function of the capital-labour ratio. Neither condition is entirely reasonable, it seems, and we must also consider important the failure to establish a unique aggregate function and "reswitching". For this, see Harris (1973), Harcourt (1969), and the literature cited there. It is not intended, in this survey, to discuss the "reswitching" problem, but the question of a stable aggregation of a consistent technology is the subject of further discussion in Section 4.3.

Our next topic concerns the empirical record for the CES function by itself and as an alternative to the CD function.[15] The original paper by Arrow *et al.* was accompanied by a set of tests for the CES model for twenty-four three-digit industries over a sample of nineteen countries. The working assumption, clearly, is that the production function is the same across countries, an heroic assumption, to say the least. The test was of equation (4.19), the marginal product of labour (with $\varepsilon = 1$); this was in the form

$$\log \frac{X}{L} = \log A + \sigma \log w + u \tag{4.23}$$

in which $\partial X/\partial L = w$ was employed. This test provided a direct estimate of σ which turned out to be significantly less than unity in fourteen cases and was never significantly greater than unity. But the assumption of a common technology is not appropriate across countries (some of which are "low wage" relatively) especially in view of the different stages of development across the sample, and Fuchs (1963), merely by introducing a dummy for developed versus underdeveloped countries, found that the estimate of σ was actually significantly different from unity in only one case, when it was significantly greater than unity. This result, consequently, favoured the constant-returns CD production function, in effect (recall, also, that $\varepsilon = 1$ in these tests).

Bodkin and Klein (1967), in a paper which we have already referred to in connection with the CD function, also tested the CES function (in single and simultaneous equation models and in a non-linear form) on US time series data. They, too, found the elasticity of substitution (σ) to be less than unity (although considerable imprecision and generally poor Durbin-Watson tests did not permit them to reject the CD model unequivocally). We noted above a paper by Coen and Hickman (1970) which used a production-function constraint in a direct test of an investment demand and a labour demand function. On Swedish time series data, Bergström and Melander (1979) turned the problem around using a CES production function. That is, they derived factor demand functions of

$$\left(\frac{K}{X}\right)^* = \delta^{\sigma}\gamma^{-(1-\sigma)}e^{-(1-\sigma)z_1 t}(P_K^*)^{-\sigma} \tag{4.24}$$

$$\left(\frac{L}{X}\right)^* = (1-\delta)^{\sigma}\gamma^{-(1-\sigma)}e^{-(1-\sigma)z_2 t}(P_L^*)^{-\sigma} \tag{4.25}$$

from a CES production function. To get desired (*) values, they assumed partial adjustment and then estimated (by FIML) these functions with the appropriate constraints (implied by the common production function). This enables identification of the parameters of the production function. The test produced significant coefficients for the aggregate CES function, although OLS and FIML estimates were not significantly different from each other. The CES function was one with embodied technical change,

$$x^* = \gamma[\delta(e^{z_1 t}K^*)^{-\rho} + (1 - \delta)(e^{z_2 t}L^*)^{-\rho}]^{-1/\rho} \quad (4.26)$$

with $\rho = (1 - \sigma)/\sigma$. The elasticity of substitution was less than unity in this test (on Swedish data).

Turning to single equation studies or comparisons, Ferguson (1965) looked at a sample of nineteen two-digit US manufacturing industries, for the 1949-61 period, and found three cases in which σ was significantly less than unity and four cases in which it was significantly greater than unity.[16] This mixed result does not necessarily run against an aggregate CD function, but it does certainly suggest that formation of an aggregate from a set of micro-CD functions may not be possible (generally they must all be CD, as we shall see). The CES function was also tested by Hildebrand and Liu (1965) in comparison with the CD function, and they reported that the CD was not necessarily inferior although the assumption of constant returns to scale does not appear to work particularly well. In another paper, Zarembka (1970) pointed out that the failure to adjust for differences in labour quality from industry to industry (or state to state, since industries are not spread evenly over the United States) could produce heteroscedasticity (and hence inefficiency) since most of the tests described so far have used the wage term as an independent variable. When Zarembka corrected the wage data for differences in earning power, as measured by the education level in the state, he found that apparent differences in production functions across states and even over time (1957-8) tended to disappear. In his battery of tests in only rare instances was the elasticity of substitution significantly different from unity (generally lower). He pronounced in favour of the CD production function. This work was extended in a paper by Zarembka and Chernicoff (1971), to the same effect.[17]

There are really numerous studies of the elasticity of substitution, and activity in this sector continues. The consensus of comments runs toward an elasticity less than unity on time series and perhaps near unity on cross-sections, but recent work (1972 +) has succeeded in boosting the time series estimate to unity (usually). Arrow *et al.* noted that their procedure for estimating σ is actually biased upward because of the effect of an admitted difference in efficiency (as represented by the parameter A in equation (4.18)) between countries using the same (assumed) production technology.[18] We have noted Zarembka's claim that differences in labour quality bias the estimates downward and Fuch's that ignoring different stages of development (whatever the cause) does likewise; similarly, Schydlowsky and Syrquin (1972), testing for the influence of differences in exchange rates, found the Arrow test downward biased.[19] In the note, there are detailed a number of other important studies, some on US, some on non-US data usually, but not always, contradicting the CES model (in favour of the CD).[20] Several surveys are especially worth mentioning here; two are by Jorgenson (1972, 1973) who concludes that the evidence just cited, and a lot more, implies that the CD form is supported by the research to 1972 at least. The second is by Berndt (1976), who remarks on the disparity of results - and notes how sensitive the estimation seems to be to both model choice and method of estimation. In his case - on the US time series data - a new data set for capital and a two-stage least squares method of estimation produced results slightly in excess of unity, results which did not depend on the model choice.[21] Again, one can accept the CD model on this evidence, and we offer that as a provisional judgment with respect to the studies we have seen.

The foregoing CES (and CD) functions are homothetic or homogeneous and carry the implication in the two-input problem that the capital-labour ratio depends only on the relative factor price ratio (see equation (4.23)) or, alternatively, only on the marginal rate of substitution. This is almost certainly not adequate for time series tests over cycles, and so R. Sato (1977) has developed some material on non-homothetic CES and CD functions which, of course, treat the latter as special cases. The non-homothetic versions are

$$F(K, L, x) = C_1(x)K^{-\rho} + C_2(x)L^{-\rho} - 1 = 0 \qquad (4.27)$$

for the elasticity of substitution (ρ) $\neq 1$ (i.e. for the CES function) and

$$F(K, L, x) = C_1(x) \log K + C_2(x) \log L - 1 \qquad (4.28)$$

in the event that $\sigma = 1$ (i.e. for the CD function). In equation (4.27), $\rho = (1 - \sigma)/\sigma$. More importantly, the marginal rate of substitution between capital and labour now depends both on the capital-labour ratio and on the output level (so that we are not restricted to a linear expansion path). Furthermore, it is also worth noting that the distribution of income now depends on the substitution parameter and on the level of output. For the distribution of income, we have that

$$\frac{S_L}{S_K} = (\frac{K}{L})^{1/\sigma - 1} C(x) \tag{4.29}$$

This result has an empirical dimension (Sato employs a "non-homotheticity parameter" which he finds to be non-zero for a majority of US two-digit industries), but of possibly more macro-interest, it has the possibility of providing a more realistic description of (e.g.) the share of labour (we found the CD and CES generally too rigid). In particular, if the capital-labour ratio falls, as it may well do during a cyclical expansion, then labour's share can rise or fall depending either on the sign of σ and on the sign of the "non-homotheticity parameter" or on K/L. This can be seen in the following derivatives calculated from equation (4.29)

$$\frac{\partial(S_L/S_K)}{\partial(K/L)} = (\frac{1}{\sigma} - 1)(\frac{K}{L})^{1/\sigma - 2} C(x) \tag{4.30}$$

$$\frac{\partial(S_L/S_K)}{\partial x} = (\frac{K}{L})^{1/\sigma - 1} C'(x) \tag{4.31}$$

$C'(x)$ is the "non-homotheticity" parameter (since it measures the curvature of the expansion path); it was generally negative in Sato's empirical work.[22]

4.2.3 VARIABLE ELASTICITY OF SUBSTITUTION (VES) PRODUCTION FUNCTIONS

It is a natural extension of the foregoing to permit the elasticity of substitution to vary over the data space, especially in view of the evidence already presented with regard to the CES function that this parameter may well vary from industry to industry and (possibly) over time. The potential number of interesting VES functions is large, however, although only a few have gained acceptability; one of the limitations has been the empirical track record. The latter, as one might expect from our discussion to this point, is very provisional and inconclusive, though.

We can approach the VES production function either as a generalization of the CD production function or of the CES function. A particularly interesting version of the VES function, obtained in effect from the CD, is due to Revankar (1971) although a similar model appears in R. Sato and Hoffman (1968); here we reproduce the Revankar model as in equation (4.32).

$$x = AK^{\gamma(1 - \delta\rho)}[L + (\rho - 1)K]^{\gamma\delta\rho} \tag{4.32}$$

Here, if $\rho = 1$, we obtain

$$x = AK^{\gamma(1 - \delta)}L^{\gamma\delta}$$

which is CD and is constant returns CD for $\gamma = 1$. Note that some restrictions have to be placed on the values of the parameters in order to ensure that the neoclassical properties exist (non-negative marginal products and diminishing marginal productivity).[23]

For later use, as before, we need the expressions for the marginal products of labour and of capital. For the former, we obtain (4.33) directly from equation (4.32).

$$\frac{\partial x}{\partial L} = \gamma\delta\rho\frac{x}{L + (\rho - 1)K} \tag{4.33}$$

Similarly,

$$\frac{\partial x}{\partial K} = \gamma(1 - \delta\rho)\frac{x}{K} + \gamma\delta\rho(\rho - 1)\frac{x}{L + (\rho - 1)K} \tag{4.34}$$

a complicated expression, unfortunately. Note, then, the role of the restrictions (in note 23) in keeping this function within the neoclassical framework.

We may arrange an empirical confrontation for this model as follows (we discuss this now because this will help to make clear the nature of the model). If we assume $\gamma = 1$ (i.e. assume constant returns to scale) and a competitive solution in factor and product markets, then we may equate each factor's marginal product to the ratio of that factor's price to the product price (as in equation (4.4)); this yields

$$\delta\rho\frac{x}{L^*} = \frac{P_L}{P_x} \tag{4.35}$$

$$(1 - \delta\rho)\frac{x}{K} + \delta\rho(\rho - 1)\frac{x}{L^*} = \frac{P_K}{P_x} \tag{4.36}$$

where $L^* = L + (\rho - 1)K$. This exercise provides two equations in x, K, L at the optimum and can be dealt with (for example) by dividing (4.36) by (4.35). In this event we have

$$\frac{L}{K} = G_0 + G_1\frac{r}{w} \tag{4.37}$$

where $r = P_K/P_x$ is the real rate of return on capital and w

$= P_L/P_X$ is the real wage. Here

$$G_0 = \frac{1 - \rho}{1 - \delta\rho}$$

and

$$G_1 = \frac{\delta\rho}{1 - \delta\rho}$$

and are restricted in the values they can take if the neo-classical properties are to hold, as described in note 23.[24] In any event, in the Revankar form of the VES function, the output - labour (and capital - labour) ratio is a function of both the real wage and the real rate of return on capital; this is one way of expressing the generalization over the CES function, since the latter has X/L depending only on w (and X/K on r) and the dependence is log-linear.[25]

Turning now to the variable elasticity of substitution, we may derive its function as follows. The marginal rate of substitution of capital for labour is calculated by dividing the (negative of) the marginal product of labour by the marginal product of capital; using equations (4.33) and (4.34), this yields

$$MRS_{\frac{K}{L}} = \frac{\rho - 1}{1 - \delta\rho} + \frac{1 - \delta\rho}{\delta\rho}\left(\frac{L}{K}\right)$$

and since

$$\sigma = \frac{\frac{K}{L}d\frac{L}{K}}{\frac{1}{MRS}dMRS}$$

is an alternative form for the elasticity of substitution, we have, for the Revankar-VES function

$$\sigma = \sigma(K, L) = 1 + \frac{\rho - 1}{1 - \sigma\rho}\left(\frac{K}{L}\right) \qquad (4.38)$$

This is a linear function of K/L around an intercept of unity; for $\rho = 1$ we have that $\sigma = 1$ (as Revankar reported for five of twelve industries studied in his 1957 cross-section US data).

For the distribution of income in the Revankar-VES model, if we assume constant returns to scale, we can proceed as follows. Equations (4.35) and (4.36) represent the competitive solution in factor markets; dividing (4.36) by (4.35), we obtain

$$\frac{L}{K} = \frac{1 - \rho}{1 - \delta\rho} + \frac{\delta\rho}{1 - \delta\rho}\frac{r}{w}$$

for $r = P_K/P_X$ and $w = P_L/P_X$ as before. Since by definition

$$\frac{S_L}{S_K} = \frac{MP_L}{MP_K}\left(\frac{L}{K}\right) = \frac{wL}{wK}$$

we directly have that

$$\frac{S_L}{S_K} = \frac{1 - \rho}{1 - \delta\rho}\frac{w}{r} + \frac{\delta\rho}{1 - \delta\rho} \tag{4.39}$$

a linear function of the w/r ratio.[26] This relation, under the popular (but not necessarily correct) wage-lag hypothesis, would (as for the CES) show a contra-cyclical behaviour for the relative share of labour. If there really is a wage lag and the share of labour actually moves pro-cyclically, then the VES model is falsified, for $\rho \geq 1$ and $\delta\rho \geq 1$ (as we have assumed to meet the conditions of the general neoclassical production model). But in any event, one can hardly claim a major advance in this area for the Revankar-VES model, in comparison to the CES.[27]

We mentioned above that there are several VES functions in the literature, and at this point we should describe some of them, although we will not exhibit as much information on their properties as we just did with the Revankar model; we follow Revankar's outline. An early generalization of the CES function is due to Hildebrand and Liu (1965) and Bruno (1962) and is given as equation (4.40).

$$X = A[(1 - \delta)K^{\eta} + \delta K^{m\eta}L^{(1 - m)\eta}]^{1/\eta} \tag{4.40}$$

This function has a variable elasticity of substitution given as

$$\sigma = \frac{1}{1 - \eta + \frac{m\eta}{S_K}}$$

where S_K is the share of capital. This model has two interesting properties, but, even so, the model has not been widely employed in either empirical or theoretical studies; these properties are that (1) S_K (and hence S_L) appear explicitly in the formula for the elasticity of substitution, and that (2) an implication of the model is that

$$\log \frac{X}{L} = h_0 + h_1 \log W + h_2 \log \frac{K}{L}$$

which is easily approached econometrically (and can be compared readily with the comparable equation for the CES, which was given as equation (4.23)). Note that for $m = 0$, the Hildebrand-Liu VES function reduces to the CES.

A version of the VES model which is also not widely employed is due to Halter, Carter, and Hocking (1957); this is

$$X = Ae^{\beta_1 K + \beta_2 L} K^{1 - \alpha} L^{\alpha}$$

which has as its elasticity of substitution the rather complicated expression

$$\sigma = \frac{(1 - \alpha + \beta_1 K)(\alpha + \beta_2 L)}{(1 - \alpha)(\alpha + \beta_2 L)^2 + \alpha(1 - \alpha + \beta_1 K)^2} \qquad (4.41)$$

Equation (4.41) reduces to the CD for $\beta_1 = \beta_2 = 0$. Another variation on the CD is known as the "constant marginal share" (CMS) production function of Bruno (1968); this is

$$X = AK^{\alpha}L^{1 - \alpha} - mL \qquad (4.42)$$

and it reduces to the CD for $m = 0$. Note that the elasticity of substitution for equation (4.42) is

$$\sigma = 1 - \left(\frac{m\alpha}{1 - \alpha}\right)\frac{L}{X}$$

which, of course, is unity for $m = 0$. Finally, another generalization of the CD model, but one which is in much greater use, is due to Lovell (1968, 1973b); this is

$$X = Ae^{\beta K/L} K^{1 - \alpha} L^{\alpha} \qquad (4.43)$$

which reduces to the constant-returns CD for $\beta = 0$. Here we need the restriction that $\alpha/\beta \geq K/L$ to keep the marginal product of labour non-negative; the function's variable elasticity of substitution is

$$\sigma = \frac{(\beta\frac{K}{L} + 1 - \alpha)(\alpha - \beta\frac{K}{L})}{(\beta\frac{K}{L} + 1 - \alpha)(\alpha - \beta\frac{K}{L}) - \beta\frac{K}{L}} \qquad (4.44)$$

which is, actually, merely a function of K/L.[28]

The VES has an interesting empirical record although there are some problems in direct tests of the model (depending on which form one uses). Revankar (1971), as noted, tests his VES function on 1957 US Census of Manufacturing data; on this data set he found five of twelve two-digit industries having $\sigma < 1$ (and meeting the requirements of the VES form) which has the implication from equation (4.36) that σ decreases with the capital-labour ratio (i.e. as an industry gets more capital intensive, it shows a decline in the elasticity of substitution between capital and labour - and this is certainly not an unreasonable finding). But, of course, seven of the twelve are not VES, a fact which is not particularly promising in the aggregate. There is also a series of tests performed by Sato and Hoffman (1968) using the Revankar model, with some variations on both US and Japanese data. They find that the share of national income going to labour does (especially in the Japanese case) depend on the capital - labour ratio, as is implied in the derivation of equation (4.37); this is a non-CD result as are some of their other tests on the (trend-dominated) time series. Ramsey and Zarembka (1971) perform a series of "specification error tests" on the 1957 US data and find that the CES performs better, with $\sigma > 1$. The specification errors tested for were for omitted variables, incorrect functional form, simultaneous equations problems, heteroscedasticity, and non-normality.

A comparison of the CD, the CES, the Revankar/Sato-Hoffman and Lovell models was made by Harvey in two papers (1975, 1977) directed mostly at statistical problems rather than at problems of modelling macro-technology. Harvey points out that the CD and the CES functions are nested, which leads to an easy comparison, but the CES and the VES are not, and this creates interesting econometric problems; furthermore, the VES function of Lovell (equation (4.43)) is actually a version of the Revankar/Sato-Hoffman models. Perhaps on this account Lovell actually tests, in a follow-up paper (1973a) to his original one, a three-variable VES function more in the spirit of the Sato-Hoffman model[29]:

$$X = \gamma[(1 + \beta)KL^{\beta}M^{\delta} + \alpha L^{1 + \beta}M^{\delta}]^{1/(1 + \beta + \delta)} \qquad (4.45)$$

M, of course, is simply any other factor (it does not figure in his tests). Lovell actually does a full-scale comparison of the VES, CD, and CES functions for seventeen US industries at the two-digit level. He found that the CD function could not be refuted in seven industries but that in ten industries a result of $\sigma > 1$ implied the rejection of the CD model. In those ten industries five were CES and one was

VES, while the winner for four industries could not be determined. In Lovell's words (p. 719),

> The primary conclusion to be drawn from this study is that we simply do not live in a CD world; nor do we live in a CES world or a VES world, for that matter. Different industries have different technological characteristics and require different production functions to portray their behavior accurately.

This, again, may be a pessimistic conclusion for macroanalysis since it was on the two-digit level, with the next step up being the ultimate aggregation (i.e. an across-industry aggregation); of course, one may still get a CD "approximately" at the macro-level. There are other empirical papers providing such comparisons.[30]

4.2.4 TECHNICAL PROGRESS IN PRODUCTION STUDIES

Generally speaking, theoretical work on technical progress (in production studies) has concentrated on establishing benchmark cases ("neutralities") while empirical work has concentrated more on the question of the style of technological change, which is usually, but not always, found to be labour-saving (at least in two-factor studies). The usual neutralities considered are Harrod, Solow, and Hicks, and they are formally defined as follows (in, e.g., Phelps, 1966, or D. Ott, A. Ott, and Yoo, 1975).

> *Harrod Neutrality*: Technical progress is Harrod-neutral if and only if, for a given X/K, when the average product of capital is constant, so too is the marginal product of capital.

Indeed, the shares are also constant. A theorem by Uzawa (1961), further, establishes that it is necessary and sufficient, for Harrod-neutrality, that the aggregate production function be of the form

$$\phi(K, L; t) = F[K, A(t)L] \tag{4.46}$$

which defines "purely labour-autmenting" technical change. If so, there exists a steady-state capital-labour ratio.

> *Solow Neutrality*: Technical progress is Solow-neutral if and only if, for a given X/L, when the average product of labour is constant, so too is the marginal product of labour.

Again, distributive shares are constant. It is, then, necessary and sufficient, for Solow neutrality, that the aggregate production function be of the form

$$\phi(K, L; t) = F[A(t)K, L] \tag{4.47}$$

which defines "purely capital-augmenting" technical change. In this case, though, no steady-state capital - labour ratio exists (it diminishes), and so no "golden path" (best consumption path - see Phelps, 1966) exists.

> *Hicks Neutrality*: Technical progress is Hicks-neutral if and only if, at a given K/L, when K/L is constant, the average and marginal product of capital increase at the same rate.

Here, too, distributive shares are constant. In other words, when the marginal rate of technical substitution of capital for labour decreases, technological change is "capital-using" etc. A production function which satisfies Hicks neutrality is

$$\phi(K, L; t) = F[A(t)K_0, A(t)L_0] = A(t)F(K, L) \tag{4.48}$$

With regard to specific functional forms, a number of results exist. To begin with, the CD production function has constant shares (and a unitary elasticity of substitution), and so it would seem to be a natural case to use to explore (empirically) the differences between the three neutralities. Indeed, the three neutralities co-exist (for a particular K/L and t) if and only if the elasticity of substitution is unitary (if and only if the aggregate production function is CD). This would pose an almost intractable empirical problem in the event that one wished to find out which neutrality has ruled in practice.

A CES production function does permit some leverage on the problem. If technical progress is labour saving, then under *Hicks* non-neutrality this can be identified (for a given K/L and t) with reference to a value of $\sigma > 1$. If technical progress is labour saving, then under *Harrod* non-neutrality this can be identified (for a given K/L, t) when capital's share is rising. If technical progress is labour saving, then, under *Solow* non-neutrality this can be identified (for a given K/L, t) when labour's share is rising. If, then, both kinds of augmentation exist and $\sigma > 1$ (as many believe), then technical progress is both capital saving (in Harrod's sense) and labour saving (in Solow's sense). Of course, if $\sigma = 1$, the CES degenerates to the CD and if (for all K/L, t) aggregate production is CD, then all three neutralities hold.

To illustrate, assume a constant returns CES production function of

$$x = \gamma[\delta K^{-\rho} + (1 - \delta)L^{-\rho}]^{-1/\rho} \tag{4.49}$$

If technical change affects only γ, then, from above, we have that

$$\frac{r}{w} = \frac{\delta}{1 - \delta}\left(\frac{L}{K}\right)^{1 + \rho} \tag{4.50}$$

Thus constancy of L/K implies constancy of r/w and hence of distributive shares; this is a Hicks-neutral result. We may, then, define Harrod neutrality (for $L^* = e^{at}L$) and Solow neutrality (for $K^* = e^{bt}K$). Empirical tests can then be constructed, in the event that $\sigma \neq 1$.

In the VES model, the elasticity of substitution is the variable

$$\sigma = \sigma(K, L) = 1 + \frac{\rho - 1}{1 - \delta\rho}\frac{K}{L} \tag{4.51}$$

in which case

$$\frac{L}{K} = \frac{1 - \rho}{1 - \delta\rho} + \frac{\delta\rho}{1 - \delta\rho}\frac{r}{w} \tag{4.52}$$

This is two equations in two unknowns (σ and K/L), and so the study of neutrality theorems is particularly complicated in the event of the VES. It is obvious, though, that constancy of L/K - as in Hicks neutrality - implies constancy of σ, which is a degenerate case of the VES.

Many of the empirical studies referred to above shed light on questions of technical change. In one such, Bergström and Melander (1979) find labour-saving technical change in Swedish industry using a two-factor CES function in aggregate and (slightly) disaggregated form. A study by Ringstad (1978), when compared to an earlier study (by Griliches and Ringstad, 1971), showed labour-saving technical change on Norwegian data. The first study found $\sigma = 1$ and the second $\sigma > 1$. For the US, Brown and de Cani (1963) found epochs of labour-saving or labour-using technological change (using a CES production function), while a recent study by May and Denny (1979) utilizes the TL function in rejecting Hicks neutrality in favour of factor (capital and labour) augmented growth (in a three-factor model which included materials). Their data were 1957-70. Again for the US data, using the R. Sato (1970) model of

$$Q(t) = F[Ae^{\lambda_L t} L(t), Be^{\lambda_K T} K(t)] \tag{4.53}$$

which permits Hicks, Harrod, and Solow neutrality, Kalt (1978) found labour-saving technical change using a CES production function (for $\sigma < 1$). Kalt presents a summary of previous studies which generally favours either Hicks-neutral (e.g. Arrow *et al.*, 1961, and Kendrick and Sato, 1963) or factor augmenting (e.g. Brown and de Cani, 1963, or R. Sato, 1970) technical change. Of course, we should note that much of this work is contradicted by other studies which find $\sigma = 1$, as noted above.

4.3 WEAK SEPARABILITY AND THE AGGREGATE PRODUCTION FUNCTION

In Chapter 1 we focused attention on the various problems of aggregation, with special emphasis on (a) aggregation over commodities, where the composite goods theorem was invoked; (b) aggregation over demand functions, where considerations of a statistical nature were emphasized; and (c), in Chapter 3, aggregation over financial commodities, where questions of the underlying macro-research strategy were considered. In fact, in many ways the most basic (and most pessimistic) literature is yet to be considered, that on the necessary and sufficient conditions for the existence of a specific aggregate production function. We note, again, that the whole question can be ducked - albeit at a cost - if one does not wish to create micro-foundations for macro-constructs. We also note that this material is merely the production function version of the "composite goods" approach, with a unique literature here primarily because of the tendency to specialize the production function. It is of broader interest, of course, as we drift toward comparable specializations of the other basic macroeconomic functions.

The unique interest in the production function emanates not from any special bias toward production studies in the aggregation literature but from three stylized facts:

(a) the production function is intermediate between inputs and outputs, and so aggregation at three levels (and, of course, over time) must be undertaken;
(b) economists seem more willing to specialize the production function, leading to the possibility of more precise results for specific representations of the

micro-technology; and

(c) considerable use of precise functional forms for the production function is made on macro-questions concerning labour and capital markets and on the functional distribution of income.

Consider equation (4.54) as our point of departure for the production function version of this literature.

$$x_i = \phi_{ij}(K_k, L_l) \tag{4.54}$$

Here we can conceive of the aggregation problem as being worked over three distinct stages:

(1) the replacement of each of K_k and L_l with composites representing the stock of capital and the stock of labour;
(2) the aggregation across j technologies (whether speialized or not) representing the way outputs are produced by different firms/industries; and
(3) the construction of an aggregate output (over i), itself required because different technologies are (assumed to be) producing more than one good at a time.

The last mentioned, of course, would be achieved with reference to the composite goods theorem provided that the aggregations over j, k, l had been carried out previously (and so will not further be discussed here).

In addition to the purely theoretical problems just alluded to, there are further aggregative issues which arise. If we visualize equation (4.54) as a structural equation in a specialized form (e.g. CD), then we should tack on an error term to describe all factors omitted by the specific hypothesis in hand. The working set of assumptions, then, is that all firms

(a) face the same function;
(b) exploit their opportunities equally efficiently; and
(c) desire and succeed in maximizing their profits thereby, regardless of industry, firm identity, location, or size.[31]

Thus, for example, even within an industry a firm which is slow to react, "satisfices", faces excess capacity, faces financial constraints which its rivals do not, is subject to locational advantages or disadvantages in comparison with its rivals, or is possessed of unusual market power in any of the factor or product markets in which it deals[32], will not aggregate successfully with the other (dissimilar) firms even within its industry. These matters seem serious enough in view of the results of a vast literature in industrial organization which seems to believe in them, but, even so, we should also note that we have not yet considered the problems of construction of K, L, ϕ from K_k, L_L, and ϕ_j, the basic topic of this section.

The general conditions for a safe aggregation over the inputs available to the jth firm are as follows. If the inputs in the production function

$$x_j = \phi_j(K_{1j}, \ldots, K_{mj}, L_{1j}, \ldots, L_{nj}) \tag{4.55}$$

can be grouped and written as

$$\begin{aligned} K_j &= \gamma_j(K_{1j}, K_{2j}, \ldots, K_{mj}) \\ L_j &= \delta_j(L_{1j}, L_{2j}, \ldots, L_{nj}) \end{aligned} \tag{4.56}$$

where the elements of γ are independent of those in δ and vice versa, then this condition of "strong separability" provides a necessary and sufficient condition for an aggregate production function of the alternative forms given in equation (4.57).

$$\begin{aligned} X_j &= \phi_j[\gamma_j(K_1, K_2, \ldots, K_m), \delta_j(L_1, L_2, \ldots, L_n)] \\ &= \phi_j(K_j + L_j) = \phi_j(V_j) \end{aligned} \tag{4.57}$$

Note, again, that all of the elements of (4.57) are firm-specific, and so a remaining aggregation is still required.[33]

Alternatively, a more general condition is available - and it produces a more general production function. In particular, if (4.55) can be grouped and written as (4.56), then if the marginal rate of substitution between any pair of elements in γ_j is independent of any of the elements in δ_j and vice versa, then this condition of "weak separability" is necessary and sufficient for the existence of an aggregate production function in the form of equation (4.58); note, again, that this is an aggregation of the firm's inputs and we have yet to aggregate over the firms in the industry and across industries.

$$X_j = F_j(K_j, L_j) \tag{4.58}$$

Let us seek to prove part of this proposition in order to demonstrate its implications.[34]

Consider the function given as equation (4.57), and, for the moment, let us drop the firm notation (the index j). Formally, the theorem states that a necessary and sufficient condition for equation (4.55) to appear as equation (4.58), where K and L can be written in the form of equation (4.58), is that

$$\frac{\dfrac{\partial\phi}{\partial K_i}}{\dfrac{\partial\phi}{\partial K_j}} = \phi_{ij}(K_i, K_j) \qquad i, j = 1, \ldots, m \tag{4.59}$$

and that

$$\frac{\dfrac{\partial\phi}{\partial L_i}}{\dfrac{\partial\phi}{\partial L_j}} = \phi_{ij}(L_i, L_j) \qquad i, j = 1, \ldots, n \tag{4.60}$$

Let us consider the details of the proof of necessity, leaving the rather complicated proof of sufficiency as outside the scope of this study (see the presentation by H.A.J. Green, 1964, pp. 13-15).

The conditions in equations (4.59) and (4.60) imply that

$$\begin{aligned} d\phi &= \sum_{i=1}^{m} \frac{\partial\phi}{\partial K_i} dK_i + \sum_{j=1}^{n} \frac{\partial\phi}{\partial L_j} dL_j \equiv dF \\ &= \frac{\partial F}{\partial K} dK + \frac{\partial F}{\partial L} dL \end{aligned} \tag{4.61}$$

i.e. that the total derivative of the micro-functions is identical to that of the macro-function (we are assuming that the aggregate exists as specified in the theorem and showing that conditions (1) and (2) are necessary). Furthermore, and more to the point, the theorem implies that

$$d\phi = \sum_{i=1}^{m} \frac{\partial F}{\partial K} \frac{\partial K}{\partial K_i} dK_i + \sum_{j=1}^{n} \frac{\partial F}{\partial L} \frac{\partial L}{\partial L_j} dL_j \tag{4.62}$$

i.e. that if the aggregate exists, then the contribution of each micro-factor to the aggregate factor $(\partial K/\partial K_i)$ along with the contribution of each macro factor to the macro-output $(\partial F/\partial K)$ sums to the aggregate (and hence micro-) output effect, when taken over both (all) factors. Looking at K, for example, we have from (4.61) and (4.60) that

$$\frac{\partial \phi}{\partial K_1} = \frac{\partial F}{\partial K}\frac{\partial K}{\partial K_1}$$

and

$$\frac{\partial \phi}{\partial K_2} = \frac{\partial F}{\partial K}\frac{\partial K}{\partial K_2}$$

whence

$$\frac{\dfrac{\partial \phi}{\partial K_1}}{\dfrac{\partial \phi}{\partial K_2}} = \frac{\dfrac{\partial K}{\partial K_1}}{\dfrac{\partial K}{\partial K_2}}$$

Since K is a function only of the variables $K_1, \ldots, K_m$, then the same must be true of its partial derivatives or of the ratios of its partial derivatives. It then follows, as we sought to show, that if the theorem holds it is necessary that equations (4.59) and (4.60) also hold.[35]

We have, to this point, established the importance of weak separability in the construction of consistent indices of a reasonably general sort[36]; it remains to show what this means in the case of specific functional forms for the input functions (γ, δ) and the output function (ϕ), itself taken across firms in the industry. Generally, the functions must be linear and linear-homogeneous (or, equivalently, isoquants must be identical for all units in the aggregation and expansion paths must be straight lines through the origin) for an aggregation to go through. Since a simple additive production (or input) function can be one such, further interest attaches to the CD, CES, etc. functions, used either for the input or output functions, as things stand. The first thing to note is that the CD and CES functions do have a constant returns (linear-homogeneous) case, and both can be written in a form which is linear in the logs of K and L, and so in these cases a consistent aggregation is possible. Note how this discussion dovetails with that in Chapter 1 where we considered the construction of an aggregate spending function from micro- (but linear) spending functions. Finally, let us set up the details of the CD aggregation across firms. If

$$x_i = A_i L_i^{\alpha 1} K_i^{\beta 1} \qquad i = 1, \ldots, n$$

and if

$$\log x = \frac{1}{n} \sum_{i=i}^{n} \log x_i$$

$$\log A = \frac{1}{n} \sum_{i=1}^{n} \log A_i$$

and if

$$\alpha = \frac{\Sigma\alpha_i \log L_i}{\Sigma \log L_i}$$

$$\beta = \frac{\Sigma\beta_i \log K_i}{\Sigma \log K_i}$$

then

$$\log x = \log A + \alpha \log L + \beta \log K \qquad (4.63)$$

would be a consistent aggregation for the CD case. The CES function can be written in a log-linear form and has a linear-homogeneous version, so it, too, has an aggregative case.[37] We will not discuss aggregation for the VES models here but will make some brief notes for the TL function in Section 4.4.

4.4 THE TRANS-LOG PRODUCTION FUNCTION

Another generalization of the CD production function is the Trans-log (for transcendental-logarithmic) production function (TL). This is often written as

$$\log x = \log \alpha_0 + \sum_{i=1}^{n} \alpha_i \log V_i + \alpha A \log A$$

$$+ \frac{1}{2} \sum_{i=1}^{n} \sum_{j=1}^{n} \gamma_{ij} \log V_i \log V_j$$

$$+ \sum_{i=1}^{n} \gamma_{iA} \log V_i \log A + \frac{1}{2}\gamma_{AA}(\log A)^2 \qquad (4.64)$$

where A is the efficiency parameter and the V_i are inputs. A somewhat simpler version of equation (4.64) is provided by Humphrey and Moroney (1975); this will be the basis of the discussion in this section.

$$\log x = \log \alpha_0 + \sum_{i=1}^{n} \alpha_i \log V_i$$

$$+ \frac{1}{2} \sum_{i=1}^{n} \sum_{j=1}^{n} \gamma_{ij} \log V_i \log V_j \qquad (4.65)$$

Note that this form results from dropping the terms involving A in equation (4.64). As seen in the note, this function can provide weak separability under certain conditions.[38]

The version of the TL function appearing in equation (4.65) clearly collapses to the CD for all of the substitution terms $\gamma_{ij} = 0$ or for all of the sums in the last term equal to zero; it is linear-homogeneous for $\Sigma\, \alpha_i = 1$ in this event. Turning to the marginal products of a three-factor TL production function, we have that

$$\frac{\partial x}{\partial L} = \frac{x}{L}(\alpha_L + \sum_{j=1}^{3} \gamma_{Lj} \log V_j) \qquad (4.66)$$

$$\frac{\partial x}{\partial K} = \frac{x}{K}(\alpha_K + \sum_{j=1}^{3} \gamma_{Kj} \log V_j) \qquad (4.67)$$

$$\frac{\partial x}{\partial M} = \frac{x}{M}(\alpha_M + \sum_{j=1}^{3} \gamma_{Mj} \log V_j) \qquad (4.68)$$

where M is any other factor and L and K denote labour and capital. Note that in the calculation of these terms we assumed for convenience that $\gamma_{ij} = \gamma_{ji}$ - i.e. we assumed symmetry of the matrix of substitution terms. One property of (4.66) to (4.68) is that they could be negative, especially in the event that the γ_{ij} are negative, and so, to avoid negative marginal products (and a violation of the neoclassical assumptions), we would have to impose a restriction. Similarly, another restriction is necessary, if we wish to hold to the neoclassical case, since the second derivative of these expressions could be positive.[39]

We may derive the distributive shares for the TL model as follows. In the economic region of our problem we must have equations (4.66), (4.67), and (4.68) strictly positive. Writing those expressions as elasticities (transposing X/V_j), we obtain

$$\frac{\partial x}{\partial V_i}\frac{V_i}{x} = \frac{\partial \log x}{\partial \log V_i} = \alpha_i + \sum_{j=1}^{3} \gamma_{ij} \log V_j > 0 \qquad (4.69)$$

for $i, j = 1, \ldots, 3$. If we assume that all markets are competitive, we have that

$$\frac{\partial x}{\partial V_i} = \frac{P_i}{P_x} \qquad (4.70)$$

which we may compare directly with the first part of equation (4.69) to show that

$$S_i = \frac{P_i V_i}{P_x} = \alpha_i + \sum_{j=1}^{3} \gamma_{ij} \log V_j > 0 \qquad (4.71)$$

which provides a directly testable expression for shares in terms of the substitution terms as well as an implied restriction that each of these shares must be positive (under the assumption that the function is to meet the neoclassical restriction of positive marginal products). Furthermore, as we can see, these expressions for shares are seen to depend on the quantities of the factors (in a specific way) and are, of course, non-constant functions. Note that equation (4.71) reduces to the CD result for all $\gamma_{ij} = 1$ or $\Sigma\gamma_{ij} = 0$, as one might have anticipated.

The main early test of the TL is offered by Berndt and Christensen (1973a); there a comparison on a time series of US manufacturing firms (1929-68) between CD, CES, Sato (1963) and Uzawa (1962) CES functions, and the Trans-log is carried out. The TL is declared the winner in general, and the various estimates of σ between the three inputs (labour, structures, and equipment) were generally above unity and variable on these data. Humphrey and Moroney (1975) also test the TL function in the same basic way on United States two-digit industries for 1963. They find for "product groups", positive values for σ usually in excess of unity (capital, labour, and resources are the three inputs), except for capital and labour in two (of seven) cases and capital and resources in one. They find, though, that if resources are not an important item in any sector, the TL function does not appear to work well (in that sector); otherwise, it does. Turning to studies of aggregation in the TL model, Berndt and Christensen (1974) test for consistency of an aggregation of labour inputs in US manufacturing using a TL technology. Arguing that the literature tends to focus on (admittedly) non-homogeneous capital, Berndt and Christensen test (in effect) earlier propositions by Griliches (1969) and Welch (1970) that skilled labour is more complementary with capital than is unskilled labour. Their results imply that this is the case (the TL does not constrain the solution) and run against successful aggregation even of the labour input. In a separate paper they reject capital aggregation (1973b).[40]

There is, as well, a literature using the TL cost function.[41] Berndt and Wood (1975) test the TL cost model with four inputs (K, L, Materials, and Energy) on the US manufacturing data for 1947 - 71 and find that energy is a substitute for most other factors but is actually a complement for capital; so, too, do Hudson and Jorgenson (1974).[42] Fuss (1977), on Canadian data, used a TL cost function approach with the same four variables; he finds moderate substitution between energy and the other inputs but at the same time substantial interfuel substitution (so that energy price increases are not transmitted to product prices). Then, Griffin and Gregory (1976)(see note 41) look at pooled international data (to avoid time series problems) using the TL cost model; they were particularly concerned with the possibility that the complementarity observed by Berndt and Wood and Hudson and Jorgenson was actually merely a short-run response, incorrectly interpreted as a long-run result in a model which could not discern with the annual US manufacturing whether or not the working assumption of long-run equilibrium is appropriate. In a nutshell, Griffin and Gregory report long-run substitution between energy and capital. They also note that their model is not CD in the three inputs (they did not deal with materials on account of data limitations) and found the elasticity of substitution between capital and labour less than unity; with two inputs the model was CD. These results are, of course, quite tentative, but they do point to an important reason why earlier CD, CES, etc. studies often came up with different results for σ_{KL}. That is, to be explicit, the influence of omitted but relevant variables (inputs or their prices) results in biases in the actual empirical studies.

In recent years even further generalizations of the flexible production structure have appeared, and it is interesting to conclude with reference to some of these. A basic paper is by Berndt and Khaled (1979) who employ a non-neutral

Box-and-Cox cost function in which the TL cost function is one among a number of special cases.[43] The model is rather complicated and appears as equation (4.72)

$$C = [1 + \lambda G(P)]^{1/\lambda} X^{\beta(X,\ P)} \tag{4.72}$$

where

$$G(P) \equiv \alpha_0 + \sum_i \alpha_i P_i(\lambda) + \frac{1}{2}\sum_{ij}\sum \gamma_{ij} P_i(\lambda) P_j(\lambda)$$

and

$$\beta(X,\ P) = \beta + \frac{\theta}{2} \log X + \sum_i \phi_i \log P_i$$

and where the functions $P_i(\lambda)$ contain the Box-and-Cox specification. The TL is produced when one takes the limit of (4.72) - after certain restrictions - as $\lambda \to 0$. Berndt and Khaled apply their model to US manufacturing data and reject homotheticity and constant returns to scale (they are increasing!). They also reject the TL model (but not the generalized Leontief). They did not locate any strong overall "energy price" effects, although, to be sure, their data were 1947-71.[44] We turn to some work on a fifth productive input (money).

4.5 MONEY AND THE PRODUCTION FUNCTION[45]

In Chapter 3 we referred to some empirical work in which money was directly inserted into the production function; the rationale used there was that money saved time in the hiring of inputs. One can easily quarrel with this rationale, since the direct insertion of money into a production function - even a highly aggregative production function - in this way runs up against a strong prejudice in the profession against assuming that money has a direct productivity. Part of this prejudice stems from a reluctance to treat the producer in the same way as the consumer; in particular, the consumer has a preference relation (into which it is often "permissible" to insert money directly[46]) and generally no technology, while the producer has a technology (often a very specific technology), an objective, but no preferences. Putting money directly into the utility function does not seem to tie one's hands (at least if all one is doing is working out results in a general equilibrium framework) while inserting it into the production function (the technology) does, in the sense that money is thereby held to be directly productive rather than just to be an aid in the productive process (to be quite vague). In Bernstein's words (1978, p. 247)

> The problem, then, is the following: without using a corporate preference function and without making money a factor of production, how can money meaningfully enter the decision process of the firm (in ways other than just by affecting costs)? . . . The answer to this question lies in the realization that, although money is not a factor of production, it is "productive".

We are, then, advised to put money into the constraints, and the following approaches represent a fair cross-section of how economists have contrived to do this, to date; we begin, though, with the "direct productivity" theory, such as it is.

Bailey (1971, p. 54) argued that "whether or not [real] cash balances help determine consumption, they assuredly are a factor of production". The implication, thus, of writing

$$x = \phi(L, m)$$

is that the marginal product of labour derived from that function, and consequently the demand for labour, also depend on real money balances (m). So, too, would aggregate supply. Mundell (1971) in a parallel study wrote

$$x = \phi(K_f, m_f)$$

for firms and gave the household a parallel function

$$\gamma = \gamma(K_h, m_h)$$

where γ defines "liquidity services". But Mundell offered no reason for this (and did not derive demand functions for m_f or m_h).

To begin with the indirect approaches to the problem, let us consider some work by Fischer (1974) and by Claasen (1975). Assume that the firm has a production function represented by

$$x = \phi(K, L_p) \tag{4.73}$$

where L_p is labour services used in production. Assume, also, that there is labour used in transactions (purchasing inputs, etc) - denoted by L_T - and for L = total labour, that we have

$$L_p + L_T = L \tag{4.74}$$

In this event, we may characterize this approach as one which provides a rationale for business cash balances in terms of their "indirect productivity".[47] The relation between L_T and the number of transactions can be assumed to be

$$n = \beta L_T \tag{4.75}$$

Further, average cash balances are assumed to be equal to the flow of net revenues (R) per transaction (n) as in equation (4.76).

$$\overline{M} = \frac{R}{n} \tag{4.76}$$

This means that $\overline{M} = R(\beta L_T)^{-1}$, using (4.69) and (4.70), whence we obtain the aggregate production function implicit in this approach (given as equation (4.77)).

$$x = \phi[K, L - (\frac{\overline{M}}{R})^{-1}] \tag{4.77}$$

This general form could be estimated in the various ways already discussed in the literature. But note, especially, that while money is in the function, it is not there as a factor in its own right. It was the specialization of the transactions process in (4.75) and (4.76) which accounts for this result.[48]

A further generalization of the basic model is possible, following the work of Lange (1936), Gabor and Pearce (1958), Vickers (1970), and Turnovsky (1970). Here we generalize the inventory model of equation (4.76) in a more interesting way as equation (4.78).

$$\overline{M} = g(K, L) \tag{4.78}$$

We can refer to this as a "money requirements" function similar in intent to the quantity equation often used for consumers (as discussed briefly in Chapter 3). This, in turn, means we can retain our production function in its general form as

$$x = \phi(K, L) \tag{4.79}$$

which implies, in effect, that there are two "production type" constraints. To see how this differs from the Fischer-Claasen case, consider a profit-maximizing firm; such a firm can be assumed to maximize the following

$$L^* = p\phi(K, L) - w_k K - w_L L - w_m\overline{M} - \lambda[g(K, L) - \overline{M}] \qquad (4.80)$$

which can be compared to the direct profit function which would arise if equations (4.73) to (4.77) were the basic model:

$$\pi = p\phi[K, L - (\beta\frac{\overline{M}}{R})^{-1}] - w_L L - w_k K - w_m\frac{\overline{M}}{R} \qquad (4.81)$$

To see the comparison more fully, consider the first order conditions for (4.80):

$$\frac{\partial L^*}{\partial K} = p\phi_1 - w_k - \lambda g_1 = 0$$

$$\frac{\partial L^*}{\partial L} = p\phi_2 - w_L - \lambda g_2 = 0$$

$$\frac{\partial L^*}{\partial K} = -w_m + \lambda = 0$$

$$\frac{\partial L^*}{\partial \lambda} = -g(K,L) + \overline{M} = 0$$

For equation (4.81), on the other hand, we would have, e.g.

$$\frac{\partial \pi}{\partial L} = p\phi_2 - w_L = 0$$

The difference, clearly, is embodied in λ (which, at the optimum = w_m) which is the marginal (and average) cost of money. Note, in particular, that this model avoids placing money in the production function, even in solution (as in equation (4.81)), by setting down a parallel constraint.

Bernstein also considers a further generalization of the model just described which is based on a transactions cost function of

$$C_t = T_c(K, L, \overline{M}, \overline{B}) \qquad (4.82)$$

where both bond and money holdings are considered. This is based on work by Saving (1972) as modified by Dutton, Gramm, and J. McDonald (1974). Here a money requirements function in the form of

$$\overline{M} = g\ (K, L, \overline{B})$$

is employed. The difference between the two formulations is

not in the appearance of a bond (Bernstein actually puts the bond in equation (4.78), above) but in the general transactions costs function (T_c) in which increased money holdings decrease transactions costs at the optimum (rather than *a priori*). This is, consequently, a significant generalization of the other models. It, too, avoids putting money in the production function directly or indirectly, for that matter.

Most of the foregoing has not been subjected to empirical work, and so on this important issue much remains to be done. There is some empirical work, as discussed briefly in Chapter 3, and some of this uses the methodology (and the models) stressed earlier in this chapter. In particular, Sinai and Stokes (1972) used a CD production function in the following forms

$$x_t = AK_t^{\alpha}L_t^{\beta}m_{t-1}^{\gamma}e^{u_t} \qquad (4.83)$$

and

$$x_t = AK_t^{\alpha}L_t^{\beta}m_{t-1}^{\gamma}e^{\delta t}e^{u_t} \qquad (4.84)$$

where the latter expression includes technical progress in the expression $e^{\delta t}$. Sinai and Stokes obtained strong results for the money stock, and some British results actually obtained strong and essentially nonsensical parameters; the problems had to do with misspecification not only of the dynamics but also of the simultaneous equations sort (as described in earlier sections of this chapter). A further study by Boyes and Kavanaugh (1979) uses the same data as Sinai and Stokes; they find that a two-factor CES model exhibits specification error (five types were tested for) while the same model extended to include money does not.[49]

A natural way to proceed, then, is to use the simultaneous approach recommended in equations (4.13) to (4.15) - or some variant; this is how Short (1979) proceeded.[50] Thus, for the CD model, adopt equations (4.84) and (4.85), where the latter is a set of three necessary conditions for a three input problem ($V_i = K, L, M/P$).

$$P_i = \left(\frac{\partial x}{\partial V_i}\right)P_x \qquad (4.85)$$

Alternatively, Short uses side conditions of

$$\frac{\partial x}{\partial V_i} = \frac{x}{V_i}\left(\alpha_i + \sum_j \gamma_{ij} \log V_j\right) \qquad i = 1, \ldots, 3 \qquad (4.86)$$

to obtain a parallel structural model and a more general

(because it contains the CD function) TL production function of

$$\log x = \log \alpha_0 + \beta T + \sum_{i=1}^{3} \alpha_i \log V_i$$

$$+ \frac{1}{2} \sum_{i=1}^{3} \sum_{j=1}^{3} \gamma_{ij} \log V_i \log V_j \tag{4.87}$$

This is nice work, although it does not tackle the more fundamental questions with which we started this section; that is, evidence of a significant effect from M/P does not tell us whether to put real balances in the constraints or into the technology, but it does tell us that there is an effect, via both the TL and CD technology. We should note, though, that the estimated coefficients are small and are not different for different measures of moneyness (M1, M2, M3) or different production functions (CD, TL).

A partly parallel study using the TL approach on a four-factor problem is by Dennis and V.K. Smith (1978). They distinguish between productive and non-productive labour to make up their four factors and invoke duality in order to justify the use of the following Trans-log cost function.

$$\log C = \alpha_0 + \alpha_Q \log Q + \frac{1}{2}\alpha_{QQ} (\log Q)^2 + \sum_{i=1}^{4} \beta_i \log P_i$$

$$+ \frac{1}{2} \sum_{i=1}^{4} \sum_{j=1}^{4} \gamma_{ij} \log P_i \log P_j$$

$$+ \sum_{i=1}^{4} \theta_i \log P_i \log Q \tag{4.88}$$

The restrictions are that $\sum_i \beta_i = 1$, $\sum_i \theta_i = 0$, and $\sum_i \gamma_{ij} = \sum_j \gamma_{ij}$ $= \sum\sum_{ij} \gamma_{ij} = 0$, and the application of duality implies that all but α_Q and α_{QQ} can be derived from estimates of the cost shares equations (suitably restricted):

$$\frac{P_i X_i}{C} = \beta_i + \sum_{j=1}^{4} \gamma_{ji} \log P_j + Q_i \log Q \tag{4.89}$$

Over a set of eleven industries, Dennis and Smith rejected the hypothesis of linear separability of the inputs so that, in effect, real money balances must be included in each of the input demand functions (and in the production function). Note that real money balances appear as an opportunity "cost" - in the form of a Treasury Bill rate - and that no direct measure of the return on moneyness was employed.

NOTES

1. The reader is reminded that this is the first of a two-volume survey of macroeconomic theory and policy. The discussion of aggregate supply and of aggregate labour markets is contained, arbitrarily, in the policy volume.
2. A useful survey of the theoretical issues associated with choosing specific functional forms is by Fuss, McFadden, and Mundlak (1978).
3. These topics are identified by Brown (1967).
4. Consider the general production function $\phi(K, L)$ which, along any iso-product curve is defined by $\phi(K, L) = c$. Differentiating, we obtain

$$\phi_K dK + \phi_L dL = 0$$

which gives us

$$\frac{dK}{dL} = -\frac{\phi_L}{\phi_K}$$

where the ϕ_i are the marginal physical products. The negative of this expression is called the marginal rate of substitution. We may measure the elasticity of substitution, here, by calculating the ratio of the percentage changes, as we did directly, for equation (4.5).
5. To obtain equation (4.8), we can substitute $\alpha + \beta = 1$ into (4.6) to obtain

$$x_t = AV_{Lt}^{\alpha}V_{Kt}^{1-\alpha}e^{u_t}$$

or

$$\frac{x_t}{V_{Kt}} = A\left(\frac{V_{Lt}}{V_{Kt}}\right)^{\alpha}e^{u_t}$$

6. There is some sentiment, bolstered by a long-defunct statistical regularity on British data known as "Bowley's Law" that the shares are constant in the long run; at

least in the short run this constancy is not a matter of record.

7. The marginal productivity condition for the profit-maximizing aggregate firm is, at the optimum:

$$\frac{\partial \phi}{\partial V_i} = \frac{P_i}{P}$$

This, for the 2-factor CD, is

$$\alpha \frac{x}{V_L} = \frac{P_L}{P}$$

and

$$\beta \frac{x}{V_K} = \frac{P_K}{P}$$

In this event

$$\frac{V_K}{V_L} = \left(\frac{\beta}{\alpha}\right)\left(\frac{P_L}{P_K}\right)$$

and taking logs we have

$$\log \frac{V_K}{V_L} = \log \frac{\beta}{\alpha} + \log \frac{P_L}{P_K}$$

Then, since log (β/α) is constant, we have $d \log V_K/V_L = d \log P_L/P_K$ as asserted.

8. See the discussion in Walters (1963). The cost function in this case is derived from the solution of

(a) $x = \phi(L, K)$
(b) $C = wL + rK$
(c) $0 = g(L, K)$

where (a) is the production function, (b) is the total cost *equation*, and (c) is the expansion path (along which first- and second-order conditions for a maximum are met). The system is three equations in four unknowns and may contain a solution in the form

$$C = h(x)$$

which is the cost function referred to in the text.

9. Briefness is also justified here and below in terms of the large number of textbook summaries of the CD, CES, and VES functions. See Heathfield (1971, 1976), Bridge (1971), Cramer (1969), and Wallis (1973).
10. In the same paper some empirical tests of the CES function were conducted, as we shall report below. The original functions, of course, are intrinsically non-linear, and so a non-linear method is adopted and compared to the familiar log-linear approach; non-linearity also results from the application of restrictions on coefficients which appear in more than one structural equation. The simultaneity arises from the setting up of a cost-minimizing framework with the production function appearing as a constraint. The structure thus has two stochastic equations

$$\text{(a)} \qquad x_t = A10^{\lambda t} L_t^{\alpha} K_t^{\beta} + u_t$$

$$\text{(b)} \qquad \frac{P_{Kt}}{W_t} = \frac{\beta L_t}{\alpha K_t} + v_t$$

where the latter, of course, comes from equating MP_L/P_L to MP_K/P_K. When we fit (a) alone, we are in effect looking at a reduced form. Note that just using (b) alone also is a reduced form approach since (a) has other coefficients and is observed with error. We can make yet another point here, following Wallis (1973). If our simultaneous system consists of the CD function and two marginal productivity conditions (along with the assumption of perfect competition in all markets), then in logarithmic form

$$\begin{aligned} \log x &= \log A + \alpha \log L + \beta \log K \\ \log x + \log \alpha &= \log L + \log W/P \\ \log x + \log \beta &= \log K + \log P_K/P \end{aligned}$$

which can be rearranged as

$$\begin{bmatrix} 1 & -\alpha & -\beta \\ 1 & -1 & 0 \\ 1 & 0 & -1 \end{bmatrix} \begin{bmatrix} \log x \\ \log L \\ \log K \end{bmatrix} = \begin{bmatrix} \log A \\ \log W/P - \log \alpha \\ \log P_K/P - \log \beta \end{bmatrix}$$

which has at its determinant $1 - \alpha - \beta$. Thus if we also have constant returns to scale (as many researchers have claimed), then the first matrix is singular, and we cannot determine output. Indeed, we must have decreasing returns (or abandon our assumption of pure competition).
11. There are several significant earlier studies. One, by M. Brown (1967) proposed that there were different

"epochs" in technical progress in the United States (identified by CD estimates along with the Chow test for stability) and found that for the sub-periods 1907-20, 1921-39 the coefficient for capital (β) was actually greater than that for labour (α), going as high as 0.73. For 1890-1906 and 1947-60, the usual results were obtained. This, then, is evidence of instability in the CD model. In another study, R. Solow (1957) used disembodied technical progress with the CD function and, later, considered capital-augmenting technical progress (see below).

12. This topic was introduced by Zellner, Kmenta, and Dreze (1966). They propose a Bayesian method of estimation; a follow-up paper is by Zellner and Richard (1973). Note, further, that log L and log K are correlated with u_0 (this can be seen from the reduced form) in the original model. The reformulation by Zellner *et al.* removes this bias since their method of estimation is such that the inputs do not depend on the disturbance term in the production function (see Ullah, Batra, and Singh, 1975, who extend the analysis by making use of the assumption that the firm is risk averse). Another important early paper in this sequence is by Mundlak (1963), and a recent study by Raj and Vinod (1978) summarizes the approaches used in the literature (two-stage least squares etc.) and proposes a "random coefficients" approach. Another approach employed on the investment and labour demand functions by Coen and Hickman (1970) is to estimate the production function subject to restrictions on its coefficients implied by the simultaneous choice of desired capital and labour stocks. Coen and Hickman estimate investment and labour demand functions subject to a production function (which implies restrictions) but not the converse; see Chapter 5 for a brief discussion of their approach. A similar methodology is noted below, in the discussion of a paper by Bergström and Melander (1979)

13. In his seminal cross-section study of the aggregate agricultural production function, Griliches (1964) again found the CES function inappropriate and used the CD function. The education of the labour force was again significant, and a variable measuring the contribution of public expenditures for agricultural research also was (highly).

14. The associated positive effect of K/L on S_L/S_K is contradicted on (some) empirical data for business cycles, as we shall see, although it is probably best not to address such questions on actual data which may reflect price and wage rigidities, money illusion, and (thereby) unemployment, without the assistance, at least, of an explicit aggregate labour supply function.

In the CES model, $S_L = MPP_L(L/x) = \alpha(x/L)$ when $\varepsilon = 1$. For $\rho > 0$ (and $\sigma < 1$) the share of labour should increase with x/L. Since x/L generally moves pro-cyclically, so should S_L; yet, paradoxically, many (especially Marxists) feel it does not (although the actual evidence for this view is usually not stated). There are (at least) four ways out of this:

(1) σ, actually, is greater than unity (and $\rho < 0$) as a few empirical studies have found;
(2) the share of labour actually moves pro-cyclically;
(3) there is some systematic error in the calculation of (e.g.) the marginal product of labour; and
(4) a richer aggregate demand-aggregate supply-disequilibrium framework is required to capture the various influences on the share of labour.

We will see that (1) is possible and so is (2). With regard to (3) Lucas (1970) suggests that the way the productivity data are put together over the day is at fault; this work is extended by Sargent and Wallace (1974) who show that a pro-cyclical behaviour of the wage share is possible with $\sigma < 1$. Indeed, point (2) may actually occur on the US post-World War II data. We should note an early CES study by M. Brown and de Cani (1963) who argue that if labour is scarce and σ increases, then S_L will fall. They worked on a long run of data (not cycles) and identified alternative "epochs" of labour-saving and labour-using technological change.

15. One can also derive the associated cost function and the aggregate supply function for this model as in Walters (1963). The CES function can be generalized to three or more factors, as in

$$F(L, K, M) = (\alpha L^{\rho} + \beta K^{\rho} + \gamma M^{\rho})^{1/\rho}$$

where M is any other factor, or even to

$$F(L, K, M) = (\alpha L^{\rho 1} + \beta K^{\rho 2} + \gamma M^{\rho 3})^{1/\rho}$$

The former still has the constant elasticity of substitution, but, in this event, all pairs of factors have to have the same elasticity of substitution (see Uzawa, 1962; McFadden, 1963; Solow, 1967). The latter, due to Mukerji (1963), has constant ratios of Allen partial elasticities of substitution (Allen, 1956). It is counted as a disadvantage that the extension of the CES function to the multi-factor case involves additional inflexibility. A generalization of the CES which is in some use in empirical work is by Hanoch (1971) who introduces Constant Ratios of Elasticities of Substitution - Homothetic (CRESH) production functions.

16. Note that Ferguson's tests are misspecified in that undeflated data are employed (see Bridge, 1971).
17. But note a study mentioned below, by Ramsey and Zarembka (1971) which, in a "specification error test" finds in favour of the CES, with $\sigma > 1$ (in comparison to CD, VES).
18. Arrow *et al.* (1961) show that $b = \sigma + e - e\sigma$ in the event that efficiency varies directly with the wage rate (itself an index of the quanity of the workforce). b is the regression coefficient and e is the efficiency ratio from

$$\frac{A_i}{A_j} = \left(\frac{W_i}{W_j}\right)^e$$

Rewriting the formula for the elasticity of substitution as

$$\sigma = \frac{b - e}{1 - e}$$

we see, following K. Sato (1977) that when $e > 1$ (Arrow *et al.* found it to be near 0.3, but they did so conditional on the assumption that $\sigma < 1$) then $\sigma > 1$ and can be very large indeed, for e close to unity. Sato goes on to show that the considerable evidence amassed by Arrow *et al.* is actually consistent with the possibility of a value of $\sigma > 1$.

19. These authors, essentially, argued that there were measurement errors in the original test (Arrow *et al.* dismissed this as a factor since they felt that both "overvalued exchange rates" and "high levels of protection" were unlikely to be correlated with the wage term in their test of the CES function (recall, it was a test of the marginal productivity condition)). Other studies which found bias were produced by Lucas (1969) who was neutral on the direction of the bias; Sveikauskas (1974) who contradicted Zarembka's results in effect, for cross-state data; and Moroney (1970). The latter uses a cost-minimization approach. A recent paper by Fishelson (1979) also contradicts Zarembka, on the basic 1957 (US) data much employed in this literature, but this is cancelled out somewhat in a paper by Paraskevopoulos (1979).
20. We have mentioned some US studies. Others include

Dhrymes and Zarembka (1970) for $\sigma < 1$. Tsurumi (1970) found σ near unity in his tests on Canadian data, while Kotowitz (1968) on much the same data had earlier found it to be between 0.3 and 0.5. Two other studies have found it to be somewhere between 0.63 and 0.71 with one result by Schaafsma (1978) worked out using Almon lags (see also Asher and Kumar, 1973). On British data there are tests by Feldstein (1967) and Mizon (1977); the latter found that the CD outperformed the CES and that it made no appreciable difference whether errors are treated as additive or multiplicative. Griliches and Ringstad (1971), on 1963 Norwegian data, found increasing returns to scale and (generally) a better performance from the CD function. They did caution that different methods of estimating σ produced different results but confessed to severe data limitations when they concluded that σ may be near unity. They compared the CD to an approximation to the CES developed by Kmenta (1967); the latter is in the form

$$\frac{X}{L} = BL^{h}[\delta + (1 - \delta)(\frac{K}{L})^{-\rho}]^{-\mu/\rho}$$

for which a Taylor series expansion is taken to produce

$$\log \frac{X}{L} \cong a_0 + a_1 \log L + a_2 \log \frac{K}{L} + a_3 (\log \frac{K}{L})^2$$

In a second study, using 1974 Norwegian data, Ringstad (1978) actually found in favour of the CES ($\sigma > 1$).

21. There are, of course, other issues. We noted above that failure of the competitive assumptions poses problems for the estimation of production functions. One of these concerns "capacity utilization", which, when substantially different from full capacity, may suggest a way in which factor price changes are being adjusted to, at least in the short run. Of course, some studies of the production function have taken this into account (e.g. C.A.K. Lovell, 1968, whose technology is VES and is given as equation (4.43)), but one still has the problem of finding a suitable index of utilization (see Malcomson, 1975, 1977). The general supposition is that ignoring the possibility of adjustment through capacity utilization leads to an overstatement of the elasticity of substitution.

22. Another generalization of the CD and CES is called the Generalized Quadratic by Denny (1974). This is

$$X = (\sum_{i}\sum_{j}\alpha_{ij}V_i^{\beta\gamma}V_j^{\beta(1 - \gamma)})^{\mu/\beta}$$

where μ is the scale parameter. When $\gamma = 1/2$, we can directly derive the CD and CES forms. This function, of course, permits the testing of the importance of differences in functional form. A function referred to as the Generalized Leontief (GL) due to Diewert (1971) is also derived in Denny's paper.

23. The restrictions are A_1, $\gamma > 0$, $0 < \delta < 1$, $0 \leq \delta\rho \leq 1$, and $L/K > (1 - \rho)/(1 - \delta\rho)$.
24. $L/K > G_0$ and $G_1 \geq 0$ are required under the neoclassical restrictions.
25. See equation (4.23). If we substitute from (4.35) into (4.36), we obtain $x/K = F_0 r + F_1 w$ in the VES case. In the CES case we have $\log x/K = F_0' + F_1' \log r$. A comparable expression for equation (4.37), this time for the CES function, is

$$\log\left(\frac{L}{K}\right) = G_0' + G_1' \log\left(\frac{r}{w}\right)$$

again showing a difference. The log-linear (CES) versus linear (VES) relation carries over to the theoretical results for shares, as we shall see.

26. The comparable relation for the CES function is log-linear as in $\log (S_L/S_K) = A + B \log (w/r)$.
27. Note that if $\rho = 1$, then $\sigma = 1$ in equation (4.39) and $S_L/S_K = \delta/(1 - \delta)$, a constant. δ, in this model, is a distribution parameter.
28. Another form of the VES is due to Kadiyala (1972) as discussed and compared (empirically) to other functions in Meyer and Kadiyala (1974). This function is

$$x = A(\delta_1 V_1^{2\rho} + 2\delta_2 V_1^{\rho_1} V_2^{\rho_2} + \delta_3 V_2^{2\rho})^{\varepsilon/2\rho}$$

and reduces to the CES for $\delta_2 = 0$, to the Sato-Hoffman (1968) for $\delta_1 = 0$, to the CD for $\rho \to 0$ and $\delta_2 = 0$, and to the Lu-Fletcher (1958) for $\delta_3 = 0$. The last named is

$$x = \gamma[\delta K^{-\rho} + (1 - \delta) \left(\frac{K}{L}\right)^{-c(1 + \rho)} L^{-\rho}]^{-1/\rho}$$

29. This function was restricted to have β, $\delta > 0$ and $-(\alpha/\beta) < K/x$. A three-factor CES model, attributed to Uzawa (1962), is

$$x = \gamma(\delta_K K^{-\rho} + \delta_L L^{-\rho} + \delta_m M^{-\rho})^{-1/\rho}$$

where $0 < \delta_K, \delta_L, \delta_m < 1$ and $\rho > -1$ are necessary restrictions. C.A.K. Lovell has another 1973 paper (1973b) comparing the CES and the two VES functions on US manufacturing data for 1947-68. He found the elasticity of substitution to be around 0.5 and the CES function somewhat better (statistically) than the two VES functions.

30. A study on Dutch data by Kuipers (1974) compares CD, CES, and VES functions for the short and long run. Kuipers finds that the short-run elasticity of substitution is less than the long run and that the latter may be greater than unity. Direct production function estimates are used (since the two-stage method (see equations (4.13) to (4.15)) requires perfect competition), and the long run is distinguished from the short run by assuming that the production function for the latter depends on the actual labour input as well as the long run labour input. This permits excess capacity and implied bounds on the value of elasticity of substitution. The data are time series (1948-71) for the "Dutch private sector".

31. We should note the existence of an important study by K. Sato (1975) which works on the "efficiency distribution" of firms in order to reduce (somewhat) the severity of the aggregation requirements.

32. Recognition of these factors is not necessarily damaging to empirical work if suitable parameters are postulated *and* successfully estimated. For example, Makepeace (1978) suggests an aggregation of a CD production function in the face of imperfect competition. Starting with the non-monopolistic version, we have for each firm

(a) $$x_i = K_i^{\beta} N_i^{1-\beta} \qquad i = 1, \ldots, n$$

Optimization, then, requires that

(b) $$\frac{N_i}{N} = \frac{K_i}{\left(\sum_{i=1}^{n} K_i\right)}$$

where

$$N = \sum_{i=1}^{n} N_i$$

i.e. that the distribution of the K-stock among firms is the same as the distribution of labour. Total output, then, is

(c) $$x = \sum_{i=1}^{n} x_i = \Sigma K_i^{\beta}\left(\frac{K_i}{\Sigma K_i}\right)^{1-\beta} N^{1-\beta} = K^{\beta} N^{1-\beta}$$

where

$$K = \sum_{i=1}^{n} K_i$$

If, though, firms with monopoly power have higher marginal products, then Makepeace shows that

(d) $$x = MK^{\beta}N^{1-\beta} = Mx_p$$

where

$$M = \left(\frac{\Sigma z_i^{-(1/\beta)}K_i}{\Sigma K_i}\right)^{\beta}\left(\frac{\Sigma z_i^{-(1-\beta)/\beta}K_i}{\Sigma z_i^{-(1/\beta)}K_i}\right)$$

the parameter in question, depends on z_i ($z_i = 1$ for a competitive firm and is > 1 for a monopoly firm). $M = 1$ for $z_i = 1$, of course, and is less than unity otherwise (so that x_p in equation (d) is "potential" output).

33. We are drawing here on the work of Berndt and Christensen (1973a); as we continue, we will incorporate material drawn from Walters (1963), H.A.J. Green (1964), and F. Fisher (1969).

34. As Berndt and Christensen (1973a) point out following Lau, we are therefore able to argue that the conditions necessary and sufficient for weak (strong) separability of a strictly quasi-concave homogeneous production function are also the conditions necessary and sufficient for weak (strong) separability of the dual cost function.

35.

(a) $$\frac{\partial\phi/\partial K_i}{\partial\phi/\partial K_j} = h_{ij}(K_1, \ldots, K_n)$$

(b) $$\frac{\partial\phi/\partial L_i}{\partial\phi/\partial L_j} = g_{ij}(L_1, \ldots, L_n)$$

We know, in general, that the marginal product of capital is a function of both capital and labour inputs, as in

$$\frac{\partial\phi}{\partial K_j} = m_j(K_j, L_j)$$

This implies, when combined with (a), that

(c) $\frac{\partial \phi}{\partial K_i} = h_{ij}(K_1, \ . \ . \ . \ , K_n)m_j(K_j, L_j) = \frac{\partial \phi_i}{\partial K_i}$

where the last expression recognizes the restriction that the aggregate marginal product of capital is equal to the firms' marginal product when the micro-functions are summed. Then the expression (c) implies that

$$\frac{\partial}{\partial L_i}\left(\frac{\partial \phi_i}{\partial K_i}\right) = 0$$

and clearly that

$$\frac{\partial}{\partial K_i}\left(\frac{\partial \phi_i}{\partial L_i}\right) = 0$$

This is what we sought to prove.

36. The problem stated in this section is an index number problem, formally. What we have shown with the composite goods theorem (see Chapter 1) is equivalent to showing that a price index with initial period weights may be (in the event of no changes in taste and no biased technological change) a "true" index in the event that individual prices change equi-proportionately. It is natural, then, to inquire into the usefulness of a Divisia Index in the production function context, rather than to use a CD (e.g.) function as we will proceed to do. The Divisia Index works with derivatives as in

$$dx = \frac{x}{\sum_{i=1}^{n} P_i x_i} \sum_{i=1}^{n} w_i dx_i$$

but itself only formally provides a "true" index for the production problem when the change in output is entirely due to changes in a single factor of production. This is not entirely satisfactory and leads one back to separable functions; see L.R. Klein (1946).

37. The CES can be written in the form

$$\gamma^{\rho} X^{-\rho} = \delta L^{-\rho} + (1 - \delta) K^{-\rho}$$

which then has the required separability property.

38. Equation (4.64) is the version which appears in Berndt and Christensen (1972a). Use of this model directly requires additional restrictions on the aggregator functions

(for K, L, etc.) requiring them to be Cobb-Douglas, in effect. (See Blackorby, Primont, and Russell, 1977.) This topic is continued below, when some empirical results are discussed.

39. The second derivative for L, for example, is

$$\frac{\partial}{\partial L} \cdot \frac{\partial x}{\partial L} = \frac{x}{L^2}[\gamma_{LL} + (\alpha_L + \sum_{j=1}^{3} \gamma_{Lj} \log V_j - 1)$$

$$(\alpha_L + \sum_{j=1}^{3} \gamma_{Li} \log V_i)]$$

which, though, would be negative for $\gamma_{Lj} < 0$, for all j.

40. The TL model (unless it degenerates to the CD) is a non-separable function, and so restrictions (linearity) must be placed on the "aggregator" functions for the inputs when one is testing for aggregation; the test is actually biased against weak separability, as pointed out by Blackorby, Primont, and Russell (1977) and Denny and Fuss (1977). Woodland (1978) suggests using a TL profit function to evade the restrictions and on US manufacturing data concludes that there may be a consistent aggregator for capital (two kinds) but not for labour (two kinds).

41. Following Griffin and P.R. Gregory (1976), we note that for the twice-differentiable production function $x = \phi(K, L, M, E)$ there is a (dual) twice-differentiable cost function of the form

$$C = C(x, P_K, P_L, P_M, P_E)$$

where the P_i identify the input price. A homothetic TL version of this is

$$\log C' = \log \alpha_0 + \sum_{i=1}^{n} \alpha_i \log P_i$$

$$+ \frac{1}{2} \sum_{i=1}^{n} \sum_{j=1}^{n} \gamma_{ij} \log P_i \log P_j$$

and one produces "cost shares" in the form of the following in the event that M (for materials) is excluded from the problem by a separability restriction (hence C'),

$$S_K = \alpha_K + \gamma_{KK} \log P_K + \gamma_{KL} \log P_L - (\gamma_{KK} + \gamma_{KL}) \log P_E$$

$$S_L = \alpha_L + \gamma_{KL} \log P_L + \gamma_{LL} \log P_L - (\gamma_{KL} + \gamma_{LL}) \log P_E$$

and one factor (energy) is dropped as redundant. All of this is produced under certain assumptions, as explained by Appelbaum (1978), and it needs to be verified that these conditions are met (in practice). Among the things one might look at is whether or not the production function results (for "inverse demand share equations") yield results consistent with the cost function results (for "derived demand share equations") - it does - and whether or not the direct production (cost) function estimates of parameters agrees with the corresponding share equation - it does not - on US aggregate time series data. Note that a motive for using cost data is the avoidance of measurement problems of X, K, L.

42. Berndt and Wood express some doubts as to whether the earlier production function studies meet the conditions of weak separability required for empirical work at the aggregate level.
43. A useful survey paper on the Box-and-Cox specification as a generalization is by Appelbaum (1979); Appelbaum's paper applies to utility and production functions and their associated indirect functions. Other recent papers surveying and extending this literature are by D.W. Caves and Christensen (1980) - who compare the generalized Leontief and the TL - and Guilkey and C.A.K. Lovell (1980) - who look at a CRESH technology via a TL approximation. The CRESH technology is a generalized CES due to Hanoch (1971).
44. There are, of course, many recent studies of the energy problem, which are somewhat beside the point for this survey. A general paper is by Pindyck (1979), and there are studies on US and Canadian data (e.g. Denny, Fuss, and Waverman, 1980) and on Dutch data (by Magnus, 1979). This is only a small sample.
45. In this section we draw on the work of Bernstein (1978).
46. As in Samuelson (1947) and Patinkin (1965).
47. That is, if we calculate the marginal productivity of money in (4.73), we obtain

$$\frac{dx}{dm} = \frac{\partial x}{\partial L_p} \frac{\partial L_p}{\partial m}$$

where $\partial L_p / \partial m$ would be calculated from some specific representation of the transactions process. In particular, if

$$L_T = \beta \frac{T}{m}$$

where T/m is transactions velocity, then, via (4.74)

$$\frac{L_p}{m} = \beta\frac{T}{m^2}$$

48. This model can then be embedded in a more detailed model of, e.g., investment or the demand for money; Bernstein (1978) does this for the demand for money and produces a standard result here, in terms of the role of the wage rate on the demand for money.
49. The British study is by D. Fisher (1975). The most effective criticism seems to have come from Prais (1975) and Khan and Kouri (1975). In a study on Canadian data using the CD function, You (1978) compares equation (4.84) with the following:

$$X_t = Ae^{rt + \lambda m_t} L_t^{\alpha} K_t^{\beta} e^{u_t}$$

to the advantage of the latter. You notes that the latter - with m as an "efficiency augmenting factor" rather than an input - produces a much lower estimate of r (it "all but disappears") and implies one way in which technical progress may have been exaggerated in this literature. The "specification errors" tested for in the Boyes and Kavanaugh paper are for omitted variables, incorrect functional form, simultaneity, non-normality of the residuals, and heteroscedasticity. An early paper on "specification error" but not on the role of money was by Ramsey and Zarembka (1971).
50. We should note an earlier study by Butterfield (1975) which supports the real money balances argument. Butterfield uses a generalized Leontief production function with three inputs.

5 The Investment Function

5.1 INTRODUCTION

The theory discussed in Chapter 4, on the production function, can also form the basis of a study of the demand for labour and the demand for capital, whether the equipment, structures, inventory, or cash of business firms, as well as, by stretching a point, the demand for consumer durables, including especially that for housing. We may, for businesses at least, assume a profit-maximizing neoclassical aggregate firm and investigate its optimal capital and labour decisions; we may also adopt a cost-minimization framework, and this is often recommended on account of its ease of manipulation (and the existence of certain types of data). Note that we get from the profit/cost framework to the investment decision of the aggregate firm by introducing some explicit dynamics involving both (a) a formal stock flow dimension and (b) lags in decision-making and in implementing capital spending (once decisions to invest have been made). These matters will be taken up in Section 5.3, after we have considered some of the work prior to the synthesis now in common use; this latter may be referred to as a "neoclassical investment function" with a "flexible accelerator" mechanism.

Among the list of topics generally considered in a discussion of the investment function, one finds the development of the accelerator-multiplier model near the front; indeed, tradition refers to this major development of Keynesian economists as "the" investment multiplier. Of course, the underlying dynamics of the investment decision - the lags just mentioned and the ability to delay action even after a project has been started up - are what provide the model with its potential for an internally-generated instability, but we should not be dogmatic about this topic

(a) either in limiting its identification to the

Keynesians

(b) or in limiting its application to the capital stock decision without considering other "capital-like" decisions (such as "permanently" hiring workers or "permanently" holding cash inventories) for which lags and delays (or accelerations) are appropriate.

We shall also try to be especially cautious in interpreting the empirical record here as the problems introduced by both dynamic and disequilibrium aspects of the investment problem seem to have resulted in an uncommonly large variation in result and in interpretation.

The topic of discussion in Section 5.2 is, somewhat arbitrarily, the Keynesian-style investment function, and it starts with Keynes himself. Briefly, the Keyneisans put the accelerator into growth and cycle models, first in a rigid and then in a flexible form, and postulated an investment function which was often both unstable and dependent on (primarily) exogenous factors; they also considerably downgraded the role of the interest rate in the investment decision. As the Keynesian Revolution aged, the investment function became more empirical, and while the accelerator was adapted to Koyck, Almon, and other lag structures, emphasis on non-neoclassical assumptions (sales maximization, excess capacity, monopoly power) also increased in this literature. This literature, especially in its empirical version, is still growing rapidly.

The neoclassical investment function - recently with a flexible accelerator to deal with the dynamics - is built on the standard competitive model of a business firm, as already described in Chapter 4. While the early work of I. Fisher (1930) lays out the structure of the neoclassical model, the standard recent treatment is due to Jorgenson, as described in Section 5.3.1; this latter is built on the same foundations as laid down by Fisher but has the considerable advantage of a more exact technique and an enormous amount of material covering both its theoretical needs and its empirical track record. The empirics, on the whole, are promising, although serious questions still remain about the more aggregative versions; these latter revolve around the questions raised by the Keynesians - as discussed in Section 5.2 - and, more specifically, about the dependence of the aggregate function on the success of both competitive and Cobb-Douglas assumptions in product and factor markets. These problems, along with the description of the reigning neoclassical investment function, will be the topics of discussion in Section 5.3.

In the remaining sections of this chapter a variety of extensions of the basic investment literature will be considered. These include, in Section 5.5, a consideration of the theory of investment in inventories and, in Section 5.6, a discussion of the literature on the demand for housing (call it "investment" in structures); furthermore, some material on financial influences on the investment decision will be discussed in Section 5.4. Finally, we should note that the material in Section 5.6.3 includes the remainder of our discussion of disequilibrium macroeconomics (continued from Chapter 1), along with a brief survey of the related literature on "credit rationing" (as it affects the housing market).

Before beginning our discussion of specific investment functions, let us consider how one might use the production literature of Chapter 4 to derive a standard neoclassical investment function depending on the real interest rate and real income. Let us start by assuming that the following production function represents the technology of the aggregate firm; this is a "vintage" production model as discussed by R.G.D. Allen (1967).

$$x = A(K) + I^{\alpha}L^{1 - \alpha} \tag{5.1}$$

Here we have aggregate output (x) produced both by existing capital $A(K)$ - actually a function - which has a certain amount of labour attached to it in a proportional manner ("locked in") and by new capital (I) and its associated labour. Note, of course, that $I = dK/dt$ and that we have capital of two vintages, both old $(A(K))$ and new (I). Investment, in equation (5.1), is thus basically treated as a factor of production.

We now desire to find a specific result for the investment function, $I(x, r, K)$, and to ascertain, as one may well desire *a priori*, the conditions under which $I_1 > 0$, $I_2 < 0$, and $I_3 < 0$ (i.e. the conditions under which we obtain the traditional signs). This, of course, is the standard investment function that appears in much of the textbook literature. Note that the function (5.1) will be assumed to have the usual neoclassical properties of positive and diminishing marginal products for the two factors I and L (being Cobb-Douglas in those inputs); we will also assume $A'(K) > 0$. We may, next, calculate the marginal product for investment; this is

$$\frac{\partial x}{\partial I} = \alpha \frac{x - A(K)}{I} = a \tag{5.2}$$

The expression $x - A(K)$ is the output produced by new capital. Let us assume that new output is always proportional to investment so that (5.2) reduces to the parameter a, as is also noted in equation (5.2). That is, let us assume that the marginal yield on investment is expected to be constant over time.

As the next step, assume that the present value of a is given by equation (5.2).

$$PV(a) = a \int_{t=0}^{T} e^{-rt}dt \qquad (5.3)$$

This, when integrated and evaluated at $t = T$, produces

$$PV(a) = \frac{a}{r}(1 - e^{-rT}) \qquad (5.4)$$

whence

$$a = \frac{PV(a)r}{1 - e^{-rt}} \qquad (5.5)$$

At the optimum, then, the marginal product of investment (as given by equation (5.2)) is equated to the ratio of the factor price to the product price (= 1, for convenience); the factor price (P_I) is given by equation (5.4), but we choose, instead, to eliminate a between (5.2) and (5.5); this produces our neoclassical-vintage investment function of

$$I = \frac{\alpha}{P_I}[x - A(K)]\frac{1 - e^{-rt}}{r} \qquad (5.6)$$

which has, as arguments P_I, K, x, r, where P_I, the price of investment goods, is a datum. This function can then be shown to be well-defined in x, K, and r - and to have the desired signs - and consequently a neoclassical-vintage rationale can be used to support the standard textbook model version of the investment function in which the level of real income (x) and the real rate of interest are arguments, provided K is also included as a variable.[1]

Before going on, we should point out that the theory just laid out calls for a real (*ex ante*) interest rate - along the lines of the discussion for consumption in Chapters 1 and 2 - and for real income as the determinant of real investment expenditures. We will, though, in what follows, find little interest in "the" interest elasticity or "the" income elasticity of investment demand and, regrettably, little interest in the real (rather than the nominal) interest rate. The lack of concern with specific elasticities reflects the complexities of the models used (for example, a "cost of capital" concept may contain several interest rates), and in the one case in which we return to simpler models, in the study of housing demand, we are able to report more exact results. The failure to use a real interest rate - or both a nominal and a real rate separately constructed - may help to account for the generally weak results one finds for the interest rate effect on investment. At least in one case, for inventory investment, this distinction has sharpened tests for the interest rate, as we shall report below. Of course, there are many problems in connection with the estimation of the *ex ante* real rate of interest, as discussed in earlier chapters, and this is certainly the main reason most investment studies work with nominal interest rates.

5.2 KEYNESIAN INVESTMENT THEORY

The modern theory of investment dates to the 1920s in large part, although strands go back at least as far as the Austrian School (who took an approach which is by no means extinct). It is not intended in this survey to dig into the complex issues raised in that voluminous and fascinating literature; equally, it is not intended to consider Marxist-inspired criticisms of the mainstream of thinking on investment decisions, however well-taken those criticisms might be. Instead, we will follow the development of the (mainly) neoclassical tradition in investment theory, with occasional ventures into the literature on financial aspects and on the neo-Keynesian adjustments to this tradition. In this context, Keynes himself is very much a neoclassical economist although, one finds, many of the major developments in investment theory have been created by economists who have explicitly rejected some of the other (mostly monetary) propositions emanating from neoclassical or monetarist sources. We will, of course, concentrate on results which are promising from the point of view of macroeconomic studies, recognizing, though, that there is considerable "micro-analytical" material that is going to be of interest. For the most part we will begin our survey after 1960, letting stand a careful summary of that literature by Eisner and Strotz (1963).

We begin with Keynes's (1936) version of the neoclassical theory. In Klein's (1954) appraisal of the "Keynesian Revolution", the following main points are made about this theory. To begin with, the investment function is derived directly from the "demand-for-capital-goods" function. The latter is built on the neoclassical assumptions of profit maximization subject to technological and market constraints. In particular, putting it in a way *not* in Keynes's words, a business firm will purchase capital goods up to the point where the discounted stream of expected net profits is equal to the cost of the new capital goods.[2] The rate of discount which achieves this equality is referred to as the "marginal efficiency of capital", and in a fully-employed competitive economy it is equal to the market interest rate (representing the cost of borrowed funds). The arguments of the investment function, then, are the market interest rate and anything which affects expected net revenues. The list of the latter could include expected interest rates (of, for example, different maturities), the cost of equipment, changes in tax laws, and so forth; technological change, perhaps by shifting the production function, also has a bearing on the investment function. Note that we can go from "capital" demand to "investment" demand by specifying suitable dynamics.

In the early days of the study of the investment function, considerable evidence was amassed which suggested that investment was essentially "autonomously" determined (see, e. g. J.R. Meyer and Kuh, 1954). Much of this evidence was essentially microeconomic in nature - indeed, some came from sample surveys of business executives - and while interesting, clearly could not be said to throw much light on the aggregate investment function. Similarly, a long debate over whether the firm - micro or macro - ought to be treated as if it were operating in competitive markets has shown no sign of abating or of being conducted rigorously, for that matter. To begin with, while L.R. Klein (1954) was optimistic over aggregation over firms (mainly because there was no need to specify business "preferences"), there are severe problems if various non-competitive (and non-Cobb-Douglas) possibilities are actually important. Indeed, our research in Chapter 4 into the aggregate production function (itself built on the same neoclassical assumptions) hardly permits us to be over-confident here. If we can simply sum individual functions then, following L.R. Klein (1954, p. 63), "the . . . fundamental Keynesian relationship" is that "the demand for capital goods depends upon the real value of national income, the interest rate and the stock of accumulated capital", a formulation which is consistent with practically all recent macro-investment functions, whatever their intellectual origins.

At that date (1954) and even up to the J.R. Meyer and Glauber (1964) study, it seems that non-competitive or random factors were generally thought to be especially important in the determination of investment demand. Klein mentions Keynes's faith in Schumpeterian innovators (see Schumpeter, 1934), the result of their activities striking the system as random shocks; similarly, Klein felt that the evidence suggested that investment would not depend on the interest rate. This was because of large subjective risk premiums, which implied that

(a) the risk premium dominates the interest rate such that the latter is "irrelevant" (when it changes);
(b) business firms act very conservatively, requiring immediate (up to five years) pay-offs;
(c) business men, especially representing large firms, have "psychological preferences" for using retained earnings;

and, even,

(d) the study of the subjective-risk discount "belongs as much to the study of psychology as to economics".

Klein claimed and documented empirical support for points (a) to (c).

The foregoing - much of which dominates the standard textbooks to this day - is essentially illogical, at least if it is intended as a description of a useful macroeconomic investment function. Micro-studies of "competitive failure" are built into theories of investment demand which are then cheerfully aggregated as if that were possible. More usually, but based on the same unsteady foundations, one finds extensive treatment of the economics of the firm, often in imperfect competition, as the apparent explanation of aggregate investment. Indeed, the often-remarked "inefficiency" of Keynes's "marginal efficiency of investment" approach is generally derived in an imperfectly competitive (and microanalytical) framework; this distinction, in fact, is unimportant if the (competitive) conditions for aggregation are met.

Returning to the Keynesian literature, then, J.R. Meyer and Glauber (1964), basically working in the Keynesian tradition, attempted a synthesis which they referred to as the "accelerator-residual funds hypothesis". For one thing, they downgraded the interest rate as a variable (although it actually does figure in their empirical tests): "Today, indeed, it is counted as something of a revival when the interest rate is even asserted to have at least *some* influence on investment outlays" (p. 2). For another, they felt that profit motivation (the "marginal efficiency approach") was not working well because its main variable, the level of recent past values of profits, was a poor proxy for expected profits and because it was at the same time a potentially good proxy for retained earnings (the preferred source of funds); this point was also made earlier in an important study by Grunfeld (1960).[3] The result, in their view, is a theory which has investment expenditures controlled by capacity - i.e. the accelerator - when capacity is fully utilized (in the later stages of the business upturn) and by the supply of residual funds (in downturns). Some empirical support is mustered for their view, and the idea of a non-market "funds constraint" survives to this day in the form of the credit rationing hypothesis. We will discuss credit rationing in Section 5.6.

We will continue our discussion of the Keynesian literature in a moment, but for now we can conclude this introductory section by noting a distinction between Keynes and the Keynesians that is parallel to that developed in Chapter 3 on the demand for money; this is also due to Leijonhufvud (1968). The Keynesian theory just discussed combines some empirical findings on the interest elasticity of investment with a reading of Keynes in which the master is seen as doubting the effectiveness of monetary policy because of the low interest elasticity of investment. Whatever we might think of the validity of the empirical work, it is simply not true that Keynes had this view; indeed, there is considerable textual evidence to the effect that he regarded the interest rate as especially influential in decisions on fixed investment expenditures (1930, vol. I, pp. 255-7, 364; 1936, pp. 136, 252). The reconciliation - since Keynes also doubted the efficacy of monetary policy - goes as follows. While investment would be expected to alter significantly when the long-term interest rate changes, the long-term interest rate itself depends on expectations, themselves often sticky (particularly in the face of a short-run and easily reversible monetary policy). Thus, attempts to reach investment via monetary policy would be frustrated because investors would simply ignore the on-off type of monetary policy which is the most one could expect from politically self-conscious governments in modern times. One might parenthetically note the remarkable stability of business fixed investment in the United States in most of the recessions since World War I.

Keynes himself did not develop the accelerator theory, but the Keynesians did. In particular, having dismissed the interest rate and downgraded the profit motive, the Keynesians were left with an intellectually vague theory of an autonomously determined, yet critical, spending function. The solution was to endogenize the function by making it depend on expectations, themselves depending on the recent dynamic history of sales or income. What ultimately resulted was a simple - and still popular - theory of the business cycle known as the accelerator-multiplier theory; its early versions were those of Samuelson (1939) and Hicks (1950), work which emanated from or coincided with that of Kahn (1931) and Harrod (1948). We will discuss these developments briefly, before returning to what we may provisionally term the Keynesian version of the accelerator; our discussion of these topics will be as brief as possible at this point, since we will have more to say about this in Section 5.3 on the flexible accelerator.

5.2.1 THE BASIC ACCELERATOR-MULTIPLIER MODEL

In the early days of the Keynesian Revolution, two sorts of investment-based dynamic models were available; there were the Harrod-Domar and the accelerator-multiplier models.[4] The accelerator itself, as a model of investment behaviour, begins with a simple proportion, as in

$$K^* = \alpha Y \tag{5.7}$$

where K^* is the desired capital stock. We can differentiate (5.7) with respect to time - and use the fact that $I \equiv dK/dt$ - to obtain

$$I^* = \alpha\frac{dY}{dt} \tag{5.8}$$

To this one might tack on a depreciation rate (δ) to get

$$I^* = \alpha\frac{dY}{dt} + \delta K_t^* = \alpha\frac{dY}{dt} + \delta\alpha Y \tag{5.9}$$

itself a differential equation in Y, of a degree determined by the lag (unspecified) in dY/dt.

One use of the accelerator is in the accelerator-multiplier model of the business cycle; this is often worked in period analysis so that the examination of the stability conditions is straightforward (in simple cases). The Harrod-Domar growth model is one such, although we will forbear to discuss it in detail here, and the Samuelson-Hicks accelerator is another. The latter appears as a consumption function

$$C_t = \beta Y_{t-1} \tag{5.10}$$

and an investment function

$$I_t = \alpha(Y_{t-1} - Y_{t-2}) \tag{5.11}$$

which in "equilibrium" yields the difference equation

$$Y_t = (\alpha + \beta)Y_{t-1} - \alpha Y_{t-2} \tag{5.12}$$

This equation has properties that can be analyzed directly (see the discussion of inventory investment theory in Section 5.5 for some further notes on the accelerator model).

The early literature on the accelerator utilized the foregoing in simple experiments, many of which suggested to their perpetrators that one might generally expect instability in the economic system (particularly as α and β become large); for a case in point see Hicks (1950) who entered "free" coefficients into the accelerator-multiplier model toward that conclusion. More to the point, an empirical literature grew up - in the Keynesian tradition - in which a more complete and certainly satisfying investment theory was developed, using the accelerator to explain the dynamics. The general idea, then, is to derive an investment demand schedule which depends on the profitability of employing capital in production, where the inputs in the function come from some specification of the firm's opportunity set. This set contains a potentially large list of variables, although, to simplify considerably, two main approaches are apparent: the Keynesian line (the subject of this section) and the neoclassical (which is discussed in the next section).

We mentioned above the J.R. Meyer and Glauber study (1964) as a typical study written in the Keynesian style. Their methodology was eclectic and empirical and accordingly well-suited to macroeconomics (since the problems of aggregation from a formal micro-model are evaded). In the earlier J.R. Meyer and Kuh study (1954) the authors had discovered

(a) a "senility effect" in the form of a negative correlation between investment and the age of the firm's capital stock;
(b) financial "conservatism" in that
    (1) older firms had a larger liquid capital stock and
    (2) firms were reluctant (1946-50) to use external financial sources;
(c) small firms were sensitive both to the level of internally generated funds and to general business conditions; and
(d) the behaviour of investment over the cycle is "accelerator" or "residual" funds (in expansions or contractions).

They did not find a relation between investment and the debt - equity ratio, any distinction between sales and profits, and any effect from certain price and interest rate variables.

The later model produced by Meyer and Glauber is based on the foregoing (obviously) and on three somewhat unusual equilibrium conditions (for a firm):

(1) that an optimal or least-cost relation exists between available capacity and the firm's average output;
(2) that the ratio of dividends to net profit (D/π) is at a long-run target level; and
(3) that investment spending is set at a level which requires little outside financing.

Thus, if demand for the product rises, D/π would fall, retained earnings would rise (releasing (3)) so that the optimal capacity could expand. Then, when the capacity additions are completed, the dividend payout is increased to the long-run target level. In an upturn, firms would be constrained by their residual funds (and would therefore be forced into the equity and bond markets) and stimulated by demand to expand capacity (thus turning on the accelerator). In (mild?) contractions, the accelerator cuts out, for the most part, and residual funds are sufficient to finance investment. The formal model, then, consists of two main equations. For full capacity we have

$$I = f_1\left(\text{capacity}, \frac{\text{price}}{\text{lowest ATC}}, \text{depreciation charges}, \frac{\dot{S}}{N}, \dot{E}\right) \qquad (5.13)$$

where $\dot{S}/N$ is a growth proxy (average growth of sales) and $\dot{E}$ is a business confidence index (the increase in the equity price). Here price divided by lowest ATC is an index of market power. For less than full capacity the investment function is given by

$$I = f_2\ (\text{retained earnings, depreciation charges}) \qquad (5.14)$$

One might also possibly add the growth and confidence indices to this latter formulation.

The foregoing cannot represent aggregate investment readily, since constant returns is not assumed and there are no factor prices specified. Further, equation (5.13) is non-competitive in the product market, and both (5.13) and (5.14) are non-competitive in financial markets. What we can do, of course, is interpret (5.13) and (5.14) as the direct picture of an aggregate firm - without the underlying micro-theory specified above - or we may look at highly disaggregated data. Meyer and Glauber actually can be interpreted as doing both in their time series and cross-section tests (and forecasts). They did not do well on the cross-sections, but the more aggregated time series show more support for the bifurcated function - and show a strong interest rate effect on investment when interest rates are "high" (at business cycle peaks). This, they feel, implies a non-linear and multiplicative effect of interest rates on investment; similarly, the residual funds variable acted in a discontinuous fashion, which suggests to them the not-unreasonable proposition that firms set their dividend payout rate low so that they are able to generate internal funds on average over the cycle. In any event, they conclude

> No simple theory, or even one as complex as the accelerator-residual funds theory, is likely to be accurate in all these different circumstances.
>
> Still, the accelerator-residual funds theory, with its embodied simplifications, may have a role to play. (p. 251).

This last seems a modest enough conclusion.

There is also some direct evidence on the accelerator theory, some of it produced around the time of the Meyer and Glauber book. One of these papers is the work of Smyth (1964). Smyth notes that the theory is actually asymmetrical in that gross disinvestment is not possible and in that excess capacity may "suspend" the investment; he also notes that a firm's liquidity position might be expected to influence its investment decision. Smyth discusses the econometric problems (auto-correlation, simultaneous equation, etc.) and also surveys the empirical literature available at the time; he notes

> statistical studies unfavourable to the acceleration principle have typically used crude formulations and unsatisfactory methods of analysis but more sophisticated models and analytical methods have almost invariably produced results favourable to the acceleration principle. (p. 194)

The simple studies referred to use such methodology as comparing time series turning points (e.g. Hickman, 1959) or simple and multiple regression and correlation (e.g. Tinbergen, 1938, and Chenery, 1952). The more sophisticated methods are the "capacity form" ($I_t = \alpha Y_{t-n} - \beta K_{t-1}$) or the "distributed lag form". The latter is a flexible accelerator model and is discussed below.

The work of Eisner is in the Keynesian tradition with both "non-competitive" and "accelerator" underpinnings, yet it follows the Meyer-Glauber "eclectic" perception fairly closely; we consider a recent (1978) effort.[5] Eisner had early rejected the questionnaire approach in favour of a body of hard data on sales, profits, etc. His main guiding perception has business investment resulting from the solution of a problem in which one maximizes the present value of expectations of future income *subject to*

(a) information and adjustment costs,
(b) a production function, and
(c) factor supply and product demand functions.

Where it becomes Keynesian (in the sense defined in this section) is in stressing differences between borrowing and lending rates, imperfections in (other) factor markets, expectations, and lags in construction (etc.). Out of these theoretical perceptions Eisner feels that the major elements of the investment function are the levels of, and changes in, the expected demand for the final product, and relative prices. One also needs the parameters from the functions specified in (b) and (c), but in actual estimations, what appears in Eisner's work (on fixed capital) are sales, profits, and depreciation, with increases in sales being the dominant factor. The effect of profits seems to have been (mainly) that of affecting the timing rather than the magnitude of investment. But unexplained variances are large, even though satisfaction is expressed in "changes in sales" and "expected sales" as variables and with the harmony of his work with the flexible accelerator model.[6]

5.3 FLEXIBLE (AND NEOCLASSICAL) ACCELERATOR MODELS

In Section 5.1 we provided a derivation of a standard textbook neoclassical investment function, but that derivation made it clear that the specialization of the production function was the key to the results obtained. That specialization was termed a "vintage" production function, but more formally it was an additively separable function in which the stocks (K and its associated stock of labour) were separated from the flows (I and new labour services). This is certainly one way to handle the stock-flow problem, and it is well within the Keynesian tradition, where (at least in some cases) the flow contribution of net investment is highlighted while its contribution to the stock of capital is neglected (additive separability achieves this). But of more interest at this point is the development of a stock flow solution in which both K and I are variable and in which more potentially relevant interaction can be permitted. We will develop the Jorgenson model in Section 5.3.1 and then consider a wide range of criticisms of the approach (as well as a few generalizations) in Section 5.3.2; then, in Section 5.3.3 we will undertake a survey of the empirical record regarding the wider range of neoclassical investment functions consistent with the Jorgenson framework.

As discussed in earlier sections of this chapter, an integral part of any investment theory is the specification of the time-path of investment, and our first comments in this section are designed to bridge the gap between the Keynesian and the neoclassical investment theories. The earliest flexible accelerator model appears in the work of Chenery (1952) and Koyck (1954) and amounts to imposing the following relation between actual capital and past desired capital.

$$K_t = (1 - \lambda) \sum_{i=0}^{\infty} \lambda^i K^*_{t-i} \qquad (5.15)$$

In the non-flexible form $(1 - \lambda) = 1$. This "Koyck lag", with $\lambda < 1$, has declining weights, and thus one can convert unobservables into observables by summing the right-hand side; we may refer to this as a "permanent" capital stock in the language of Friedman's (1957) permanent income hypothesis for consumption; in this respect Eisner's "Keynesian-style" models (discussed in Section 5.2.3) are properly included as flexible-accelerator models (in sales). We note that the early models were not "choice-theoretic", and the lags were essentially *ad hoc*.

Work on the flexible lag structure of investment models (more of which is discussed later in this section) began with the Koyck format but reached somewhat of a peak - in terms of developing a flexible functional form at least - with the development of what is now known as the Almon lag by Almon (1965, 1968). Almon's procedure is by now well-known and widely used in problems where lags are felt to exist (as discussed in Chapters 2 and 3 in this survey); her actual investment framework is quite simple, though, and approximately fits the Keynesian form. In her paper, capital appropriations (A) are explained in terms of

$$A = b_2 IP + b_3 IF + (b_1 + b_4 i)\, capacity \qquad (5.16)$$

where IP is industrial production (representing the accelerator), *IF* is internal funds, and i is a nominal interest rate (Moody's), representing the cost of external funds. After dividing through by capacity, "Almon lags" (parabolic with end points restricted to zero) were placed on the three variables to the effect that all variables were significant and that *IF* slightly dominated *IP* (the accelerator); the interest rate, when added to *IP* and *IF*, had a small but significant effect and other variables, such as the debt - equity ratio and stock prices, were not significant. We shall report numerous successful results for the debt - equity ratio below; a recent study utilizing the Almon lag (and a variable to measure the backlog of capital appropriations) is by Warner (1978), who also finds the long-term interest rate influential on investment decisions. In any event, Almon's results are not often discussed although they are by no means unusual, but her "lagrangean polynomial interpolation" technique, which is certainly very flexible is, and it is also widely used.[7]

5.3.1 THE JORGENSON MODEL FOR DESIRED INVESTMENT SPENDING

As Jorgenson developed his investment function (1965, 1967, and Jorgenson and Stephenson, 1967), there are five main problem areas to consider. These involve the economics of the (aggregate) firm, the choice of functional form for the production function, the economics of the lag problem, the choice of functional form for the lag distribution, and the mathematical optimization technique. We will begin here with the first two and the fifth of these, taking up the questions concerning lags in Section 5.3.2. We will defer most questions concerning the validity of this framework - and those referring to its empirical possibilities - to later sections as well.

In his basic derivation of the investment function Jorgenson employs equation (5.17) to define the Lagrangean of the firm, assuming it wishes to maximize net worth.

$$L = \int_0^\infty \{e^{-rt}[Z(t) - T(t)] + \lambda_1(t)F(x, L; K) + \lambda_2(t)(\dot{K} - I + \delta K)]\}dt \qquad (5.17)$$

Here, to take the ingredients from left to right, we have the rate of discount (r), the dynamic behaviour of profits $Z(t)$, the dynamic behaviour of taxes $T(t)$, and two constraints represented by the two dynamic Lagrangean multipliers $[\lambda_1(t), \lambda_2(t)]$; the first is for the production function and the second is for depreciation (the rate of depreciation is δ). The integral is taken over the remaining life of the firm.

Taking the functions first, let us consider $Z(t)$, the profit function, in (5.18).

$$Z(t) = px - sL - qI \tag{5.18}$$

This function lists revenues (px) and expenditures $(sL + qI)$ and we once again encounter the idea that new capital expenditures (I) are costs and are (hence) one of the decision variables of the firm; q is the price of new capital goods (we will encounter a version of q again in our discussion of financial variables), and s is the wage rate. Note that the right-hand expressions are not written as functions of time explicitly (for convenience). The second function in equation (5.17) is the tax function; its calculation makes $Z(t) - T(t)$ equal to net profits (profits after taxes).

$$T(t) = u(t)\{px - sL - q[V(t)\delta + w(t)r - z(t)\frac{\dot{q}}{q}]K\} \tag{5.19}$$

Here the expression in the curly brackets is total taxable income for the firm, and $u(t)$ is the applicable corporate income tax rate; the latter is a function of time since it depends on which bracket the average firm is in and, of course, is liable to be changed. In the square brackets we have three tax rates: $V(t)$, the tax allowance on depreciation (the expression is $qV(t)\delta K$, where δ is the rate of depreciation; $w(t)$, the allowance permitted because interest expenses are deductible (the expression is $qw(t)(rK)$, where, as before, q puts it in money terms); and $z(t)$, the tax rate on capital gains (where $\dot{q}/q$ represents the percent rate of change of capital goods prices).

Turning to the constraints, we note that Jorgenson writes the firm's production function in implicit form as

$$F(x, L; K) = 0 \tag{5.20}$$

The reason for the separation of the capital stock is that K is not treated in the optimization in the same way as x, L, although it is a choice variable, as well. Note that $\partial F/\partial K$ will enter into the optimization (see below) and that Jorgenson intends here to treat the capital item in equation (5.20) as capital services, not as the capital stock. The other constraint which is applicable, as mentioned, is

$$\dot{K} + \delta K = I \tag{5.21}$$

where $\dot{K}$ is dK/dt. Here gross investment consists of new capital stock ($\dot{K}$), plus replacement investment (δK), where δ is the rate of replacement (or rate of depreciation); net investment, of course, is $I - \delta K$.

The actual optimization involves the use of the basic calculus of variations model. The choice variables for the firm are x, L, I, K in this problem, and the stock flow problem we have here has to be resolved by also finding the function which maximizes equation (5.17). Let us, for simplicity, write equation (5.17) as

$$L = \int_0^\infty f(t)\,dt \tag{5.22}$$

in which case the marginal conditions necessary for a maximum are

$$\frac{\partial f}{\partial x} = e^{-rt}[1 - u(t)]p + \lambda_1(t)\frac{\partial F}{\partial x} = 0 \tag{5.23}$$

$$\frac{\partial f}{\partial L} = -e^{-rt}[1 - u(t)]s + \lambda_1(t)\frac{\partial F}{\partial L} = 0 \tag{5.24}$$

$$\frac{\partial f}{\partial I} = -e^{-rt}q - \lambda_2(t) = 0 \tag{5.25}$$

$$\frac{\partial f}{\partial \lambda_1} = F(x, L; K) = 0 \tag{5.26}$$

$$\frac{\partial f}{\partial \lambda_2} = \dot{K} - I + \delta K = 0 \tag{5.27}$$

and the Euler condition expressing the function which maximizes equation (5.17); this equation describes the time path of the capital stock.

$$\frac{\partial f}{\partial K} - \frac{d}{dt}\frac{\partial f}{\partial \dot{K}} = e^{-rt}u(t)q[V(t)\delta + w(t)r - z(t)\frac{\dot{q}}{q}]$$

$$+ \lambda_1(t)\frac{\partial F}{\partial K} + \lambda_2(t)\delta - \frac{d}{dt}\lambda_2(t) = 0 \tag{5.28}$$

In the foregoing, we can view equation (5.28) as the net marginal product (really the net after-tax marginal revenue product) of capital, where the adjustment $(d/dt)(\partial f/\partial \dot{K})$ has to do with any change over time in the net marginal product of net investment (recalling that $\dot{K} = I - \delta K$). We can also view equation (5.28) formally as the solution to a problem in functional analysis, or we can interpret it more prosaically as a kind of stock $(\partial f/\partial K)$-flow $(d/dt)(\partial f/\partial \dot{K})$ solution, where the term $(d/dt)(\partial f/\partial \dot{K})$ adjusts the marginal product of capital for interactions between K and I (net) on account of the passage of time.

The solution to this system involves the replacement of the functions of $u(t)$, etc., with parameters u, etc. We may obtain an expression for $\lambda_2(t)$ from equation (5.25); then, working with equation (5.28) and carrying out the differentiation d/dt, we obtain

$$\lambda_1(t)\frac{\partial F}{\partial K} = e^{-rt}q\{[1 - uv]\delta + [1 - uw]r - [1 - uz]\frac{\dot{q}}{q}\} \quad (5.29)$$

where, as noted, we have replaced the functions $u(t)$, $w(t)$ etc., with the parameters u, w, etc. Since $\partial x/\partial K = (\partial x/\partial F)(\partial F/\partial K)$, we can directly calculate the marginal product of capital as

$$\frac{\partial x}{\partial K} = \frac{e^{-rt}q\{[1 - uv]\delta + [1 - uw]r - [1 - uz]\dot{q}/q\}}{e^{-rt}[1 - u]p} \quad (5.30)$$

combining equations (5.23) and (5.29) and eliminating $\lambda_1(t)\cdot(\partial F/\partial K)$ between them. This can be rearranged as

$$\frac{\partial x}{\partial K} = \frac{C}{p} \quad (5.31)$$

where

$$C = q\{[\frac{1 - uv}{1 - u}]\delta + [\frac{1 - uw}{1 - u}]r - [\frac{1 - uz}{1 - u}]\frac{\dot{q}}{q}\} \quad (5.32)$$

is the "user cost of capital". Specializing the production function to the constant returns Cobb-Douglas form, for which the marginal product of capital yields

$$\frac{\partial x}{\partial K} = \beta\frac{x}{K} \quad (5.33)$$

produces the following expression for the desired capital stock.[8]

$$K^* = \beta\frac{p}{C}x^* \quad (5.34)$$

Jorgenson goes on to substitute actual output for desired output and to employ (5.27), to construct the investment function; this relation depends on p, C, and desired output.[9]

5.3.2 JORGENSON'S FLEXIBLE ACCELERATOR

The foregoing is a stock (as opposed to flow) model of the demand for capital by the firm and thus requires - at the least - a stock-adjustment equation to capture the flow aspect of desired investment spending. In fact, Jorgenson also puts a considerable effort into laying out the dynamic structure of the investment problem. Noting that there are really five distinct stages to any investment programme,

initiation of project	(t_1)
appropriation of funds	(t_2)
letting of contracts	(t_3)
issuing of orders	(t_4)
actual investment	(t_5)

Jorgenson shows that a lag clearly must exist in the investment function and that one simply cannot combine equations (5.34) and (5.21) to arrive at the investment function as in

$$I^* = (\alpha\frac{p}{c})dx^* + \delta K \qquad (5.35)$$

Jorgenson's work here is worth considering in some detail.

Investment expenditures (in t_5) are the result of previously or currently started projects, some of which are finished in the current period and some of which are carried over from previous periods. If W_0 represents the percentage of an investment project completed in its first year, then the relation between "starts" and investment expenditures in time period "t" is

$$I_t = \sum_{i=0}^{n-1} W_i S_{t-i} \qquad (5.36)$$

where the "0" weight, again, is assigned to the first year of the project. Using the lag operator, we may rewrite equation (5.36) as

$$I_t = W(L)S_t = (W_0 + W_1 L + \ldots + W_{n-1}L^{n-1})S_t \qquad (5.37)$$

which generalizes the lag problem.

The stock of capital desired at the end of t $(= K_t^*)$, used in equation (5.34), of course, consists of the sum of new starts in t, the backlog of uncompleted projects, and the existing capital stock. This we may express as equation (5.3*) in which the expressions in parentheses are the uncompleted parts.

$$K_t^* = S_t + (S_{t-1} - W_0 S_{t-1}) + (S_{t-2} - W_0 S_{t-2} - W_1 S_{t-2}) + \ldots + K_{t-1} \quad (5.38)$$

Reorganizing this expression, we have $K_t^* - K_{t-1} = S_t + (1 - W_0)S_{t-1} + (1 - W_0 - W_1)S_{t-2} + \ldots$, or converting by means of lag operators

$$K_t^* - K_{t-1} = \frac{[1 - LW(L)]}{1 - L} S_t \quad (5.39)$$

Then, since $I_{t-1} = LI_t = K_{t-1} - K_{t-2} = W(L)S_{t-1}$ from equation (5.37) and $(1 - L)K_{t-1} = K_{t-1} - K_{t-2}$, we have

$$W(L)S_{t-1} = (1 - L)K_{t-1}$$

or

$$K_{t-1} = \frac{W(L)S_{t-1}}{1 - L}$$

Putting this into equation (5.39), we obtain

$$K_t^* - \frac{W(L)}{1 - L} S_t = \frac{[1 - LW(L)]}{1 - L} S_t \quad (5.40)$$

which, when combined with equation (5.37), yields an equation in the first difference of the desired stock of capital

$$I_t = W(L)[K_t^* - K_{t-1}^*] + \delta K_{t-1} \quad (5.41)$$

with the depreciation term being carried over from equation (5.21). The next step, of course, has already been carried out, and that is to provide expressions for K_t^*, K_{t-1}^*. What Jorgenson has provided here is an analysis of the lag problem in investment studies in terms of incomplete projects; the derivation shows us how one obtains the standard model (5.41)

Jorgenson's method of approach to the lag problem is outlined in his paper on rational distributed lags (1966). When we write a general lagged relation, where both the dependent and the independent variables are lagged *a priori*, then in the equivalent expressions of equation (5.42)

$$Y_t = P(L)X_t = \frac{U(L)}{V(L)} X_t \quad (5.42)$$

the function $P(L)$ is a rational distributed lag function, where $U(L)$ and $V(L)$ are polynomials in the lag operator, if $U(L)$ and $V(L)$ have no characteristic roots in common. Letting

$$V(L) = 1 + V_1 L + \ldots + V_n L^n$$

$$U(L) = U_0 + U_1 L + \ldots U_m L^m$$

then we may convert a function such as

$$I_t = \frac{\alpha U(L)}{V(L)}\left(\frac{p_t x_t}{C_t} - \frac{p_{t-1} x_{t-1}}{C_{t-1}}\right) + \delta K_{t-1} \qquad (5.43)$$

into an estimating equation for particular choices of polynomial for $U(L)$ and $V(L)$. Practice varies in the profession, but adherence to "rationality" and the use of the Pascal distribution caused Jorgenson to employ a second-degree polynomial for $V(L)$ and a fifth-degree polynomial for $U(L)$, with the latter containing no linear or quadratic terms.[10] When he fitted the model on the data, Jorgenson obtained reasonably good results; again, however, the lags were relatively short (L^5 taking us back only five quarters) on capital spending data (t_5).[11]

We have mentioned the problems which occur if the scale parameter in the production function is greater than unity and if the elasticity of substitution between capital and labour is not unity. It is interesting to consider the results of a British study by Boatwright and Eaton (1972) which utilizes (a) a simple definition of the cost of capital, $C + q(1 - A)(\delta + r)/(1 - u)$, where all terms are as before except A (for the discounted value of tax savings due to investment allowances); (b) the Almon lag (which gets a longer lag on quarterly data running out from two quarters to fourteen quarters); and (c) the CES production function.[12] The best value for the elasticity of substitution (the one which minimized the standard error of estimate) is 0.47 (although the gain from $\sigma = 1$ to $\sigma = 0.47$ is not great in terms of the test statistic, and there are the usual problems in interpreting the Almon lags). Even so, the modified Jorgenson model does well on these tests.

5.3.3 CRITICISMS AND EMPIRICAL EXTENSION OF THE NEOCLASSICAL MODEL

At this point we will take up some of the major criticisms

of the Jorgenson model that have appeared in the literature over the years. On the positive side, the model is still in wide use in studies of aggregate investment, particularly in the advanced textbooks; furthermore, the method has been employed on other problems for which the solution of a stock adjustment problem seems especially apt.[13] This having been said, it is still important that the model's limitations be appreciated, particularly as they involve the need to employ the strong Cobb-Douglas/constant returns production function to rationalize Jorgenson's simple solution. The problems, then, are

(a) that actual output is used in place of desired output in equation (5.34), requiring the assumption that constant returns to scale exist;
(b) that the first-order condition for labour is ignored on the justification that the chosen production function has a unitary elasticity of substitution between the two inputs of capital and labour (and no other relevant inputs);
(c) that the product market is competitive (Jorgenson has a fixed price for the output of the firm);
(d) that the model requires a second-hand market in capital goods; and
(e) that an entire term structure of interest rates appears to be necessary, at least as the theory is outlined above.

Furthermore, we will ignore potentially serious problems of excess capacity, uncertainty, "non-optimal" methods of pricing, and so forth, first mentioned at the beginning of Chapter 4. Note that in this section we are actually appraising much of the empirical work on the neoclassical investment function; that being the case, no separate empirical section will be included in this chapter.

The first problem mentioned, then, is that the production function in the investment model specifies desired output levels; as such, the variables are not directly observable (Jorgenson uses actual output for desired output in equation (5.34)), and a jointly-estimated equation may well be needed for each input - or a two-stage procedure adopted - if a simultaneous equations bias is to be avoided.[14] What Coen and Hickman (1970) do is to derive parallel expressions for K^* and L^* in terms of expected prices and desired output and then use two "permanent-style" measures for these items, using a distributed lag of the Koyck form. One implication of their approach is that in the short run the K^* equation is formally independent of the L^* equation. In particular, when there is a shock to aggregate demand, the aggregate firm is jolted off its production function while the labour input is adjusted slowly. This non-binding of the short-run production constraint permits the independence of K^* and L^*.[15] But the Coen-Hickman model fits poorly, and says Jorgenson (1973), uses faulty data and an inappropriate method of estimation (they should have used 2SLS); when the adjustments are made by Berndt (1976), Jorgenson's results again obtain. We should note, somewhat parenthetically, that the question of endogeneity of the output variable - as raised, for example, by Gould (1969) - is somewhat beside the point, since the investment equation is a structural equation, not a reduced form, and there exist methods for estimation in such a situation; indeed, output need not appear at all, if K^* and L^* are the choice variables.[16] Of course, problems of serial correlation and the like are especially important in the event that the lags are long (see Hall, 1977).

With regard to the second question raised above, Eisner and Nadiri (1968) point out that equation (5.34) assumes, in effect, that the following elasticities are unity - $\varepsilon_{K \cdot x} = \partial \log K^*/\partial \log x = \varepsilon_{K \cdot p/C} = \partial \log K^*/\partial \log p/C = 1$ - conditions that result from the use of the homogeneous Cobb-Douglas production function. The first of these conditions is true of any homogeneous function and is not really in dispute (although we did note non-constant returns to scale in empirical studies of the production function in Chapter 4), but the latter is contradicted by the fairly widespread (but far from unanimous) view that the elasticity of substitution (σ) between labour and capital is actually less than unity. Eisner and Nadiri then test Jorgenson's data as in

$$\Delta \log K_t = \sum_{i=m}^{7} \gamma_i \, \Delta \log \left(\frac{px}{C}\right)_{t-i} + \sum_{j=m}^{3} w_j \, \Delta \log K_{t-j} + u_t \quad (5.44)$$

in which case the product of the elasticities for K and px/C varied between 0.038 and 0.464 and in all cases was significantly less than unity. In several extensions the elasticities were separated and calculated, and the long-term interest rate was employed in lieu of the complicated expression for the cost of capital (C) with the result that both elasticities were low.[17] Jorgenson, in his turn (1971), notes that an implication of their model is that $\varepsilon = (1 - \varepsilon_p)/(\varepsilon_x - \varepsilon_p)$ is the estimate of the returns to scale parameter and that their results imply that it is greater than unity (increasing returns to scale). This, then, is incompatible with their working assumption of competitive equilibrium. Furthermore, as Bischoff demonstrates (1971), the Eisner-Nadiri results (in the first differences of a time series) are inconsistent on account of serial correlation (as pointed out in a classic paper by Griliches, 1967). When the required adjustment is made, claims Bischoff, the model fits better, and one cannot reject the hypotheses that $\sigma = \varepsilon = 1$. Jorgenson also argues (1972), more directly, that a large body of empirical work (including Bischoff's) supports the idea of a unitary elasticity of substitution for new capital equipment (with labour), although not necessarily for old (after installation). This latter fact does suggest that Jorgenson's model may be less effective in the short run (macro-policy) context.[18]

With regard to the assumption of perfect competition in the product market, Jorgenson may appear vulnerable since this might be an unreasonable assumption to make in some industries; but as Hall points out (1977), the theory can be restructured, provided one is willing to assume instead that firms produce at minimum cost.[19] This seems to be a point which perhaps could be conceded by those who find the assumption of perfect competition unpalatable. Competitive assumptions and the Cobb-Douglas production function deal with most of the objections raised above - for example, we need not include the first-order condition for labour if, in a two-factor problem, the Cobb-Douglas is employed (on account of the unitary elasticity of substitution) - but several of the issues mentioned above remain. These concern the need for a "second-hand" market in capital goods already alluded to and the need for a term-structure of interest rates or, at the least, for both a long-term and a short-term rate of interest. Both of these problems arise from the apparent long-term view which the Jorgenson model requires. In the case of the second-hand market, the problem concerns what the firm is to do with old and sub-optimal capital equipment when the equation is recalculated from period to period and a different capital stock is required (given technological change). In the case of the interest rate, a long-lived capital decision would seem to require a long-term interest rate.

Hall (1977) also tackles these two interrelated questions by restating the Jorgenson investment problem as a cost-minimization rather than a profit-maximization problem (see note 19). Doing things this way enables Hall to avoid setting down a lot of structure and enables him to derive the investment function in such a way that it is apparent that the investor's view need only be one period ahead, rather than over all periods until the capital good finally expires. With regard to the age of the capital equipment, the firm, in this theory, takes account of existing, new, and expected capital, including any relevant interaction among equipment of different ages, in its decision to undertake a new investment. This seems to do away with the need for a second-hand market. With regard to the interest rate, the problem is similar to one which appears in the literature on the term structure of interest rates (see Malkiel, 1966). This is that the firm can take a long-term view - over the entire range of future periods - or a short-term view - looking over interest rates for all maturities, but only looking one period ahead. That is, in the second approach, the firm (or investor) looks at rates for all maturities and makes its predictions for only one period ahead - in effect predicting changes in the long-term rate for the next period. Since the main reason for a change in any rate is undoubtedly a corresponding change of the short-term rate, the firm - in its investment decision - will respond to changes in the short-term rate (primarily) even though the long-term rate is the relevant (and used) yardstick to use to compute the present value of the project. This has, however, been challenged by Hartman (1980) who argues that both a long-term and a short-term rate would be necessary under reasonable descriptions of the investment environment.[20]

The most obvious omissions in the discussion to this point are the numerous papers by Jorgenson himself, especially with other authors, which expand the analysis and/or offer tests on fresh data sets. In one such, Jorgenson and Siebert (1968) compare the neoclassical model (with and without capital gains) with an accelerator model $(K^* = \alpha_1 X_t)$, an expected profits model $(K^*_t = \alpha_2 V_t)$, and a liquidity model $(K^*_t = \alpha_3 L_t)$. Each of the five models is combined with an *ad hoc* rational lag formulation on a time series of fifteen large US manufacturing corporations; the winner in this microeconomic exercise is the neoclassical model with capital gains $(\dot{q}/q)$ included. Following another line, Hall and Jorgenson (1967) look at the effect of tax policy on investment spending in the United States; the model is roughly similar to that outlined above (which included tax variables). Hall and Jorgenson, on US aggregate data, estimate the model and then calculate the effects of accelerated depreciation (1949), shortening of capital lifetimes (1962), an investment tax credit (1962), and a hypothetical experiment involving a first-year write-off (in 1954). They conclude that the effects of accelerated depreciation (1954) are substantial and so are those of an investment tax credit; this finding, of course, has been revived in the recent "supply-side" controversy.

The Hall-Jorgenson work has not gone unchallenged, and a debate in the *American Economic Review* in 1969 added new evidence on the role of taxation. Coen (1969) suggests that the use of the Cobb-Douglas production function implies a price-elasticity of demand for capital of unity when, in fact, it should be less than unity (on the Hall-Jorgenson data), and argues that the firm has to be modelled as choosing its inputs and its outputs. He suggests a CES production function to deal with the first problem and, in view of an elasticity of substitution of less than unity, finds the Hall-Jorgenson claim of a strong tax effect unfounded. Eisner (1969) also joins the debate, criticizing the failure of Hall and Jorgenson to estimate the tax effect directly; Hall and Jorgenson estimated the model and then calculated the tax effect. The underlying problems, though, are still the CD production function and the exogeneity of output. Eisner re-estimates the model, suggesting that output is relatively important and that relative prices are relatively unimportant and, as a consequence, finds no significant effect on investment of changes in tax policy (on the US data). Hall and Jorgenson (1969) reply to these charges by reviewing the extensive literature on the elasticity of substitution (i.e. on the use of the CD function). This material is discussed in Chapter 4 and while inconclusive, especially at the micro-level, does permit Hall and Jorgenson to use the CD function at the more aggregative level (and for some industries). If this empirical justification is accepted, then the Hall-Jorgenson procedure is correct; if not, a simultaneous equations structure is appropriate. At this date (1981) the debate seems to be in a suspended state, although estimates of "the" elasticity of substitution still appear from time to time, firmly supporting neither view. Note that there is a "q" theory version of this literature, too (as discussed below).[21]

Finally, a much discussed problem which Jorgenson actually did deal with concerns a logical problem with the investment function, as discussed by Haavelmo (1960) and Witte (1963); we follow Nickell's presentation (1978). The investment function can be written as

$$I^*(t) = \dot{K}^*(t) + \delta K^*(t) \qquad (5.45)$$

where the asterisk indicates a demand. Haavelmo argued that while there is a demand schedule for K, there is an on-off character to$I^*(t)$ - in effect, a discontinuity - such that a smooth functional relationship between I and r cannot be derived; indeed, it is frequently observed that investment expenditures (even aggregate expenditures) are "lumpy". The problem lies in the lack of dynamics - in the failure to specify transactions costs - and, in Haavelmo's words (1960)

> the demand for investment cannot simply be derived from the demand for capital. Demand for a finite addition to the stock of capital can lead to any rate of investment, from almost zero to infinity, depending on the additional hypothesis we introduce regarding the speed of reaction of the capital-users. (p. 216)

The answers are to specify the adjustment function - i.e. to parameterize it - as in the flexible accelerator model (see above), to aggregate in such a way that the discontinuity disappears, or to specify a cost of transactions. Nickell (1978) takes the latter approach, specifying a convex cost function of the form $C[I(t)]$ which, in the constant-returns case, produces a well-defined cost function of present and future (expected) prices; there are other contribution, in a literature which is often very complex.[22]

5.4 MONETARY, FISCAL, AND FINANCIAL CONSIDERATIONS IN THE THEORY OF INVESTMENT

As noted earlier, the neoclassical model of investment is a structural stock adjustment model in which the structure consists of a series of constraints (e.g. the production function); an explicit statement of the cost of capital utilizing market interest rates, tax rates, and (sometimes) balance sheet relations (e.g. the debt - equity ratio); and an explicit parameterization of the adjustment process. An alternative, following a line laid down by Tobin (1969) is a flow-oriented approach which emphasizes financial variables (or ratios), in which the formal structure is much less visible (much of it being buried in market valuations in the manner of the rational expectations theory). The starting point in this latter stream of work is usually the paper by Tobin, although this is also the place to take up some of the issues raised in the Modigliani and Miller (1958) literature on the cost of capital (and on other work on financial matters and taxation not fitting so neatly into the framework just outlined). We will also briefly discuss several proposed measures of the cost of capital itself. Note that in this section the survey is considerably more representative than in other parts of this chapter, primarily because the material (and evidence) is mostly microeconomic.

5.4.1 FINANCE AND INVESTMENT

The principal alternative theory to that proposed by Jorgenson is known as Tobin's "q" theory of investment. Tobin's work (1969) is the outgrowth of some earlier work on financial intermediaries undertaken with Brainard (in Hester and Tobin, 1967). The basic approach taken is to assume that the objective of the firm is a neoclassical one, that of maximizing the present net worth of the outstanding shares of common stock. An investment project, in this case, would be undertaken if it increased this value with the securities market expected to assess the relative values of the expected returns and expected risks associated with the new project. The key variable is "q" - the market value of the firm relative to the replacement costs of its assets - which if greater than unity should stimulate investment activity (and if less than unity, discourage it).

Recent reformulations of the q theory emphasize that it is a neoclassical model not really in conflict with the Jorgenson model although it puts the emphasis in a different place; among these works are papers by Hall (1977), Yoshikawa (1980), and Ciccolo and Fromm (1979). Following the latter, we may assume that the market value of the firm is

$$V = \int_0^{\infty} (px - wL)e^{-(i + \delta - g)t}dt \tag{5.46}$$

where g is the expected rate of increase of the price of capital goods relative to wage rates (w) and output prices (p). Assuming that the marginal product of labour is always equal to the wage - and employing Euler's theorem - we then have that

$$V = \frac{p(\frac{\partial x}{\partial K})K}{i + \delta - g} = \frac{\alpha px}{i + \delta - g} \tag{5.47}$$

where α is the elasticity of output with respect to the capital (K) input. Defining q as $q = V/p_K K$, we then have that

$$q = \frac{\alpha px/K}{p_K(i + \delta - g)} \tag{5.48}$$

The desired stock of capital, calculated from the first-order conditions which go with equation (5.48), is $K^* = \alpha px/p_K(i + \delta - g)$, whence

$$qK = \frac{V}{p_K} = K^* \tag{5.49}$$

Thus q, itself the ratio of the value of capital to the replacement cost of the capital, depends on the ratio of the desired capital stock to the actual. V, of course, is determined by the financial markets.

When one moves to the empirical level, one must still deal with lags - and one must now measure q. The lags can be done in the fashion of the flexible accelerator (etc.), and a literature has grown up about this, which we have touched on elsewhere in this survey. This involves such topics as formally modelling adjustment costs, introducing different forms of flexible accelerator models (and/or using specific or general functional forms - such as the Almon lag), and dealing with serial correlation (existing or induced by one's specification). For the lag, one might assume a simple flexible accelerator as in $I = \lambda(K^* - K) + \delta K$, in which case combined with equation (5.49), we have $\Delta K/K = \lambda(q - 1)$. This highlights the potential interdependence between q and the lag distribution (represented here by λ) in the event that $q \neq 1$.

Several explanations have been given in the literature as to why q might exceed unity. Tobin suggests that lags in the delivery of capital goods could generate a short-run discrepancy and that adjustment costs of investment might rise more in proportion to the rate of investment, bringing both transitional and permanent departures of q from unity. That is, the long-run price of capital goods can be assumed to be set on the basis of normal production and capital utilization, while in the short run there are increasing costs of production - and, for that matter, of planning, labour training, and the like. At any rate, the more rapidly the firm presses on resources, the wider this discrepancy (and *vice versa*) in the short run. Monetary policy, too, may work through q - as Tobin suggested in his original paper (1969) - driving a wedge between rates of return on financial assets and non-financial assets (e.g. capital equipment) and thus (for "easy money") encouraging production of the latter (for $q > 1$).[23]

A few other extensions and references to empirical tests are in order, before we move on. Von Furstenberg (1977) added q to an equation containing capacity utilization and the debt/asset ratio (among other variables) and found that q added little to the regression (on US manufacturing investment), although it was significant. By itself - as if q contained all of the relevant information (after accounting for noticeable tax effects) - q did not work well (evidence of misspecification abounded). In a later study, utilizing a rational expectations framework, Malkiel, Von Furstenberg, and Watson (1979) found that capacity utilization or the level of output (related to trend) did not affect investment while q did. The reason for the poor performance of output (and capacity utilization) is that firms apparently expected it (rationally) to return to trend and hence ignored it; q, on the other hand, apparently contains the new information which makes the rational expectations theory go. This finding underscores a fundamental unity among the various investment theories so long as markets are found to be efficient and competitive and investors rational.

The q model has also provided the framework for the study of tax effects on investment. Ciccolo (1979) argues that tax regulations affect the calculation of q materially; on US data this is shown to have a strong effect on expenditures by firms on "producer's durables" and structures. Even more recently, Summers, in two papers (1980a, 1980b), uses the q approach to investigate the potential role of tax policy in stimulating investment (and economic growth). In the first paper it is pointed out that changes in tax policy (especially investment tax credits and accelerated depreciation) have substantial effects (on US data) - with long lags. This work is extended in the second paper in which the design of a sympathetic "savings policy" is considered. Taken together, it seems, Summers is arguing in favour of a "supply-side" policy aimed at stimulating investment and saving.

The second major financial literature referred to above is an intensely microeconomic one involving the financial structure of the firm as it affects the investment decision; its macroeconomic implications are, however, readily apparent. While an informal literature stretches back a good way, the first major paper in the modern sequence is that of Modigliani and Miller (1958). Modigliani and Miller (MM) argue that the value of a company (itself equal to the value of debt plus the value of equity) is simply equal to the discounted value of the earnings stream generated by the company and that the market for securities would tend to make this so by arbitraging away any potentially abnormal gains due to the method of finance (debt versus equity).[24] In a nutshell, the debt - equity (D/E) ratio, in a perfectly competitive market without government interference of any kind, would not be a factor in any investment decision, with the stock market's reaction to a firm's leverage wiping out any apparent gain associated with any particular change in the leverage ratio (D/E). A derivative proposition, then, is that the value of the firm is not affected by the firm's decision as to whether to retain earnings or to pay them out as dividends. Finally, of special relevance to the way we have formulated the investment problem earlier in this chapter, we should note that a further implication is that the cost of capital is also not dependent on these financial factors (on whether funds are raised by debt, equity, or retained earnings).

This analysis has been extended considerably by Stiglitz (1969, 1974), who argues that not only does the firm choose its debt - equity ratio and its dividend-retention ratio but also that it chooses the maturity structure of its debt and its holdings of the securities of other firms. Stiglitz points out that MM strictly do not make a strong case for a macroeconomic dictum that the D/E is indeterminate but that their proof does involve indeterminacy for the firm. Stiglitz, in his turn, establishes the condition under which D/E is irrelevant for both firms and individuals (investors). This, then, by simple aggregation, has the implication that the D/E is irrelevant in the macroeconomic investment function. Stiglitz, incidentally, does not rely on a perfectly competitive capital market (just non-discriminatory security pricing), individual rationality (just consistency), special financial models (such as the mean-variance), homogeneous expectations, and market clearing at all future points. His model does have uncertainty and is weakest in not permitting bankruptcy (default risk).[25]

It can be recalled that the Jorgenson investment function did contain financial factors (especially interest payments and capital gains), and one reason for this is the US tax law which creates an environment conducive to all sorts of special financial effects on investment. This was recognized by MM (1963, 1967) who also accepted that brokerage costs may provide an explanation as to why the percentage of funds raised by retained earnings may also influence the investment decision. In addition, and quite naturally, the MM assumption about perfect markets has been questioned; Durand (1959), for example, argues that perfect arbitrage through the stock market is generally not possible - because bonds and stocks are quite different contracts (involving voting rights, prior claims on assets, and, of course, tax breaks) - and that numerous imperfections in the market will vitiate the basic MM proposition.[26] He mentions restrictions on margin buying (via the US Regulation T) as especially important. Durand also discusses risk in connection with margin buying, but a more basic objection to MM is that of Lintner (1965, 1967) who argues that the correct assumption to make is the (usual) one that default risk rises with the D/E ratio so that the cost of capital does too; indeed, Lintner argues that the cost of retained earnings also depends on

D/E and so on both grounds offers a direct contradiction to MM; these papers also provide some empirical support for his proposition.[27]

Empirical work often shows taxes, "retentions", and D/E influencing investment of course, and so a truly enormous literature has developed (since, obviously, such a finding can be explained in various ways, the MM theory merely being adapted (e.g.) for tax laws); representative studies are as follow.[28] On the apparent relevance of the D/E, we have studies by Davenport (1972) and Taggart (1977), as well as many of the studies already mentioned. Earlier, for the homogeneous and regulated electric utility industry, Miller and Modigliani (1966) found no strong effects for D/E or for "dividend" effects. On the importance of long-versus-short debt (a proxy for risk), we have studies by Jaffee (1971) and W.L. White (1974). On dividends and retentions, empirical papers which support MM (that it does not matter how the project is financed) are by Black and Scholes (1974), Fama (1974), and Morgan and Saint-Pierre (1978), the last on Canadian data; while contrasting work is by Spies (1974), who distinguishes between short-run and long-run investment, and (possibly) by Dhrymes and Kurz (1967) who use the simultaneous equations framework appropriate for testing the interaction between financial and real decisions (but their results are not especially strong). The latter study was amended by McCabe (1979) who worked on the dynamics to the effect that an interaction (a non-MM result) occurred. Other empirical issues have also surfaced.[29]

5.4.2 MONEY AND THE INVESTMENT FUNCTION

We have produced a variety of demand for money models in this study, especially in Chapter 3 and in the discussion of money in the production function in Chapter 4. In Chapter 3 one such presentation was the neoclassical approach of Motley (1969), who actually built a Jorgenson-style model to rationalize money holding. That was a utility function approach, however, and applied literally to the consumer's demand for money, and so it is interesting to consider an extension of the production function problem of Chapter 4 - utilizing the neoclassical investment model - to the business demand for money. We will follow the work of Coates (1976).

Firstly, let us assume a production function of

$$X = \phi(K, L, M/P) \qquad (5.50)$$

Assume that the firm's after tax cash flow is given by $R =$

$px - wL - qI - \dot{M} - T$, where T is tax payments and $\dot{M}$ is the change in the firm's money balances. For a simple cost-of-capital of r, we will assume the firm seeks to maximize

$$PV = \int_0^\infty e^{-rt} \frac{R}{P} dt \tag{5.51}$$

subject to (5.50) and to a depreciation condition $\dot{K} - I + \delta K = 0$.

The necessary conditions for a maximum, following Jorgenson's notation, include

$$\frac{\partial f}{\partial x} = e^{-rt}\left(\frac{P_x}{P} - \frac{\partial T/P}{\partial x}\right) + \lambda_0 = 0 \tag{5.52}$$

$$\frac{\partial f}{\partial m} - \frac{d}{dt}\frac{\partial f}{\partial \dot{m}} = e^{-rt}\left(- \frac{\partial T/P}{\partial m} - \frac{\dot{P}}{P}\right) - \lambda_0 \frac{\partial \phi}{\partial m} + \frac{d}{dt} e^{-rt} = 0 \tag{5.53}$$

as well as conditions for $\partial f/\partial L$, $\partial f/\partial K$, $\partial f/\partial I$, $\partial f/\partial \lambda_0$, and $\partial f/\partial \lambda_1$. Note that all variables and the multipliers (λ_0, λ_1) are functions of time, that $m = M/P$, that P is the general price level, and that Euler conditions are presented for both K and m (the latter is equation (5.53), of course). We may combine (5.52) and (5.53), assuming that $(\partial T/P)/(\partial x) = (\partial T/P)/(\partial m)$, in which case we have the familiar result that

$$\frac{P_x}{P}\frac{\partial \phi}{\partial m} = r + \frac{\dot{P}}{P} = 1 \tag{5.54}$$

Continuing to ignore taxes (Coates does not) and specializing the production function (equation (5.50)) to the Cobb-Douglas, $x = AK^{\alpha}L^{\beta}m^{\gamma}$, so that $\partial \phi/\partial m = \gamma x/m$, we have an explicit demand for real balances by the firm of

$$m^* = \frac{\gamma \frac{P_x}{P} x}{r + \frac{\dot{P}}{P}} \tag{5.55}$$

which, then, could be lagged. This formulation has the interesting property that while r, the real rate, is appropriate for all investment decisions, i, the nominal rate, is appropriate for the user cost of real cash balances. This came out of the theory, in equation (5.53), in fact, and provides a neat theoretical justification for a distinction first noted in Chapter 1. We also note that Coates did some empirical work with his model, converting to nominal balances, and found some evidence of instability (he had a time series of data for 103 firms). He also found substantial economies of scale in the holding of cash balances.[30]

Another way money might influence investment, of course, is by means of changes in the price level - or by changes in the rate of inflation. In Chapter 1 and elsewhere we argued that the appropriate interest rate for investment - at least in the abstract version of the theory - is the real rather than the nominal interest rate, and so here we note that most empirical studies in this literature actually use the nominal rate. Part of this, no doubt, is the consequence of not having a good proxy for expected inflation (in $i = r + [(\Delta P/P)_e])$, and part has to do with the modest rates of inflation during most of the period actually studied, but since the early 1970s such complacency is certainly unwarranted. A paper rewriting the Sharpe-Lintner-Mossin capital asset pricing model in terms of real rates of return is by Chen and Boness (1975), who develop the idea of inflation-preferred, inflation-neutral, and inflation-averse stocks on the basis of the covariance between the stock's rate of return and the (expected) inflation rate. For the investment decision, though, Chen and Boness argue that the firm tends to invest less when uncertain inflation is expected (that is, the cost of capital is biased upward in uncertain inflation). Finally, as to the method of finance, Chen and Boness show that in the absence of corporate income taxes, uncertain inflation will not induce any effect from D/E or from dividend payout rates. Other studies (e.g. Van Horne, 1971; Cooley, Roenfeldt, and Chew, 1975; Nelson, 1976; and Cross, 1980) confirm that inflation is a factor, although the tendency in these studies is to emphasize the effect via tax laws and accounting practices rather than through the *ex ante* real rate of return as such. These studies are also at the firm level.

It is clear, of course, that individual firms can gain from expected inflation if the net effect on their present value between tax (etc.) advantages and depreciation (etc.) disadvantages is favourable. One further way the firm might gain occurs if the Keynesian idea that a little inflation is beneficial to growth is correct. (This is because it is (somehow), in this hypothesis, a stimulus to overall growth.) This introduces an interesting macroeconomic dimension to the problem. To assess this, Kim (1979)uses a model similar to that of Chen and Boness to measure the impact of inflation on the net operating income of 317 firms selected from the US COMPUSTAT tapes; three separate inflationary regimes were tested to the effect that the more rapid inflation (1971-76) showed a stronger positive effect of inflation on corporate earnings. This is not an aggregate result, but it is, at least, suggestive of what such a study might reveal.

There is a further important question raised by the Chen and Boness study involving the proper use of the formula for the real rate of interest. It is not entirely clear to this reader that Chen and Boness are distinguishing between the *ex post* and *ex ante* real interest rates (see Chapter 1), but at any rate what is appropriate for their proposition is r in $i = r + (\Delta P/P)_e$. In one view, then, $(\Delta P/P)_e$ is simply tacked on to i, and no interaction with r need occur (outside of tax and other similar considerations). This is why it is generally argued that r is appropriate for the investment and consumption functions (and i is not). Now it is an empirical question as to whether or not r and $(\Delta P/P)_e$ are interrelated, and so we may briefly comment on the evidence (we may take Kim's study as suggesting they are). Fama (1975), thus, argued that US Treasury Bill rates exhibited "rational" predictions of inflation (and so r and $(\Delta P/P)_e$ were unrelated). Fama, actually went further and argued that r was constant, but in subsequent studies (Nelson and Schwert, 1977, Garbade and Wachtel, 1978, and Fama and Gibbons, 1980) this was shown to be untrue. In the last of these, Fama and Gibbons actually found *some* evidence of a connection between r and $(\Delta P/P)_e$.[31]

5.5 INVENTORY INVESTMENT

In the foregoing, which was devoted to any type of investment expenditure but which probably is most apt for business fixed investment, it was possible to hope for a proportional relation between the capital stock and output, at least when resources are fully employed. Inventory investment, though, is planned for a short term, and thus it is simply not going to be designed to bridge the cycle; rather, the typical firm may well seek to adjust its inventories at several times during the business cycle, even possibly using the inventory to mitigate the effect of the cycle in some way. Complicating the problem is the fact that inventories are both demand and supply determined in a way which seems especially compelling in this context. That is, a firm can pick its desired capital stock and its desired rate of investment (and more or less aim to achieve them), but its desired level of inventories is itself (a) contingent on estimated sales figures and (b) fluctuates with the demand for the product. In fact, it is at least conceivable that a firm can cut production to zero, mark down the price of its stock-in-trade, and still not easily reach its desired level of inventories in particular (recessed) circumstances. Also of considerable significance is the fact that inventory investment behaviour - at least over recent American business cycles - has provided a large measured "contribution" to overall instability (accounting for as much as 75 per cent of the change in real GNP in recent cycles.[32] Of course, whether or not this is added instability or instability in lieu of some more costly (or more socially undesirable) form of adjustment to cyclical pressures is something which (a) must be studied in the context of a specific macroeconomic model admitting of both possibilities and (b) is unknown, essentially, in the present state of the art.

There are various ways to organize the theoretical and empirical material on this topic, but one of the more interesting is that of Rowley and Trivedi (1975) who suggest transactions, precautionary, and speculative approaches, just as if inventories were money balances. The essence of the "transactions cost" approach is the minimization of the cost of holding an inventory when the fluctuation in sales (or expected sales) can be described by some statistical distribution and when penalty (or brokerage) and interest costs can be assigned; the inventories are then useful because there is a lack of synchronization between sales and production (for example). A transactions cost approach, though, does not convey the idea of a "buffer stock" very clearly, since a buffer stock, on the whole suggests the existence of a "precautionary motive" for holding inventories. The buffer stock, then, is held (at least partly) to offset fluctuations in a firm's business; in this connection one must distinguish between "production for stocks" versus "production for order" since these may well produce different responses. In particular, when firms produce for order, they may well carry very small stocks - in effect holding an inventory of orders - compared to the "production for stocks system", when all sales are made directly out of stocks.[33] Finally, there may well be a "speculative demand" for certain types of inventories, based on price expectations or on expected input shortages. We will pursue this analogy with the demand for money in what follows, although we will also refer to some studies which do not fit this overall scheme.

5.5.1 THE TRANSACTIONS DEMAND FOR INVENTORIES

A natural way to begin with the transactions demand for inventories is to formulate an investment-in-inventories model by means of the inventory theoretic model of Chapter 3; indeed, that model is really more obvious in the present context, since cash inventories are much more liquid (in general) than are goods inventories.[34] Without derivation, then, a starting point could be the simple "square root formula" in the form of

$$I_I^* = \left(\frac{2bS^e}{r}\right)^{1/2} \tag{5.56}$$

where S^e represents expected sales, r the real (*ex ante*) interest rate, and b is a (penalty) brokerage fee per item ordered from the firm's suppliers.

The problem with (5.56) is that it is naive; in practice, S^e will be unequal to S^a - actual sales - and firms will undertake some adjustment for this stochastic factor in advance. Thus, following the Miller and Orr (1966) model of Chapter 3, suppose that the distribution of the inventory is expected to follow a Bernoulli process. If p is the probability of the inventory increasing by I during a day and $q = 1 - p$, then over n weeks the distribution of changes in inventories can be represented by

$$\begin{aligned} \mu_n &= ntI(p - q) \\ \sigma_n^2 &= 4ntpqI^2 \end{aligned} \tag{5.57}$$

If we assume $p = q = 1/2$, then $\mu_n = 0$ and $\sigma_n^2 = nI^2t$. Let the expected cost $(E(C))$ per day (T) of managing the inventory be given by

$$E(C) = rE(\overline{I}) + \frac{bE(N)}{T} \tag{5.58}$$

where $E(\overline{I})$ is the average level of inventories (and r is the real interest foregone by holding them) and $E(N)/T$ is the number of inventory adjustments per week (b is the cost per order). Following the discussion of Chapter 3, then, without repeating the derivation, we can derive a demand for inventory investment (in the stochastic framework) of

$$I_I^* = \frac{4}{3}\left(\frac{3b}{4r}\sigma_I^2\right)^{1/3} \tag{5.59}$$

which is certainly a general enough version (in spite of its apparent rigidity, the scale parameters here can vary over a wide range). At any rate, this is a two variable model with r and σ_I^2 rather than sales; it emphasizes that a proportionality to sales is not to be expected in the event that stochastic elements are (as they must be) relevant. One can also use a portfolio (mean-variance) model here, but we will forbear for the time being.

5.5.2 THE PRECAUTIONARY DEMAND FOR INVENTORIES

The main development in the "precautionary demand for stocks" is the inventory-accelerator model designed both to provide an *ad hoc* rationale for the holding of "buffer" stocks and to show how "reasonable" inventory behaviour can lead to business cycles. Indeed, the accelerator model, with sales usually providing the momentum, is the most widely used inventory investment model in the literature.

Actually, firms will hold inventories for a number of (interrelated) buffer stock reasons, involving the firm's overall capital stock (fixed and variable) in the limit. The typical case of an inventory is (a) the finished good (held above the quantity of orders), but firms also hold (b) inventories of materials and goods-in-process, (c) inventories of liquid assets, and, even, (d) inventories of excess capacity and labour skills. These items can offset each other and certainly depend on forecasted interest rates, prices, shortages, etc., and so a very complicated "portfolio" problem may well exist, involving capital from fixed to totally liquid, in the task of minimizing adjustment costs (and/or raising profits). We will generally not concentrate on (c) and (d) in this summary, generally limiting the discussion to the items in (a) and (b). At any rate, such interactions are at the heart of the economic (micro and macro) functions of inventories, as we shall see.[35]

To begin with, we follow the work of A. Ott, D. Ott, and Yoo (1971) and Rowley and Trivedi (1975). Metzler (1941) is responsible for an early version of the accelerator-inventory investment model. In one of his models Metzler assumes that firms try to hold their inventories in proportion to expected sales as in $K^*_{It} = \alpha S^e_t$. Assuming, then, that expected sales in t are equal to actual sales in $t - 1$, that is, assuming that $S^e_t = S_{t-1}$, and assuming that $I_{It} = K^*_{it} - K_{It-1}$, we have a simple relation for inventory investment of

$$I_{It} = \alpha S_{t-1} - K_{It-1} \qquad (5.60)$$

K_{It-1}, itself, is the inventory of investment goods at the end of $t - 1$. This is equal to the stock at the end of $t - 2$ $(= K_{t-2})$ less the change in sales in period $t - 1$ $(= \Delta S_{t-1})$. With this further substitution, we have

$$I_{It} = \alpha S_{t-1} - K_{It-2} + \Delta S_{t-1} \tag{5.61}$$

where the substitutions for past capital stocks are arbitrarily stopped.[36] We may, then, embed this result in a simple model of national income determination in order to obtain an "inventory cycle" in national income. Thus, if we interpret S_{t-1} as consumption (recall that S is "sales" here) and impose the condition that $C_t = \beta Y_t$, then with $Y_t = C_t + I_{It} + \overline{I}_{Ft}$ and with fixed investment $(\overline{I}_{Ft})$ exogenous, we clearly have a second-degree difference equation in national income; this is, of course, merely the simple accelerator-multiplier model, with inventories in the role of investment in that model.

Metzler, in another version of the model in his early paper, also defines a "coefficient of expectations" as in $\eta = \Delta S^e_t / \Delta S_{t-1}$, and with this providing a new version for S^e_t $S^e_t = S_{t-1} + \eta \Delta S_{t-1}$, we have an investment function of

$$I_{It} = \alpha S_{t-1} + (1 + \alpha\eta)\Delta S_{t-1} - \eta \Delta S_{t-2} - K_{It-2} \tag{5.62}$$

Again we might include this as one equation in a model with I_{Ft} and C_t (for S_t) proportional to lagged income.[37] The result in this case is a third-degree difference equation (if we substitute $C_t = \beta Y_{t-1}$ and $Y_t = C_t + I_{It} + \overline{I}_{Ft}$) whose stability properties include the possibility of sharp swings in national income. We note that a separate accelerator, perhaps with a longer lag, could be introduced for $\overline{I}_{Ft}$ and that longer lags for C_t can be assumed.[38]

Turning to the flexible accelerator and other developments, we first consider work by L.R. Klein (1950), Darling (1959), and M.C. Lovell (1961); summaries of this work appear in Evans (1969) and D. Ott, A. Ott, and Yoo (1975). Klein used the relation $I_{It} = \lambda(K^*_{It} - K_{It-1})$, which implies a partial adjustment of the stock of inventories; this is the flexible accelerator. When we substitute this into Metzler's formulation in equation (5.60), it produces an inventory investment function of

$$I_{It} = \lambda\alpha S_{t-1} + \lambda(1 + \alpha\eta)\Delta(S_{t-1}) - \lambda\eta\Delta(S_{t-2}) - \lambda K_{It-2} \tag{5.63}$$

which is in exactly the same form as equation (5.62) but with a different interpretation of the coefficients. Darling, in the second of these models, suggests that α - the ratio of inventory to sales - may well vary inversely with the cycle (in addition to the relations already specified in equation (5.60)); thus let

$$a = a_0 + a_1\left(\frac{\Delta U}{S}\right)_{t-1}$$

where ΔU is the change in unfilled orders, and substitute this variable accelerator equation into (5.60), adding λ for "flexibility" and dropping S_{t-1}; this produces an inventory investment demand of

$$I_{It} = \lambda a_0 S_{t-1} + \lambda a_1 \Delta(U_{t-1}) - \lambda K_{It-2} \tag{5.64}$$

His tests produced strikingly firm results in terms of $\bar{R}^2$, the von Neumann ratio (which is, though, biased towards 2 in this case), the significance of the coefficients, and (possibly) the stability of the formulation over quarterly US manufacturing data for 1947-58.

Finally, M.C. Lovell (1961) assumes both the flexible accelerator (λ) and a partial adjustment (β) in $I_{It} = \lambda(K^*_{It} - K_{It-1}) + \beta(S^e_t - S_t)$ with $S^e_t - S_t = \zeta(S_t - S_{t-1})$ and with $K^*_{It} = \gamma S^e_t$. Lovell justifies the term $\beta(S^e_t - S_t)$ in terms of the reasonableness of having a lag in lining up expectations with sales. Thus, if β is equal to zero, then we have "static expectations", while with $0 < \beta < 1$, the implication is that firms will adjust their expectations in a "sticky" way (i.e. predictions understate actual events). The resulting inventory investment demand function is then

$$I_{It} = \lambda\gamma S + \zeta(\lambda\gamma + \beta)\Delta(S_t) - \lambda K_{It-1} \tag{5.65}$$

Lovell estimates this on quarterly US data for 1948-55 for all manufacturing and finds that it works well (in terms of standard errors, etc.) for durable but not for non-durable manufacturing; in fact, β was close to 0.8. Lovell also provides a useful distinction between "purchased material plus goods in process" and "finished goods". The latter may well respond more quickly to changes in demand, while the former would require further production and possibly unfilled orders.

In the foregoing, t could refer to a period of any length although the empirical tests have tended to work with quarterly data. It does not seem reasonable to work with two and three quarter lag structures in some industries (especially in heavy industry), but one should also remember that the models described here are "temporally reduced" forms and that when the empirical estimates appear, lags implying quarterly adjustment of as little as 10-20 per cent are not uncommon. Darling (1959), indeed, felt strongly that an *a priori* lag of two quarters was too long, and M.C. Lovell (1967) also found that the lags were unreasonably long. One real-world problem is that when firms face an increase in demand, three things are involved: they must replace their depleted stocks; they might wish to increase the size of their buffer stocks; and they may wish to acquire quickly a "speculative balance" in anticipation of (further) price rises. With this much pressure on suppliers, it may be some time before stock orders are actually filled, at least in some cases.

Another concern, more in the spirit of the accelerator model itself, is that the researcher actually has no *a priori* reason to believe that lags are short and thus to doubt his results; Carlson and Wehrs (1974) refer to this as "implicit theorizing" and attribute it to an analogy with some (usually) unstated microeconomic perception. Carlson and Wehrs also suggest distinguishing the decision period from the (quarterly) data period, where the decision period is presumably shorter; while the Lovell formulation in equation (5.64) does this, they propose to add an objective function - a quadratic cost function - where an "out of equilibrium" cost is added to the basic production cost. Their empirical work rejects their model, however.

An earlier study which tackles the question of decision variables more completely is by Hay (1970b). Hay notes that the Darling and Lovell models assume production is "given" and that the product price is constant; instead, Hay proposes an "integrated model" with a single optimization process.[39] In Hay's model desired unfilled orders are assumed to be a linear function of production $U_t^* = a_1 + a_2X_t$ (recalling that unfilled orders could be deliberate and could be industry- and firm-specific); the cost of deviating from the desired level of unfilled orders is a quadratic, $a_3 + a_4(U_t - U_t^*)^2$; desired inventories are proportional to sales, $H_t^* = b_1 + b_2S_t$, and they also have a quadratic deviation $b_3 + b_4(H_t - H_t^*)^2$; unit costs of production are a quadratic $c_2(X_t - X_{t-1})^2$; and new orders (the demand for the product) are $\theta_t = d_1 - d_2P_t$, with the cost of changing price a quadratic $c_3(P_t - P_{t-1})^2$, itself justified in terms of firms' conservatism. Hay, then, sets up a Lagrangean which recognizes that $\theta_t - S_t \equiv U_t - U_{t-1}$ and $X_t - S_t \equiv H_t - H_{t-1}$ and derives "linear decision rules" for X_t, P_t, and H_t; the latter is in the form

$$H_t = f(X_{t-1}, P_{t-1}, H_{t-1}, U_{t-1}, Q_t, Q_{t+1}, \dots, V_{t-1}, V_t, \dots) \qquad (5.66)$$

with Q_{t+1}, V_t, etc. being expected variables. Hay tests his model for its sensitivity to specification error and is not dissatisfied. But just as happened with Carlson and Wehrs, the inventory equation generally failed to perform on US monthly data, 1953-66 (partly because *a priori* values were often close to zero). At any rate the mutual endogenizizing of price, output, and inventories in an optimizing framework is a sensible way to proceed, especially, one might conjecture, for aggregate studies.[40]

The conflict between the "theoretical" expectation of a short lag and the empirical estimation of a long lag in the adjustment of inventories is, as noted, a very frequent result in the literature; this has prompted the development of a "target-adjustment" model, assuming adjustment within the quarter, by Feldstein and Auerbach (1976). Feldstein and Auerbach note five important characteristics of the data on manufactured durable goods:

(1) actual changes in inventories represent the outputs and inputs of very short periods (a day, potentially!);
(2) investment in materials and goods-in-process inventories is three times that in finished goods;
(3) as before, fluctuations in inventories (both types) are large compared to fluctuations in GNP;
(4) these two types of inventory investment are uncorrelated (0.2 or so); and
(5) the former component fluctuates in a destabilizing and the latter in a stabilizing fashion.

First of all, with regard to finished goods inventories, the Lovell model is estimated (as a bench-mark) on 1961-76 quarterly data; the lags are very long (less than 35 per cent adjustment in a year).[41] The essence of their "within quarter" model is in two equations. In the first

$$I_{It} = I^*_{It} + \gamma_0(S^e_{t,\,t} - S_t) + u_t \qquad (5.67)$$

where both I^*_{It} and $S^e_{t,\,t}$ (for sales) are measured at t, and γ_0 is, in any event, expected to be small. In the second, *desired* inventories (I^*_I) are assumed to adjust slowly, as in

$$I^*_{It} - I^*_{It-1} = \mu(\gamma_1 + \gamma_2 S^e_{t,\,t} - I^*_{It-1}) + e_t \qquad (5.68)$$

where μ measures the speed of adjustment. Combining (5.67) and (5.68), and lagging (5.67) to obtain I^*_{It-1}, Feldstein and Auerbach produce an equation in which two parameters, μ and γ_0, represent the new hypothesis. γ_0 turns out to be small, supporting the idea that unanticipated changes in sales are adjusted for within the quarter.

Turning to the more volatile component - materials and goods in process - Feldstein and Auerbach again obtain very long lags when they employ Lovell-type accelerator models. Because goods-in-process stockpiling is a partial substitute for materials stockpiling, Feldstein and Auerbach find it necessary to set up separate equations. The equation for materials investment recognizes that orders placed for materials are not deliveries (and orders can be cancelled easily). Again, assuming within-quarter "target adjustment", the result is an equation of the form

$$I_{IMGt} = \eta a_0 + \eta a_1 N\theta_{t-1} + \eta a_2 U\theta_{t-1} + (1-\eta) I_{IMGt-1} + v_t \quad (5.69)$$

were $N\theta$ is new orders and $U\theta$ is unfilled orders. The result is again a successful regression on the US data. The two models are then used to predict the behaviour of inventories in the 1974 - 75 recession (the two equations were re-estimated up to the end of 1973) when (in 1974) inventories fell sharply, exacerbating the downturn of that year. Their equations correctly predict the events (missing the turning point) without reference to the inflation rate, interest rates, and energy prices. This, of course, is because these elements are endogenized into sales expectations (and sales) which the model reacts quickly to. They are probably also swamped by sales changes.

Maccini and Rossana (1981), in a recent paper, utilize a model developed by Maccini (1978) in which a buffer stock model is employed and the aggregate manufacturing firm chooses prices, output, and the size of the inventory of finished goods (with the price and output decision used to set the optimal inventory). In their model, in contrast to Feldstein and Auerbach, desired inventories respond slowly because the variables they depend on change slowly. These variables are "normal" variables (expected variables) which themselves respond slowly to changes in the underlying data. Their equation for desired inventories is

$$\log I^*_{1t} = a_0 + a_1 \log S^*_t + a_2 \log \frac{W^*_t}{P^*_t} + a_3 \log \frac{V^*_t}{P^*_t} + a_4 r^*_t \quad (5.70)$$

where S_t^* is expected normal orders and V_t^* is the expected normal level of raw material prices. Raw material inventories are included explicitly in the analysis, and Maccini and Rossana also incorporate "production smoothing" and (of course) an assumption about expectations (they are "regressive" - really auto regressive). Over the US total manufacturing sector the results indicate quick adjustment between desired and actual inventories and slow adjustment of desired inventories. Normal real interest rates (measured by a distributed lag of past real interest rates) do not work, but the rates were *ex post* real rates which is not the correct concept (see Chapter 1). An attempt to use a "normal" real rate to correct for this was also unsuccessful. At any rate, this is the usual result, and the Maccini and Rossana paper does go further than most other studies in giving this appealing hypothesis a chance.

Not only does the holding of buffer stocks of inventories provide a force which may contribute to or alleviate the business cycle, but their use has a number of interesting implications for macroeconomic studies. For one thing, inventories, acting as a buffer, can cushion the shock on business firms so that they are not forced to alter their prices frequently (Blinder, 1981a, 1981b). The existence of buffer stocks of goods, in a word, can explain the existence of sticky prices. For another, buffer stock inventories - embedded in a Keynesian model - help explain why real wages move pro-cyclically (the usual Keynesian model predicts they move contra-cyclically (via sticky money wages)); what happens (see Blinder, 1977) is that the demand for labour shifts considerably, compared to the supply, so that money wages pick up much of the effect of the cycle directly. For yet another, there is a short-run reaction in inventories, when the demand for final output swamps the revision in desired inventories; this could imply a kind of short-run stagflation, at least in Keynesian models in which price setting is neither "rational" nor competitive. Finally, the consideration of buffer stocks of inventories provides us with a compelling reason for doubting the usefulness, at least for mild fluctuations, of the Barro-Grossman disequilibrium models. In particular, the effects of spillovers between markets discussed in Chapter 1 would not occur if firms absorb the impact of an unexpected disequilibrium in their inventories (of goods and money). This is also discussed in a paper by Leijonhufvud (1973).

In an interesting extension of the basic Metzler model, M. C. Lovell (1974) considers how monetary policy might be employed to alleviate the effects of inventory cycles; he builds on the paper by M.C. Lovell and Prescott (1968) which was considered earlier in this chapter as an addition to the basic accelerator-multiplier model. Lovell assumes that desired inventories depend on expected sales and on the interest rate, as in

$$I^*_{It} = a_0 + a_1 S^e_t - a_2 i_t \tag{5.71}$$

and also adopts the basic Metzler model. Assuming consumption is proportional to output and with fixed capital investment and government spending both assumed to be exogenous, Lovell derives a third-order difference equation for income as in

$$y_t = b_1 y_{t-1} + b_2 y_{t-2} + b_3 y_{t-3} + b_4 (i_t - i_{t-1}) + b_5 G^*_t \tag{5.72}$$

where G^*_t is composed of current and lagged values of the exogenous variables. Equation (5.71) represents a "financial" influence on inventories of the kind generally not successfully estimated in the literature (see e.g. Trivedi, 1970); here "monetary policy" is assumed to be one of direct *nominal* interest rate control. Lovell also amends his money supply hypothesis to permit the authorities to adjust the interest rate to changing economic conditions; this is done by assuming equation (5.73)

$$i_t - i_n = \pi (y_{t-1} - y^*_t) \tag{5.73}$$

where i_n is a target or "neutral" interest rate and y^*_t is a targel level of GNP. The achievement of an interest rate target by means of open market operations requires the use of a demand for money function, which is the standard

$$M_d = c_0 + c_1 y - c_2 i \tag{5.74}$$

This leads to a money supply rule of

$$M_s = c_0 + c_2 (\pi y^* - i_n) + (c_1 - c_2 \pi) y_{t-1} \tag{5.75}$$

The parameter π, then, becomes the key to the monetary authority's control over the inventory cycle; equation (5.73) is substituted into equation (5.75) - for $M_t - M_{t-1}$ - as if the demand for money were stable, and the (complicated) roots of the resulting third-order difference equation in income are examined. Lovell discovers that while monetary policy can be stabilizing it can also be set in such a way that it adds to instability. Furthermore, as was the case with the general accelerator-multiplier model, Lovell shows that there are admissable values of the parameters for which no monetary offset to inventory-induced instability exists. All of this, and some further work with a stochastic specification, is somewhat under a cloud in view of the inability of researchers to measure any direct financial influences on inventory investment; the interest rate, in particular, has generally not worked. Of course, one should also sound a note of caution about whether one should take inventory fluctuations as producers of rather than productions of general instability.[42] One might, then, conjecture that a rational expectations approach, use of the distinction between nominal and real rates, and, even, a wealth/real balance effect variable may sharpen the hypothesis about financial influences on inventory investment.

One of the things one might do to add to the monetary approach is to construct a model of inventory demand under "rational expectations" and then to shock it, with unexpected monetary policy. Haraf (1978) does some work on this problem in a paper which explains why the lags on "monetary policy" in rational expectations models are so long (up to three years); Haraf refers to work by Barro (1978). The hypothesis is that inventories and backlogs of orders absorb the impact of monetary surprises, enabling firms to spread the effect over a longer period; in effect, the monetary policy proxy "picks up" the longer inventory adjustment in the Barro equation. Haraf's empirical work supports his argument.[43] With regard to the interest rate itself, some work by Lieberman (1980b) shows that cost-of-capital concepts (balance sheet variables, essentially) work at the firm level, while Irvine (1981) found that retail inventories respond to a Hall-Jorgenson cost-of-capital measure and so did merchant wholesale inventories (1980). In the latter study the Hall-Jorgenson expression used, in effect, a real interest rate (with price expectations modelled over past price changes). In all cases the cost-of-capital variable worked, statistically. Finally, on US data, Rubin (1979-80) obtains both a nominal interest rate effect and short lags (54 per cent adjustment in a quarter) in a model built on a flexible accelerator and a "planned" versus "unplanned" inventory relation; the rate of inflation (of inventory prices) does not work in this case.

5.5.3 THE SPECULATIVE DEMAND FOR INVENTORIES

The speculative demand for inventories leads one rather

quickly from a Keynesian notion to one of rational expectations; indeed, Muth's classic paper (1961) on rational expectations is worked on a micro-inventory price-expectation problem. A "differences of opinion" rationale - as in Keynes - could provide a plunger's demand for inventories by firms. Since firms will tend to have diversified portfolios of inventories, a more reasonable approach is the mean-variance. Thus, we could suppose that inventory speculators have a profit function (net of all storage and transactions costs) of

$$E(\pi_t) = I_{It}(P^e_{t+1} - P_t) \qquad (5.76)$$

that

$$u = U(E(\pi), \sigma^2_\pi) \qquad (5.77)$$

with $U_1 > 0$, $U_2 < 0$ and that

$$E(u) = a - cE[e^{-b\pi}] \qquad (5.78)$$

provides a specific functional form for expected utility. With π distributed normally and both π and σ^2_π describing a vector of inventory opportunities, the general model of Section 3.4 on the demand for money could be applied literally here. It would lead to "demand for inventory" functions with expected price changes (as in equation (5.76)) as arguments. There could even be, in this framework, "portfolio effects" (such as complementarity). Finally, note that this model may well be appropriate in aggregate studies, not as a "pure" price expectations model, but in the event that it proxies an expectation of future shortages (or delays in orders); inflation (a rise in all money prices) would not generally have an impact here, and so a total aggregate $(C + I + G)$ would not be expected to show a speculative demand for inventories unless general shortages or delays were expected.[44]

Muth, indeed, writes the expected utility function as in equation (5.79); we follow Rowley and Trivedi (1978).

$$E[U(\pi_t)] = U(0) + U'(0)E(\pi_t) + \tfrac{1}{2}U''(0)E(\pi^2_t) + \ldots \qquad (5.79)$$

Substituting from (5.76) and using the definition of σ^2_{t+1} and the first two terms of the expansion, he obtains

$$I^s_t = \frac{-U'(0)(P^e_{t+1} - P_t)}{U''(0)[\sigma^2_{t+1} + (P^e_{t+1} - P_t)^2]} \qquad (5.80)$$

With $U''(0) < 0$, then, an increase in the expected compared to the actual price would cause an increase in speculative inventory investment. Finally, this model can be turned into the often-used empirical form of

$$I_{It} = \alpha(P^e_{t+1} - P_t) + u_t$$

with the assumption that $(P^e_{t+1} - P_t)^2$ is small, provided that our measure of risk aversion $U'(0)/U''(0)$ is constant and σ^2_{t+1} is independent of P^e_{t+1}.

5.6 HOUSING "INVESTMENT"

A house, of course, is a consumer durable, and so its inclusion in a chapter on investment needs to be justified. For one thing, new housing expenditure is a large sector in the national accounts, and, for another, housing starts seem unusually responsive to cyclical pressures, especially those involved with fluctuations in nominal interest rates. Then, too, a house is a personal "investment" - along with money, consumer stocks, bonds, etc. - and so standard investment theory, real or financial, may be appropriate in approaching the housing market. Further, a house can be thought of as a (particularly) durable consumer good, one, quite possibly, subject to erratic swings of the accelerator type. Finally, and by no means peripherally, there are some unique "model aspects" to this literature that are of direct interest to the macro-economist.

This section, then, considers three main topics. To begin with, there is a short discussion of the housing market itself which is needed to clarify the special nature of the market; the survey here is suggestive only, primarily because detailed concentration on one industry is unlikely to have much of a macroeconomic pay off in anything other than fairly disaggregated models. The second topic concerns the housing investment models themselves, from early *ad hoc* models to recent dynamic consumption forms. Finally, we return to the topic of financial influences on investment by considering the topic of "credit rationing" as it applies to the housing market. This is both a justification for using a disequilibrium approach and a justification for designing specific policies to prevent "housing disequilibrium" as a result of, for example, a tight money policy. We will discuss credit availability in Section 5.6.2 and the estimation of (housing) disequilibrium models in Section 5.6.3.

A house is manufactured by a business firm, which may also be a dealer in houses (may also have an inventory of houses), for a final consumer of housing services. The latter will likely regard his house as a personal investment, and its durability and expense will require that careful long-term plans be laid when the purchase is initially effected. The house, indeed, along with short- and medium-term savings accounts (up to M3 in the US monetary data) and human capital often represents the bulk of a private wealth holder's assets. Constraining both the supplier of houses and the demander - in view of the mass of capital tied up in a housing investment - is the cost and availability of funds. Usually, in this context, it is the flow of funds to the demander (the "investor") in the form of mortgage funds which is discussed in connection with the housing market. Indeed, the institutional structure here is radically different from that facing the housing supplier, whose framework is similar to that discussed above (under the heading of business fixed investment), although there are some alleged differences here, too.

Among the issues most frequently discussed in connection with the housing market itself, one finds the following "stylized facts" on most lists. For one thing, it is frequently argued that business fixed investment and (other) consumer expenditures pre-empt physical inputs and credit so that the housing market receives residual supplies of both real and financial resources. We will discuss the "credit rationing" hypothesis below, but here we should note that the "residual real inputs" hypothesis seems to be based on an alleged preference of construction workers for the less seasonal fixed investment projects and on the alleged ability of the fixed investment projects to hire away workers from housing construction contractors. This factor is argued to provide a contra-cyclical nature to housing expenditures, since business fixed investment is pro-cyclical. Poor "credit availability", too, is supposed to hurt the housing industry during the later stages of the typical business expansion, and this factor is accentuated by the (alleged) relatively high credit needs of the housing sector which involves both purchasers and builders. Thus two main factors are adduced to explain an alleged contra-cyclical pattern to housing expenditures.[45]

5.6.1 SOME BASIC RESULTS FOR HOUSING

The following section considers the housing market by means of analogies with consumption and investment demand models. Naively, one might begin by postulating a connection between income and housing demand, in which case a "permanent income" measure - along the lines of Chapter 1 - would seem to be most appropriate in a model which emphasizes the consumption of housing services; to get to "new starts" or "housing expenditures", then, one needs to consider how stocks of housing and inventories of finished and unfinished housing are influential on the housing decision. We will not follow this literature in great detail, primarily because it is essentially microeconomic (especially in its use of data), but a few words are in order here, before we consider three approaches which are more in the spirit of macro-modelling (and do not require disaggregation beyond the total of housing expenditure itself).

In a basic paper, Muth (1960) provides what is now the standard demand for housing - given here by equation (5.81) - in which i_H could be a mortgage interest rate (Muth uses a bond rate).

$$H_D = a_0 + a_1 P_H + a_2 Y_P + a_3 i_H \tag{5.81}$$

This expression needs to be combined with expressions to deal with the dynamics in order to construct some sort of minimum empirical test; it also can use other variables and can be estimated as part of a structure. Muth tests the simple model and ends up with appropriate signs for his variables and with permanent income as his income variable. This model, as noted, has formed the basis of a large number of studies, often over very disaggregated data. With our interest here primarily in macroeconomic topics, we will discuss below papers on aggregation bias; on simultaneous equations bias, involving, for example, the supply of housing; and on which variables should be expected to work best, how they should be measured and estimated, and what sort of response elasticities actually emerge (in simple cases).

Turning to more specifically macroeconomic approaches, we may try to construct a housing demand model as if it were a consumption-expenditure problem. The first consideration is that by breaking out a particular component of consumption (by disaggregating), we necessarily introduce relative prices into the framework. Muth, as already noted, has permanent income and the price of housing, but, instead, let us refer again to the Boughton (1976) consumption model in which food, other non-durables, and durable goods were distinguished and equation (5.83) was estimated

$$C_k^*(t) = \beta_0 + \beta_1 Y_P(t) + \beta_2 \left(\frac{P_k}{P}\right)(t) + \beta_3 L(t) + u(t) \tag{5.82}$$

for $k = 1, \ldots, 3$ categories of consumption. For purposes of this section, $y_p(t)$ would represent permanent income, and $L(t)$ would represent a measure of liquid assets (perhaps as a wealth proxy or even as a supply of funds proxy)[46]; k, then, could be disaggregated into "non-durables", "durables", and "housing" expenditures. Putting a lag structure in for y_p would be equivalent to postulating a difference between $C_k^*(t)$ and $C_k(t)$ - i.e. between desired and actual housing consumption expenditures (Boughton did not find slow adjustment for *his* categories and his y_p lags were the same across categories). The hypothesis, then, is that housing investment is a consumption expenditure that substitutes for (or complements) other expenditures (P_k/P), that may have a different lag pattern (for y_p) due to its durability and postponability, and that may well strengthen the influence of liquid assets (L) on consumption, on account of the influence of "credit rationing" in housing markets. There do not seem to have been consumption or investment studies with just this rationale, but it is logical enough, and it is a potentially rewarding disaggregation, depending on the strength of the substitution effects (etc.) and on the availability of suitable data.[47]

The foregoing is not really adequate in that the investment aspect of housing is not accounted for, and this could be accomodated in a consumption-investment model. One way to do this is to follow the neoclassical investment model, but in this case to produce a neoclassical new-housing-demand function. We consider a model developed by Kalchbrenner (1972), as explained by D. Ott, A. Ott, and Yoo (1975). Assume, firstly, a per capita demand for housing services of

$$\frac{c_h}{N} = \gamma\left(\frac{P_h}{P}, \frac{c}{N}\right) \qquad (5.83)$$

where c is total consumption services (Kalchbrenner had permanent income), and P_h is the rent per unit of housing. To convert from the flow to the stock demand, we note that for a perpetual stream of rents $P_h/i = P_H$ where P_H is the average price of a new house. Deducting property and income taxes (in the form of T, a tax rate) from P_H, we have

$$P_h = P_H(1 - T)i$$

With this substitution we may directly model the desired stock of housing as in

$$\frac{K^*_H}{N} = \gamma\left(\frac{P_H(1 - T)i}{P}, \frac{c}{N}\right) \qquad \gamma_1 < 0;\ \gamma_2 > 0 \qquad (5.84)$$

which Ott, Ott, and Yoo and Kalchbrenner take in the Cobb-Douglas form. Here K_H^* increases with rises in T and P and decreases with rises in i and P_H. Finally, one can simply tack on a depreciation rate (δh), assume that one does not achieve his desired housing stock instantly, and then derive an investment-in-housing function in the manner of the Jorgenson investment function.

$$I_{Ht}^* = W(L)[K_{Ht}^* - K_{Ht-1}^*] + \delta_h K_{Ht-1} \quad (5.85)$$

The life-cycle model of consumption - in which the consumer uses his wealth to smooth his consumption stream depending on his age - would seem a natural way to model home ownership. As Tobin (1972) suggests, much of an individual's wealth is actually in a very illiquid form - a house - and so it might be more relevant to solve a "liquidity constraint" problem, in which case interest rate effects would be downgraded and the appropriate income constraint would be the level of income rather than some measure of permanent income. Dolde and Tobin (1971), then, find that this may well apply to younger and poorer households, at least, suggesting, for one thing, the existence of an interesting aggregation problem. Artle and Varaiya (1978) point all this out and then go on to develop a life-cycle, "tenure" decision model in which the consumption of housing services is constant over the life-cycle, while the house may be purchased at any time. A renter gains liquidity at the cost of the greater utility in the consumption of housing services, and so renting, even over the entire life-cycle, is certainly rational (it is also rational as a part of an overall portfolio strategy). While much of the Artle and Varaiya paper is technical, there are some interesting results. For one thing, since home owners find it difficult to "borrow on their equity", there is a market imperfection which must be considered; this is overcome by entering the market as soon as a down payment is scratched together in full knowledge that a period of "forced saving" will ensue. This helps explain why housing demand is sensitive to the non-price terms of the loan (without reference to "credit rationing"). For another thing, the inability to borrow on equity introduces a discontinuity in the "tenure" decision-age profile. This discontinuity, of course, may well arrive at an early age.

We may derive a neoclassical expression for housing expenditure directly, following Motley's (1969) work on the demand for money. Let consumers maximize life-time utility.

$$U = \int_0^\infty \gamma(t)U[c_h(t), c_n(t)] \quad (5.86)$$

Here $\gamma(t)$ represents time preference; c_h and c_n are service flows from housing and all other consumer goods; and a specific functional form such as

$$U[c_h(t),\ c_n(t)] = Ac_h^{\alpha}c_n^{\beta} \tag{5.87}$$

could be adopted.

Much of the economics of this problem lies in the constraints; let housing depreciate at the rate δ so that

$$\dot{K}_h = I_h + \delta K_h \tag{5.88}$$

Furthermore, suppose that the aggregate consumer has a resources constraint of

$$\int_0^{\infty} e^{-rt}[Y(t) - P_n(t)c_n(t) - P_h(t)c_h(t)]dt \tag{5.89}$$

P_h, here, represents an appropriately scaled rental rate (or an implicit rental rate for owner-occupied housing) for housing, and $Y(t)$ is national income, presumably including an estimate of the implicit income generated in home ownership as well as direct rental income. It is taken as after-tax income as in equation (5.90).

$$Y(t) = Y(t) - \mu(t)\{Y^*(t) - P_H[w(t)r + x(t)\frac{\dot{P}_H}{P_H}]K_h\} \tag{5.90}$$

Here $\mu(t)$ is an income tax rate applied to that part of income $(Y^*(t))$ which is taxable (recall that houses generate implicit income); $w(t)$ represents the interest deduction (in the US tax code); and $x(t)$ represents the different tax treatment of realized capital gains in the housing market.[48] Note that the latter would have to come from actual house sales in the cases where taxes were not completely avoided in some way.

In the foregoing the consumer chooses c_h, c_n, and I_h with the latter representing the aggregate housing investment function. It will depend, in general, on the relative price of housing services P_h/P_n, on expected income (itself dependent on expected taxes and capital gains in housing), and on the real interest rate. Even so, an increase in the interest rate will clearly have an ambiguous effect since it will have income, substitution, and wealth effects complicated by the tax deduction of the interest payments of consumers. An increase in income would have a positive effect, normally, but a rise in the relative price of housing increases the implicit (and explicit) rental payment as well as offering the chance to convert a capital gain to cash (and earn r).

Increases in the income tax rate would tend to depress net income (which would reduce housing investment), but at the same time they would stimulate the production of non-taxable sources of income such as housing, where non-taxable income can be generated and stored as unrealized capital gains.[49]

The next topic concerns the actual empirical consensus, granting the usual (and growing) profusion of models and methods of estimation. Beginning with the variables, we note that practically all work suggests that permanent income (often just an average of past incomes) is the appropriate income variable. With regard to the permanent income elasticity, while micro-work runs toward an inelastic demand (between 0.5 and 0.7, often), aggregative studies come closer to unity. Recent work by Polinsky (1977) and Polinsky and Ellwood (1979) study the effect of numerous specification problems; here one finds an income elasticity around 0.4 (or a little more) - see also Roistacher (1977) and Kearl, Rosen, and Swan (1975). The (earlier) aggregative studies of Winger (1968) and Wilkinson (1973) ran toward an income elasticity around unity. There were argued to be biased upward on account of their (implicit) use of microanalysis on macro-data; the critical paper is by B.A. Smith and Campbell (1978), and their instrumental variables approach reduces the (permanent) income elasticity to between 0.5 and 0.7. On the other hand, Vaughn (1976) argues that grouping to achieve homogeneity in individual data may bias the income elasticity downward; Vaughn also argues that ignoring the supply of housing produces a downward bias (for more aggregative studies).

With regard to the "own" price elasticity, again, the Polinsky and Ellwood (1979) paper provides an inelastic result - of about -0.7. There is also not really much disagreement with this magnitude.[50] With regard to the interest rate elasticity, one usually finds a pretty strong negative effect, possibly greater than (minus) unity; for an example, see Kearl, Rosen, and Swan (1975), who use nominal mortgage or nominal long-term interest rates (as in Muth). Finally, note that while this is not the place to consider micro-oriented or demographic variables - and these are very popular in this literature - one should note that their frequent presence in empirical studies suggests the existence of aggregation problems.

With regard to inflation, a separate literature has grown up that is at least partly inspired by the proposition that housing has been an effective hedge against inflation (in the 1970s). Of course, it matters to what extent inflation has been a surprise - and produced windfall gains and losses - but the literature has settled on two major themes:

(a) that in view of the conventional practice of long-term fixed payment contracts, the existence of inflation has induced mortgage lenders to increase their interest rates and the size of their required down payments and thus home buying is reduced (as in Kearl, 1979) and
(b) that expected capital gains are sufficient to induce a considerable move into housing as if it were an especially useful investment opportunity (as in H. Rosen and K. Rosen, 1980, and Summers, 1980c).

The latter discusses the move into housing and out of corporate common stock as a joint inflation-induced phenomenon. There are tax burdens at the root of this, affecting both corporations' profits adversely and house prices favourably. Kearl (1979) argues that the practice of having a long-term nominal rate mortgage, partly on account of regulation, forces lenders to increase the initial burden (implying a "forced saving" by prospective house buyers) to compensate for the expected depreciation of their assets. He estimates a standard model which has, in addition to the cost of capital, permanent income, and housing stock variables, a variable measuring the initial quarterly mortgage payment and a variable measuring the duration of the mortgage. The last two have a negative effect on the relative price of housing, and their effect is attributable to inflation (the suppliers of funds shortened the duration and raised the down payment - and this reduced the demand for housing and hence the relative price of housing). This, though, is nothing new, and the theoretical case for it is not particularly strong - at least as evidence of inflationary effects as such.[51] On point (b) a recent study by Boehm and McKenzie (1980) found (on US micro-data) that in the early 1970s inflationary expectations (measured by a distributed lag of past house price changes) affected the decision whether to rent or own (the "tenure decision") and in the later 1970s actually effected household expenditures via windfalls (the expenditures of "prior owners" was the only category which showed this response). In this connection, Diamond (1979) points out that while inflation in the 1970s has raised house prices relative to the average of consumer prices, it has at the same time lowered *ex post* real rates of interest and real operating costs. The combination of these and the other inflation-related factors associated with the boom in housing in the 1970s at the same time suggests a vulnerability of this boom to a slow-down in the rate of inflation.

Aggregation problems are also important in housing markets, and some attempts have been made to identify them. In one such, Gerking and Boyes (1980) use a flexible functional form (Box-and-Cox) of

$$H_i^{(\lambda_0)} = \alpha_0 + \alpha_1 Y_i^{(\lambda_1)} + \alpha_2 P_i^{(\lambda_2)} + \alpha_3 T_i^{(\lambda_3)} + u_i \qquad (5.91)$$

where the appropriateness of the usual log-linear specification can be tested (this is approximately the same as the test of the liquidity trap, as discussed in Chapter 3); T_i are transportation costs. The results suggested a rejection of an aggregation across SMSAs, rejection of the log-linear model, and rejection of the T_i variables. Note that Gerking and Boyes present a derivation (from utility theory) of the Muth model which emphasizes its *a priori* vulnerability to aggregation problems. Polinksy and Ellwood (1979) use a CES production function (of housing) as the basis for calculating a CES cost function for the "own price" of housing; this is

$$P_H = [\alpha^{\sigma} P_s^{(1 - \sigma)} + \delta^{\sigma} P_K^{(1 - \sigma)}]^{1/(1 - \sigma)} \qquad (5.92)$$

where s denotes land (space) and K denotes housing capital (the two inputs in the production function). The data are on individual households, and the authors do not locate any serious aggregation problem (across individuals). Note, finally, two studies already mentioned in which aggregation problems are alleged to lead to biased estimates of the demand for housing; these are by B.A. Smith and Campbell (1978) - ε_y is "too high" - and by Vaughn (1976) - arguing it may be too low (because of the grouping needed to achieve a measure of homogeneity in the sample).

5.6.2 CREDIT RATIONING IN HOUSING MARKETS

The idea that "tight money" discriminates against housing (and other sectors) goes back a long way and is the cornerstone of the "credit rationing" hypothesis as this more general view has come to be known. In its broad form it is not dissimilar to the "residual funds" hypothesis described above (although it is a symmetrical effect) and it is used to help explain the contra-cyclical pattern of housing expenditure (the residual funds hypothesis, it should be recalled, was part of a hybrid with the accelerator which actually explains a pro-cyclical pattern). "Credit rationing" refers to the use by lenders of variables other than interest rates to control the size (and composition) of their loan portfolios. It can certainly result from a situation in which there are legal ceilings on interest rates, but the more interesting allegation concerns its existence even when interest rates could be flexible. The main reason for placing what might seem to be a market failure in such a predominant role is the frequency of what have become known as "credit crunches"; in recent years these are periods when it seems as if tight money has driven funds away from the firms which typically finance house purchases so that they are forced to ration the available funds among potential users. This condition is (was) exacerbated by legal ceilings on mortgage rates and by (alleged) financial lending and regulatory practices which favour rules of thumb rather than marginal rules for pricing decisions. Of course, there is also a complicated issue of the effectiveness of monetary policy, but that is beyond the scope of this study; see, though, Tucker (1968) for some of the basic issues.

One way to deal with the phenomenon of credit rationing is to employ a "tightness" proxy in one's basic "housing investment" equation. For example, D. Ott, A. Ott, and Yoo (1975) propose adding in a distributed lag on the difference between long and short rates to pick up "general credit conditions" as in

$$\sum_{i=0}^{N} \beta_i (i_L - i_s)_{t-i}$$

and tack it onto their basic housing investment equation. Presumably, the cyclical pattern in $i_L - i_s$ (as noted in Kessel, 1966) would then show tightness and ease, in so far as these ideas are correlated with the cycle. While no formal explanation for this variable is given in D. Ott, A. Ott, and Yoo, one might be advanced, as follows. Kessel, actually, considers whether or not the evident cyclical pattern in $i_L - i_s$ is due to the influence of interest rate expectations. At cyclical peaks, then, if long-term rates are averages of expected future short-term rates (i.e. are predictions) and these are expected (reasonably) to fall, then the actual short-term rates may well be greater than the weighted sum of expected short rates (i_L); at the business cycle trough $i_s < i_L$ by the same reasoning. In contrast, if supplies of funds are uneven across the structure of interest rates, that is, if short-term funds are in scarce supply relative to long and these influences are not readily transmitted across the structure, then this variable also can proxy "credit availability" to (say) the housing sector. The reasons for poor transmission are "market segmentation" or the gathering of funds into "preferred habitats".[52]

The early literature on credit rationing itself was surveyed in 1972 by B.M. Friedman and again by Baltensperger

(1978); Jaffee (1971) also has a survey. Friedman's review presents an essentially microeconomic interpretation in terms of the behaviour of commercial banks. Friedman argues that rationing - that is, the use of non-price variables to control loan demand - may well be part of a rational strategy by banks; indeed, many proponents of the theory had often made it unclear as to exactly why banks might do this. Thus, Scott (1957) proposed a mean-variance explanation; in this case, banks, in the face of increased uncertainty during tight money periods, move into less risky government securities and away from (e.g.) the housing market. Others have postulated "lock-in effects" - that is, effects emanating from particular non-rational constraints (liquidity ratios, etc.) - perceived differences in borrowers (especially involving their credit-worthiness), or downward rigidities in interest rates. Other significant early papers along these lines are by Hodgman (1963) and Guttentag (1961). Hodgman most notably postulated the existence of a back-bending supply of funds curve whose slope was rationalized on the basis of lender's reluctance to lend because of default risk. In particular, with a fixed wealth (assumed), a borrower's status becomes increasingly risky as interest rates rise (obviously).[53] Finally, one might construct a model in which the variation of the non-price terms of a loan is the rational way to maximize profits and some other objectives. This is what Harris does (1973), employing a "characteristics" approach in the event that a bank's "soundness" could be identified as a second objective; Harris provides some empirical support in a second paper (1974).

It is not entirely clear that legal ceilings on lending rates are binding, although during the tight money period of 1979-81 in the United States, there were frequent notices of this effect. The reason for doubt is simply that legal jurisdictions may well recognize the problem and raise the ceiling; in addition, funds can be gathered by syndication from non-regulated markets (toward which they would tend to flow from regulated markets). Similarly, the back-bending supply curve of funds does not actually produce "rationing" since it does not require reading points off two curves (as discussed in Chapter 1). In place of these Jaffee and Modigliani (1969) initiated what has now become a never-ending stream of more formal "rationing" models, which culminate in formal disequilibrium models (to be discussed below in Section 5.6.3). Attention is directed to the firm doing the rationing - the bank in this case - and these authors distinguish between "equilibrium" rationing (which occurs when the loan rate is arbitrarily set at its long-run equilibrium level) and "dynamic" rationing (which occurs in the short run in the event that the loan rate is not fully and quickly adjusted to its long-run equilibrium level). Both types of rationing involve supply and demand schedules for loans and an explanation of the determinants of the loan rate. Even if the long rate is set at its optimum level, both the existence of uncertainty and imperfect discrimination in loan markets implies some "rationing"; if the rate is not set at its optimal level (for whatever reason), then dynamic rationing (positive or negative) would arise. Changes in the interest rate do not affect equilibrium rationing in any predictable way, but if the current rate is less than the equilibrium (market) rate, then dynamic credit rationing will increase so long as the quoted loan rate is somewhat sticky compared to the market rate. In short, where $\hat{R}$ is the market rate and R is the (sticky) loan rate

$$\textit{Credit rationing} = \beta(\hat{R} - R)$$

where $\beta > 0$. It should be noted that this proposition is Keynesian in spirit, involving sticky interest rates and an oligopolistic banking industry; banks, of course, will be shifting their funds to more attractive opportunities, and the impact will generally be greatest on marginal customers who would be rationed in equilibrium anyway (because of risk etc.).

In their paper, Jaffee and Modigliani consider empirical proxies for credit rationing. Arguing that dynamic rationing is more systematic (in being related to economic variables) and larger, they propose the model

$$H = a_0 + a_1(i_L^* - i_L) \tag{5.93}$$

where i_L^* is the long-run equilibrium rate and i_L is the actual average loan rate. For i_L^* they recommend the return on Treasury Bills, as described in the note.[54] This, it seems, is a more exact formulation than the $i_L - i_s$ discussed above.

One problem with the foregoing is the increasing ability of commercial banks (and now savings banks) to utilize the market for secondary funds (Euro-dollars, RPs, CDs. etc.) to obtain funds to meet unforeseen drains. Another, quite simply, is that self-imposed quantity limits are still generally non-optimal from the firm's point of view; indeed, as Meltzer (1974) points out, much of this literature is based on the asusmption of "generally unspecified market failures".[55] Further, one should note, it was B.M. Friedman's judgment in 1972 that no firm empirical case for credit rationing had yet been made.[56] A later survey of the evidence by Kearl, Rosen, and Swan (1975) also doubts that "interest rate ceilings" are as important as once thought in view of their apparent flexibility when they are challenged.[57] The latter paper catalogues many of the non-price financial variables which have been used successfully in "housing start" equations - loan to value ratios, inflow of funds to financial institutions, amortization periods and down payments - to show how the (alleged) deficiency in institutional arrangements leads to rationing. These factors are also used to show how markets with sticky interest rates adjust to changes in the supply of funds. This, of course, is a reduced form approach - and a short-run approach - and while the sifting of evidence of Kearl, Rosen, and Swan suggests that one can still hold to the availability hypothesis without risk of empirical refutation, the issue is still clearly an open one.[58] One should note that the loan to value ratio appears to be a particularly strong variable in these studies.

No one is really quarrelling with the potentially important role of "disintermediation" in accentuating housing cycles, but one should also emphasize that a complicated simultaneous equations problem exists, involving demand and supply in both housing and credit markets. The dynamics, too, are a problem in view of both the durability of housing and the potential lags in decisions. To deal with some of these problems a paper by Gramlich and Jaffee (1972) combines three markets (and the results of several other studies) - savings deposit, mortgage, and housing - in a simulation experiment. They conclude that fiscal policy exerts little leverage on housing (it operates via income and the income elasticity is low) but monetary policy does, via its sharp impact on nominal interest rates. This breaks down to strong short-run rationing effects on the mortgage market and a somewhat less violent longer run effect on the cost-of-capital (recall the finding that the nominal interest rate effect on the demand for housing is strong). They, too, doubt that ceilings are important. In contrast, in a paper involving only consumer debt markets and the housing market, Kearl and Mishkin (1977) find no strong support for credit availability. Kearl and Mishkin argue that two additional channels for the effect of monetary policy (other than the interest rate and "availability") are its effect

(a) on the value of consumer financial assets and
(b) - via past interest rates and "availability" - on the size of consumer debt holdings.

In combination, these provide a "liquidity" hypothesis. On

(a) a house is a very illiquid asset, so that when a householder faces a "crunch", he reduces his housing - as it becomes possible - attempting to restore or retain his liquidity. At the same time, high debt in his balance sheet presents a risk to the home owner - a risk which increases with an increase in debt service and a decrease in the value of financial assets. Tight money, of course, has both effects, and Kearl and Mishkin's empirical work suggests that these factors - rather than availability or direct interest rate effects - may explain the sensitivity of housing markets to monetary policy. Another doubter, whose paper utilizes consumers' balance sheets, is based on the Brainard and Tobin "pitfalls" approach; this is by De Rosa (1978). De Rosa argues that mortgage credit is fungible and that consumers are not limited to the allegedly "segmented" mortgage market in being able to appeal to other lenders for funds; he employs a Brainard and Tobin (1968) portfolio model and finds no evidence, either in terms of cross-elasticities between housing and other durables (they show fungibility) or in the form of significant changes in the coefficients of the model when "credit crunch" periods are contrasted with "normal" periods.[59]

5.6.3 DISEQUILIBRIUM IN HOUSING MARKETS

The possible existence of credit rationing immediately suggests that one might well use direct "disequilibrium econometrics" in order to avoid the problem of bias which would result if the working assumption is that observations are read off the intersections of long-run curves. We have discussed disquilibrium theory in Chapter 1, and so it remains to consider here - in the area (housing) in which most of the estimation has been done - just what one might do in the event that supply is thought to be unequal to demand for a time. We should note (a) that we have already used disequilibrium as a rationale for introducing partial adjustment into studies of housing (in the short run) and (b) that the remaining material in this chapter, being generally econometric, is only representative of the literature.

The problem, quite simply, is to provide estimates of the parameters of demand and supply functions in a situation in which supply is unequal to demand and in which (e.g.) the market quantity is given by $x = min\ (Q_S, Q_D)$. One approach, and the first in the literature, is that of Fair and Jaffee (1972) as, for example, it appears in the short-run forecasting model of Fair (1971). In the latter, the problem arises in the housing sector, in view of the likelihood that the housing and mortgage markets are not always in equilibrium; the underlying rationale is that of "credit availability" - or rather unavailability.[60] The demand for housing starts, then, is

$$H_{Dt} = f(\tilde{X}_{Dt}, \varepsilon_{1t}) \tag{5.94}$$

where ζ_{1t} is an error term, and the supply is

$$H_{st} = g(\tilde{X}_{st}, \varepsilon_{1t}) \tag{5.95}$$

where the $\tilde{X}_i$ are vectors of relevant variables. There is also a mortgage market - that is, a market for mortgage funds - and the two functions here are the demand function

$$\frac{M_{Dt}}{H_{Dt}} = a_0 + a_1 T \tag{5.96}$$

where T is the time trend, and the supply function, itself depending of a vector (Z) of variables (including the flow of funds into the "savings" banks), of

$$M_{st} = h(\tilde{Z}, \varepsilon_{3t}) \tag{5.97}$$

Finally, it is assumed that actual housing starts are given by

$$H_t = min\left(H_{Dt}, H_{st}, \frac{M_{Dt}}{a_0 + a_{1T}}\right) \tag{5.98}$$

with the last term introducing the "credit availability" already mentioned.

This is not the point to take up the analysis of the components of these expressions (the members of $\tilde{X}$, $\tilde{Z}$); instead, we consider the suggested approaches of Fair and Jaffee (1972). For one, they suggest a maximum-likelihood method for finding the optimal separation of the sample into supply and demand regimes. For a second, they propose a simple directional method of estimation; write the change of price as a simple proportion of the difference between quantity demanded and quantity supplied.

$$\Delta P = k(M_{Dt} - M_{st}) \tag{5.99}$$

Then, if $M_{Dt} > M_{st}$, $\Delta P > 0$, and so forth; this implies $H_t = H_{st}$, for $\Delta P > 0$, and $H_t = H_{Dt}$, for $\Delta P < 0$, ignoring the trend adjustment term for the moment. This approach has several obvious problems; these are that the estimates are inconsistent, that there are potential problems of serial correlation, that (5.99) has a strict proportionality, and that (5.96), (5.97), and (5.98) are treated as non-stochastic. These matters are discussed and dealt with in later studies (e.g. Fair and Kelejian, 1974, and Goldfeld and Quandt, 1975).[61]

In the original paper and in the book by Fair there is yet another approach taken to the problem of disequilibrium estimation. In this approach an attempt is made to adjust the observed quantity for the effects of rationing so that the demand and supply schedules can be estimated directly. If we assume that the change in the mortgage interest rate is given by

$$\Delta i_m = q(H_{Dt} - H_{st}) \qquad q \geq 0 \tag{5.100}$$

then, where q is a parameter, we can estimate the parameters of the original functions and q. Indeed, the system would be set up as follows:

$$H_t = H_{Dt} - \frac{1}{q}\Delta i^*_{mt} + \varepsilon_{5t} \tag{5.101}$$

for

$$\Delta i^*_{mt} = \begin{cases} \Delta i_{mt} \text{ for } \Delta i_m \geq 0 \\ 0 \text{ otherwise} \end{cases}$$

$$H_t = H_{st} - \frac{1}{q}\Delta i^{**}_{mt} + \varepsilon_{6t} \tag{5.102}$$

for

$$\Delta i^{**}_{mt} = \begin{cases} -\Delta i_{mt} \text{ for } \Delta i_m \leq 0 \\ 0 \text{ otherwise} \end{cases}$$

This generalizes the approach taken in equation (5.100) by actually estimating the parameter q but presents problems of its own since i_{mt} is endogenized in equation (5.100) - introducing a potential simultaneous equations bias - while with q appearing in both (5.101) and (5.102), there is an identification problem. The authors assume that the errors in equations (5.101) and (5.102) are directly uncorrelated (although each is assumed to be serially correlated) and basically dealt with the q problem by imposing across-equation constraints; the simultaneity problem was ignored. The Δi_{mt} terms were significant in the two equations on US data.

In a paper roughly along these lines, Laufenberg (1974) estimates a supply and demand model for mortgage credit (by S & Ls) with separate equations for (a) changes in the deposit flow to S & Ls, (b) changes in the net worth of households, and (c) changes in the mortgage interest rate. The latter is rationalized on disequilibrium grounds and is

$$\Delta_{im} = f(\Delta m, \Delta i_D, \Delta m_B) \tag{5.103}$$

Here the mortgage term (Δm) is non-significant, while the Federal Reserve discount rate and the monetary base are significant. This paper, then, goes further in attributing the disequilibrium to a specific cause (but Δ_{im} is significant only in the demand and not the supply of mortgage credit function) and in carefully describing the structure underlying each reduced form (of which (5.103) is one such). In a study of the same problem, Ostas and Zahn (1975) consider the role of non-price factors adjusting in the event that mortgage interest rates are sticky. The stickiness is captured by partial adjustment, and the non-price term used to achieve equilibrium is the "rate of downpayment" (in tight money it increases to clear the market). This is also (like Laufenberg) a "structural" approach - compared to Fair and Jaffee - but in their case both the supply and demand for mortgage credit were influenced by the "disequilibrium proxy". Their data were also on S & Ls.[62]

NOTES

1. We may calculate $\partial I/\partial Y$ directly, for $Y = P_X X$ and it is positive since $(1 - e^{-rT}) > 0$. The expression

(a) $$-\frac{\partial I}{\partial r} = \frac{\alpha}{P_I}[x - A(K)]\frac{1 - (1 + rT)e^{-rT}}{r^2}$$

is also positive, for $[x - A(K)] > 0$. The expression

(b) $$-\frac{\partial I}{\partial K} = \frac{\alpha}{P_I}\frac{1 - e^{-rT}}{r}A'(K) > 0$$

for $A'(K) > 0$ as was assumed. Note that as $T \to 0$, that is, as the horizon for the investment decision shortens, the investment function becomes decreasingly interest-elastic.

2. Note that we are not, here, phrasing the relation in ex-

actly the way Keynes (or Klein) put it. See Branson (1979) for a discussion of a point of no particular importance if we are willing to adopt a neoclassical competitive framework here.

3. Grunfeld (1960) argued that the use of past profits also leads to understatement of the role of the interest rate. He proposed and tested the "market value of the firm" as a variable, thus anticipating Tobin's "q" to some extent. See below for a discussion of the latter.

4. We will not discuss the well-known Harrod-Domar model in this book, but a brief discussion may be of use; this can be compared to the neoclassical growth model which we will also paraphrase.

Defining national income as $Y = C + I + A$, where A is autonomous (exogenous) expenditure, the multiplier is contained in $C = cY$ for $0 < c < 1$ and the accelerator in $I = g(dY/dt)$ for $g > 0$; the combination yields $dY/dt = s/g(y - A/s)$ where $s = 1 - c$. With $A = A_0e^{rt}$ - that is, in nonhomogeneous dynamic form - the solution of the resulting differential equation is

$$y = \overline{Y}_0 e^{rt} + (Y_0 - \overline{Y}_0)e^{st/g}$$

with $\overline{Y}_0 = A_0/g(s/g - r)$ being the initial value of income. If we start off at $Y_0 = \overline{Y}_0$, then income grows steadily at r; but if we start at $Y_0 \neq \overline{Y}_0$, income steadily deviates from r at the rate s/g. This sensitivity is called the "knife-edge" result of the Harrod-Domar model.

The neoclassical model (of Phelps, 1966) begins with a constant returns production function meeting neoclassical conditions, $X(t) = F[K(t), e^{\lambda t}L(t)]$, an expression for the supply of labour, $L(t) = L_0e^{(\gamma + \lambda)t}$ (γ is the quality improvement and λ the quantity increase in labour), an investment function, $I(t) = \dot{K}(t) + \delta K(t)$, and an equilibrium condition $c(t) = X(t) - I(t)$. If we increase both $K(t)$ and $L_0e^{(\gamma + \lambda)t}$ by $1/L_0e^{(\gamma + \lambda)t}$, we obtain

$$X(t) = L_0e^{(\gamma + \lambda)t}F[\frac{K(t)}{L_0e^{(\gamma + \lambda)t}}, 1]$$

then, for the capital - labour ratio (in the square brackets) constant - let us call it k, we have $X(t) = L_0e^{(\gamma + \lambda)t}F(k, 1)$, which says that output will grow at $\gamma + \lambda$ in this labour-augmenting model. It turns out that all variables which grow will grow at the rate of $\gamma + \lambda$ along the "golden path" of growth. This includes investment, of course. The expression for this is $I(t) = (\gamma + \lambda + \delta)kL_0e^{(\gamma + \lambda)t}$. Finally, the interest rate is a constant in this model.

5. In an influential early paper (1963a) Eisner tested a "permanent acceleration hypothesis" based on a direct analogy with the permanent income hypothesis for consumer spending. This produced evidence (on pooled cross-section data) of a hump-shaped "sales" accelerator; lagged profits and a "depreciation" dummy were also successful.
6. Eisner formally espouses the "permanent income" model of investment in the 1967 study. In his 1978 survey he returns to this theme in trying to rationalize the difference between time series and cross-section estimates of sales elasticities (lower for cross-section). In particular, if cross-sections are divided into homogeneous groups in terms of "permanent sales", then transitory components in sales would dominate the inter-group variances and bias downward the investment - sales relation (in terms of slopes and elasticities). He notes some statistical support. A paper by Birch and Siebert (1976) uses uncertainty to help explain why the adjustment of the actual capital stock to the desired capital stock is so "sticky". The model used is an accelerator in sales.
7. Perhaps the clearest standard treatment of the method without much critical comment is in Johnston (1972). Suppose we have a lagged relation as in $y_t = \beta_0X_t + \beta_1X_{t-1} + \ldots + \beta_sX_{t-s} + u_t$. What we can do is express the βs as functions of arbitrary variables $a_0 \ldots, a_r$ (their number representing the degree of the approximating polynomial) such that a_0 represents the constant term, a_1 the linear term, etc. The idea, then, is to reduce the s lag terms to r variables of a standard (and preferably simple) approximating function. We would obtain our estimates for the a_i by the regression of the original y_t on the expanded values of X (each X, constant, linear, etc., is a new variable). The results, after estimation, are then unscrambled and standard errors (also interpolated) attached.

   The principle virtue of the approach is that an agnostic on the correct lag structure can add polynomials and extend the lag on purely statistical grounds, by watching $\bar{R}^2$, permitting the shape and length of the lag structure to emerge from the data. Indeed, more than one independent variable can be so treated, with different r and s, and different lags, variable to variable. The principle problems - as any user of the technique can verify - are that (often) big differences in the appearance and length of the lag structure are not attended by big differences in the test statistics and that more than one (local) maximum often appears. Indeed, lag structures often get implausibly long (although other structures such as the Koyck have been known to be implausibly long, too).

8. If we assume the CES production function, then since

$$\frac{\partial x}{\partial K} = \beta\varepsilon A^{1 - (\rho + \varepsilon)/\varepsilon} \frac{x^{\frac{\rho + \varepsilon}{\varepsilon}}}{K^{1 + \rho}}$$

we would have the following equation in place of (5.34), in the event that $\varepsilon = 1$, $K^* = \beta^{\sigma}(\rho/c)^{\sigma}x^*$, where σ is the elasticity of substitution. For an empirical test of the CES version of the model in which $\sigma < 1$, see Boatwright and Eaton (1972).

9. This model provides the sign of the interest rate effect on the demand for investment (negative). Let the cost of capital be the simpler $C = q(r + \delta) - \dot{q}$ and recall that the demand for capital goods is $K = K(w, C, p)$. In this event

$$\dot{K} = \frac{\partial K}{\partial w}\frac{\partial w}{\partial t} + \frac{\partial K}{\partial C}\frac{\partial C}{\partial t} + \frac{\partial K}{\partial p}\frac{\partial p}{\partial t}$$

where w is the wage and p the product price. Assuming $\partial w/\partial t = \partial p/\partial t = 0$, differentiating the cost of capital equation with respect to time, and combining these with $\dot{K} = I - \delta K$, Jorgenson (1967) obtains

$$I = \frac{\partial K}{\partial C}\left[\frac{\partial q}{\partial t}(\delta + r) + q\frac{\partial r}{\partial t} - \frac{\partial^2 q}{\partial t^2}\right] + \delta K$$

He then calculates $\partial I/\partial r$ and deduces that it is equal to $(\partial K/\partial C)C$ which is (*a priori*) negative.

10. The application of the expressions $U(L) = \gamma_3 L^3 + \gamma_4 L^4 + \gamma_5 L^5$ and $V(L) = 1 + W_1 + W_2 L^2$ to equation (5.3) yields

$$I_t = \alpha\gamma_3\left[\frac{p_{t-3}X_{t-3}}{C_{t-3}} - \frac{p_{t-4}X_{t-4}}{C_{t-4}}\right] + \alpha\gamma_4\left[\frac{p_{t-4}X_{t-4}}{C_{t-4}}\right.$$

$$\left. - \frac{p_{t-5}X_{t-5}}{C_{t-5}}\right] + \alpha\gamma_5\left[\frac{p_{t-5}X_{t-5}}{C_{t-5}} - \frac{p_{t-6}X_{t-6}}{C_{t-6}}\right]$$

$$- W_1[I_{t-1} - \delta K_{t-2}] - W_2[I_{t-2} - \delta K_{t-3}] + \delta K_{t-1}$$

This is the equation actually fitted by Jorgenson.

11. There is further early work on "rational flexible accelerators", which is essentially firm-oriented; important papers are by Lucas (1967) and Treadway (1969).

12. They estimated

$$I_t = \sum_{i=0}^{n} w_i \Delta[\alpha^\sigma (\tfrac{p}{c})^\sigma x]_{t-i} + \delta K_{t-1}$$

and produced an $\overline{R}^2$ of 0.977 and a Durbin-Watson statistic of 1.38 (δ was estimated as 0.02). The Almon polynomial was quadratic. See note 7 for the definition of the Almon lag.

13. The function presents a solution for the demand for labour, for example, and can even be adapted to deal with a human capital type problem, although I have not seen such an application. There is a study of the neoclassical demand for money by Motley (1969) which directly carries the model over, as described in Chapter 4.

14. Direct estimates also ignore the information contained in marginal productivity conditions; if relevant, the (direct) estimates are inefficient and inconsistent. This can be dealt with by including the equation of the expansion path (see Coen and Hickman, 1970).

15. The two functions are $L^* = a_0(p_1^*)^{a_1}(x_1^*)^{a_2}e^{-a_3t}$ and $K^* = b_0(p_2^*)^{b_1}(x_2^*)^{b_2}e^{-b_3t}$, where the p_i^* are expected factor prices, the x_i^* are expected outputs, and the coefficients are combinations of the parameters of the production function. One, then, converts to observed p_i, x_i using permanent-style measures of the expected variables. Note that output here is expected and not desired output.

16. We should point out that there is an apparent difference between simple accelerator models (they are "mechanistic" in linking Δx to I without any "choice-theoretic" framework) and the neoclassical investment model (which is "choice-theoretic"). Grossman (1972) constructs an accelerator model along neoclassical lines that is also "choice-theoretic". In the neoclassical investment theory with adjustment - as described in this paragraph - the investment demand function (when the firm chooses K, L) is $I = I(r, w, K_{t-1})$, and output does not appear (it is "maximized out"). In contrast, Grossman argues that an accelerator (Δx) variable will actually appear if the firm is unable to sell all that it wants to produce (this, presumably, implies excess capacity). This situation of excess capacity may seem "non-neoclassical" to some, but, in any event, it does re-introduce output (and the accelera-

tor).

17. The elasticity for equation (5.44) is

$$\varepsilon_{K \cdot px/C} = \frac{\sum_{i=m}^{7} \hat{\gamma}_i}{1 - \sum_{i=1}^{3} \hat{W}_j}$$

For the separated form Eisner and Nadiri employ

$$\Delta \log K_t = \sum_{i=m}^{7} [\gamma_{pi} \Delta \log (\tfrac{p}{C})_{t-i} + \gamma_{xi} \Delta \log x_{t-i}]$$

$$+ \sum_{j=1}^{3} W_j \Delta \log K_{t-j} + V_t$$

where the two elasticities are

$$\hat{\varepsilon}_p = \frac{\sum_{i=m}^{7} \hat{\gamma}_{pi}}{1 - \sum_{j=1}^{3} \hat{W}_j} \qquad \hat{\varepsilon}_x = \frac{\sum_{i=m}^{7} \hat{\gamma}_{xi}}{1 - \sum_{j=1}^{3} \hat{W}_j}$$

$\hat{\varepsilon}_p$ turns out to be close to 0 and $\hat{\varepsilon}_x$ close to 0.5.

18. An argument about whether time series and cross-section studies were providing differences (cross-section lower) was laid to rest, for the time being, by Berndt (1976), who found both near unity.

19. Hall sets up the problem as follows. Total cost, which is the present discounted value of future costs is

$$\sum_{s=t}^{\infty} R_{s,t}[C_s(x_s, K_o, \ldots, K_s) + p_s K_s]$$

where $R_{s,t}$ is the present value (in t) of a dollar received in s; C_s is the variable cost function in s; and $p_s K_s$ is the value of new capital equipment installed in s. A minimum is achieved when $\Sigma R_{s,t} M_{s,t} = p_t$, i.e. when the marginal value (in s) of investment in $t (M_{s,t} \equiv -\partial x_s / \partial K_t)$ is equal to the current value of capital goods. From this (see below) Hall shows that when there is sufficient interaction among vintages of capital equipment, $M_{t,t} = p_t - (p_{t+1})/(1 + i_t)(1 + \delta)$. Here δ is the depreciation rate, and i_t, the current short-term nominal interest rate. This is the rental cost of capital as derived by Jorgenson.

20. Hartman argues that when there is a distribution of completion of lags of projects, when there are adjustment costs, and in the presence of uncertainty (and risk aversion), then the supply price of capital (and current investment expenditures) may well depend on a term structure of capital opportunities. This does not really alter Hall's conclusions - if Hall's premises concerning interest rate expectations can be accepted - but it certainly suggests an empirical confrontation would be in order. This is the investment analogue to a more developed literature on the demand for money (see Chapter 3) which has replaced a "which interest rate" (long or short) with a term structure approach at both a theoretical and empirical level.
21. There is an early study on British data, using the Jorgenson model, by Feldstein and Flemming (1971). They show that both investment allowances and a tax designed to stimulate investment by discouraging dividends have the desired effect.
22. Eisner and Strotz (1963) have one of the earliest studies in which an attempt was made to study the dynamics (and the dynamic interaction between the desired capital stock and the constraints on adjustment). Jorgenson's procedure was *ad hoc* (but it got the job done). Later studies are by Gould (1968), Treadway (1971), Nadiri and S. Rosen (1973), and Brechling (1975). The latter surveys the literature - and the last two present some empirical work (in an essentially microeconomic framework). The empirical studies also feature interaction between capital demand and labour demand functions; a recent paper on this topic is by Faurot (1978) on aggregate US data.
23. An interesting examination of the role of q in monetary policy by Ciccolo (1978) concluded in favour of the q model of investment; q was measured using data from Standard and Poor's 500 non-financial firms in a series produced by Ciccolo.
24. The way this is worded intentionally emphasizes the overlap of the MM theory with that of q. See the paper by Ciccolo and Fromm (1979) for a formal statement of this overlap.
25. An extension is by Baron (1974) who argues that default risk, differences in borrowing rates between firms and individuals, and risk aversion could lead to a role for D/E.

For a summary discussion of this and other adjustments to the literature, see Chen and E.H. Kim (1979).

26. If capital funds are not "available" - see below on "credit availability" - then financial variables will affect the cost of capital (see Vickers, 1970). It is not really in dispute that D/E affects the cost of capital, as noted already, and most empirical studies confirm this (although measurement problems abound).
27. Another approach, but one still implying that the retention rate has an influence on the investment decision, is that of Lerner and Carleton (1964). They set up a model with a capital-budgeting schedule and a stock-valuation schedule and treat the latter as the firm's objective function. The debt - equity ratio does not matter (and rules of thumb, in general, are dismissed as sub-optimal). a paper following the Lintner approach is by V.L. Smith (1972), who shows how the "homemade leverage theorem" of MM is vulnerable to default risk. Stiglitz (1969, 1974), as noted above, also argued for the importance of "no default risk", but this is disputed by Fama and Miller (1972) who propose that default risk would not matter if the stock and bond holders achieve protection from each other by operating "me-first" rules. Fama (1978) subsequently altered his judgment here, arguing that stability of equilibrium and the pressure of a perfectly competitive capital market on the firm are sufficient to make the firm's financial decision irrelevant. Fama has a careful summary of the literature in this paper. Two other basic papers along the lines of Lintner are by Mossin (1966) and Sharpe (1964).
28. We should note that what follows refers, primarily, to studies in which investment is jointly determined with financial variables. This precludes discussion of a considerable body of material in which investment is "given", in which the effect of tax laws on financial decisions is discussed and estimated.
29. Part of the empirical discussion involves the measurement of the cost of capital, and it seems safe to say that this literature reflects the fragmented state of the theoretical debate, as well as the intrinsic difficulty of finding specific numbers to match each theoretical concept. For equity, one finds the dividend yield, various measures of the earnings yield, the rate of return on common stocks (particularly for a group of stocks) as the most widely used measures. For bonds, one finds constructs varying from a simple interest rate, right up to the complicated measure employed by Jorgenson (as discussed above). As Elliott (1980) points out, there are really two

questions: that of the effect of the cost of capital itself and the question of the relative merits of the different candidates (ranging from a simple nominal interest rate to a measure involving the various financial ratios). Elliott's results suggest that when one separates these questions, a clear answer can be given to the role of the cost of capital (it matters) but not to which measure one ought to prefer. His data are US macro. Finally, one notes that some are beginning to doubt the usefulness of the concept of the cost of capital itself, preferring more complex concepts (see Haley and Schall, 1978).

30. We should, at this point, note that there is an interesting literature linking money growth with investment via Tobin's q. The originating paper is by Tobin (1965), and there are many other contributions, but those which are of direct interest to investment studies are rare. In one such, Gertler and Grinols (1979) built a complete macromodel, concluding that an increase in the average rate of growth of money stimulates investment, but that an increase in its variance - by also inducing an increase in the variance of inflation - actually lowers investment (by increasing total risk, since one must borrow (in some way) to finance investment).

31. This is certainly the tip of the iceberg on the "Fisher Effect". We plan to be considerably more complete on these matters in our survey on monetary and fiscal policy.

32. We should note here, as pointed out by Blinder (1981b) that the principle source of this fluctuation is in inventories of finished goods (for retailers) and that manufacturers' inventories of finished goods or works in progress are not important in these fluctuations. That notwithstanding, most of the analysis of this section is on the latter two categories.

33. Abramovitz (1950) makes this distinction, and Trivedi (1970) sets up a model and presents some evidence which suggests that British industries do differ considerably in this respect. He proposes that the industries producing "to order" would tend to ignore the fluctuations in inventories and concentrate on the length of the backlog. His model did not work particularly well and, in any event, showed signs of instability. Rowley and Trivedi (1975) also tackle the question briefly. The stacking of orders is actually peculiar to certain industries - such as furniture or specialized durable capital equipment (e.g. airplane manufacturers) - who use the list of unfilled orders as a buffer stock to smooth production. While an unfilled order in some ways is merely a negative inventory, it does differ by industry, and, more importantly, it is often ne-

gotiated at a pre-arranged nominal price. Thus, the risk of fluctuation in input costs and the risk of cancelled orders (or delays) are elements that are not involved in the direct holding of inventories (but product prices, storage costs, and interest costs (and risk thereof) are). Several early studies on this topic are by Childs (1967) and Belsey (1969).

34. The distinction between "inventories" of money, stocks of finished goods and materials, and "inventories" of fixed capital equipment is essentially arbitrary here. The drift of this section is, consequently, often toward particular types of investment models rather than toward inventories themselves.

35. There are also inventories of orders, of inputs, and, even, outputs - perhaps for future delivery - and inventories of labour skills. In a recent paper by Caves, Jarrett, and Loucks (1979), a basically *ad hoc* structure for the four types of inventories mentioned in the text - on a fairly disaggregated set of US data - produced some evidence of interaction. Inventories of goods may enable a firm to economize on inventories of labour skills, and, in any case, there is an interesting interaction here - in the face of cyclical pressures - which has obvious macroeconomic implications. But it does seem to vary from industry to industry (depending partly on the industry's competitive structure).

36. Bosworth (1970) estimates this model; he looks at four sectors (durable trade, non-durable, equipment and defence, and durable manufacturing for the United States for 1953-69). His results are not particularly well-determined and contained many insignificant variables (e.g. no version had lagged sales and current sales simultaneously significant).

37. Assuming that $S_t^e = (1 + \eta)S_{t-1} - \eta S_{t-2} = [(1 + \eta)\beta] Y_{t-1} - (\eta\beta)Y_{t-2}$, where β describes the relation between actual sales (consumption) and income, then with $S_t = \beta Y_{t-1}$, we have $S_t^e - S_t = \eta\beta(Y_{t-1} - Y_{t-2})$ with η being the "coefficient of expectations".

38. Bergstrom (1966) extends the lag on the consumption decision and endogenizes the fixed investment decision; he also produces a solution for national income which highlights the role of inventories in inducing aggregate instability.

39. In a published exchange Hay (1970a) and Darling and M.C. Lovell (1971) debated the validity of a "production smoothing" rationale for inventory holding. Hay advanced the hypothesis (as described in the text), and Darling and Lovell replied that (a) earlier work was often consistent

with production smoothing and, even, (b) sometimes rejected it. This discussion is continued below.

40. Childs (1974) combines a buffer stock model - with forecasting errors - with an "input accelerator" for materials stocks, to obtain a "generalized accelerator"; it is basically an extension of the Hay (1970b) and Lucas (1967) models. His results, on a time series of US manufacturing data, suggest (for durables, at least) that both an accelerator-input and accelerator-buffer stock model work. There is also a suggestion that firms use inventories partly to absorb their forecasting errors. Inventories, then, are seen to serve a purpose for the firm which might help to mitigate the effect of demand fluctuation of the economy. A study which supports Hay is by Bryant (1978). Bryant uses a Brunner-Meltzer (1972) financial model to the effect that adjustment of inventories to desired levels - by output variations - occurs within the year.

41. Feldstein and Auerbach also present estimates for the Holt *et al.* (1960) model (which is also used by Belsey, 1969; Childs, 1967; and Hay, 1970b); we have already described Hay's version, and Feldstein and Auerbach, in an appendix, carefully explain the Holt *et al.* model.

42. We have remarked on this issue at several points (see Hay, 1970a, 1970b). In a study of the aggregate annual US data, Bryant (1978) suggests that inventories (really unddesired inventories) ought to be treated as evidence of disequilibrium. Using a Brunner-Meltzer (1972) model, three sector (two financial, one real) model, inventories are used in their own right (as assets) and provide a driving force pushing the economy toward equilibrium. The role of the interest rate is downgraded in this model, and monetary policy plays a direct role.

43. While not in line with the rational expectations model, there is an empirical paper by Levi (1975) which provides at least a suggestion that such work might be successful. Levi considers both monetary and fiscal influences on inventories. Assuming policy effects are on buffer stocks (a monetary expansion reduces stocks in the first instance), Levi estimates (essentially without derivation)

$$I_{It} = a_0 + a_1 S_{t+1} + \sum_{i=m}^{q} a_{2i} D_{t-i} + \sum_{i=0}^{n} a_{3i} \Delta\Delta M_{t-i}$$

$$+ \sum_{i=0}^{n} a_{4i} \Delta E_{t-i} + \sum_{i=0}^{n} a_{5i} \Delta R_{t-i}$$

Here D represents days lost in strikes $(m = -3,\ q = 3)$, and the ΔΔ notation for (narrow) money reflects deviations from trend growth rates. E represents real high employment government expenditures, and R represents real high employment receipts. The Almon lags used are long (sixteen quarters); M shows a negative effect, as does E, while R shows a positive effect, as postulated. Significantly, inclusion of an interest rate and a rate of inflation produced no changes in the results.

44. It is not entirely clear that we can go from a micro or even a sectoral specification to a totally aggregative one; as noted, the "portfolio of inventories approach", here, is a disaggregated one, essentially. The reason for the concern is that the price level becomes the price proxy at the aggregative level, and errors in predicting this (or anticipations different from those of the economy as a whole) should not affect the real plans of economic agents. Thus, one frequently hears that "consumers buy now in anticipation of inflation", although this stocking of consumer goods is essentially illogical if incomes are expected to keep pace with inflation (as they generally must). This idea has a firm hold on the public and may have some slight empirical validity (thereby?); of course, if one is looking only at consumption inventories and relative prices are included in one's consumption framework (see Chapter 2 for some results suggesting this), then the personal inventory motive has some scope.

45. Surveys of these issues appear in Evans (1969) and D. Ott, A. Ott, and Yoo (1975). Influential early papers in this sequence are by Guttentag (1961), Alberts (1962), and Maisel (1963). Maisel constructs a theory and tests it in the reduced form, in which there are separate equations for final housing demand, removals (net losses), changes in inventories of finishing housing, and changes of housing in the construction pipeline (both of the latter fluctuate considerably). The dependent variable of the reduced form equation was "housing starts", and the inventory fluctuations of housing contractors were shown to be influential and credit conditions shown to be uninfluential (Alberts, for one, thought them important). One should note - as the discussion to this point should make clear - that some accounting for "housing supply" is going to be necessary for completely satisfactory work on these (and other) topics. The papers discussed below often do have a supply side, but problems abound, among them being issues (already discussed elsewhere in this survey) relating to "housing investment" and "housing production" functions to put the matter broadly. See B.A. Smith (1976) for a sum-

mary and some estimates of the "elasticity of supply" for a US cross-section and Vaughn (1976) for the effect on the income elasticity (biased downward) of ignoring the supply function.

46. As a wealth proxy β_3 would be expected to have a positive sign. As a proxy for "credit availability", especially for the purchase of houses (we might use M3, for example), it would also have a positive sign, but it would not be expected to affect non-durables and, even, durables although it may well affect housing. Boughton did not succeed in obtaining any effect here, but, of course, he may well have improved his fit if housing had been his third (or fourth) category.

47. We should note, as pointed out by Evans (1969), that the new housing expenditure data are essentially construction data and not sales data and that the turnover of existing housing is also unaccounted for. Indeed, as the discussion of this section continues, these (and other) factors are taken up.

48. $\dot{P}_H/P_H$ represents capital gains. As with the D. Ott, A. Ott, and Yoo model, P_H is the present value of (after tax) rental payments.

49. Home-owners are also permitted to deduct local property taxes and mortgage interest payments when calculating their income tax. On net one would expect a stimulation to both "tenure" and "housing" demand functions, as pointed out by Laidler (1969b); indeed, this "subsidy" would be positively associated with the level of income taxes (and, of course, the level of income), as pointed out by Aaron (1971). Laidler calculates the welfare cost of the subsidy, and two recent studies by H.S. Rosen (1979a, 1979b) confirm that tax rule changes would have a substantial effect on the demand for housing (on US cross-section data). With regard to the "tenure decision", again on US data (a time series), H.S. Rosen and K.T. Rosen (1980) find that as much as one-fourth of the increase in the quantity of owner-occupied housing since 1945 is due to the favourable tax treatment just mentioned.

50. See also studies by Lee (1968), Carliner (1973), Maisel, Burnham, and Austin (1971), and Gramlich and Jaffee (1972) which offer broad agreement. The Gramlich and Jaffee paper is part of the "credit rationing" literature which is discussed below.

51. Kearl qualifies his (indirect) result by noting that (a) nominal tax rates are tax deductible, (b) capital gains in housing are often not taxed, (c) many households actually received windfall capital gains in the period (increasing their liquidity), and (d) houses, as real property, became

more important in the portfolio of private investors. These factors would all increase the relative price of housing in this period (but were not included in his tests). The idea of "multiple terms" (some being "non-price") is not new, of course, and an early paper by R.F. Muth (1962) considered the theoretical argument behind this idea and argued against it - arguing, instead, that different maturities (etc.) are essentially different contracts (i.e. different products) and could be expected to have different prices (and, presumably, different response elasticities). He was explaining the correlation between i, maturity, and down payment length which is the essence of Kearl's problem.

52. See the survey in D. Fisher (1976).
53. The idea of credit-worthiness is pursued formally by Jaffee and Russell (1976b) in a paper which extends the (microeconomic) analysis in terms of "moral hazard and adverse selection". The idea is to show how imperfect information (about the honesty and dishonesty of borrowers) and uncertainty (about lucky and unlucky borrowers) affect the situation. The feature of interest is that in their model honest borrowers, who cannot be distinguished from dishonest, must pay a premium above the opportunity cost (competitive interest rate); this premium is reduced at a smaller (equilibrium) loan size - where there is less failure - a fact which suggests a willing participation by honest borrowers in a less-than-equilibrium solution. The idea of the failure of the market to develop default insurance (other than by tacking on a risk premium) is considered by Jaffee and Russell in another paper (1976a).
54. Jaffee and Modigliani point out that commercial banks appear to adjust their loan rates to Federal Reserve discount rate changes, in effect speeding up the adjustment in the loan market and reducing the need to ration credit. This assumes, of course, that the discount rate change is a signal as to the actual direction of open market operations.

This return is calculated from

$$i_L^* = C_0 + C_1\{i_T + b_1(\frac{DEP}{TB} - 1) - b_2D_{62} + b_3C$$

$$+ b_4(\frac{L}{A - L}) + b_5\Delta(\frac{L}{A - L})\}$$

where DEP/TB is the deposit/TBill ratio $(b_1 > 0)$, D_{62} is a dummy variable for the arrival of the large-scale certificates of deposits (CD) market, C is another dummy for the case when the market CD rate exceeds the ceiling CD rate, and $L/(A - L)$ represents the share of the loan portfolio in total assets.

55. In a comment on the original Jaffee and Modigliani paper, Azzi and Cox (1976) argue that failure to equate actual supply and demand at a given interest rate is not the same as failure to equate effective demand. The latter involves the collateral and equity of the borrower who may not satisfy the lender at the going rate. This is, no doubt, a short-run possibility, but note a paper by Kearl and Mishkin (1977) - see the discussion below - who also argue that consumer collateral is important (providing some empirical support).
56. The results do seem to cancel out somewhat, but, on net, something seems to be left. Huang (1966), for example, constructs a complete supply and demand model for the mortgage market; he finds that monetary ease or tightness affects the supply of mortgage loans with a lag of three (calendar) quarters. When this result is coupled with Sparks's (1967) results in which housing starts are seen to be influenced by the supply of mortgage funds, one has a strong suspicion that an empirical case for credit rationing can be made.
57. Baltensperger (1978), who surveys this literature, points out that certain so-called rationing devices - and even lags in the process - may well be rational and even efficient lending practices in a market such as this, where lenders differ in (default) quality, where products are far from homogeneous, and where information is costly to obtain (and not a little ambiguous). These factors might well suggest the use of non-price methods to make adjustments rationally. A case in point - but out of context - is the use of the Prime Rate in the United States; this is a rate which is *not* the rate to the bank's most credit-worthy corporate customers in spite of its acceptance (in the Press) as such. The point is that certain non-price rationing devices may be more efficient than prices, given the nature of existing loan contracts (for one thing).
58. Another study which finds availability effects is by L. B. Smith (1969) on Canadian data (with a reduced form of the housing and mortgage markets).
59. Another way house buyers can avoid a credit crunch - through their intermediaries - is to approach US government agencies for funds. Meltzer (1974) argued that agencies' activities are offset by private sector lenders, and an early study by Jaffee (1972) agreed, at least with respect to the mortgage market alone, but in a recent paper, Jaffee and K.T. Rosen (1978) disagreed, finding agency in-

tervention significant in a monthly three-sector (mortgage, housing, and capital market and deposit) model. This does not deal directly with fungibility, but, on the other hand, De Rosa did not deal directly with Federal agency activity, either. There is, actually, a literature on how the (US) Federal Home Loan Banks (FHLB) supply funds to the savings banks (they do so partly to offset alleged "credit rationing" by savings banks). In an interesting turnabout, Goldfeld, Jaffee, and Quandt (1980) study whether the FHLB Board itself rations credit, concluding that it does not, in a disequilibrium context (see their paper for the relevant bibliography).

60. A useful survey of the failure of earlier studies on credit availability (and housing models) to deal with the apparent disequilibrium in the housing market is by Fair (1972).

61. Maddala and F.D. Nelson (1974) compare four models and apply their results to housing starts data. The models all have a supply function, a demand function, and a "min" condition; model (1), then, is that just stated; model (2) has conditions on ΔP_t (e.g. $\Delta P_t > 0$ if $D > S$); model (3) has $\Delta P_t = \gamma(D_t - S_t)$; and model (4) makes the equation added in model (3) stochastic. The results seem to favour model (2), although this was only in illustration (of their maximum likelihood approach). Sealey (1979) has recently reopened the question, with an estimate of model (4), in which the ΔP_t equation is stochastic; he argues that the disequilibrium model shows that price adjustment is incomplete in each period. This requires, then, that non-price terms adjust, and, in the fashion of the literature, this "lends support" to the credit-rationing hypothsis.

62. In a study on (micro) Australian data, Bowden (1978) used the mortgage free assets ratio of savings banks - checked with reference to a shorter series of offers "fallen through". The dependent variable - also unique to this micro-experiment - was the price of housing. But the results were generally poor. Bowden's work has been extended by Ueda (1980) to a consideration of the prime rate in Japan and the United States. This test of "disequilibrium rationing" provided evidence that the Japanese prime rate tends to be adjusted very slowly (compared to the US) suggesting the existence (really the need for) short-run rationing.

Bibliography

Aaron, H. (1972), *Shelter and Subsidies* (Washington: The Brookings Institution).

Abel, A., R. Dornbusch, J. Huzinga and A. Marcus (1979), "Money Demand during Hyperinflation", *Journal of Monetary Economics* (Jan.).

Abramovitz, M. (1950), *Inventories and Business Cycles* (New York: National Bureau of Economic Research).

Ahmad, S. (1977), "Transactions Demand for Money and the Quantity Theory of Money", *Quarterly Journal of Economics* (May).

Akerlof, G.A. (1979), "Irving Fisher on His Head: The Consequences of Constant Threshold-Target Monitoring of Money Holdings", *Quarterly Journal of Economics* (May).

Akerlof, G.A. and R.D. Milbourne (1978), "The Sensitivity of Monetarist Conclusions to Monetarist Assumptions: Constant Lag Versus Constant Target - Threshold Monitoring", *Special Studies Paper* no. 117 (New York: Federal Reserve Bank of New York, June).

Akerlof, G.A. and R.D. Milbourne (1980), "The Short Run Demand for Money", *Economic Journal* (Dec.).

Akhtar, M.A. and B.H. Putnam (1980), "Money Demand and Foreign Exchange Risk: The German Case, 1972-1976", *Journal of Finance* (June).

Alberts, W.W. (1962), "Business Cycles, Residential Construction Cycles, and the Mortgage Market", *Journal of Political Economy* (June).

Allen, R.G.D. (1956), *Mathematical Analysis for Economists* (London: Macmillan).

Allen, R.G.D. (1967), *Macro-Economic Theory* (London: Macmillan).

Allen, S.D. and R.W. Hafer (1980), "Money Demand and the Term Structure of Interest Rates: Some Consistent Estimates", mimeo, University of North Carolina at Greensboro (Nov.).

Almon, S. (1965), "The Distributed Lag between Capital Appropriations and Expenditures", *Econometrica* (Jan.).

Almon, S. (1968), "Lags between Investment Decisions and Their Causes", *Review of Economics and Statistics* (May).

Ando, A. and F. Modigliani (1960), "The Permanent Income and Life Cycle Hypothesis of Saving Behavior: Comparison and Tests", in I. Friend and R. Jones, *Consumption and Saving* (Philadelphia: University of Pennsylvania Press).

Ando, A. and F. Modigliani (1963), "The 'Life Cycle' Hypothesis of Saving: Aggregate Implications and Tests", *American Economic Review* (Mar.).

Ando, A. and F. Modigliani (1964), "The 'Life Cycle' Hypothesis of Saving: A Correction", *American Economic Review* (Mar.).

Applebaum, E. (1978), "Testing Neoclassical Production Theory", *Journal of Econometrics* (Feb.).

Applebaum, E. (1979), "On the Choice of Functional Forms", *International Economic Review* (June).

Arak, M. (1978), "The Geometrically Weighted Average of Past Incomes as a Representation of Permanent Income: A Reconsideration", *Southern Economic Journal* (Apr.).

Archibald, G.C. and G. Rosenbluth (1978), "Production Theory in Terms of Characteristics: Some Preliminary Considerations", mimeo, University of British Columbia (May).

Arena, J.J. (1964), "Capital Gains and the 'Life Cycle' Hypothesis of Saving", *American Economic Review* (Mar.).

Arrow, K.J., H.B. Chenery, B.S. Minhas, and R.M. Solow (1961), "Capital Labor Substitution and Economic Efficiency", *Review of Economics and Statistics* (Aug.).

Artis, M.J. and M.K. Lewis (1976), "The Demand for Money in the United Kingdom, 1963-1973", *Manchester School* (June).

Artle, R. and P. Varaiya (1978), "Life Cycle Consumption and Homeownership", *Journal of Economic Theory* (June).

Asher, E. and T.K. Kumar (1973), "Capital-Labor Substitution and Technical Progress in Planned and Market-Oriented Economies: A Comparative Study", *Southern Economic Journal* (July).

Attfield, C.L.F. (1976), "Estimation of the Structural Parameters in a Permanent Income Model", *Economica* (Aug.).

Attfield, C.L.F. (1977), "Estimation of a Model Containing Unobservable Variables Using Grouped Observations: An Application to the Permanent Income Hypothesis", *Journal of Econometrics* (July).

Attfield, C.L.F. (1980), "Testing the Assumptions of the Permanent-Income Model", *Journal of the American Statistical Association* (Mar.).

Azzi, C.F. and J.C. Cox (1976), "A Theory and Test of Credit Rationing: Comment", *American Economic Review* (Dec.).

Bailey, M.J. (1979), *National Income and the Price Level*,

second edition (New York: McGraw-Hill).

Ball, R.J. and P.S. Drake (1964), "The Relationship between Aggregate Consumption and Wealth", *International Economic Review* (Jan.).

Baltensperger, E. (1978), "Credit Rationing", *Journal of Money, Credit, and Banking* (May).

Barnett, W.A., E.K. Offenbacher, and P.A. Spindt (1981), "New Concepts of Aggregated Money", *Journal of Finance* (May).

Barnett, W.A. and P.A. Spindt (1979), "The Velocity Behavior and Information Content of Divisia Monetary Aggregates", *Economic Letters* (vol. 4, no. 1).

Baron, D.P. (1974), "Default Risk, Homemade Leverage, and the Modigliani-Miller Theorem", *American Economic Review* (Mar.).

Baron, D.P. (1977), "On the Utility Theoretic Foundations of Mean-Variance Analysis", *Journal of Finance* (Dec.).

Barro, R.J. (1974), "Are Government Bonds Net Wealth?", *Journal of Political Economy* (Nov./Dec.).

Barro, R.J. (1976), "Integral Constraints and Aggregation in an Inventory Model of Money Demand", *Journal of Finance* (Mar.).

Barro, R.J. (1977), "Permanent Income and Expected Future Income in a Time Series Study of Consumer Expenditure", mimeo, University of Rochester.

Barro, R.J. (1978), "Unanticipated Money, Output, and the Price Level in the United States", *Journal of Political Economy* (Aug.).

Barro, R.J. (1979), "Second Thoughts on Keynesian Economics", *American Economic Review* (May).

Barro, R.J. and H.I. Grossman (1971), "A General Disequilibrium Model of Income and Employment", *American Economic Review* (Mar.).

Barro, R.J. and A.M. Santomero (1975), "Household Money Holding and the Demand Deposit Ratio", *Journal of Finance* (Mar.).

Baumol, W.J. (1952), "The Transactions Demand for Cash: An Inventory Theoretic Approach", *Quarterly Journal of Economics* (Nov.).

Becker, W.E., Jr (1975), "Determinants of the United States Currency-Demand Deposit Ratio", *Journal of Finance* (Mar.).

Belsey, D.A. (1969), *Industry Production Behaviour: The Order-Stock Distinction* (Amsterdam: North-Holland).

Benassy, J. (1975), "Neo-Keynesian Disequilibrium in a Monetary Economy", *Review of Economic Studies* (Oct.).

Bergstrom, A.R. (1966), "Nonrecursive Models as Discrete Approximations to Systems of Stochastic Differential Equations", *Econometrica* (Jan.).

Bergström, V. and H. Melander (1979), "Production Functions and Factor Demand Functions in Postwar Swedish Industry", *Scandinavian Journal of Economics* (no. 4).

Berndt, E.R. (1976), "Reconciling Alternative Estimates of the Elasticity of Substitution", *Review of Economics and Statistics* (Feb.).

Berndt, E.R. and L.R. Christensen (1973a), "The Translog Function and the Substitution of Equipment, Structures, and Labor in U.S. Manufacturing, 1929-68", *Journal of Econometrics* (Mar.).

Berndt, E.R. and L.R. Christensen (1973b), "The Internal Structure of Functional Relationships: Separability, Substitution, and Aggregation", *Review of Economic Studies* (July).

Berndt, E.R. and L.R. Christensen (1974), "Testing for the Existence of a Consistent Aggregate Index of Labor Inputs", *American Economic Review* (June).

Berndt, E.R. and M.S. Khaled (1979), "Parametric Productivity Measurement and Choice among Flexible Functional Forms", *Journal of Political Economy* (Dec.).

Berndt, E.R. and D.O. Wood (1975), "Technology, Prices, and the Derived Demand for Energy", *Review of Economics and Statistics* (Aug.).

Bernstein, J.I. (1978), "The Demand for Money by the Firm", Appendix B, in D. Fisher, *Monetary Theory and the Demand for Money* (London: Martin Robertson).

Bernstein, J.I. and D. Fisher (1978), "Consumption, the Term Structure of Interest Rates, and the Demand for Money", mimeo, Concordia University.

Bernstein, J.I. and D. Fisher (1981), "The Demand for Money and the Term Structure of Interest Rates: A Portfolio Approach", *Southern Economic Journal* (Oct.).

Bernstein, J.I. and D. Fisher (1982), "The Demand for Money and the Term Structure of Interest Rates: British Tests from a Portfolio Model", mimeo, McGill University.

Bhalla, S.S. (1979), "Measurement Errors and the Permanent Income Hypothesis: Evidence from Rural India", *American Economic Review* (June).

Bhatia, K.B. (1972), "Capital Gains and the Aggregate Consumption Function", *American Economic Review* (Dec.).

Bhattacharyya, D.K. (1979), "On Measuring the Nearness of Near-Moneys: An Econometric Experiment with the U.K. Personal Sector Data", University of Leicester, *Discussion Paper*, no. 9 (Aug.).

Bierwag, G.O. and M.A. Grove (1967), "A Model of the Term Structure of Interest Rates", *Review of Economics and Statistics* (Feb.).

Bilson, J.F.O. (1980), "The Rational Expectations Approach

to the Consumption Function - A Multi-Country Study", *European Economic Review* (May).

Bilson, J.F.O. and J.E. Glassman (1979), "A Consumption Function with Rational Forecasts of Permanent Income", mimeo, University of Chicago.

Birch, E.M. and C.D. Siebert (1976), "Uncertainty, Permanent Demand, and Investment Behavior", *American Economic Review* (Mar.).

Bird, R.C. and R.G. Bodkin (1965), "The National Service Life-Insurance Dividend of 1950 and Consumption: A Further Test of the 'Strict' Permanent-Income Hypothesis", *Journal of Political Economy* (Oct.).

Bischoff, C.W. (1971), "The Effect of Alternative Lag Distributions", in G. Fromm (ed.), *Tax Incentives and Capital Spending* (Washington: Brookings Institution).

Black, F. (1974), "Uniqueness of the Price Level in Monetary Growth with Rational Expectations", *Journal of Economic Theory* (Jan.).

Black, F. and M.S. Scholes (1974), "The Effects of Dividend Yield and Dividend Policy on Common Stock Prices and Returns", *Journal of Financial Economics* (May).

Blackorby, C., D. Primont, and R.R. Russell (1977), "On Testing Separability Restrictions with Flexible Functional Forms", *Journal of Econometrics* (Mar.).

Blejer, M.I. (1979), "The Demand for Money and the Variability of the Rate of Inflation: Some Empirical Results", *International Economic Review* (June).

Blinder, A.S. (1975), "Distribution Effects and the Aggregate Consumption Function", *Journal of Political Economy* (June).

Blinder, A.S. (1976), "Intergenerational Transfers and Life Cycle Consumption", *American Economic Review* (May).

Blinder, A.S. (1977), "A Difficulty with Keynesian Models of Aggregate Demand", in A.S. Blinder and P. Friedman, *Natural Resources, Uncertainty, and General Equilibrium Systems* (New York: Academic Press).

Blinder, A.S. (1981a), "Inventories and Sticky Prices: More on the Microfoundations of Macroeconomics", *Working Paper* no. 620, National Bureau of Economic Research (Jan.).

Blinder, A.S. (1981b), "Inventories and the Structure of Macro Models", *American Economic Review* (May).

Boatwright, B.D. and J.R. Eaton (1972), "The Estimation of Investment Functions for Manufacturing Industry in the United Kingdom", *Economica* (Nov.).

Bodkin, R.G. (1959), "Windfall Income and Consumption", *American Economic Review* (Sept.).

Bodkin, R.G. and L.R. Klein (1967), "Nonlinear Estimation of Aggregate Production Functions", *Review of Economics and*

Statistics (Feb.).

Boehm, T.P. and J.A. McKenzie (1980), "The Investment Demand for Housing", mimeo, Federal Home Loan Bank Board (Sept.).

Bomberger, W.A. and G.E. Makinen (1980), "The Demand for Money in Open Economies: Alternative Specifications", *Southern Economic Journal* (July).

Bomhoff, E.J. (1980), *Inflation, the Quantity Theory, and Rational Expectations* (Amsterdam: North-Holland).

Boskin, M.J. (1978), "Taxation, Saving, and the Rate of Interest", *Journal of Political Economy* (Apr.).

Bosworth, B. (1970), "Analyzing Inventory Investment", *Brookings Papers*, no. 2.

Boughton, J.M. (1976), "The Aggregate Permanent Income Consumption Function", *Economic Inquiry* (Mar.).

Bowden, R.J. (1974), "Risk Premiums and the Life Cycle Hypothesis", *American Economic Review* (Mar.).

Bowden, R.J. (1978), *The Econometrics of Disequilibrium* (Amsterdam: North-Holland).

Boyd, J.H. (1976), "Household Demand for Checking Account Money", *Journal of Monetary Economics* (Jan.).

Boyes, W.J. (1978), "An Application of Specification Error Tests - The Liquidity Trap", *Manchester School* (June).

Boyes, W.J. and D.C. Kavanaugh (1979), "Money and the Production Function: A Test for Specification Errors", *Review of Economics and Statistics* (Aug.).

Brainard, W.C. and J. Tobin (1968), "Pitfalls in Financial Model Building", *American Economic Review* (May).

Branson, W.H. (1979), *Macroeconomic Theory and Policy*, second edition (New York: Harper and Row).

Branson, W.H. and A.K. Klevorick (1969), "Money Illusion and the Aggregate Consumption Function", *American Economic Review* (Dec.).

Brechling, F.P.R. (1975), *Investment and Employment Decisions* (Manchester: Manchester University Press).

Brenner, R. and F.S. Mishkin (1979), "Bankruptcy, the Price Level, and the Real Balance Effect", mimeo, University of Chicago.

Bridge, J.L. (1971), *Applied Econometrics* (Amsterdam: North-Holland).

Broer, D.P. and J.C. Siebrand (1978), "A Simultaneous Disequilibrium Analysis of Product Market and Labor Market", mimeo, Erasmus University (Rotterdam).

Bronfenbrenner, M. and T. Mayer (1960), "Liquidity Functions in the American Economy", *Econometrica* (Oct.).

Brown, M. (1967), *The Theory and Measurement of Technological Change* (New York: Columbia University Press for the National Bureau of Economic Research).

Brown, M. and J.S. deCani (1963), "Technological Change and

the Distribution of Income", *International Economic Review* (Sept.).

Brown, R.L., J. Durbin, and J.M. Evans (1975), "Techniques for Testing the Constancy of Regression Relationships over Time", *Journal of the Royal Statistical Society* (no. 2, series B).

Bruce, N. (1977), "The IS-LM Model of Macroeconomic Equilibrium and the Monetarist Controversy", *Journal of Political Economy* (Oct.).

Brunner, K. and A.H. Meltzer (1967), "Economies of Scale in Cash Balances Reconsidered", *Quarterly Journal of Economics* (Aug.).

Brunner, K. and A.H. Meltzer (1971), "The Uses of Money: Money in the Theory of an Exchange Economy", *American Economic Review* (Dec.).

Brunner, K. and A.H. Meltzer (1972), "Money, Debt, and Economic Activity", *Journal of Political Economy* (Sept./Oct.).

Bruno, M. (1962), "A Note on the Implications of an Empirical Relationship between Output per Unit of Labor, the Wage Rate, and the Capital - Labor Ratio", mimeo, Stanford University (July).

Bruno, M. (1968), "Estimation of Factor Contribution to Growth under Structural Disequilibrium", *International Economic Review* (Feb.).

Bryant, J. (1978), "Relative Prices and Inventory Investment", *Journal of Monetary Economics* (Jan.).

Buchanan, J.M. (1969), "An Outside Economist's Defense of Pesek and Saving", *Journal of Economic Literature* (Sept.).

Buiter, W.H. and C.A. Armstrong (1978), "A Didactic Note on the Transactions Demand for Money and Behavior Towards Risk", *Journal of Money, Credit, and Banking* (Nov.).

Butkiewicz, J.L. (1979), "Outside Wealth, the Demand for Money, and the Crowding Out Effect", *Journal of Monetary Economics* (Apr.).

Butterfield, D.W. (1975), *Money as a Productive Factor: A Study of Business Money Balances*, PhD thesis, University of California at Berkeley.

Cagan, P. (1956), "The Monetary Dynamics of Hyper-Inflation", in M. Friedman (ed.), *Studies in the Quantity Theory of Money* (Chicago: University of Chicago Press).

Cameron, N. (1979), "The Stability of Canadian Demand for Money Functions", *Canadian Journal of Economics* (May).

Campbell, T. and L. Brendsel (1977), "The Impact of Compensating Balance Requirements on the Cash Balances of Manufacturing Corporations: An Empirical Study", *Journal of Finance* (Mar.).

Carliner, G. (1973), "Income Elasticity of Housing Demand",

Review of Economics and Statistics (Nov.).

Carlson, J.A. and J.R. Frew (1980), "Money Demand Responsiveness to the Rate of Return on Money: A Methodological Critique", *Journal of Political Economy* (June).

Carlson, J.A. and W.E. Wehrs (1974), "Aggregate Inventory Behavior", in G. Horwich and P.A. Samuelson (eds.), *Trade, Stability, and Growth* (New York: Academic Press).

Caves, D.W. and L.R. Christensen (1980), "Global Properties of Flexible Functional Forms", *American Economic Review* (June).

Caves, R.E., J.P. Jarrett, and M.K. Loucks (1979), "Competitive Conditions and the Firm's Buffer Stocks: An Exploratory Analysis", *Review of Economics and Statistics* (Nov.).

Chant, J.F. (1976), "Dynamic Adjustments in Simple Models of the Transactions Demand for Money", *Journal of Monetary Economics* (July).

Chen, A.H. and A.J. Boness (1975), "Effects of Uncertain Inflation on the Investment and Financing Decisions of Firms", *Journal of Finance* (May).

Chen, A.H. and E.H. Kim (1979), "Theories of Corporate Debt Policy: A Synthesis", *Journal of Finance* (May).

Chenery, H.B. (1952), "Overcapacity and the Acceleration Principle", *Econometrica* (Jan.).

Chetty, V.K. (1969), "On Measuring the Nearness of Near Monies", *American Economic Review* (June).

Childs, G.C. (1967), *Unfilled Orders and Inventories: A Structural Analysis* (Amsterdam: North-Holland).

Childs, G.C. (1974), "Inventories and the Generalized Accelerator", in G. Horwich and P.A. Samuelson (eds.), *Trade, Stability, and Macroeconomics* (New York: Academic Press).

Chow, G.L. (1966), "On the Long-run and Short-run Demand for Money", *Journal of Political Economy* (Apr.).

Ciccolo, J.H. (1978), "Money, Equity Values, and Income", *Journal of Money, Credit, and Banking* (Feb.).

Ciccolo, J.H. (1979), "Tobin's q and Tax Incentives", mimeo, Southern Economic Association Annual Meetings (Nov.).

Ciccolo, J.H. and G. Fromm (1979), "'q' and the Theory of Investment", *Journal of Finance* (May).

Claasen, E. (1975), "On the Indirect Productivity of Money", *Journal of Political Economy* (Apr.).

Clark, C. (1973), "The Demand for Money and the Choice of a Permanent Income Estimate: Some Canadian Evidence, 1926-65", *Journal of Money, Credit, and Banking* (Aug.)

Clinton, K. (1973a), "The Demand for Money in Canada, 1955-70: Some Single-Equations Estimates and Stability Tests", *Canadian Journal of Economics* (Feb.).

Clinton, K. (1973b), "Pitfalls in Financial Model Building: Comment", *American Economic Review* (Dec.).

Clower, R.W. (1965), "The Keynesian Counter-Revolution: A Theoretical Appraisal", in F.H. Hahn and F.P.R. Brechling (eds.), *The Theory of Interest* (London: Macmillan).

Clower, R.W. and P.W. Howitt (1978), "The Transactions Theory of the Demand for Money: A Reconsideration", *Journal of Political Economy* (June).

Coates, C.R. (1976), *The Demand for Money by Firms* (New York: Marcel Dekker).

Cobb, C.W. and P.H. Douglas (1928), "A Theory of Production", *American Economic Review* (Mar.).

Coen, R.M. (1969), "Tax Policy and Investment Behavior: Comment", *American Economic Review* (June).

Coen, R.M. and B.G. Hickman (1970), "Constrained Joint Estimation of Factor Demand and Production Functions", *Review of Economics and Statistics* (Aug.).

Cooley, P.L., R.L. Roenfeldt, and I. Chew (1975), "Capital Budgeting Procedures under Inflation", *Financial Management* (Winter).

Cooley, T.F. and E.C. Prescott (1973), "Systematic Variation Models Varying Parameter Regression: A Theory and Some Applications", *Annals of Economic and Social Measurement* (Oct.).

Corbo, V. (1974), *Inflation in Developing Countries* (Amsterdam: North-Holland).

Corbo, V. (1976), "Second-Order Approximations for Estimating Production Functions", *Annals of Economic and Social Measurement*, (vol. 5, no. 1).

Courchene, T.J. and A.K. Kelly (1971), "Money Supply and Money Demand: An Econometric Analysis for Canada", *Journal of Money, Credit, and Banking* (May).

Courchene, T.J. and H.T. Shapiro (1964), "The Demand for Money: A Note from the Time Series", *Journal of Political Economy* (Oct.).

Craig, G.D. (1974), "Money Illusion and the Aggregate Consumption Function", *American Economic Review* (Mar.).

Cramer, J. (1969), *Empirical Econometrics* (Amsterdam: North-Holland).

Cropper, M.L. (1976), "A State-Preference Approach to the Precautionary Demand for Money", *American Economic Review* (June).

Cross, S.M. (1980), "A Note on Inflation, Taxation and Investment Returns", *Journal of Finance* (Mar.).

Crouch, R.L. (1967), "A Model of the United Kingdom's Monetary Sector", *Econometrica* (July/Oct.).

Cukierman, A. (1972), "Money Illusion and the Aggregate Consumption Function: Comment", *American Economic Review* (Mar.).

Daniere, A. (1975), "The Optimum Lifetime Distribution of

Consumption Expenditures: Comment", *American Economic Review* (Sept.).

Darby, M.R. (1972), "The Allocation of Transitory Income among Consumers' Assets", *American Economic Review* (Dec.).

Darby, M.R. (1974), "The Permanent Income Theory - a Restatement", *Quarterly Journal of Economics* (May).

Darling, P.G. (1959), "Manufacturers' Inventory Investment, 1947-1958", *American Economic Review* (Dec.).

Darling, P.G. and M.C. Lovell (1971), "Inventories, Production Smoothing, and the Flexible Accelerator", *Quarterly Journal of Economics* (May).

Davenport, M. (1972), "Leverage and the Cost of Capital: An Empiricist Approach", Oxford Institute of Statistics *Bulletin* (Nov.).

Davidson, J.E.H., D.F. Hendry, F. Srba, and S. Yeo (1978), "Econometric Modelling of the Aggregate Time-Series Relationship between Consumers' Expenditure and Income in the United Kingdom", *Economic Journal* (Dec.).

Davidson, P. (1973), *Money and the Real World* (London: Macmillan).

Deane, P. (1979), *The First Industrial Revolution*, second edition (Cambridge: Cambridge University Press).

Deaton, A.S. (1972), "Wealth Effects on Consumption in a Modified Life Cycle Model", *Review of Economic Studies* (Oct.).

Deaton, A.S. (1977), "Involuntary Saving through Unanticipated Inflation", *American Economic Review* (Dec.).

Deaver, J. (1970), "The Chilean Inflation and the Demand for Money", in D. Meiselman (ed.), *Varieties of Monetary Experience* (Chicago: University of Chicago Press).

Della Valle, P.A. and N. Oguchi (1976), "Distribution, the Aggregate Consumption Function, and the Level of Economic Development: Some Cross Country Results", *Journal of Political Economy* (Dec.).

Dennis, E. and V.K. Smith (1978), "A Neoclassical Analysis of the Demand for Real Cash Balances by Firms", *Journal of Political Economy* (Oct.).

Denny, M.G. (1974), "The Relationship between Functional Forms for the Production System", *Canadian Journal of Economics* (Feb.).

Denny, M.G. and M.A. Fuss (1977), "The Use of Approximation Analysis to Test for Separability and the Existence of Consistent Aggregates", *American Economic Review* (June).

Denny, M.G., M.A. Fuss, and L. Waverman (1980), "The Substitution Possibilities for Energy: Evidence from U.S. and Canadian Manufacturing Industries", mimeo, University of Toronto, no. 8013.

Denton, F.T. and B.G. Spencer (1974), "Household and Population Effects on Aggregate Consumption", McMaster University, *Working Paper* (June).

DeRosa, P. (1978), "Mortgage Rationing and Residential Investment", *Journal of Money, Credit, and Banking* (Feb.).

Dhrymes, P.J. and M. Kurz (1967), "Investment, Dividends, and External Finance Behavior of Firms", in R. Ferber (ed.), *Determinants of Investment Behavior* (New York: National Bureau of Economic Research).

Dhrymes, P.J. and P. Zarembka (1970), "Elasticities of Substitution for Two-Digit Manufacturing Industries: A Correction", *Review of Economics and Statistics* (Feb.).

Diamond, D.B., Jr (1979), "Taxes, Inflation, Speculation and the Cost of Homeownership: 1963-1978", mimeo, North Carolina State University (May).

Dickson, H.D. and D.R. Starleaf (1972), "Polynomial Distributed Lag Structures in the Demand Function for Money", *Journal of Finance* (Dec.).

Diewert, W.E. (1971), "An Application of the Shephard Duality Theorem: A Generalized Leontief Production Function", *Journal of Political Economy* (May/June).

Diewert, W.E. and C. Parkan (1979), "Linear Programming Tests of Regularity Conditions for Production Functions", mimeo, University of British Columbia (Jan.).

Dixon, P.B. and C. Lluch (1977), "Durable Goods in the Extended Linear Expenditure System", *Review of Economic Studies* (June).

Diz, A. (1970), "Money and Prices in Argentina, 1935-1962", in D. Meiselman (ed.), *Varieties of Monetary Experience* (Chicago: University of Chicago Press).

Dolde, W. (1978), "Capital Markets and the Short-Run Behavior of Life Cycle Savers", *Journal of Finance* (May).

Dolde, W. and J. Tobin (1971), "Monetary and Fiscal Effects on Consumption", *Consumer Spending and Monetary Policy: the Linkages* (Boston: Federal Reserve Bank of Boston).

Donovan, D.J. (1978), "Modeling the Demand for Liquid Assets: An Application to Canada", *International Monetary Fund Staff Papers* (Dec.).

Drazen, A. (1978a), "Government Debt, Human Capital, and Bequests in a Life-Cycle Model", *Journal of Political Economy* (June).

Drazen, A. (1978b), "Consumption Theory and Secular Aggregate Saving: A Reexamination", mimeo, University of Chicago (Nov.).

Drazen, A. (1980a), "Recent Developments in Macroeconomic Disequilibrium Theory", *Econometrica* (Mar.).

Drazen, A. (1980b), "A Quantity-Constrained Macroeconomic Model with Price Flexibility", mimeo, University of Chicago (Aug.).

Dreze, J.H. (1975), "Existence of an Exchange Equilibrium under Price Rigidities", *International Economic Review* (June).

Duesenberry, J.S. (1949), *Income, Saving and the Theory of Consumer Behavior* (Cambridge: Harvard University Press).

Durand, D. (1959), "The Cost of Capital, Corporation Finance, and the Theory of Investment: Comment", *American Economic Review* (Sept.).

Dutton, D.S. (1971), "The Demand for Money and the Price Level", *Journal of Political Economy* (Sept./Oct.).

Dutton, D.S. and W.P. Gramm (1973), "Transactions Costs, the Wage Rate, and the Demand for Money", *American Economic Review* (Sept.).

Dutton, D.S., W.P. Gramm, and J. McDonald (1974), "Transactions Costs, the Wage Rate and the Firm's Demand for Money", mimeo, University of Iowa (Apr.).

Dutton, D.S., R. Rozek, and S. Wu (1974), "Uncertainty, Transactions Motive, and the Demand for Money", mimeo, University of Iowa (May).

Eden, B. (1976), "On the Specification of the Demand for Money during the Hyperinflation", mimeo, Hebrew University.

Edwards, F.R. (1972), "More on Substitutability between Money and Near-Monies", *Journal of Money, Credit, and Banking* (Aug.).

Eisner, R. (1958), "The Permanent Income Hypothesis: Comment", *American Economic Review* (Dec.).

Eisner, R. (1963a), "Investment: Fact and Fancy", *American Economic Review* (May).

Eisner, R. (1963b), "Another Look at Liquidity Preference", *Econometrica* (July).

Eisner, R. (1967), "A Permanent Income Theory of Investment: Some Empirical Explorations", *American Economic Review* (June).

Eisner, R. (1969), "Tax Policy and Investment Behavior: Comment", *American Economic Review* (June).

Eisner, R. (1971), "Non-Linear Estimates of the Liquidity Trap", *Econometrica* (Sept.).

Eisner, R. (1978), *Factors in Business Investment* (Cambridge: Ballinger for the National Bureau of Economic Research).

Eisner, R. and M.I. Nadiri (1968), "Investment Behavior and Neo-Classical Theory", *Review of Economics and Statistics* (Aug.).

Eisner, R. and R.H. Strotz (1963), "Determinants of Business Investment", in Commission on Money and Credit, *Impacts of Monetary Policy* (Englewood Cliffs, NJ: Prentice-Hall).

Elliott, J.W. (1980), "The Cost of Capital and U.S. Capital

Investment: A Test of Alternative Concepts", *Journal of Finance* (Sept.).

Enzler, J., L. Johnson, and J. Paulus (1976), "Some Problems of Money Demand", *Brookings Papers*, no. 1.

Evans, M.K. (1967), "The Importance of Wealth in the Consumption Function", *Journal of Political Economy* (Aug.).

Evans, M.K. (1969), *Macroeconomic Activity* (New York: Harper and Row).

Fair, R.C. (1971), *A Short-Run Forecasting Model of the United States Economy* (Lexington, Mass.: D.C. Heath).

Fair, R.C. (1972), "Disequilibrium in Housing Models", *Journal of Finance* (May).

Fair, R.C. and D.M. Jaffee (1972), "Methods of Estimation for Markets in Disequilibrium", *Econometrica* (May).

Fair, R.C. and H.H. Kelejian (1974), "Methods of Estimation for Markets in Disequilibrium: A Further Study", *Econometrica* (Jan).

Fama, E.F. (1974), "The Empirical Relationship between the Dividend and Investment Decisions of Firms", *American Economic Review* (June).

Fama, E.F. (1975), "Short-Term Interest Rates as Predictors of Inflation", *American Economic Review* (June).

Fama, E.F. (1978), "The Effects of a Firm's Investment and Financing Decisions on the Welfare of Its Security Holders", *American Economic Review* (June).

Fama, E.F. and M.R. Gibbons (1980), "Inflation, Real Returns, and Capital Investment", *CRSP Working Paper* (Chicago: Graduate School of Business (Aug.)).

Fama, E.F. and M.H. Miller (1972), *The Theory of Finance* (New York: Holt, Rinehart and Winston).

Farrell, M.J. (1959), "The New Theories of the Consumption Function", *Economic Journal* (Dec.).

Faurot, D.J. (1978), "Interrelated Demand for Capital and Labor in a Globally Optimal Flexible Accelerator Model", *Review of Economics and Statistics* (Feb.).

Feige, E.L. (1964), *The Demand for Liquid Assets* (Englewood Cliffs, NJ: Prentice-Hall).

Feige, E.L. (1967), "Expectations and Adjustments in the Monetary Sector", *American Economic Review* (May).

Feige, E.L. (1974), "Alternative Temporal Cross-Section Specifications of the Demand for Demand Deposits", in H.G. Johnson and A.R. Nobay (eds.), *Issues in Monetary Economics* (Oxford University Press).

Feige, E.L. and D.K. Pearce (1977), "The Substitutability of Money and Near-Monies", *Journal of Economic Literature* (June).

Feige, E.L. and P.A.V.B. Swamy (1974), "A Random Coefficient Model of the Demand for Liquid Assets", *Journal of Money,*

Credit, and Banking (May).
Feldstein, M.S. (1967), "Alternative Methods of Estimating a CES Production Function for Britain", *Economica* (Nov.).
Feldstein, M.S. (1974), "Social Security, Induced Retirement, and Aggregate Capital Accumulation", *Journal of Political Economy* (Sept./Oct.).
Feldstein, M.S. (1978), "The Rate of Return, Taxation, and Personal Savings", *Economic Journal* (Sept.).
Feldstein, M.S. (1981), "Social Security, Induced Retirement, and Aggregate Capital Accumulation: A Correlation and Updating", mimeo, National Bureau of Economic Research *Working Paper*, no. 583.
Feldstein, M.S. and A. Auerbach (1976), "Inventory Behavior in Durable-Goods and Manufacturing: The Target-Adjustment Model", *Brookings Papers*, no. 2.
Feldstein, M.S. and J.S. Flemming (1971), "Tax Policy, Corporate Saving and Investment Behavior in Britain", *Review of Economic Studies* (Oct.).
Ferber, R. (1962), "Research in Household Behavior", *American Economic Review* (Mar.).
Ferber, R. (1973), "Consumer Economics: A Survey", *Journal of Economic Literature* (Dec.).
Ferguson, C.E. (1965), "Time Series Production Functions and Technological Progress in American Manufacturing Industry", *Journal of Political Economy* (Apr.).
Ferguson, J.D. and W.R. Hart (1980), "Liquidity Preference or Loanable Funds: Interest Rate Determination in Market Disequilibrium", *Oxford Economic Papers* (Mar.).
Fischer, S. (1974), "Money and the Production Function", *Economic Inquiry* (Dec.).
Fishelson, G. (1979), "Elasticity of Factor Substitution in Cross-Section Production Functions", *Review of Economics and Statistics* (Aug.).
Fisher, D. (1968), "The Demand for Money in Britain: Quarterly Results, 1951 to 1967", *Manchester School* (Dec.).
Fisher, D. (1970), "Real Balances and the Demand for Money", *Journal of Political Economy* (Nov./Dec.).
Fisher, D. (1973), "The Speculative Demand for Money: An Empirical Test", *Economica* (May).
Fisher, D. (1975), "Wealth Adjustment Effects in a Macroeconomic Model", in M. Parkin and A.R. Nobay (eds.), *Contemporary Issues in Economics* (Manchester University Press).
Fisher, D. (1976), "The Term Structure of Interest Rates", in R.S. Thorn (ed.), *Monetary Theory and Policy*, second edition (New York: Praeger).
Fisher, D. (1978), *Monetary Theory and the Demand for Money* London: Martin Robertson).
Fisher, F.M. (1969), "The Existence of Aggregate Production

Functions", *Econometrica* (Oct.).

Fisher, G. and M. McAleer (1979), "Theory and Econometric Evaluation of a Systems Approach to the Demand for Money: The Canadian Case", mimeo, Institute for Economic Research, Queens University (Dec.).

Fisher, I. (1934), *Mastering the Crisis* (London: George Allen).

Fisher, I. (1963), *The Purchasing Power of Money* (New York: Augustus M. Kelley).

Fisher, I, (1965), *The Theory of Interest*, reprint of 1930 edition (New York: Augustus M. Kelley).

Fisher, M.R. (1956), "Explorations in Savings Behaviour", Oxford Institute of Statistics *Bulletin* (Aug.).

Floyd, J.E. and J.A. Hynes (1972), "The Contribution of Real Money Balances to the Level of Wealth", *Journal of Money, Credit, and Banking* (May).

Foot, D.K. (1977), "The Demand for Money in Canada: Some Additional Evidence", *Canadian Journal of Economics* (Aug.).

Frenkel, J.A. (1977), "The Forward Exchange Rate, Expectations, and the Demand for Money: The German Hyperinflation", *American Economic Review* (Sept.).

Frenkel, J.A. (1979), "Further Evidence on Expectations and the Demand for Money during the German Hyperinflation", *Journal of Monetary Economics* (Jan.).

Frenkel, J.A. and C. Rodriquez (1975), "Wealth Effects and the Dynamics of Inflation", *Journal of Money, Credit, and Banking* (May).

Freund, R.J. (1956), "The Introduction of Risk into a Programming Model", *Econometrica* (July).

Friedman, B.M. (1972), "Credit Rationing: A Review", Board of Governors of the Federal Reserve System *Staff Economic Studies*, no. 72 (June).

Friedman, M. (1956), "The Quantity Theory of Money - A Restatement", in M. Friedman (ed.), *Studies in the Quantity Theory of Money* (Chicago: University of Chicago Press).

Friedman, M. (1957), *A Theory of the Consumption Function* (Princeton: Princeton University Press).

Friedman, M. (1963), "Windfalls, the Horizon, and Related Concepts in the Permanent Income Hypothesis", in C. Christ (ed.), *Measurement in Economics* (Stanford, Cal.: Stanford University Press).

Friedman, M. (1959), "The Demand for Money: Some Theoretical and Empirical Results", *Journal of Political Economy* (Aug.).

Friedman, M. (1970), "A Theoretical Framework for Monetary Analysis", *Journal of Political Economy* (Mar./Apr.).

Friedman, M. (1971), "A Monetary Theory of Nominal Income", *Journal of Political Economy* (Mar./Apr.).

Friedman, M. (1977), "Time Perspective in Demand for Money", *Scandinavian Journal of Economics* (Dec.).

Friedman, M. and D. Meiselman (1963), "The Relative Stability of Monetary Velocity and the Investment Multiplier in the United States, 1897-1958", in E.C. Brown *et al.*, *Stabilization Policies* (Englewood Cliffs, NJ: Prentice-Hall).

Friedman, M. and A.J. Schwartz (1963), *A Monetary History of the United States, 1867-1960* (New York: Columbia University Press).

Friedman, M. and A.J. Schwartz (1970), *Monetary Statistics of the United States* (New York: Columbia University Press).

Friend, I. and C. Lieberman (1975), "Short-Run Asset Effects on Household Saving and Consumption", *American Economic Review* (Sept.).

Frodin, J.H. and R. Startz (1979), "The NOW Account Experiment and the Demand for Money", mimeo, Wharton School, University of Pennsylvania, no. 11-79.

Frost, P.A. (1970), "Banking Services, Minimum Cash Balances, and the Firm's Demand for Money", *Journal of Finance* (Dec.).

Fuchs, V.R. (1963), "Capital-Labor Substitution: A Note", *Review of Economics and Statistics* (Nov.).

Fuss, M.A. (1977), "The Demand for Energy in Canadian Manufacturing", *Journal of Econometrics* (Jan.).

Fuss, M.A., D. McFadden, and Y. Mundlak (1978), "A Survey of Functional Forms in the Economic Analysis of Production", in M.A. Fuss and D. McFadden (eds.), *Production Economics: A Dual Approach to Theory and Applications*, vol. 1 (Amsterdam: North-Holland).

Gabor, A. and I.F. Pearce (1958), "The Place of Money Capital in the Theory of Production", *Quarterly Journal of Economics* (Nov.).

Gandolfi, A.E. and J.R. Lothian (1976), "The Demand for Money from the Great Depression to the Present", *American Economic Review* (May).

Ganjarerndee, S. (1972), "The Effects of Temporal Aggregation on a Model of the Australian Monetary Sector", *Economic Record* (Dec.).

Garbade, P.J. and P. Wachtel (1978), "Time Variation in the Relationship between Inflation and Interest Rates", *Journal of Monetary Economics* (Nov.).

Garcia, G. and S. Pak (1979), "Some Clues in the Case of the Missing Money", *American Economic Review* (May).

Gerking, S.D. and W.J. Boyes (1980), "The Role of Functional Form in Estimating Elasticities of Housing Expenditures", *Southern Economic Journal* (Oct.).

Gertler, M. and E. Grinols (1979), "Monetary Randomness and

Investment", mimeo, Cornell University (Oct.).
Gibson, W.E. (1972), "Demand and Supply Functions for Money in the United States: Theory and Measurement", *Econometrica* (Mar.).
Gibson, W.E. (1976), "Demand and Supply Functions for Money: A Comment", *Econometrica* (Mar.).
Girton, L. and D. Roper (1981), "Theory and Implications of Currency Substitution", *Journal of Money, Credit, and Banking* (Feb.).
Goldberger, A.S. (1967), "Functional Form and Utility: A Review of Consumer Demand Theory", Social Systems Research Institute, University of Wisconsin.
Goldfeld, S.M. (1973), "The Demand for Money Revisited", *Brookings Papers*, no. 3.
Goldfeld, S.M. (1976), "The Case of the Missing Money", *Brookings Papers*, no. 3.
Goldfeld, S.M., D.M. Jaffee, and R.E. Quandt (1980), "A Model of FHLBB Advances: Rationing or Market Clearing?", *Review of Economics and Statistics* (Aug.).
Goldfeld, S.M. and R.E. Quandt (1975), "Estimation in a Disequilibrium Model and the Value of Information", *Journal of Econometrics* (Nov.).
Goldsmith, R. (1955), *A Study of Saving in the United States* (Princeton, NJ: Princeton University Press).
Goodhart, C.A.E. and A. Crockett (1970), "The Importance of Money", Bank of England, *Quarterly Bulletin* (June).
Gould, J.P. (1968), "Adjustment Costs in the Theory of Investment of the Firm", *Review of Economic Studies* (Jan.).
Gould, J.P. (1969), "The Use of Endogenous Variables in Dynamic Models of Investment", *Quarterly Journal of Economics* (Nov.).
Graham, J. (1979), "The Household Production Theory of Consumption: Aggregate Implications and Tests", mimeo, University of Illinois (Urbana-Champaign (Oct.)).
Gramlich, E.M. and D.T. Hulett (1972), "The Demand for and Supply of Savings Deposits", in E.M. Gramlich and D.M. Jaffee (eds.), *Savings Deposits, Mortgages, and Housing* (Lexington, Mass.: Lexington Books).
Gramlich, E.M. and D.M. Jaffee (1972), "The Behavior of the Three Sectors Together", in E.M. Gramlich and D.M. Jaffee (eds.), *Savings Deposits, Mortgages, and Housing* (Lexington, Mass.: Lexington Books).
Grandmont, J. (1973), "On the Short-Run and Long-Run Demand for Money", *European Economic Review* (Oct.).
Grandmont, J. (1977), "Temporary General Equilibrium Theory", *Econometrica* (Apr.).
Gray, M.R. and M. Parkin (1973), "Portfolio Diversification as Optimal Precautionary Behaviour", in M. Morishima (ed.),

Theory of Demand, Real and Monetary (Oxford: Clarendon Press).
Green, H.A.J. (1964), *Aggregation in Economic Analysis* (Princeton, NJ: Princeton University Press).
Green, H.A.J. (1976), *Consumer Theory*, revised edition (London: Macmillan).
Green. J. (1971) "A Simple General Equilibrium Model of the Term Structure of Interest Rates", Harvard Institute of Economic Research, *Discussion Paper*, no. 133 (Mar.).
Gregory, A.W. and M. McAleer (1980), "Exogeneity and the Demand for Money in a Small Open Economy: The Canadian Case", mimeo, Queens University, no. 401 (Sept.).
Griffin, J.M. and P.R. Gregory (1976), "An Intercountry Translog Model of Energy Substitution Responses", *American Economic Review* (Dec.).
Griliches, Z. (1961), "A Note on Serial Correlation Bias in Estimates of Distributed Lags", *Econometrica* (Jan.).
Griliches, Z. (1964), "Research Expenditures, Education, and the Aggregate Agricultural Production Function", *American Economic Review* (Dec.).
Griliches, Z. (1967a) "Distributed Lags: A Survey", *Econometrica* (Jan.).
Griliches, Z. (1967b), "Production Functions in Manufacturing: Some Preliminary Results", in M. Brown (ed.), *The Theory and Empirical Analysis of Production* (New York: National Bureau of Economic Research).
Griliches, Z. (1969), "Capital-Skill Complementarity", *Review of Economics and Statistics* (Nov.).
Griliches, Z. and V. Ringstad (1971), *Economies of Scale and the Production Function* (Amsterdam: North-Holland).
Grossman, H.I. (1971), "Money, Interest, and Prices in Market Disequilibrium", *Journal of Political Economy* (Sept./Oct).
Grossman, H.I. (1972), "A Choice-Theoretic Model of an Income-Investment Accelerator", *American Economic Review* (Sept.).
Grossman, H.I. (1974), "The Nature of Quantities in Market Disequilibrium", *American Economic Review* (June).
Grossman, H.I. (1979), "Why Does Aggregate Employment Fluctuate?", *American Economic Review* (May).
Grossman, H.I. and A.J. Policano (1975), "Money Balances, Commodity Inventories, and Inflationary Expectations", *Journal of Political Economy* (Dec.).
Grunfeld, Y. (1960), "The Determinants of Corporate Investment", in A. Harberger (ed.), *The Demand for Durable Goods* (Chicago: University of Chicago Press).
Guilkey, D.K. and C.A.K. Lovell (1980), "On the Flexibility of the Translog Approximation", *International Economic Re-*

view (Feb.).

Gupta, K.L. (1980), "Some Controversial Aspects of the Demand for Money", *Journal of Money, Credit, and Banking*, part I (Nov.).

Gurley, J.G. and E.S. Shaw (1960), *Money in a Theory of Finance* (Washington, DC: Brookings Institution).

Guttentag, J.M. (1961), "The Short Cycle in Residential Construction, 1946-59", *American Economic Review* (June).

Haavelmo, T. (1960), *A Study in the Theory of Investment* (Chicago: University of Chicago Press).

Hacche, G. (1974), "The Demand for Money in the United Kingdom: Experience since 1971", Bank of England *Quarterly Bulletin* (Sept.).

Hafer, R.W. and S.E. Hein (1979), "Evidence on the Temporal Stability of the Demand for Money Relationship in the United States", Federal Reserve Bank of St Louis *Review* (Dec.).

Hafer, R.W. and S.E. Hein (1980), "The Dynamics and Estimation of Short-Run Money Demand", Federal Reserve Bank of St Louis *Review* (Mar.).

Haley, C.W. and L.D. Schall (1978), "Problems with the Concept of the Cost of Capital", *Journal of Financial and Quantitative Analysis* (Dec.).

Hall, R.E. (1977), "Investment, Interest Rates, and the Effects of Stabilization Policies", *Brookings Papers*, no. 1.

Hall, R.E. (1978), "Stochastic Implications of the Life Cycle-Permanent Income Hypothesis: Theory and Evidence", *Journal of Political Economy* (Dec.).

Hall, R.E. and D.W. Jorgenson (1967), "Tax Policy and Investment Behavior", *American Economic Review* (June).

Hall, R.E. and D.W. Jorgenson (1969), "Tax Policy and Investment Behavior: Reply and Further Results", *American Economic Review* (June).

Halter, A.N., H.O. Carter, and J.G. Hocking (1957), "A Note on the Transcendental Production Function", *Journal of Farm Economics* (Nov.).

Hamburger, M.J. (1967), "Interest Rates and the Demand for Consumer Durable Goods", *American Economic Review* (Dec.).

Hamburger, M.J. (1969), "Alternative Interest Rates and the Demand for Money: Comment", *American Economic Review* (June).

Hamburger, M.J. (1977a), "The Demand for Money in an Open Economy: Germany and the United Kingdom", *Journal of Monetary Economics* (Jan.).

Hamburger, M.J. (1977b), "Behavior of the Money Stock: Is There a Puzzle?", *Journal of Monetary Economics* (July).

Hanoch, G. (1971), "CRESH Production Functions", *Econometrica* (Sept.).

Hanoch, G. and M. Rothschild (1972), "Testing the Assumptions of Production Theory: A Nonparametric Approach", *Journal of Political Economy* (Mar./Apr.).

Haraf, W.S. (1978), "Inventories, Orders and the Persistent Effects of Monetary Shocks", in *West Coast Academic/Federal Reserve Economic Research Seminar* (San Francisco: Federal Reserve Bank of San Francisco).

Harcourt, G.C. (1969), "Some Cambridge Controversies in the Theory of Capital", *Journal of Economic Literature* (June).

Harris, D.G. (1973), "A Model of Bank Loan Term Adjustment", *Western Economic Journal* (Dec.).

Harris, D.G. (1974), "Credit Rationing at Commercial Banks: Some Empirical Evidence", *Journal of Money, Credit, and Banking* (May).

Harris, D.J. (1973), "Capital, Distribution, and the Aggregate Production Function", *American Economic Review* (Mar.).

Harrod, R.F. (1948), *Towards a Dynamic Economics* (London: Macmillan).

Hartman, R.C. (1980), "The Term Structure of Interest Rates and the Demand for Investment", *Quarterly Journal of Economics* (May).

Harvey, A.C. (1975), "Testing for Functional Form in Regression with Special Reference to Production Functions", University of Kent *Discussion Paper*, no. 22 (July).

Harvey, A.C. (1977), "Discrimination between CES and VES Production Functions", *Annals of Economic and Social Measurement*, vol. 6, no. 4.

Havrilesky, T.M. and J.T. Boorman (1980), *Current Issues in Monetary Theory and Policy* (Arlington Heights, Ill.: AHM Publishing).

Hay, G.A. (1970a), "Adjustment Costs and the Flexible Accelerator", *Quarterly Journal of Economics* (Feb.).

Hay, G.A. (1970b), "Production, Price, and Inventory Theory", *American Economic Review* (Sept.).

Heathfield, D. (1971), *Production Functions* (London: Macmillan).

Heathfield, D. (1976), "Production Functions", in D. Heathfield (ed.), *Topics in Applied Macroeconomics* (London: Macmillan).

Heckman, J. (1974), "Life Cycle Consumption and Labor Supply: An Explanation of the Relationship between Income and Consumption over the Life Cycle", *American Economic Review* (Mar.).

Heien, D.M. (1972), "Demographic Effects and the Multiperiod Consumption Function", *Journal of Political Economy* (Jan./Feb.).

Hein, S.E. (1980), "Dynamic Forecasting and the Demand for

Money", Federal Reserve Bank of St Louis *Review* (June/July).

Heller, H.R. and M.S. Khan (1979), "The Demand for Money and the Term Structure of Interest Rates", *Journal of Political Economy* (Feb.).

Heller, W.P. and R.M. Starr (1979), "Capital Market Imperfection, the Consumption Function, and the Effectiveness of Fiscal Policy", *Quarterly Journal of Economics* (Aug.).

Hester, D.D. and J. Tobin (1967), *Financial Markets and Economic Activity* (New York: Wiley).

Hickman, B.G. (1959), "Diffusion, Acceleration and Business Cycles", *American Economic Review* (Sept.).

Hicks, J.R. (1946), *Value and Capital* (Oxford: Clarendon Press).

Hicks, J.R. (1950), *A Contribution to the Theory of the Trade Cycle* (Oxford: Clarendon Press).

Hildebrand, G.H. and T. Liu (1965), *Manufacturing Production Functions in the United States, 1957* (Ithaca, NY: Cornell University Press).

Hock, I. (1958), "Simultaneous Equation Bias in the Context of the Cobb-Douglas Production Function", *Econometrica* (Oct.).

Hodgman, D.R. (1963), *Commercial Bank Loan and Investment Policy* (Champaign, Ill.: University of Illinois).

Hoffman, S.G. (1979), "An Empirical Analysis of Sectoral Money Demand in the Southeast", Federal Reserve Bank of Atlanta *Working Paper Series* (Feb.).

Holbrook, R.S. (1967), "The Three-Year Horizon: An Analysis of the Evidence", *Journal of Political Economy* (Oct.).

Holbrook, R.S. and F.P. Stafford (1971), "The Propensity to Consume Separate Types of Income: A Generalized Permanent Income Hypothesis", *Econometrica* (Jan.).

Holmes, J.M. (1974), "A Test of the Permanent-Income Hypothesis: Comment", *Journal of Political Economy* (Jan./Feb.).

Holt, C.A., F. Modigliani, J.F. Muth, and H.A. Simon (1960), *Planning Production, Inventories, and Work Force* (Englewood Cliffs, NJ: Prentice-Hall).

Honkapohja, S. and T. Ito (1979), "A Stochastic Approach to Disequilibrium Macroeconomics", mimeo, University of Minnesota (Sept.).

Howard, D.H. (1976), "The Disequilibrium Model in a Controlled Economy: An Empirical Test of the Barro-Grossman Model", *American Economic Review* (Dec.).

Howard, D.H. (1978), "Personal Saving Behavior and the Rate of Inflation", *Review of Economics and Statistics* (Nov.).

Howitt, P.W. (1979), "Evaluating the Non-Market-Clearing Approach", *American Economic Review* (May).

Huang, D.S. (1966), "The Short-Run Flows of Nonfarm Residen-

tial Mortgage Credit", *Econometrica* (Apr.).
Hudson, E.A. and D.W. Jorgenson (1974), "U.S. Energy Policy and Economic Growth, 1975-2000", *Bell Journal* (Autumn).
Hulett, D.T. (1971), "More on an Empirical Definition of Money: Note", *American Economic Review* (June).
Humphrey, D.B. and J.R. Moroney (1975), "Substitution among Capital, Labor, and National Resource Products in American Manufacturing", *Journal of Political Economy* (Feb.).
Irvine, F.O. (1980), "Merchant Wholesaler Inventory Investment and the Cost of Capital", mimeo, Board of Governors of the Federal Reserve System (Sept.).
Irvine, F.O. (1981), "Retail Inventory Investment and the Cost of Capital", *American Economic Review* (Sept.).
Isachsen, A.J. (1976), *The Demand for Money in Norway* (Oslo: Norges Bank).
Ito, T. and K. Ueda (1980), "Tests of the Equilibrium Hypothesis in Disequilibrium Econometrics: An International Test of Credit Rationing", mimeo, Center for Economics, University of Minnesota (July).
Jacobs, R.L. (1974), "Estimating the Long-Run Demand for Money from Time-Series Data", *Journal of Political Economy* (Nov./Dec.).
Jacobs, R.L. (1975), "A Difficulty with Monetarist Models of Hyperinflation", *Economic Inquiry* (Sept.).
Jaffee, D.M. (1971), *Credit Rationing and the Loan Market* (New York: Wiley).
Jaffee, D.M. (1972), "An Econometric Model of the Mortgage Market", in E.M. Gramlich and D.M. Jaffee (eds.), *Savings Deposits, Mortgages, and Housing* (Lexington, Mass.: Lexington Books).
Jaffee, D.M. and F. Modigliani (1969), "A Theory and Test of Credit Rationing", *American Economic Review* (Dec.).
Jaffee, D.M. and K.T. Rosen (1978), "Estimates of the Effectiveness of Stabilization Policies for the Mortgage and Housing Markets", *Journal of Finance* (June).
Jaffee, D.M. and T. Russell (1976a), "A Simplification of Credit Rationing Theory in Terms of Insurance Market Failure", mimeo, Princeton University.
Jaffee, D.M. and T. Russell (1976b), "Imperfect Information, Uncertainty, and Credit Rationing", *Quarterly Journal of Economics* (Nov.).
Johnson, H.G. (1970), "Recent Developments in Monetary Theory - A Commentary", in D. Croome and H.G. Johnson (eds.), *Money in Britain, 1959-1969* (Oxford University Press).
Johnson, H.G. (1977), "The Monetary Approach to Balance of Payments Theory and Policy: Explanations and Policy Implications", *Economica* (Aug.).
Johnston, J. (1972), *Econometric Methods* , second edition

(New York: McGraw-Hill).

Jorgenson, D.W. (1963), "Capital Theory and Investment Behavior", *American Economic Review* (May).

Jorgenson, D.W. (1965), "Anticipations and Investment Behaviour", in J. Duesenberry *et al.*, *The Brookings Quarterly Econometric Model of the United States* (Amsterdam: North-Holland).

Jorgenson, D.W. (1966), "Rational Distributed Lag Functions", *Econometrica* (Jan.).

Jorgenson, D.W. (1967), "The Theory of Investment Behavior", in R. Ferber (ed.), *Determinants of Investment Behavior* (New York: National Bureau of Economic Research).

Jorgenson, D.W. (1971), "Econometric Studies of Investment Behavior: A Survey", *Journal of Economic Literature* (Dec.).

Jorgenson, D.W. (1972), "Investment Behavior and the Production Function", *Bell Journal* (Spring).

Jorgenson, D.W. (1973), "Investment and Production: A Review", in M. Intriligator and D. Kendrick (eds.), *Frontiers of Quantitative Economics*, vol. II (Amsterdam: North-Holland).

Jorgenson, D.W. and C.D. Siebert (1968), "A Comparison of Alternative Theories of Corporate Investment Behavior", *American Economic Review* (Sept.).

Jorgenson, D.W. and J.A. Stephenson (1967), "The Time Structure of Investment Behavior in United States Manufacturing, 1947-1960", *Review of Economics and Statistics* (Feb.).

Jump, G.V. (1980), "Interest Rates, Inflation Expectations, and Spurious Elements in Measured Real Income and Saving", *American Economic Review* (Dec.).

Juster, F.T. and L.D. Taylor (1975), "Towards a Theory of Saving Behavior", *American Economic Review* (May).

Juster, F.T. and P. Wachtel (1972a), "Inflation and the Consumer", *Brookings Papers*, no. 1.

Juster, F.T. and P. Wachtel (1972b), "A Note on Inflation and the Saving Rate", *Brookings Papers*, no. 3.

Kadiyala, K.R. (1972), "Production Functions and Elasticity of Substitution", *Southern Economic Journal* (Jan.).

Kahn, R.F. (1931), "The Relation of Home Investment to Unemployment", *Economic Journal* (June).

Kalchbrenner, J.A. (1972), "A Model of the Housing Sector", in E.M. Gramlich and D.M. Jaffee (eds.), *Savings Deposits, Mortgages, and Housing* (Lexington, Mass.: Lexington Books).

Kalt, J.P. (1978), "Technological Change and Factor Substitution in the United States: 1929-1967", *International Economic Review* (Oct.).

Karni, E. (1973), "The Transactions Demand for Cash: Incorporation of the Value of Time into the Inventory Approach", *Journal of Political Economy* (Sept./Oct.).

Karni, E. (1974), "The Value of Time and the Demand for Money", *Journal of Money, Credit, and Banking* (Feb.).

Karni, E. (1975), "The Value of Time and the Demand for Money: Evidence from U.K. Time Series Data", *Australian Economic Papers* (Dec.).

Katz, B.G. (1979), "The Disequilibrium Model in a Controlled Economy: Comment", *American Economic Review* (Sept.).

Katzimbris, G.M. and S.M. Miller (1980), "Distribution Effects and the Business Demand for Money", *Journal of Macroeconomics* (Fall).

Kavanagh, N.J. and A.A. Walters (1966), "Demand for Money in the U.K., 1877-1961: Some Preliminary Findings", Oxford Institute of Statistics *Bulletin* (May).

Kazi, U.A. (1976), "Production Functions with a Variable Elasticity of Substitution: Analysis and Some Empirical Results", mimeo, University of Durham.

Kearl, J.R. (1979), "Inflation, Mortgages, and Housing", *Journal of Political Economy* (Oct.).

Kearl, J.R. and F.S. Mishkin (1977), "Illiquidity, the Demand for Residential Housing and Monetary Policy", *Journal of Finance* (Dec.).

Kearl, J.R., K. Rosen, and C. Swan (1975), "Relationships between the Mortgage Investments, the Demand for Housing, and Mortgage Credit: A Review of the Empirical Studies", in F. Modigliani and D.R. Lessard (eds.), *New Mortgage Designs for Stable Housing in an Inflationary Environment*, Conference Series No. 14, Federal Reserve Bank of Boston (Jan.).

Kendrick, J.W. and R. Sato (1963), "Factor Prices, Productivity, and Economic Growth", *American Economic Review* (Dec.).

Keran, M.W. (1970), "Selecting a Monetary Indicator - Evidence from the United States and Other Developed Countries", Federal Reserve Bank of St Louis *Review* (Sept.).

Kessel, R.A. (1966), *The Cyclical Behavior of the Term Structure of Interest Rates* (New York: National Bureau of Economic Research).

Keynes, J.M. (1930), *A Treatise on Money*, 2 vols. (London: Macmillan).

Keynes, J.M. (1936), *The General Theory of Employment, Interest and Money* (New York: Harcourt, Brace).

Keynes, J.M. (1937), "Alternative Theories of the Rate of Interest", *Economic Journal* (June).

Khan, M.S. (1977a), "The Variability of Expectations in Hyperinflations", *Journal of Political Economy* (Aug.).

Khan, M.S. (1977b), "Variable Expectations and the Demand for Money in High Inflation Countries", *Manchester School* (Sept.).

Khan, M.S. and P.J.K. Kouri (1975), "Real Money Balances: An Omitted Variable from the Production Function", *Review of Economics and Statistics* (May).

Kim, M.K. (1979), "Inflationary Effects in the Capital Investment Process: An Empirical Examination", *Journal of Finance* (Sept.).

Klein, B. (1974), "Competitive Interest Payments on Bank Deposits and the Long-Run Demand for Money", *American Economic Review* (Dec.).

Klein, B. (1977), "The Demand for Quality-Adjusted Cash Balances: Price Uncertainty in the U.S. Money Demand Function", *Journal of Political Economy* (Aug.).

Klein, L.R. (1946), "Macroeconomics and the Theory of Rational Behavior", *Econometrica* (Apr.).

Klein, L.R. (1950), *Economic Fluctuations in the United States, 1921-1924* (New York: Wiley).

Klein, L.R. (1954), *The Keynesian Revolution* (New York: Macmillan).

Klein, L.R. and N. Liviatan (1957), "The Significance of Income Variability on Savings Behaviour", Oxford Institute of Statistics *Bulletin* (May).

Klein, M.A. and N.B. Murphy (1971), "The Pricing of Bank Deposits: A Theoretical and Empirical Analysis", *Journal of Financial and Quantitative Analysis* (Mar.).

Klovland, J.T. (1977), "Maximum Likelihood Estimation of Geometric Distributed Lag Models: A Case Study of Aggregate Consumption Functions of Ten European Countries", mimeo, Norwegian School of Economics and Business (May).

Klovland, J.T. (1978), "The Stability of the Demand for Money in Norway 1925-1937", mimeo, Norwegian School of Economics and Business (Nov.).

Kmenta, J. (1967), "On Estimation of the CES Production Function", *International Economic Review* (June).

Kochin, L.A. (1974), "Are Future Taxes Anticipated by Consumers?", *Journal of Money, Credit, and Banking* (Aug.).

Kohli, U.R. (1978), "Permanent Income in the Consumption and the Demand for Money Functions", Econometric Society, mimeo, Chicago Meetings.

Kotowitz, Y. (1968), "Capital-Labour Substitution in Canadian Manufacturing, 1926-39 and 1946-61", *Canadian Journal of Economics* (Aug.).

Koyck, L.M. (1954), *Distributed Lags and Investment Analysis* (Amsterdam: North-Holland).

Kreinin, M.E. (1961), "Windfall Income and Consumption: Additional Evidence", *American Economic Review* (June).

Kuipers, S.K. (1974), "On the Estimation of Short Run and Long Run Production Equations", in F.L. Altmann, O. Kyn, and H.J. Wagener, *On the Measurement of Factor Productivities* (Göttingen: Vandenhoeck & Ruprecht).

Kuipers, S.K. and B.S. Wilpstra (1977), "A Simple Disequilibrium Model of the Dutch Monetary Sector", mimeo, University of Groningen (Jan.).

Kuznets, S. (1946), *National Product since 1869* (New York: National Bureau of Economic Research).

Ladenson, M.L. (1971), "Pitfalls in Financial Model Building: Some Extensions", *American Economic Review* (Mar.).

Laidler, D. (1966), "The Rate of Interest and the Demand for Money: Some Empirical Evidence", *Journal of Political Economy* (Dec.).

Laidler, D. (1969a), "The Definition of Money: Theoretical and Empirical Problems", *Journal of Money, Credit, and Banking* (Aug.).

Laidler, D. (1969b), "Income Tax Incentives for Owner-Occupied Housing", in A.C. Harberger and M.J. Bailey (eds.), *The Taxation of Income from Capital* (Washington: Brookings Institution).

Laidler, D. (1977), *The Demand for Money: Theories and Evidence* (New York: Dun-Donnelly).

Laidler, D. and M. Parkin (1970), "The Demand for Money in the United Kingdom, 1956-1967: Preliminary Estimates", *Manchester School* (Sept.).

Laidler, D. and M. Parkin (1975), "Inflation: A Survey", *Economic Journal* (Dec.).

Landsberger, M. (1970), *Restitution Receipts, Household Savings and Consumption Behavior* (Jerusalem: Bank of Israel).

Landsberger, M. (1971), "Consumer Discount Rate and the Horizon: New Evidence", *Journal of Political Economy* (Nov./Dec.).

Lange, O. (1936), "The Place of Interest in the Theory of Production", *Review of Economic Studies* (June).

Lau, L.J. (1969), "Duality and the Structure of Utility Functions", *Journal of Economic Theory* (Dec.).

Laufenberg, D.E. (1974), "An Econometric Model of Channeled Monetary Effects on Conventional Mortgage Credit", Board of Governors of the Federal Reserve, *Special Studies Paper*, no. 39 (Jan.).

Laumas, G.S. (1968), "The Degree of Moneyness in Savings Deposits", *American Economic Review* (June).

Laumas, G.S. (1977), "Liquidity Functions for the United States Manufacturing Corporations", *Southern Economic Journal* (Oct.).

Laumas, G.S. (1978), "A Test of the Stability of the Demand for Money", *Scottish Journal of Political Economy* (Nov.).

Laumas, G.S. (1979), "The Stability of the Demand for Money by the Household Sector - A Note", *Southern Economic Journal* (Oct.).

Laumas, G.S. and Y.P. Mehra (1976), "The Stability of the Demand for Money Function: The Evidence from Quarterly Data", *Review of Economics and Statistics* (Nov.).

Laumas, G.S. and Y.P. Mehra (1977), "The Stability of the Demand for Money Function, 1900-1974", *Journal of Finance* (June).

Laumas, P.S. (1969), "A Test of the Permanent Income Hypothesis", *Journal of Political Economy* (Sept.).

Laumas, P.S. (1978), "Monetization, Economic Development and the Demand for Money", *Review of Economics and Statistics* (Nov.).

Lee, T.H. (1966), "Substitutability of Non-Bank Intermediary Liabilities for Money: The Empirical Evidence", *Journal of Finance* (Sept.).

Lee, T.H. (1968), "Housing and Permanent Income: Tests Based on a Three-Year Reinterview Survey", *Review of Economics and Statistics* (Nov.).

Lee, T.H. (1972), "On Measuring the Nearness of Near-Moneys: Comment", *American Economic Review* (Mar.).

Leijonhufvud, A. (1968), *On Keynesian Economics and the Economics of Keynes* (New York: Oxford University Press).

Leijonhufvud, A. (1973), "Effective Demand Failures", *Swedish Journal of Economics* (Mar.).

Leimer, D.R. and S.D. Lesnoy (1980), "Social Security and Private Saving", mimeo, US Social Security Administration (Sept.).

Lerner, E.M. and W.T. Carleton (1964), "The Integration of Capital Budgeting and Stock Valuation", *American Economic Review* (Sept.).

Levi, M.D. (1975), "Effectiveness of Monetary vs. Fiscal Policy as Revealed by the Behavior of Inventory Stocks", *Journal of Monetary Economics* (Apr.).

Levin, J.H. (1974), "IS, LM and External Equilibrium: Some Extensions", *Economic Internazionale* (May).

Lieberman, C. (1977), "The Transactions Demand for Money and Technological Change", *Review of Economics and Statistics* (Nov.).

Lieberman, C. (1979), "A Transactions vs. Asset Demand Approach to the Empirical Definition of Money", *Economic Inquiry* (Apr.).

Lieberman, C. (1980a), "The Long-Run and Short-Run Demand for Money, Revisited", *Journal of Money, Credit, and Banking* (Feb.).

Lieberman, C. (1980b), "Inventory Demand and Cost of Capital Effects", *Review of Economics and Statistics* (Aug.).

Lintner, J. (1965), "The Valuation of Risk Assets and the Selection of Risky Investments in Stock Portfolios and Capital Budgets", *Review of Economics and Statistics* (Feb.).

Lintner, J. (1967), "Corporation Finance: Risk and Investment", in R. Ferber (ed.), *Determinants of Investment Behavior* (New York: National Bureau of Economic Research).

Liviatan, N. (1963), "Tests of the Permanent Income Hypothesis Based on a Reinterview Saving Survey", in C. Christ (ed.), *Measurement in Economics* (Stanford, Cal.: Stanford University Press).

Lloyd, C. (1968), "Two Classical Monetary Models", in J. Wolfe (ed.), *Value, Capital and Growth* (Edinburgh: Edinburgh University Press).

Lorie, H.R. (1978), "Price-Quantity Adjustments in a Macro-Disequilibrium Model", *Economic Inquiry* (Apr.).

Lovell, C.A.K. (1968), "Capacity Utilization and Production Function Estimation in Postwar American Manufacturing", *Quarterly Journal of Economics* (May).

Lovell, C.A.K. (1973a), "CES and VES Production Functions in a Cross-Section Context", *Journal of Political Economy* (May/June).

Lovell, C.A.K. (1973b), "Estimation and Prediction with CES and VES Production Functions", *International Economic Review* (Oct.).

Lovell, M.C. (1961), "Manufacturers' Inventories, Sales Expectations, and the Acceleration Principle", *Econometrica* (July).

Lovell, M.C. (1967), "Sales Anticipation, Planned Inventory Investment, and Realizations", in R. Ferber (ed.), *Determinants of Investment Behavior* (New York: National Bureau of Economic Research).

Lovell, M.C. (1974), "Monetary Policy and the Inventory Cycle", in G. Horwich and P.A. Samuelson (eds.), *Trade, Stability, and Macroeconomics* (New York: Academic Press).

Lovell, M.C. and E.C. Prescott (1968), "Money, Multiplier-Accelerator Interaction and the Business Cycle", *Southern Economic Journal* (July).

Lu, Y. and L.B. Fletcher (1968), "A Generalization of the CES Production Function", *Review of Economics and Statistics* (Nov.).

Lucas, R.E., Jr (1967), "Optimal Investment Policy and the Flexible Accelerator", *International Economic Review* (Feb.).

Lucas, R.E., Jr (1969), "Labor-Capital Substitution in U.S. Manufacturing", in A. Harberger and M. Bailey (eds.), *The Taxation of Income and Capital* (Washington: Brookings Institution).

Lucas, R.E., Jr (1970), "Capacity, Overtime, and Empirical Production Functions", *American Economic Review* (May).

McCabe, G.M. (1979), "The Empirical Relationship between Investment and Financing: A New Look", *Journal of Financial and Quantitative Analysis* (Mar.).

Maccini, L.J. (1978), "The Impact of Demand and Price Expectations on the Behavior of Prices", *American Economic Review* (Mar.).

Maccini, L.J. and R.J. Rossana (1981), "Finished Good Inventory Investment: An Analysis of Adjustment Speeds", *American Economic Review* (May).

McDonald, I.M. (1980), "On the Comparison of the Stability Implications of Marshallian and Walrasian Adjustment Schemes: Note", *American Economic Review* (Sept.).

McElroy, M.B. and J.C. Poindexter (1975), "Capital Gains and the Aggregate Consumption Function: Comment", *American Economic Review* (Sept.).

McFadden, D. (1963), "Constant Elasticity of Substitution Production Functions", *Review of Economic Studies* (June).

MacKay, R.J. and W.E. Weber (1977), "Consumer Behavior and Quantity Constraints", *Journal of Money, Credit, and Banking* (Feb.).

Maddala, G.S. and F.D. Nelson (1974), "Maximum Likelihood Methods for Models of Markets in Disequilibrium", *Econometrica* (Nov.).

Magnus, J.R. (1979), "Substitution between Energy and Non-Energy Inputs in the Netherlands, 1950-1976", *International Economic Review* (June).

Maisel, S.J. (1963), "A Theory of Fluctuations in Residential Construction Starts", *American Economic Review* (June).

Maisel, S.J., J.B. Burnham, and J.S. Austin (1971), "The Demand for Housing: A Comment", *Review of Economics and Statistics* (Nov.).

Makepeace, G.H. (1978), "Aggregate Production Possibilities in the Presence of Imperfect Competition", *Manchester School* (Dec.).

Malcomson, J.M. (1975), "Capacity Utilization, the User Cost of Capital and the Cost of Adjustment", *International Economic Review* (June).

Malcomson, J.M. (1977), "Capital Utilization and the Measurement of the Elasticity of Substitution", *Manchester School* (June).

Malkiel, B.G. (1966), *The Term Structure of Interest Rates* (Princeton: Princeton University Press).

Malkiel, B.G., G.M. von Furstenberg, and H.S. Watson (1979), "Expectations, Tobin's q, and Industry Investment", *Journal of Finance* (May).

Marschak, J. and W.J. Andrews (1944), "Random Simultaneous Equations and the Theory of Production", *Econometrica* (July-Oct.).
Marwah, K. (1976), "Competitive Interest Payments on Bank Deposits and the Long-Run Demand for Money: Comment", *American Economic Review* (Dec.).
May, J.D. and M.G. Denny (1979), "Factor-Augmenting Technical Progress and Productivity in U.S. Manufacturing", *International Economic Review* (Oct.).
Mayer, T. (1972), *Permanent Income, Wealth and Consumption* (Berkeley: University of California Press).
Mayer, T. (1978), *The Structure of Monetarism* (New York: Norton).
Mayshar, J. (1979), "Transaction Costs in a Model of Capital Market Equilibrium", *Journal of Political Economy* (Aug.).
Mehra, Y.P. (1978), "Is Money Exogenous in Money Demand Equations?", *Journal of Political Economy* (Apr.).
Meiselman, D. (1962), *The Term Structure of Interest Rates* (Englewood Cliffs, NJ: Prentice-Hall).
Meiselman, D. (ed.) (1970), *Varieties of Monetary Experience* (Chicago: University of Chicago Press).
Melitz, J. (1976), "Inflationary Expectations and the French Demand for Money, 1959-1970", *Manchester School* (Mar.).
Meltzer, A.H. (1963a), "The Demand for Money: The Evidence from the Time Series", *Journal of Political Economy* (June).
Meltzer, A.H. (1963b), "The Demand for Money: A Cross-Section Study of Business Firms", *Quarterly Journal of Economics* (Aug.).
Meltzer, A.H. (1974), "Credit Availability and Economic Decisions: Some Evidence for Mortgage and Housing Markets", *Journal of Finance* (June).
Metzler, L.A. (1941), "The Nature and Stability of Inventory Cycles", *Review of Economic Statistics* (Aug.).
Metzler, L.A. (1951), "Wealth, Saving, and the Rate of Interest", *Journal of Political Economy* (Apr.).
Meyer, J.R. and R.R. Glauber (1964), *Investment Decisions, Economic Forecasting, and Public Policy* (Cambridge: Harvard University Press).
Meyer, J.R. and E. Kuh (1957), *The Investment Decision: An Empirical Study* (Cambridge: Harvard University Press).
Meyer, L.H. (1974), "Wealth Effects and the Effectiveness of Monetary and Fiscal Policy", *Journal of Money, Credit, and Banking* (Nov.).
Meyer, L.H. and J.B. Yawitz (1977), "The Interest-Induced Wealth Effect and the Behavior of Real and Nominal Interest Rates: A Comment", *Journal of Finance* (June).
Meyer, P.A. and J.A. Neri (1975), "A Keynes-Friedman Money

Demand Function", *American Economic Review* (Sept.).
Meyer, R.A. and K.R. Kadiyala (1974), "Linear and Nonlinear Estimation of Production Functions", *Southern Economic Journal* (Jan.).
Miles, M.A. (1978), "Currency Substitution, Flexible Exchange Rates, and Monetary Independence", *American Economic Review* (June).
Miller, M.H. and F. Modigliani (1966), "Some Estimates of the Cost of Capital to the Electric Utility Industry, 1954-57", *American Economic Review* (June).
Miller, M.H. and D. Orr (1966), "A Model of the Demand for Money by Firms", *Quarterly Journal of Economics* (Aug.).
Miller, M.H. and D. Orr (1968), "The Demand for Money by Firms: Extension of Analytic Results", *Journal of Finance* (Dec.).
Mills, T.C. (1975), "Sensitivity and Stability of the U.K. Demand for Money Function: 1963-1974", University of Warwick *Discussion Paper* (Nov.).
Mills, T.C. (1978), "The Functional Form of the U.K. Demand for Money", *Applied Statistics*, no. 1.
Mirer, T.W. (1979), "The Wealth-Age Relation among the Aged", *American Economic Review* (June).
Mirer, T.W. (1980), "The Dissaving Behavior of the Retired Aged", *Southern Economic Journal* (Apr.).
Mishkin, F.S. (1976), "Illiquidity, Consumer Durable Expenditure, and Monetary Policy", *American Economic Review* (Sept.).
Mishkin, F.S. (1977), "A Note on Short-Run Asset Effects on Household Saving and Consumption", *American Economic Review* (Mar.).
Mizon, G.E. (1977), "Inferential Procedures in Nonlinear Models: An Application in a U.K. Industrial Cross Section Study of Factor Substitution and Returns to Scale", *Econometrica* (July).
Modigliani, F. (1971), "Monetary Policy and Consumption: The Linkages via Interest Rate and Wealth Effects in the Federal Reserve MIT-Penn Model", in *Consumer Spending and Monetary Policy: The Linkages* (Boston: Federal Reserve Bank).
Modigliani, F. and R. Brumberg (1954), "Utility Analysis and the Consumption Function: An Interpretation of Cross-Section Data", in K. Kurihara (ed.), *Post-Keynesian Economics* (New Brunswick: Rutgers University Press).
Modigliani, F. and M.H. Miller (1958), "The Cost of Capital, Corporation Finance, and the Theory of Investment", *American Economic Review* (June).
Modigliani, F. and M.H. Miller (1963), "Corporate Income Taxes and the Cost of Capital: A Correction", *American*

Economic Review (June).

Modigliani, F. and M.H. Miller (1967), "Estimates of the Cost of Capital Relevant for Investment Decisions under Uncertainty", in R. Ferber (ed.), *Determinants of Business Investment* (New York: National Bureau of Economic Research).

Mohabbat, K.A. and E.O. Simos (1977), "Consumer Horizon: Further Evidence", *Journal of Political Economy* (Aug.).

Moore, B.J. (1979), "The Endogenous Money Stock", *JPKE* (Fall).

Morgan, I. and J. Saint-Pierre (1978), "Dividend and Investment Decisions of Canadian Firms", *Canadian Journal of Economics* (Feb.).

Moroney, J.R. (1970), "Identification and Specification Analysis of Alternative Equations for Estimating the Elasticity of Substitution", *Southern Economic Journal* (Jan.).

Mossin, J. (1966), "Equilibrium in a Capital Asset Market", *Econometrica* (Oct.).

Motley, B. (1969), "The Consumer's Demand for Money: a Neoclassical Approach", *Journal of Political Economy* (Sept./Oct.).

Motley, B. and S.A. Morley (1970), "The Optimum Lifetime Distribution of Consumption Expenditures: Comment", *American Economic Review* (Sept.).

Muellbauer, J. and R. Portes (1978), "Macroeconomic Models with Quantity Rationing", *Economic Journal* (Dec.).

Mukerji, V. (1963), "A Generalized SMAC Function with Constant Ratios of Elasticity of Substitution", *Review of Economic Studies* (Oct.).

Mullineaux, D. (1977), "The Stability of the Demand for Money: Some Adaptive Regression Tests on Monthly Data", mimeo, Federal Reserve Bank of Philadelphia.

Mundell, R.A. (1971), *Monetary Theory* (Pacific Palisades, Cal.: Goodyear).

Mundlak, Y. (1963), "Estimation of Production and Behavioral Functions from a Combination of Cross-Section and Time-Series Data", in C. Christ *et al.*, *Measurement in Economics* (Stanford, Cal.: Stanford University Press).

Munnell, A.H. (1974), "The Impact of Social Security on Private Savings", *National Tax Journal* (Dec.).

Musgrove, P. (1979), "Permanent Household Income and Consumption in Urban South America", *American Economic Review* (June).

Musgrove, P. (1980), "Income Distribution and the Aggregate Consumption Function", *Journal of Political Economy* (June).

Muth, J.F. (1961), "Rational Expectations and the Theory of Price Movements", *Econometrica* (July).

Muth, R.F. (1960), "The Demand for Non-Farm Housing", in A. Harberger (ed.), *The Demand for Durable Goods* (Chicago: University of Chicago Press).

Muth, R.F. (1962), "Interest Rates, Contract Terms, and the Allocation of Mortgage Funds", *Journal of Finance* (Mar.).

Nadiri, M.I. and S. Rosen (1973), *A Disequilibrium Model of Demand for Factors of Production* (New York: National Bureau of Economic Research).

Nagatani, K. (1972), "Life Cycle Saving: Theory and Fact", *American Economic Review* (June).

Nelson, C.R. (1976), "Inflation and Capital Budgeting", *Journal of Finance* (June).

Nelson, C.R. and G.W. Schwert (1977), "Short Term Interest Rates as Predictors of Inflation: On Testing the Hypothesis That the Real Rate of Interest Is Constant", *American Economic Review* (June).

Nickell, S.J. (1978), *The Investment Decision of Firms* (New York: Cambridge University Press).

Niehans, J. (1978), *The Theory of Money* (Baltimore: Johns Hopkins University Press).

Nissanke, M.K. (1979), "The Disequilibrium Model in a Controlled Economy: Comment", *American Economic Review* (Sept.).

O'Brien, J.M. (1974), "The Covariance Measure of Substitution: An Application to Financial Assets", *Review of Economics and Statistics* (Nov.).

Offenbacher, E.K. (1980a), "The Substitutability of Monetary Assets", mimeo, Board of Governors of the Federal Reserve System.

Offenbacher, E.K. (1980b), "Disaggregated Monetary Asset Demand Systems: Estimation and an Application of the Preference Independence Transformation", mimeo, Board of Governors of the Federal Reserve System (July).

Orr, D. (1971), *Cash Management and the Demand for Money* (New York: Praeger).

Orr, D. (1974), "A Note on the Uselessness of Transaction Demand Models", *Journal of Finance* (Dec.).

Ostas, J.R. and F. Zahn (1975), "Interest and Non-Interest Credit Rationing in the Mortgage Market", *Journal of Monetary Economics* (Apr.).

Ott, D.J., A.F. Ott, and J.H. Yoo (1975), *Macroeconomic Theory* (New York: McGraw-Hill).

Pagan, A. (1977), "The Stability of the Demand for Money Reexamined", mimeo, Australian National University (June).

Paraskevopoulos, C.C. (1979), "Alternative Estimate of the Elasticity of Substitution: An Inter-Metropolitan CES Production Function Analysis of U.S. Manufacturing Industries, 1958-1972", *Review of Economics and Statistics*

(Aug.).

Park, S. (1974), "Functional Distribution of Income and Consumption: An Econometric Analysis", mimeo, Carleton University.

Parkin, M. (1970), "Discount House Portfolio and Debt Selection", *Review of Economic Studies* (Oct.).

Parkin, M., M.R. Gray, and R. Barrett (1970), "The Portfolio Behaviour of Commercial Banks", in D. Heathfield and K. Hilton (eds.), *The Econometric Model of the United Kingdom* (London: Macmillan).

Parsons, L.J., R.L. Schultz, and T.L. Pilon (1979), "The Impact of Advertising on the Aggregate Consumption Function", mimeo, Krannert School, Purdue University (May).

Patinkin, D. (1965), *Money, Interest and Prices*, second edition (New York: Harper and Row).

Patinkin, D. (1969), "Money and Wealth: A Review Article", *Journal of Economic Literature* (Dec.).

Pesando, J.E. and A. Yatchew (1977), "Real Versus Nominal Interest Rates and the Demand for Consumer Durables in Canada", *Journal of Money, Credit, and Banking* (Aug.).

Pesek, B.P. (1979a), "A Note on the Theory of Permanent Income", *JPKE* (Summer).

Pesek, B.P. (1979b), "Modern Bank Deposits and the Theory of Optimum Undefined Money", in M.B. Ballabon (ed.), *Economic Perspectives* (New York: Harwood Academic Publishers).

Pesek, B.P. and T.R. Saving (1967), *Money, Wealth and Economic Theory* (New York: Macmillan).

Phelps, E.S. (1966), *Golden Rules of Economic Growth* (New York: W.W. Norton).

Phlips, L. (1978), "The Demand for Money and Leisure", *Econometrica* (Sept.).

Pifer, H.W. (1969), "A Non-Linear Maximum Likelihood Estimate of the Liquidity Trap", *Econometrica* (Apr.).

Pigou, A.C. (1947), "Economic Progress in a Stable Environment", *Economica* (Aug.).

Pindyck, R.S. (1979), "Interfuel Substitution and the Industrail Demand for Energy: An International Comparison", *Review of Economics and Statistics* (May).

Pissarides, C.A. (1978), "Liquidity Considerations in the Theory of Consumption", *Quarterly Journal of Economics* (May).

Policano, A.J. and E.K. Choi (1978), "The Effects of Relative Price Changes on the Household's Demand for Money", *Journal of Monetary Economics* (Nov.).

Polinsky, A.M. (1977), "The Demand for Housing: A Study in Specification and Grouping", *Econometrica* (Mar.).

Polinsky, A.M. and D.T. Ellwood (1979), "An Empirical Reconciliation of Micro and Grouped Estimates of the Demand for

Housing", *Review of Economics and Statistics* (May).

Poloz, S.S. (1979), "The Stability of the Demand for Money in Canada, 1952-1977", mimeo, Queen's University (Jan.).

Prais, Z. (1975), "Real Money Balances as a Variable in the Production Function", *Journal of Money, Credit, and Banking* (Nov.).

Price, L.D.D. (1972), "The Demand for Money in the United Kingdom: A Further Investigation", Bank of England *Quarterly Bulletin* (Mar.).

Purvis, D.D. (1978), "Dynamic Models of Portfolio Behavior: More on Pitfalls in Financial Model Building", *American Economic Review* (June).

Quandt, R.E. (1978), "Tests of the Equilibrium vs Disequilibrium Hypotheses", *International Economic Review* (June).

Raj, B. and H.D. Vinod (1978), "The Specification and Estimation of Cobb-Douglas Production Function with Randomly Varying Parameters", mimeo, Wilfred Laurier University.

Ramsey, J.B. and P. Zarembka (1971), "Specification Error Tests and Alternative Functional Forms for the Aggregate Production Function", *Journal of the American Statistical Association* (Sept.).

Rausser, G.C. and P.S. Laumas (1976), "The Stability of the Demand for Money in Canada", *Journal of Monetary Economics* (July).

Reid, M.G. (1962), "Consumption, Saving, and Windfall Gains", *American Economic Review* (Sept.).

Revankar, N.S. (1971), "A Class of Variable Elasticity of Substitution Production Functions", *Econometrica* (Jan.).

Ringstad, V. (1978), "Economies of Scale and the Form of the Production Function: Some New Estimates", *Scandinavian Journal of Economics*, no. 3.

Roistacher, E.A. (1977), "Short-Run Housing Responses to Changes in Income", *American Economic Review* (Feb.).

Rosen, H.S. (1979a), "Housing Decisions and the U.S. Income Tax", *Journal of Public Economics* (Feb.).

Rosen, H.S. (1979b), "Owner Occupied Housing and the Federal Income Tax: Estimates and Simulations", *Journal of Urban Economics* (Apr,).

Rosen, H.S. and K.T. Rosen (1980), "Federal Taxes and Homeownership: Evidence from Time Series", *Journal of Political Economy* (Feb.).

Rowan, D.C. and J. Miller (1979), "The Demand for Money in the United Kingdom: 1963-1977", mimeo, University of Southampton (Jan.).

Rowley, J.C.R. and P.K. Trivedi (1975), *Econometrics of Investment* (New York: Wiley).

Rubin, L.S. (1979-80), "Aggregate Inventory Behavior: Response to Uncertainty and Interest Rates", *JPKE* (Winter).

Russell, T. (1974), "The Effects of Improvements in the Consumer Loan Market", *Journal of Economic Theory* (Nov.).

Saito, M. (1977), "Household Flow-of-Funds Equations", *Journal of Money, Credit, and Banking* (Feb.).

Salemi, M.K. and T.J. Sargent (1979), "The Demand for Money during Hyperinflation under Rational Expectations: II", *International Economic Review* (Oct.).

Samuelson, P.A. (1947), *Foundations of Economic Analysis* (Cambridge: Harvard University Press).

Samuelson, P.A. (1939), "A Synthesis of the Principle of Acceleration and the Multiplier", *Journal of Political Economy* (Dec.).

Samuelson, P.A. (1970), "The Fundamental Approximation Theorem of Portfolio Analysis in Terms of Means, Variances, and Higher Moments", *Review of Economic Studies* (Oct.).

Santomero, A.M. (1974), "A Model of the Demand for Money by Households", *Journal of Finance* (Mar.).

Santomero, A.M. and J.J. Seater (1978), "The Role of Partial Adjustment in the Demand for Money: Theory and Empirics", mimeo, Federal Reserve Bank of Philadelphia.

Sargen, N.P. (1977), "Exchange Rate Flexibility and Demand for Money", *Journal of Finance* (May).

Sargent, T.J. (1977), "The Demand for Money during Hyperinflation under Rational Expectations", *International Economic Review* (Feb.).

Sargent, T.J. (1978), "Rational Expectations, Economic Exogeneity, and Consumption", *Journal of Political Economy* (Aug.).

Sargent, T.J. and N. Wallace (1973), "The Stability of Models of Money and Growth with Perfect Foresight", *Econometrica* (Nov.).

Sargent, T.J. and N. Wallace (1974), "The Elasticity of Substitution and Cyclical Behavior of Productivity, Wages, and Labor's Share", *American Economic Review* (May).

Sato, K. (1967), "A Two-Level Constant Elasticity of Substitution Production Function", *Review of Economic Studies* (Apr.).

Sato, K. (1975), *Production Functions and Aggregation* (Amsterdam: North-Holland).

Sato, K. (1977), "A Note on Factor Substitution and Efficiency", *Review of Economics and Statistics* (Aug.).

Sato, R. (1970), "The Estimation of Biased Technical Progress and the Production Function", *International Economic Review* (June).

Sato, R. (1977), "Homothetic and Non-Homothetic CES Production Functions", *American Economic Review* (Sept.).

Sato, R. and R.F. Hoffman (1968), "Production Functions with Variable Elasticity of Factor Substitution: Some Analysis and Testing", *Review of Economics and Statistics* (Nov.).

Saving, T.R. (1970), "Outside Money, Inside Money, and the Real Balance Effect", *Journal of Money, Credit, and Banking* (Feb.).

Saving, T.R. (1971), "Transactions Costs and the Demand for Money", *American Economic Review* (June).

Saving, T.R. (1972), "Transactions Costs and the Firm's Demand for Money", *Journal of Money, Credit, and Banking* (May).

Saving, T.R. (1976), "Transactions Cost Functions and the Inventory-Theoretic Approach to Money Demand", *Journal of Money, Credit, and Banking* (Aug.).

Scadding, J.L. (1977), "An Annual Money Demand and Supply Model for the U.S.: 1924-1966", *Journal of Monetary Economics*, no. 3.

Schaafsma, J. (1978), "On Estimating the Time Structure of Capital-Labor Substitution in the Manufacturing Sector: A Model Applied to 1949-72 Canadian Data", *Southern Economic Journal* (Apr.).

Schmalensee, R. (1972), *The Economics of Advertising* (Amsterdam: North-Holland).

Schumpeter, J.A. (1934), *The Theory of Economic Development* (Cambridge: Harvard University Press).

Schydlowsky, D.M. and M. Syrquin (1972), "The Estimation of CES Production Functions and Neutral Efficiency Levels Using Effective Rates of Protection as Price Deflators", *Review of Economics and Statistics* (Feb.).

Scott, I.O. (1957), "The Availability Doctrine: Theoretical Underpinnings", *Review of Economic Studies* (Oct.).

Sealey, C.W. (1979), "Credit Rationing in the Commercial Loan Market: Estimates of a Structural Model under Conditions of Disequilibrium", *Journal of Finance* (June).

Seater, J.J. (1980), "On the Estimation of Permanent Income", mimeo, Federal Reserve Bank of Philadelphia (July).

Shapiro, A.A. (1973), "Inflation, Lags, and the Demand for Money", *International Economic Review* (Feb.).

Shapiro, I.A. (1976), "A Test of the Effect of Windfall Receipts on Consumption", *Eastern Economic Journal* (Jan.).

Sharpe, W.F. (1964), "Capital Asset Prices: A Theory of Market Equilibrium under Conditions of Risk", *Journal of Finance* (Sept.).

Shell, K. (1972), "Selected Elementary Topics in the Theory of Economic Decision-Making under Uncertainty", in G.P. Szegö and K. Shell, *Mathematical Methods in Investment and Finance* (Amsterdam: North-Holland).

Short, B.K. and D.P. Villanueva (1977), "Further Evidence on the Role of Savings Deposits as Money in Canada", *Journal of Money, Credit, and Banking* (Aug.).

Short, E.D. (1979), "A New Look at Real Money Balances as a Variable in the Production Function", *Journal of Money, Credit, and Banking* (Aug.).
Simon, J.L. and D.J. Aigner (1970), "Cross Section and Time Series Tests of the Permanent Income Hypothesis", *American Economic Review* (June).
Sinai, A. and H.H. Stokes (1972), "Real Money Balances: An Omitted Variable from the Production Function?", *Review of Economics and Statistics* (Aug.).
Slovin, M.B. and M.E. Sushka (1975), "The Structural Shift in the Demand for Money", *Journal of Finance* (June).
Slovin, M.B., M.E. Sushka, and R. Hill (1978), "Risk and the Demand for Money", mimeo, Econometric Society Meetings (Aug.).
Smith, B.A. (1976), "The Supply of Urban Housing", *Quarterly Journal of Economics* (Aug.).
Smith, B.A. and J.M. Campbell (1978), "Aggregation Bias and the Demand for Housing", *International Economic Review* (June).
Smith, G. (1975) "Pitfalls in Financial Model Building: A Clarification", *American Economic Review* (June).
Smith, L.B. (1969), "A Model of the Canadian Housing and Mortgage Markets", *Journal of Political Economy* (Sept./Oct.).
Smith, L.B. and J.W.L. Winder (1971), "Price and Interest Rate Expectations and the Demand for Money in Canada", *Journal of Finance* (June).
Smith, P. (1979), "A Reconsideration of Keynes' Finance Motive", *Economic Record* (Sept.).
Smith, V.L. (1972), "Default Risk, Scale, and the Homemade Leverage Theorem", *American Economic Review* (Mar.).
Smyth, D.J. (1964), "Empirical Evidence on the Acceleration Principle", *Review of Economic Studies* (June).
Smyth, D.J. and J.D. Jackson (1978), "A Theoretical and Empirical Analysis of Ratchet Models as Alternatives to Permanent Income and Continuous Habit Formation Consumption Functions", *Journal of Economics and Business* (Winter).
Smyth, D.J. and P.C. McMahon (1972), "The Australian Short-Run Consumption Function", *Economic Record* (June).
Solow, R.M. (1957), "Technical Change and the Aggregate Production Function", *Review of Economics and Statistics* (Aug.).
Solow, R.M. (1967), "Some Recent Developments in the Theory of Production", in M. Brown (ed.), *The Theory and Empirical Analysis of Production* (New York: National Bureau of Economic Research).
Sparks, G.R. (1967), "An Econometric Analysis of the Role of Financial Intermediaries in Postwar Residential Building

Cycles", in R. Ferber (ed.), *Determinants of Investment Behavior* (New York: National Bureau of Economic Research).
Spies, R.R. (1974), "The Dynamics of Corporate Capital Budgeting", *Journal of Finance* (June).
Spiro, A. (1962), "Wealth and the Consumption Function", *Journal of Political Economy* (Aug.).
Spitzer, J.J. (1976), "The Demand for Money, the Liquidity Trap, and Functional Form", *International Economic Review* (Feb.),
Spitzer, J.J. (1977), "A Simultaneous Equations System of Money Demand and Supply Using Generalized Functional Forms", *Journal of Econometrics* (Jan.).
Sprenkle, C.M. (1969), "The Uselessness of Transactions Demand Models", *Journal of Finance* (Dec.).
Stafford, F.P. (1968), *Graduate Student Income and Consumption*, PhD Dissertation, University of Chicago.
Starleaf, D.R., and R.R. Reimer (1967), "The Keynesian Demand Function for Money: Some Statistical Tests", *Journal of Finance* (Mar.).
Startz, R. (1979), "Implicit Interest on Demand Deposits", *Journal of Monetary Economics* (Oct.).
Stiglitz, J.E. (1969), "A Re-Examination of the Modigliani-Miller Theorem", *American Economic Review* (Dec.).
Stiglitz, J.E. (1970), "A Consumption-Oriented Theory of the Demand for Financial Assets and the Term Structure of Interest Rates", *Review of Economic Studies* (July).
Stiglitz, J.E. (1974), "On the Irrelevance of Corporate Financial Policy", *American Economic Review* (Dec.).
Summers, L.H. (1980a), "Inflation, Taxation and Corporate Investment: A q Theory Approach", National Bureau of Economic Research *Working Paper*, no. 604 (Dec.).
Summers, L.H. (1980b), "Tax Policy and Corporate Investment", National Bureau of Economic Research *Working Paper*, no. 605 (Dec.).
Summers, L.H. (1980c), "Inflation, the Stock Market, and Owner Occupied Housing", National Bureau of Economic Research *Working Paper*, no. 606 (Dec.).
Surrey, M.J.C. (1970), "Personal Incomes and Consumers' Expenditure", in K. Hilton and D. Heathfield (eds.), *The Econometric Model of the United Kingdom* (London: Macmillan).
Sveikauskas, L. (1974), "Bias in Cross-Section Estimates of the Elasticity of Substitution", *International Economic Review* (June).
Syring, E. (1966), *The Demand for Money in Norway* (Oslo: Universitetsforlagets Trykmingssentral).
Taggart, R.A. (1977), "A Model of Corporate Financial Decisions", *Journal of Finance* (Dec.).

Tanner, J.E. (1970), "Empirical Evidence on the Short-Run Real Balance Effect in Canada", *Journal of Money, Credit, and Banking* (Nov.).
Tanner, J.E. (1979), "Fiscal Policy and Consumer Behavior", *Review of Economics and Statistics* (May).
Taylor, L.D. and D. Weiserbs, (1972), "Advertising and the Aggregate Consumption Function", *American Economic Review* (Sept.).
Teigen, R.L. (1964), "Demand and Supply Functions for Money in the United States: Some Structural Estimates", *Econometrica* (Oct.).
Teigen, R.L. (1971), "The Demand for Money in Norway, 1959-1969", *Statsokonomisk Tidsskrift* (Sept.).
Thomas, J.J. (1975), "Some Aggregation Problems in the Estimation of Partial Adjustment Models of the Demand for Money", *Recherches Economiques de Louvain* (June).
Thurow, L.C. (1969), "The Optimum Lifetime Distribution of Consumption Expenditures", *American Economic Review* (June).
Thurston, T.B. (1977), "The Permanent Income Hypothesis and Monetary Influences on Consumption", *Journal of Money, Credit, and Banking* (Nov.).
Tinbergen, J. (1938), "Statistical Evidence on the Acceleration Principle", *Economica* (May).
Tinsley, P.A. and B. Garrett (with M.E. Friar) (1978), "The Measurement of Money Demand", *Special Studies Paper No. 133*, Board of Governors of the Federal Reserve System (Oct.).
Tobin, J. (1951), "Relative Income, Absolute Income, and Savings", in *Money, Trade, and Economic Growth* (for John H. Williams) (New York: Macmillan).
Tobin, J. (1956), "The Interest Elasticity of the Transactions Demand for Cash", *Review of Economics and Statistics* (Aug.).
Tobin, J. (1958), "Liquidity Preference as Behaviour Towards Risk", *Review of Economic Studies* (Feb.).
Tobin, J. (1965), "Money and Economic Growth", *Econometrica* (Oct.).
Tobin, J. (1969), "A General Equilibrium Approach to Monetary Theory", *Journal of Money, Credit, and Banking* (Feb.).
Tobin, J. (1972), "Wealth, Liquidity, and the Propensity to Consume", in B. Strumpel, J. Morgan, and E. Zahn (eds.), *Human Behavior in Economic Affairs* (New York: Elsevier).
Tobin, J. (1975), "Keynesian Models of Recession and Depression", *American Economic Review* (May).
Tower, E. (1975), "Devaluation and the Demand for Money", *Discussion Paper*, Department of the Treasury.

Townend, J.C. (1972), "Substitution among Capital-Certain Assets in the Personal Sector of the U.K. Economy: 1963-1971", mimeo, Bank of England (Sept.).

Treadway, A.B. (1969), "On Rational Entrepreneurial Behaviour and the Demand for Investment", *Review of Economic Studies* (Apr.).

Treadway, A.B. (1971), "The Rational Multivariate Flexible Accelerator", *Econometrica* (Sept.).

Trivdei, P.K. (1970), "Inventory Behaviour in U.K. Manufacturing, 1956-67", *Review of Economic Studies* (Oct.).

Tsurumi, H. (1970), "Nonlinear Two-Stage Least Squares Estimation of CES Production Functions Applied to Canadian Manufacturing Industries, 1926-1939, 1946-1967", *Review of Economics and Statistics* (May).

Tucker, D.P. (1968), "Credit Rationing, Interest Rate Lags, and Monetary Policy Speed", *Quarterly Journal of Economics* (Feb.).

Tucker, D.P. (1971), "Macroeconomic Models and the Demand for Money under Market Disequilibrium", *Journal of Money, Credit, and Banking* (Feb.).

Turnovsky, S.J. (1970), "Financial Structure and the Theory of Production", *Journal of Finance* (Dec.).

Ullah, A., R.N. Batra, and B. Singh (1975), "On the Estimation of the Cobb-Douglas Production Function under Uncertainty", University of Western Ontario Research Report 7526.

Ungar, M. and B. Zilberfarb (1980), "The Demand for Money by Firms: The Stability and Other Issues Reexamined", *Journal of Finance* (June).

Uzawa, H. (1961), "Neutral Invention and the Stability of Growth Equilibrium", *Review of Economic Studies* (Feb.).

Uzawa, H. (1962), "Production Functions with Constant Elasticities of Substitution", *Review of Economic Studies* (Oct.).

Valentine, T.J. (1977a), "Determination of the Volume of Money", *Working Paper* No. 51, Australian National University.

Valentine, T.J. (1977b), "The Demand for Money and Price Expectations in Australia", *Journal of Finance* (June).

Van Daal, J. (1980), "Money Illusion and Aggregation Bias", *De Economist*, no. 1.

Van Horne, J.C. (1971), "A Note on Biases in Capital Budgeting Introduced by Inflation", *Journal of Financial and Quantitative Analysis* (Jan.).

Varian, H.R. (1977), "Non-Walrasian Equilibria", *Econometrica* (Apr.).

Vaughn, G.A. (1976), "Sources of Downward Bias in Estimating the Demand Income Elasticity for Urban Housing", *Journal of Urban Economics* (Jan.).

Vickers, D. (1970), "The Cost of Capital and the Structure of the Firm", *Journal of Finance* (Mar.).

Vogel, R.C. (1974), "The Dynamics of Inflation in Latin America", *American Economic Review* (Mar.).

Von Furstenberg, G.M. (1977), "Corporate Investment: Does Market Valuation Matter in the Aggregate?", *Brookings Papers*, no. 2.

Von Furstenberg, G.M. and B.G. Malkiel (1977), "The Government and Capital Formation: A Survey of Recent Issues", *Journal of Economic Literature* (Sept.).

Wallis, K.F. (1973), *Topics in Applied Econometrics* (London: Gray-Mills).

Walters, A.A. (1963), "Production and Cost Functions: An Econometric Survey", *Econometrica* (Jan. - Apr.).

Warner, J.C. (1978), "Unfulfilled Long-Term Interest Rate Expectations and Changes in Business Fixed Investment", *American Economic Review* (June).

Watts, H. (1958), "Long-Run Income Expectations and Consumer Savings", in T. Dernburg, R. Rosett, and H. Watts (eds.), *Studies in Household Economic Behavior* (New Haven: Yale University Press).

Weber. W.E. (1970), "The Effect of Interest Rates on Aggregate Consumption", *American Economic Review* (Sept.).

Weber, W.E. (1971), "Interest Rates and the Short-Run Consumption Function", *American Economic Review* (June).

Weber, W.E. (1975), "Interest Rates, Inflation, and Consumer Expenditure", *American Economic Review* (Dec.).

Weinrobe, M.D. (1973), "The Demand for Money by Six Non-Bank Financial Intermediaries", *Western Economic Journal* (June).

Weintraub, E.R. (1977), "The Microfoundations of Macroeconomics: A Critical Survey", *Journal of Economic Literature* (Mar.).

Welch, F. (1970), "Education in Production", *Journal of Political Economy* (Jan./Feb.).

Whalen, E.L. (1966), "A Rationalization of the Precautionary Demand for Cash", *Quarterly Journal of Economics* (May).

White, B.B. (1978), "Empirical Tests of the Life Cycle Hypothesis", *American Economic Review* (Sept.).

White, W.H. (1976), "The Demand for Money in Canada and the Control of Monetary Aggregates: Evidence from the Monthly Data", *Staff Research Studies*, Bank of Canada.

White, W.H. (1978), "Improving the Demand for Money Function in Moderate Inflation", International Monetary Fund *Staff Papers* (Sept.).

White, W.L. (1974), "Debt Management and the Form of Business Financing", *Journal of Finance* (May).

Wilbratte, B.J. (1975), "Some Essential Differences in the Demand for Money by Households and by Firms", *Journal of Finance* (Sept.).

Wilkinson, R.K. (1973), "The Income Elasticity of Demand for Housing", *Oxford Economic Papers* (Nov.).

Winger, A. (1968), "Housing and Income", *Western Economic Journal* (June).

Witte, J.G. (1963), "The Microfoundations of the Social Investment Function", *Journal of Political Economy* (Oct.).

Wong, C. (1977), "Demand for Money in Developing Countries: Some Theoretical and Empirical Results", *Journal of Monetary Economics* (Jan.).

Woodland, A.D. (1978), "On Testing Weak Separability", *Journal of Econometrics* (Dec.).

Wright, C. (1967), "Some Evidence on the Interest Elasticity of Consumption", *American Economic Review* (Sept.).

Wright, C. (1969), "Estimating Permanent Income: A Note", *Journal of Political Economy* (Sept./Oct.).

Yaari, M.E. (1964), "On the Consumer's Lifetime Allocation Process", *International Economic Review* (Sept.).

Yoshikawa, H. (1980), "On the 'q' Theory of Investment", *American Economic Review* (Sept.).

You, J.S. (1978), "Real Money Balances, Technological Progress, and the Aggregate Production Function in Canada, 1946-1977", mimeo, Carleton University (Dec.).

Zarembka, P. (1970), "On the Empirical Relevance of the CES Production Function", *Review of Economics and Statistics* (Feb.).

Zarembka, P. and H.B. Chernicoff (1971), "Further Results on the Empirical Relevance of the CES Production Function", *Review of Economics and Statistics* (Feb.).

Zellner, A. and M.S. Geisel (1970), "Analysis of Distributed Lag Models with Application to Consumption Function Estimation", *Econometrica* (Nov.).

Zellner, A., D.S. Huang, and L.C. Chau (1965), "Further Analysis of the Short-Run Consumption Function, with Emphasis on the Role of Liquid Assets", *Econometrica* (July).

Zellner, A., J. Kmenta, and J. Dreze (1966), "Specification and Estimation of Cobb-Douglas Production Function Models", *Econometrica* (Oct.).

Zellner, A. and J.F. Richard (1973), "Use of Prior Information in the Analysis and Estimation of Cobb-Douglas Production Function Models", *International Economic Review* (Feb.).

Zwick, B. (1974), "The Interest-Induced Wealth Effect and the Behavior of Real and Nominal Interest Rates", *Journal of Finance* (Dec.).

Index